MARYSUE
RUCCI
BOOKS

Also by Rebecca Romney

Printer's Error:
Irreverent Stories from Book History (with J. P. Romney)

JANE AUSTEN'S BOOKSHELF

A Rare Book Collector's
Quest to Find the Women Writers
Who Shaped a Legend

REBECCA ROMNEY

MARYSUE
RUCCI
BOOKS

New York   Amsterdam/Antwerp   London
Toronto   Sydney   New Delhi

MARYSUE RUCCI BOOKS

An Imprint of Simon & Schuster, LLC
1230 Avenue of the Americas
New York, NY 10020

First Marysue Rucci Books hardcover edition February 2025

MARYSUE RUCCI BOOKS and colophon are trademarks of Simon & Schuster, LLC

For information about special discounts for bulk purchases, please contact Simon & Schuster Special Sales at 1-866-506-1949 or business@simonandschuster.com.

The Simon & Schuster Speakers Bureau can bring authors to your live event. For more information or to book an event, contact the Simon & Schuster Speakers Bureau at 1-866-248-3049 or visit our website at www.simonspeakers.com.

Interior design by Laura Levatino

Manufactured in the United States of America

10 9 8 7 6 5 4 3 2 1

Library of Congress Cataloging-in-Publication Data has been applied for.

ISBN 978-1-9821-9024-8
ISBN 978-1-9821-9026-2 (ebook)

For my daughter

CREDITS

I wrote *Jane Austen's Bookshelf*, but it could not have been published without the efforts of the many individuals at Simon & Schuster and Marysue Rucci Books who collaborated on this book with me. I would like to express my gratitude to everyone involved in this process across departments whose invaluable expertise were integral to the creation of this book.

Editorial
Emily Graff, *Executive Editor*
Katie McClimon, *Editorial Assistant*

Jacket Design
Chris Allen, *Designer*
Jenny Carrow, *Art Director*
Jackie Seow, *VP and Executive Art Director*
Pamela Grant, *Senior Art Manager*
Madelyn Rodriguez, *Junior Designer*

Marketing
Alyssa diPierro, *Senior Marketing Manager*
Elizabeth Breeden, *Senior Marketing Director*
Ali Kochik, *Marketing Assistant*

Production
Jessie McNiel, *Managing Editor*
Samantha Hoback, *Senior Production Editor*
Allison Har-zvi, *Senior Production Manager*
Laura Levatino, *Interior Text Designer*
Jane Phan, *Bound Galley Production Manager*
Mikaela Bielawski, *Ebook Manager*

Publicity
Clare Maurer, *Senior Publicity Manager*
Jessica Preeg, *Senior Director, Publicity and Marketing*
Grace Noglows, *Associate Publicist*

Publisher
Marysue Rucci, *VP and Publisher*

Subsidiary Rights
Nicole Bond, *VP and Executive Director of Subsidiary Rights*

CONTENTS

INTRODUCTION

"You see, but you do not observe."

**—Sherlock Holmes,
"A Scandal in Bohemia"**

It all started with a book that made me curious.

I was on a house call in Georgetown, invited to browse the personal book collection of a woman who used to be a professional rare book dealer like me. In the tree-dappled sunlight that filtered through the windows, I spent the afternoon combing through her library. As the wind grazed the branches outside, the light within the room shifted, sparkling across the antique rug, the gently worn furniture, and the bookcases. Every shelf had been filled with books that quietly spoke to her discernment. Instead of a flashy modern edition of *Pride and Prejudice*, this woman had a rather ugly one, bound in drab brown paper boards resembling dilapidated cardboard. It also bore an unusual revised title, *Elizabeth Bennet; or, Pride and Prejudice*. Despite its humble appearance, I knew the book was incredibly rare. It was the first edition of *Pride and Prejudice* published in the United States, from 1832. A woman who kept this book on her shelf knew a good book when she saw it, even if others around her might overlook it.

Jane Austen is one of my favorite writers. She was born in 1775 in the English countryside, Steventon, Hampshire, and went on to become "the first great woman writer in English," according to one of her many modern biographers. She wrote six major novels, along with a novella, two other incomplete novels, and what scholars call juvenilia (early writing she composed when she was growing up). I have always been drawn to Austen's confidence, how she guides the reader through her heroines' struggles and uncertainties. And I like her wit, which shines in the details she chooses to linger on. Austen died fairly young, at the age of forty-one, and I have often wished that she had lived to write more.

But on that house call, it wasn't *Pride and Prejudice* that made me curious. I have handled many different editions of Austen's books over the years, including a wide variety of nineteenth-century ones. We would certainly purchase this copy. It was another shelf that drew my eye, one lined with a series of books that had been published during the 1890s and early 1900s by Macmillan in London, recognizable because of their stunning emerald-green cloth bindings and elaborate gilt spines. I took one glance and knew we'd make an offer on the entire collection. Offer accepted, we boxed up our acquisitions to transport back to the shop. The book that would change my life was lying within.

———————

A few months later, I sat at my desk and opened my laptop, ready to spend a few hours cataloging new acquisitions. Before a book is offered for sale, we rare book dealers record its physical attributes: Is it bound in cloth? Leather? Does it have any damage? Signs of previous ownership? We also often write a brief summary of its importance, drawing on the work of other experts in our field and surrounding fields—not just literary critics and biographers, but also book historians, or scholars who study the history of the book. We call the result a catalog description, which becomes our official documentation for that rare book.

On that day, I had plenty of options for which book I would catalog first. I am a maker of piles: this stack has books I've cataloged but not yet put online; that stack contains a few volumes I've pulled for our next newsletter of new arrivals; yet another stack came from that Georgetown house call. I looked toward the last stack of books. Three volumes down from the top sat a novel called *Evelina* by Frances Burney.

I had seen Burney's name before, mostly on the spines of books at antiquarian book fairs in the UK. But I couldn't recall any details of her life. I certainly hadn't read any of her books. I had purchased this one primarily for the emerald-green cloth binding. Not all books are collected because they are first editions. Some are collected for their beauty. This one dated from 1903, a period when UK and US publishers commissioned artists to design eye-catching cloth bindings as a marketing tool (this, before dust jackets rose to dominance). The front board featured a woman poised with a quill pen, dressed in voluminous skirts and a plumed hat. She stood beneath a tree, clusters of leaves spreading across nearly half the binding, all stamped in gilt upon that rich, emerald-green background. Just like it had in the library in Georgetown, when the light hit it just right, it sparkled.

I have no problem admitting that I've bought books for their covers. But even when I do, I care about the story in the book—and the story *of* the book. I want to know what the book is about. What happens? How was it different than the stories that came before? How was it similar? I want to know about the author. Who was she? How did she come to be a writer? I want to know about the book itself. How was it made? What does that say about its publisher's view of its target audience? I want to know about the book's publication. What did people think about it then? What do they think of it now? I want to know where it has been. Who owned this book? How did they care for it (or not)? Why was it saved for so long? To be a rare book dealer is to appreciate that the book itself—the object—can be as interesting as its text.

I've made a career out of that curiosity. I like to ask questions, approaching books like a detective. My job is to investigate each book's story, its importance. When I present my findings, I anticipate interrogation for every statement, as if a judge were leaning over my shoulder asking, "What's your evidence?" If I call a book a first edition, what's my evidence? If I say this book is rare, how do I know? If I call an author influential, where's my source? I take pride in doing work that Sherlock Holmes would compliment. So how was I to catalog this book by an author I knew nothing about? I pulled down a stack of reference books from my shelves.

I quickly gathered that *Evelina* was Burney's first and most famous novel, published to acclaim in 1778. Then, with my finger keeping my place in one reference book while I used my other hand to flip through another, I ran across something electric. If my job is to investigate a book's importance, a detail like this becomes the star evidence in my case.

This is the moment I savor. I chase this feeling across auctions, in book fairs from London to San Francisco, through labyrinths of institutional special collections and private libraries, and on the pages in reference books.

The star evidence: the phrase "pride and prejudice" came from Burney's second novel, *Cecilia* (1782). Frances Burney, it turns out, had been one of Austen's favorite authors. She wrote courtship novels very like Austen's, focused on young heroines navigating the difficulties of finding love. Or rather, Austen wrote books very like *hers*: Burney was one of the most successful novelists of Austen's lifetime. I'd had no idea. Me, a reader and re-reader of Austen's work over decades. I had overlooked this important English author, one with deep significance to another I admired. In spite of my supposed professional curiosity, I realized I had missed something. And it stung.

In the Sherlock Holmes short story "A Scandal in Bohemia," the detective famously scolds Watson, "You see, but you do not observe." After *Evelina* crossed my desk (or rather, sat for months in that pile, stacked between *Gulliver's Travels* and *The Compleat Angler*), I returned to Austen's books and began to observe new traits in them. Every character in *Northanger Abbey* who isn't a boor sings the praises of the gothic writer Ann Radcliffe. The play that causes so much controversy in *Mansfield Park* is in fact a real one adapted by the playwright Elizabeth Inchbald. I was picking up on clues, sprinkled about in the works of Austen like bread crumbs, that pointed toward the women writers she admired.

Why hadn't I noticed these authors before? I had researched the rise of the English novel for my job (and, who am I kidding, because I enjoyed it).

The authors whom Austen referenced in her work had barely entered that discourse. Baffled, I headed to my bookshelf and pulled off a 2005 book on the English novel written for students "by one of the world's leading literary theorists," as the back panel assured me. I opened the first page. The period when Austen did most of her formative reading "was one of the most fertile, diverse, and adventurous periods of novel-writing in English history," the author asserted—for one more paragraph, before moving straight to Austen and Walter Scott. The previous chapter had examined Laurence Sterne. I stared at the ceiling and did the math. *Tristram Shandy*'s last volume was published in 1767. Austen's first published novel, *Sense and Sensibility*, came in 1811. Forty-four years. Simply skipped.

Austen read William Shakespeare, John Milton, Daniel Defoe, and Samuel Richardson, all authors I had read. She also read Frances Burney, Ann Radcliffe, Charlotte Lennox, Hannah More, Charlotte Smith, Elizabeth Inchbald, Hester Piozzi, and Maria Edgeworth, all authors I hadn't. They were part of Austen's bookshelf, but they had disappeared entirely from mine—and largely from that Leading Literary Theorist's bookshelf as well. It was unsettling to realize I had read so many of the men on Austen's bookshelf, but none of the women. Critical authorities like this one had provided the foundation for my understanding the past. But something was wrong. There was a crack in the foundation. I began to feel unsteady.

The feeling was all the more unsettling because this type of knowledge is central to what I do as a rare book dealer. "It is my business to know what other people do not know," as the ever-quotable Sherlock Holmes says. For instance: the first edition in English of Grimms' fairy tales contains a typo on the title page because the British printers forgot an umlaut on a German word; an adventure novel in Spanish called *El Anacronópete* (1887) describes a time machine eight years before the book most believe was the first to do so, H. G. Wells's *The Time Machine*; publisher Frederick Warne's edition of *The Tale of Peter Rabbit* (1902) isn't the true first edition, but was preceded in 1901 by a run of a few hundred copies that Beatrix Potter printed privately as gifts for friends. Literary trivia is my joy and my currency. Besides the ability to quote the Great Detective in nearly any situation, I can also tell you how many steps led to his flat at 221B; I can recite Sappho in Greek and Horace in Latin; I have participated in public readings of *Ulysses*; and I have seriously considered getting a tattoo of a Catullus verse. Yet I had completely missed some of Austen's major predecessors. I've read swaths of Samuel Johnson's *Dictionary*—pages upon pages of eighteenth-century lexical entries—but I assumed these women writers from the same period weren't worth my time.

The game was afoot (and no, I won't stop quoting Holmes). When I investigated further, I learned that Austen had done all this reading during the first time in English history when more women published novels than men. Yet in my own reading, I had skipped them so entirely that it seemed almost intentional. And it was: the critics who shaped our modern idea of the novel in English so frequently dismissed women writers that the systematic excising has a name. It's called the Great Forgetting. Only Austen survived that period, becoming "the first great woman writer in English"—even though there is a passage in one of her own novels that explicitly celebrated the work of women writers who had come before her. Austen gave me a hint of my mistake in *Northanger Abbey*, as well as how I might correct it:

> while the abilities of the nine-hundredth abridger of the History of England, or of the man who collects and publishes in a volume some dozen lines of Milton, Pope, and Prior, with a paper from the *Spectator*, and a chapter from Sterne, are eulogized by a thousand pens—there seems almost a general wish of decrying the capacity and undervaluing the labour of the novelist, and of slighting the performances which have only genius, wit, and taste to recommend them. "I am no novel-reader—I seldom look into novels—Do not imagine that I often read novels—It is really very well for a novel." Such is the common cant. "And what are you reading, Miss—?" "Oh! It is only a novel!" replies the young lady, while she lays down her book with affected indifference, or momentary shame. "It is only *Cecilia*, or *Camilla*, or *Belinda*"; or, in short, only some

work in which the greatest powers of the mind are displayed, in which the most thorough knowledge of human nature, the happiest delineation of its varieties, the liveliest effusions of wit and humour, are conveyed to the world in the best-chosen language. Now, had the same young lady been engaged with a volume of the *Spectator*, instead of such a work, how proudly would she have produced the book, and told its name.

In this passage, Austen had already recognized a mechanism of the Great Forgetting: "a thousand pens" talk of works like Milton's *Paradise Lost*, while embarrassed to admit to reading novels. Austen felt no such shame. Novels display some of "the greatest powers of the mind," she argued. And then *she gave examples. Cecilia* (1782) was Frances Burney's second novel; *Camilla* (1796) was her third. *Belinda* (1801) was the second novel of another woman writer, Maria Edgeworth.

———————

To call Austen "the first great woman writer in English," really, is to call her the first British woman accepted in the Western canon. The canon is famous; it is useful. It offers a list of authors and titles that are recommended as classics by literary authorities like the author of that 2005 book on the English novel. You probably caught how loaded that sentence was; every part of it leads to more questions. Now you're thinking like a rare book dealer. What is a classic? Who gets to be a literary authority? How do these authorities determine the list? Why do we need a list of recommended books at all?

The last question is easy enough to answer: Lists are useful because we cannot read every book. Because we cannot read every book, we must be selective. Because we must be selective, we must make judgments about which books to try *before* we read them. Because we must make judgments before reading, who better to trust for recommendations than professionals, like teachers and literary critics and other scholars, whose job it is to read and analyze many books? These professionals recommend books that are valuable to read far beyond their initial publication—what we call "classics." But professionals have individual tastes, too, so a consensus of professionals is surely best. That consensus of classics, when approached as a list, is what we call the canon. The entire idea of a canon is *practical*.

Because I accepted all of that, I regularly purchased and read books like that 2005 survey of the English novel. I had also read Ian Watt's *The Rise of the Novel* (1957), perhaps the single most influential study of the eighteenth-century English novel, the era when Frances Burney published and when Austen was doing most of her formative reading. Yet it was these very literary authorities who had led me astray: they either dismissed or outright ignored these authors Austen had held so dear. The idea of a canon may be practical, but I had been relying upon it too much.

I kept investigating, and soon learned that other scholars had been noticing these clues in Austen's writings. Decades before the copy of *Evelina* became a jenga piece on my desk, feminist critics had been working to recover the stories of these women. Some would eventually become my guides. Yet even as scholars write new biographies of these women and their books are studied in university classes on the eighteenth-century English novel, their contributions are often left out of the venues that reach the widest range of people: popular books, introductory survey courses of English literature and high school curricula, film and television adaptations of literary classics, and more. Once I became aware of these gaps, I began to see them everywhere. As of this writing, the "genre and style" section of Jane Austen's Wikipedia page notes Austen's debt to Richardson and Johnson, while Burney isn't mentioned at all. Most people don't know. I didn't know either.

I felt the weight of my mistake. I spent years wishing that Austen had authored more books. It didn't even occur to me that there were women writers whom Austen had used as models—and whose books I could read, too.

Scholars have often used Austen as a gateway to study earlier writers, but my initial explorations into these books were discouraging. It felt as if every time I turned a corner, I ran into a dead end. First, I turned to one of the pioneering academic monographs on the subject, Frank W.

Bradbrook's *Jane Austen and Her Predecessors* (1966), which included an entire chapter about "The Feminist Tradition" in the English novel that influenced Austen. I thought that title boded well. I was wrong. It immediately introduced the tradition as "not particularly distinguished." He categorically dismissed the novelists whom Austen had praised in her own works, such as Ann Radcliffe, Frances Burney, Charlotte Smith, and Maria Edgeworth: "Jane Austen turns inferior work by her predecessors and contemporaries to positive and constructive uses." According to an authority like Bradbrook, this quest of mine had already been investigated and resolved: we call Jane Austen the first great woman writer in English . . . because she was.

But Austen herself had provided evidence contradicting that conclusion. Were these authorities suggesting that some of the favorite books of one of the greatest authors of all time were trash? Would an author of that caliber really have had such terrible taste?

Part of the issue, I soon grasped, was that I was using the same methods to investigate these women as had originally caused the gap in my reading. I was relying upon grand narratives covering hundreds of years in a single book. My instinct was to trust the authorities who wrote these books because the canon had served me well in the past: I had enjoyed most of the "classics" that I had read (yes, even *Ulysses*). But the Great Forgetting lurked in these broad surveys. My investigation had turned into a labyrinth, and I was lost. I needed a different approach. It hadn't been reading about important novels that led me to take interest in Frances Burney, after all. It was book collecting. I had come across that 1903 copy of *Evelina* entirely by chance. I needed to stop thinking like a twentieth-century student and start thinking like a twenty-first-century book collector.

As the cofounder of a rare book company, I work with collectors every day, helping them track down scarce editions, walking them through auction records, and introducing them to books they haven't heard of but that are perfect for their shelves. In 2017 I also cofounded a book-collecting contest, the Honey & Wax Prize, for which we judge dozens of submissions annually and grant $1,000 to the winner. And I'm a collector myself, an admittedly dangerous pastime for a dealer (who must sell most of the books she acquires in order to remain in business). I shelve my personal collections at home, separate from my business, so as to maintain a boundary between what I keep long term as a collector and what I acquire to sell quickly as a dealer. Ironically, I came to book collecting long after I had been working in the rare book trade. Before that, I hadn't even considered it. It took becoming a professional in rare books to realize that anyone can collect rare books.

I became a rare book dealer by accident. When I was a college student, I didn't know that the job I now have even existed. Sure, I knew about "rare books." I had heard of "first editions." I knew my university library had a special collections department. But I was certain I didn't belong there. The doors of the special collections department looked heavy—like a gate kept closed to people like me. I thought that if I walked in, I would be coldly escorted out. And even if I could muster a legitimate reason to get in, there was no way they would ever let me touch anything.

I graduated from college and was living back home with my parents (a sentence that made half of you wince). That's when I spotted an employment ad for an introductory position at a rare book firm. "This looks amazing!" I said to my mother. Then I remembered those heavy doors of the special collections department. "Too bad I'm not qualified enough to apply."

My mother told me to apply anyway.

It turned out I was qualified, thanks to the fact that I had spent so many years reading books—especially classics. The year before, I had read *Paradise Lost* for fun; during one interview, I was asked to talk about that very book without preparation. At another point I had to write a short description on the importance of James Joyce's *Ulysses*—a book I happened to have tucked in my bag at that very moment. The week before, I had been at my local public library exploring the stacks. I had seen *Ulysses* on one shelf and figured there was no better time to tackle a famously complex masterpiece than when I was unemployed. Instead, it got me employment.

I have always been a reader. Growing up, every evening it was lights-out—and flashlight on, sneaking in a few pages before sleep pulled me under. I was an odd child, awkward around other kids, struggling to figure out how to say the right thing, often failing. I found socializing difficult, but in books I found less perplexing company.

The fact is, it's easier for me to relate to dead people than to the living. Characters in fiction, too. What I need is some distance. Emotions are big, scary. Distance provides safety to examine them without fear. Before I finished elementary school, I had read Roald Dahl's *Matilda* (1988) about six times. In Matilda, I saw another girl who was a bit odd, a bit awkward around other kids, and who used her mind to find happiness. Perhaps I might also be able to find happiness using my mind. I didn't have Matilda's telekinesis, but I liked reading books just like she did. Of course, I couldn't articulate that when I was ten. I could only say: I love *Matilda*.

When I read, I can enjoy other people's emotions at my own pace. Sometimes a book burns through me like a fever, and I can't eat or sleep until it's through. Other times I can take months to finish a single book, picking it up and putting it back down as the whim hits me, a fallen leaf suddenly blown aloft again by a gust of wind. When I feel a connection, with a character or with an author, it soothes that ever-lurking loneliness. But I also don't have to relate to characters to appreciate them: even differences reflect back on me by their contrast. Books give us a window into the minds of others, but they also help us know our own.

If you feel a similar way about reading, then I have a recommendation: book collecting. What reading and book collecting share is that contradictory miracle of finding closeness in distance. Yet book collecting is different than reading in its approach. A reader cares first and foremost about the text. Readers may have a preference of how that text is packaged—the old-schooler's comforting weight of a print copy; the vacationer's convenient e-reader; or the commuter's talisman, the audiobook—but these choices are all in service of the optimal reading experience.

A book collector, on the other hand, looks at a book as a historical artifact. Each detail reveals something about the time and circumstances of its production, as well as the lives it has lived since. Jane Austen's books, for example, were originally published in print runs that we would consider small today, none more than two thousand copies. Books were much more expensive then, and the audience with the means to purchase them correspondingly smaller. Besides, if a thousand-copy print run sold out, a publisher could always print more. If they printed two thousand copies and sold only a thousand, then they lost money. Show me a book from any era, any country, any genre, and I will show you how it reveals something about its own historical moment.

A reader says, "Which book do I want to read?" A collector says, "Which copy of this book do I want to find?" A reader falls in love with the story in the book. A collector falls in love with the story *of* the book.

I learned all this about book collecting after I got my first job in "the trade," as it is called. In 2007, I was hired by Bauman Rare Books, which was then the biggest rare book firm in North America; for years, its iconic ads in the back of the *New York Times Book Review* provided a glimpse into the world of rare books for many casual readers. There I was trained in all the particulars of what we broadly call bibliography—the study of the book as an object, such as how to determine the physical structure of a book, whether it's a first edition, and the history of its production and use. But becoming a rare book dealer is a long-term process. Even after I left that first company and eventually cofounded one of my own, I continued to develop my expertise. Knowledge about rare books is sensory as much as it is factual. To notice how the leaves feel between your fingers, how they smell, how they have toned over time . . . all this is relentlessly, inescapably, irresistibly material.

Because sensory knowledge is so important, the best way to learn is by doing. You must get as many books as possible in your hands. Then you must allow them to speak to you. But you don't need to be a professional to do this. Most people in the rare book world are not dealers or librarians. They are collectors, and they enjoy exploring this world as a hobby. I wish I had known this when I stood in front of those heavy doors at the special collections department in college. In retrospect, I realize that the curators there would likely have loved to see me step across that threshold.

Anyone can be a collector. One may be a Silicon Valley hotshot who has been inspired by ancient Greek Stoicism, collecting expensive editions of that philosophy's classic texts, like those of Epictetus and Marcus Aurelius. Another may be a teen who came to the Hunger Games books after seeing the films, then decided to find as many different editions of the trilogy as possible, hunting them down in thrift shops and Little Free Libraries on a limited budget. What we all have in common is a topic we love and the curiosity to explore it.

Book collectors have one other thing in common: we appreciate the idea of serendipity, when you come across the exact right book at the exact right time. It is a moment when fate seems to have intervened in your life. Alice Walker talks about this phenomenon in her book *In Search of Our Mothers' Gardens* (1983) when she was seeking the work of earlier Black women writers: "My discovery of them—most of them out of print, abandoned, discredited, maligned, nearly lost—came about, as many things of value do, almost by accident." I ran across this line when cataloging a signed first edition of the book at my shop and I thought: how appropriate. It reminded me that the serendipity of book collecting had brought me to Burney, who brought me back to Austen.

It was time to begin a new book collection.

———

While book collecting can turn on chance, it also demands parameters. Collecting is not thoughtless accumulation, but mindful curation. So I started to think about what this new book collection would look like. I would use Austen's own novels and letters as if they were a map, and trace the story of the women writers whom she read and who influenced her work. I wanted to read these books. But I also wanted to collect copies of historical interest that taught me something about their lives—and afterlives. Thanks to that passage in *Northanger Abbey*, I already had the outline for it: from Frances Burney to Maria Edgeworth.

Book collecting can appear intimidating in the beginning, but it is fairly simple. Again, you need only start with a topic you love and the curiosity to explore it. It can be as unique, as obscure, as weird as you want it to be. Book collecting is very personal, just as reading is very personal. In fact, collecting is an opportunity to embrace that oddly specific topic that only you care about. It allows you the opportunity to indulge your obsession when all you get is blank looks and glazed eyes from your loved ones. (They do love you! They just aren't as obsessed as you!) I already had my topic: Austen's favorite women writers.

Second, you need to create parameters as to which books fit in the collection and why. Are you only focusing on first editions? Only on copies with an interesting history? For instance, I had initially considered whether I should only include copies of books in my collection that Austen may actually have had on her own shelves, but quickly discarded the idea. I wanted to learn not only about these women's own books, but also their literary legacies. That meant some books would be published after their deaths, and Austen's. With Sherlock Holmes in mind, I determined that my scope would include any books that produced evidence for my investigation. I was looking for the turning points, books that marked moments when these women were added to, removed from, and sometimes placed back into the canon. That is a fairly wide scope. But since I was just starting my quest, I wanted to stay open to where the evidence might take me.

Finally, as a book collector you need to decide how you feel about the little details. Do you want a book that is in pristine condition, looking like it did on the day of its publication two hundred years ago? Or do you want a book that hints to its past lives through bits of wear and owner markings? I liked both, so I would play that on a case-by-case basis. A bigger concern for me was the prices. In my work as a rare book dealer, I regularly spend big money to obtain great material. But I get that cost back (hopefully with profit) when I sell those books. In this project I was acting as a private collector: I was keeping the books as my own, not with the intent to sell them professionally.

I set a budget that made me comfortable. Anything under $50, what I would call the price of a modest dinner out with friends, I would acquire without remorse. (This is a questionable habit I developed as early as high school, when I would go without eating at school for the week so that I could spend my lunch money on used CDs on the weekend. Maybe don't be like me.) Above $50, I would have to give it more thought. Above $100, I would save money in smaller amounts for a few months before making the buy. Above $500, and I would likely purchase it only if I was buying it for resale in my business. My collection was meant to be a source of joy, not a source of stress; a modest budget ensured it would remain so. Despite what newspaper headlines may tell you, you don't have to be rich to collect rare books.

––––––––––

It has been many years since that house call in Georgetown. I have spent that time building my book collection. Through this process, I did track down the evidence I had been seeking. It was not what I had assumed before: that these women weren't remembered because they weren't interesting enough, or their works weren't good enough. I did not find a group of hacks whose devices and themes existed only to reach full perfection in Austen's use of them. Instead, I found the turning points. I traced moments when these women were attacked, elided, demeaned, and displaced from the canon. In some cases, I also saw moments when they made their way back to the canon, championed by a particular critic or given new life with a popular reprint. Each book in my collection was a clue as to how all this happened, and why.

This is the story of how I collected books by, and books about, eight women writers whose works Jane Austen read, but who no longer have the widespread readership they once enjoyed. I read and studied their works, drawing on biography, literary criticism, literary history, and, of course, the skills of my trade in rare books. Over time, my book collection became a eulogy to these writers' legacies—and an argument for their popular reassessment.

I have wondered over the years whether my project would have appealed to Austen. I'm confident she would have been horrified to hear today's popular opinion of Frances Burney or Maria Edgeworth—when they are remembered at all. As repayment for what she had given me, I hoped I could offer Austen this in return: a collection that reunites the novels she read, and a book honoring her own favorite authors. I took my Sherlockian skills from the rare book trade and turned them to this investigation. I wanted to know who these women were, what they wrote, and why they were no longer part of the canon. I would read their books and I would collect copies that appealed to me for their historical interest. I would fill Jane Austen's Bookshelf.

Chapter One

JANE AUSTEN
(1775-1817)

Mrs Martin tells us that her Collection is not to consist only of Novels, but of every kind of Literature &c &c—She might have spared this pretension to <u>our</u> family, who are great Novel-readers & not ashamed of being so.

—Letter from Jane Austen to Cassandra Austen, December 18–19, 1798

Austen's canonical status is so unassailable that she's not just included in the list of great novelists: she tops it. Claire Harman's book about Austen's path to canonicity, *Jane's Fame* (2009), is subtitled *How Jane Austen Conquered the World.* Juliette Wells's book about her American champions, *A New Jane Austen* (2023), is subtitled *How Americans Brought Us the World's Greatest Novelist. Pride and Prejudice* is "the best romance novel ever written," according to Pamela Regis, who wrote the foundational academic study of the English romance novel, *A Natural History of the Romance Novel* (2003). I happen to agree with Regis. I have read and reread Austen's six major novels: *Sense and Sensibility* (1811), *Pride and Prejudice* (1813), *Mansfield Park* (1814), *Emma* (1816), *Northanger Abbey* (1818), and *Persuasion* (1818); as well as her novella, *Lady Susan* (circa 1794), and various forms of her unfinished works, *The Watsons* (circa 1803–4) and *Sanditon* (drafted 1817). And I will read them all again.

What I turn to over and over is Austen's confidence. Her style has the ease that comes from an incredible amount of work—and a conviction in one's own voice. She leads us from conflict to resolution, from hating Mr. Darcy to loving him, with the skill of a master. She knows exactly what she's doing, and where she's going. I also love her sly wit. In much of her prose, it feels as if she is sharing a conspiratorial glance with the reader. She can narrate the dullest of behaviors with the comic timing of your most interesting friend, as in the hypochondriac Mr. Woodhouse's inane dinner patter: "let Emma help you to a *little* bit of tart—a *very* little bit. Ours are all apple tarts. You need not be afraid of unwholesome preserves here. I do not advise the custard."

Despite their narrow focus on life in the English countryside in the early nineteenth century, her books remain relatable. Every time I read about Elizabeth Bennet accidentally running into Mr. Darcy at his Pemberley estate after she has rejected him, I feel a pang of recognition: "she had not got beyond the words 'delightful,' and 'charming,' when [. . .] she fancied that praise of Pemberley from her, might be mischievously construed. Her colour changed, and she said no more." Who has not experienced being so embarrassed that you simply stop talking in the middle of a sentence? This is part of what makes Austen's novels classics: they feel fresh to readers over two centuries after their publication.

It comes as no surprise, then, that Austen's books are also highly sought on the rare book marketplace. Take *Pride and Prejudice*: I've sold first editions in "contemporary calf," leather-bound around the time of the book's publication, for prices in the six figures. I've handled countless other editions that were notable for all sorts of reasons. One of my favorite copies was a third edition bound in green moiré silk—a fabric popular in Regency-era dresses thanks to French fashion trends—sold to a collector who wanted it as a Christmas gift for a loved one. I've also sold more modest reprints for memorable occasions, such as an early-twentieth-century copy bound in simple red cloth that was used as a key prop in one man's proposal to his soon-to-be-fiancée. Then there are the crumbling "yellowbacks," so called for their bright paper boards meant to catch travelers' eyes in Victorian railway stations; the stereotyped copies that use the same printing plates across decades, but dressed up for each reissue with a new binding; and the garish books from the post–World War II paperback boom that are, ironically, more fragile than first edition copies, since their cheaply produced paper deteriorates faster than the cotton rag–based paper used in Austen's time.

All these books speak to an illustrious legacy built over centuries from humble beginnings. Jane Austen was born in 1775 in the English countryside, Steventon, Hampshire. "To generations of Austen worshippers," the modern biographer Lucy Worsley notes, her childhood home "is hallowed ground." But it wasn't always so. Austen's rise to canonical dominance occurred largely after her lifetime, and only truly began to gain momentum more than fifty years after her death. Her life and legacy provided the context for my investigation into the other women writers on my list: by tracing the turning points in Austen's trajectory, I hoped to recognize similar patterns in, and deviations from, those of her predecessors.

The Austens were a genteel family—that is, they were upper-class, but not titled—though Jane's father, George Austen, struggled to provide the lifestyle associated with this high status on his income. George was a rector of two parishes. He also ran a small school for boys. One modern biographer, John Halperin, estimates her father's annual income at "a little under £600": enough to pay for the upkeep of a carriage, employ servants, and keep his wife and daughters from the need to work, but not much else. Jane was one of eight children: James, the oldest, who also became a rector; George, who was disabled, and largely cared for in a home; Edward, who was adopted by wealthy relatives and took on the surname Knight; Henry, Jane's "favorite" brother and an ebullient businessman; Cassandra, the sister to whom Jane was devoted for the entirety of her life; and Francis and Charles, who both had distinguished careers in the Royal Navy. Jane was the second youngest, born between Francis and Charles.

The family culture was distinctly literary. They were "great Novel-readers," as Austen proudly observed in a 1798 letter to her sister. They reread favorite novels and constantly made references to their characters. The family would often read books together, with one person reading aloud. Among these was Burney's *Evelina*. As an adult, Jane Austen became known for reading aloud "remarkably well," according to her niece: "once I knew her to take up a volume of *Evelina* [. . .] and I thought it was like a play." Austen did not purchase many books for herself—they were, as I will discuss later, quite expensive at the time—but she took advantage of circulating libraries, where members paid a flat monthly fee to borrow books; she was part of a local "book club" that split the cost of a book to share among themselves; she received books as gifts; and she enjoyed access to her family members' books, including Edward's magnificent library at one of the estates he eventually inherited, Godmersham Park.

The Austens also loved the theater. When Jane was eight years old, the family began mounting their own amateur versions of plays at home. The barn was the perfect place for a summer rendition of a play written by David Garrick, the famous actor and theater manager.

James was considered the literary darling of the family. He wrote the prologues and epilogues for these plays, and he had run a small literary magazine, *The Loiterer*, during his school days at Oxford (to which Henry contributed). But in fact, most members of the family wrote in some fashion, whether poetry (Austen's mother and sister), sermons (Austen's father and two brothers), or plays (Austen's oldest brother). Austen enjoyed a supportive environment to experiment early with writing. Scholars refer to these pieces, which she composed as a child, as juvenilia.

Austen's juvenilia show a delight in parody. A typical example of her comedic bent as a teen is *Love and Freindship* [*sic*], composed in 1790 when she was fourteen. In it, the heroine relates stories of her travels and misfortunes in an extravagant and absurd manner. When one young man's father encourages his son to marry the woman he loves, the young man cries, "No! Never shall it be said that I obliged my Father."

Austen's juvenilia also contain indications, in cheeky details, of her authorly ambitions and her family's support of them. Both are visible in the beginning of her unfinished novel *Lesley Castle*, which she dedicated to her brother Henry. In thanks, Henry added a note beneath the dedication with faux pomposity, "pay Jane Austen Spinster the sum of one hundred guineas." This was meant as a humorously large amount, especially when one considers their father's annual income of under £600. Austen didn't finish every piece, but she was constantly writing. In 1794, she wrote probably her best-known work of juvenilia, the novella *Lady Susan*, about a wickedly intelligent widow who wreaks havoc in the lives of her friends and family. Though it would not appear in print until 1871, today it is often named alongside her six full-length novels published in the 1810s.

Austen was supported in her writing not only by her family but also by family friends, especially the women in her life. One of these was her neighbor Madame Anne Lefroy, whom Austen loved to visit. In December 1795, just as Austen was turning twenty, Madame Lefroy's nephew Tom came to Hampshire. Something between the young man and the aspiring writer sparked. But the precarious financial status of the Austen family (including the lack of dowry for the Austen sisters) was well known to Madame Lefroy. When she noticed the growing attraction between Tom and Jane, she quickly sent her nephew away. In Austen's surviving letters from the period immediately after, she shows a determination to remain in good humor—and continues to joke about the success that her writing will one day bring her: "I write only for Fame," she quipped in a January 14, 1796, letter to Cassandra.

In 1796 Austen began the book that would eventually be published as *Pride and Prejudice*. The manuscript was initially called *First Impressions*; it was the first of three novels that Austen would revise extensively and publish under a new title. In 1797, her father wrote a well-established publisher, Cadell, with an offer to submit *First Impressions*. Cadell declined and returned his letter. Undeterred, Austen began a new novel titled *Elinor and Marianne*, though this story of two sisters would also not see print until much later, after it too had been revised and retitled. Being a professional writer was Austen's long-standing ambition; according to the modern scholar Jan Fergus, it was, "apart from her family, more important to her than anything else in her life." But she would work for many more years and endure a number of personal tragedies before the publication of her first book.

One of the biggest shocks of Austen's life occurred in 1801, when she was twenty-five: her father retired and moved the family to Bath. Austen did not want to leave Steventon, but she had little choice. Her dismay over the move comes out in little details in her letters to Cassandra, as when she dutifully participated in the search for a house in Bath. The ones on New King Street that her mother liked were "smaller than I expected [. . .] the best of the sittingrooms not so large as the little parlour at Steventon." She reconciled herself as best she could to the situation. In one letter, she told Cassandra of a ball that was "rather a dull affair"—but "[a]fter tea we cheered up," a phrase of noble resignation you could easily expect to find in one of her novels.

Another unpleasant surprise occurred in 1802 when she visited old friends in Hampshire. Harris Bigg-Wither, the son of family friends, proposed to Austen. He was twenty-one; she was twenty-seven. Austen accepted, then changed her mind the next morning. We don't know for certain why Austen rejected his proposal. Had she married Bigg-Wither, who had a large inheritance and an ancient family estate, she would have lived comfortably for the remainder of her life. Yet she clearly did not love him. It is my guess that she first accepted him as a practicality, then rejected him as a reality. (A little over a year later, Bigg-Wither married another woman; they had ten children.) Austen would have been well aware of the implications of refusing such an offer in her late twenties. It meant that she would likely remain unmarried—and therefore financially dependent upon her family members for the rest of her life.

But Austen had new prospects: she had sold her first novel. She expected the book, titled *Susan*, to be issued soon after in 1803. But the publisher dragged his feet and the manuscript languished. *Susan* was not destined to become Austen's first published novel. Eventually it would see print and find its audience—under a new title—over a decade later.

Back in Bath, Austen began another novel that would become known as *The Watsons*, about a young woman who returns to her family after years living with a wealthy aunt. But Austen abandoned it unfinished after a tragedy occurred worse than any before. Her father died in 1804, leaving Austen, her mother, and her sister entirely dependent upon the brothers. The brothers discussed the problem: James, the eldest; Edward, inheritor of the Knight estates Chawton House (in East Hampshire) and Godmersham Park (in Kent); and Francis, moving quickly through the Royal Navy ranks during the Napoleonic Wars. They each committed to providing funds to support their mother and sisters for a total of £450 per year. For the next few years, the three women moved around between Bath; the countryside, where they visited family friends; and Southampton, where they stayed at Francis's house. Edward also gave his mother the choice of a more permanent home near one of his two estates. In 1809 she chose Chawton. Edward prepared a cottage in walking distance to Chawton House for his mother and sisters. This cottage is now legendary, as it was while living here that Austen would finally become a published author. Here she would usher into print three of her already drafted manuscripts, *Sense and Sensibility*, *Pride and Prejudice*, and—posthumously—*Northanger Abbey*. Here she would write the remainder of her three completed novels, *Mansfield Park*, *Emma*, and *Persuasion*, and begin a fourth (*Sanditon*).

Her brother Henry negotiated the business arrangements for all of the books successfully published in her lifetime. Looking at them as a whole, one can find commonalities from one to the next. They all take place in small, genteel social circles, primarily in the English countryside, but also in resort towns like Bath. All include subplots, but ultimately focus on a love story for the heroines, with a happy ending. (Today we would call these "romances," but that word had a different meaning in Austen's time. In acknowledgment of that context, I'll be calling them "courtship novels.") Yet while the settings and plots of Austen's novels are similar, each is distinctive in its prevailing tone and the temperaments of her heroines. Fellow Austen fans will have to forgive me for the next few pages: you know these books like old friends, but I'm including a quick overview of each because their plots and characters appear again in surprising ways throughout my investigation.

———

Austen's first published book was *Sense and Sensibility* in late October 1811. This novel was in fact a revision of her 1797 manuscript *Elinor and Mari-*

anne. Austen was able to secure a publisher for it only by commission, that is, by paying for all the expenses of the production herself. If the book sold well, she might make enough to see a profit after costs; if it did not, then she would simply be out that money. Henry later said his sister was so convinced "that its sale would not repay the expense of publication, that she actually made a reserve from her very moderate income to meet the expected loss." In the end the edition, probably of one thousand copies or less, sold well enough to bring her £140. It went into a second edition in 1813, and Austen was delighted. The book was issued in three volumes, as was typical in the era; all of Austen's novels were issued in multiple volumes. This practice was developed by publishers to mitigate their high-risk, high-return business, since book production entailed heavy up-front costs that a poor seller might take a long time to pay back. Multiple volumes provided the ability to charge more for a single book, as well as to coax more profits out of the popular book subscription services of this era called circulating libraries. (When Austen's characters mention "the Library," that's where they're going, not the free public libraries we enjoy today.)

In *Sense and Sensibility*, the two Dashwood sisters each experience love and disappointment while reckoning with their own financial insecurity. Due to their contrasting personalities—Elinor, stoic to a fault; Marianne, full of spirit and impetuosity—they handle these events in opposite ways. Both extremes compound the young women's trials before they each eventually settle into happy marriages. What I like most about this book is its dialogue, especially in one masterful early scene. The heroines' wealthy half brother, who promised their father he would take care of them financially, is gradually convinced by his wife to be less generous than he had intended. After planning to settle £3,000 upon his sisters, he eventually concludes: "A present [. . .] now and then, will prevent their ever being distressed for money, and will, I think, be amply discharging my promise to my father." The subtle disintegration of his intention occurs over the course of a few conversations with his wife, whose strategic sequence of questions wears him down without him even noticing. It is brilliant; it is entertaining; and it is strikingly realistic.

Sense and Sensibility received two public reviews, including a meaty one from the *Critical Review*, one of the most influential British literary newspapers. The *Review* thought it "worthy of particular commendation" and appreciated its "useful moral." Intriguingly for a reader like me, who was just beginning to learn that there were novelists like Austen before Austen, this review also noted that there was no "newness" in it. *Sense and Sensibility* followed established conventions in the novel.

Austen was proud of her first publication, writing in a letter to Cassandra that "I am never too busy to think of S&S. I can no more forget it, than a mother can forget her suckling child." But Austen's pleasure at seeing one of her books finally reach readers did not mean she wanted to draw attention to herself publicly: as with all her novels published in her lifetime, it was issued anonymously. This was not unusual. Anonymous publication was an accepted convention in this era, far more common than in our own. There were a number of reasons for this, but as we will see, many writers preferred to let their works rise or fall on their own merits, and might only reveal their authorship after an established record of success. Among genteel women, publishing under one's name could also appear to be a "boast" of one's accomplishments: it was seen as awfully forward when anonymity was a viable choice. Word spread among the family that Austen did not want her authorship to become a topic of conversation, as when one niece recorded a "Letter from At. Cass. [Jane's sister, Cassandra] to beg we would not mention that Aunt Jane wrote Sense and Sensibility." Henry, however, developed the waggish habit of "slipping" about the author's identity, and it soon became an open secret.

Austen's second book was published in January 1813. The year her first book was published, Austen had returned to another old manuscript, *First Impressions* of 1796. She revised it significantly and gave it the new title of *Pride and Prejudice*. The first edition had an estimated 1,500 copies, and it went into two further editions in Austen's lifetime. In *Pride and Prejudice*, the heroine Elizabeth Bennet brings a detached irony to the chaotic surroundings of her large household with four sisters. At a local ball she meets a wealthy and snobbish visitor, Fitzwilliam Darcy, and takes an immediate dislike to him. The feeling appears to be mutual in subsequent encounters—until Darcy surprises her with a proposal. She refuses him, then quickly comes to regret her decision. Austen loved Elizabeth Bennet, whom she called "as delightful a creature as ever appeared in print." I adore this novel for the same reason: Elizabeth Bennet is the fictional heroine I would wish to be. *Pride and Prejudice* received three public reviews, and this time critics were even more impressed: "It is far superior to almost all the publications of the kind which have lately come before us," noted the *British Critic*.

By that summer *Sense and Sensibility*'s first edition had sold out and Austen had learned that she was a profitable author—"which only makes me long for more," she bantered in a July 1813 letter to her brother Francis. She was already working on her next novel, *Mansfield Park*, which she hoped would build on the success of *Pride and Prejudice*. It was the first novel begun at the Chawton cottage.

Mansfield Park became her third published novel in May 1814. Printed in an estimated edition of 1,250 copies, it was sold out in six months and went into a second edition in February 1816. In *Mansfield Park*, Fanny Price lives with a wealthier branch of her family, the Bertrams, who take her in but do not treat her on equal terms with her cousins. The real action begins after Fanny's uncle, Sir Thomas Bertram, leaves the titular estate to check on a plantation he owns in Antigua. While he is away, the young people of the neighborhood decide to stage a rather racy play to the dismay of Fanny and her cousin, Edmund, whom she has always admired. Edmund begins to return her admiration as he observes her strength of character amid the drama that ensues.

Mansfield Park did not receive any public reviews, surely a disappointment to Austen after the praise of her first two novels. It is perhaps her most subtle work. So much pulses beneath the surface: the specter of the slave trade, the machinations of the defiant flirts, Fanny's own timidly beating heart. By now Austen's anonymity, still formally maintained on the title pages of her books, was an open secret among her friends and acquaintances. Austen began collecting their opinions on her books. Of *Mansfield*

Park, her mother did not like it "so well as P. & P." and "[t]hought Fanny insipid"; Cassandra, for her part, was "[f]ond of Fanny" but thought the book "not so brilliant as P. & P." Another family friend, Mrs. Bramstone, liked *Mansfield Park* the best, "but imagined *that* might be her want of Taste—as she does not understand Wit," the great strength of *Pride and Prejudice*.

The publication of *Mansfield Park* brought out another important fan, the prince regent. The regent was the eldest child of King George III, the acting monarch in his father's stead since 1811, due to the king's mental illness. (This is where the name for the time period we associate with Austen, "the Regency," comes from; it covers 1811 to 1820, after which the regent became King George IV.) Since Austen's authorship was an open secret, the regent's librarian was able to write to her to say that the regent "has read and admired all your publications." At the librarian's suggestion, Austen's next novel would carry a dedication to the prince regent.

That novel was *Emma*, her fourth published book, which featured a heroine whom Austen feared "no one but myself will much like." It was begun in January 1814 and published in an edition of two thousand copies in December 1815. (Its title page, however, is dated 1816: this was a common practice for books published at the end of the year in order to extend the perception of their newness into the following year.) Emma Woodhouse is the doyenne of genteel society in the fictional village of Highbury: she is smart, beautiful, capable, and witty. However, her confidence leads her to meddling in the lives of others, such as when she attempts to find a "better" match for her friend Harriet over the farmer whom Harriet actually loves. All the while Emma's neighbor and family friend, George Knightley, simultaneously argues with and admires her. Austen feared no one would like Emma, but I love how believably flawed the heroine is. Her strengths are also her weaknesses; she's so used to being right that she forgets she can be wrong.

While *Pride and Prejudice* is often the favorite of many people's hearts, *Emma* has often been praised as the most technically perfect of her novels. It received the most critical attention of any of her books in her lifetime, including a major analysis in the *Quarterly Review*—published anonymously, but in fact by Walter Scott. (In 1814 Scott had himself anonymously published a bestselling novel, *Waverley*, with three editions in a single year.) In many ways this review marked the beginning of Austen studies, and it set the tone for a number of the subsequent analyses in the nineteenth century. For instance, Scott remarked that Austen's "subjects are not often elegant, and certainly never grand; but they are finished up to nature, and with a precision which delights the reader." That is, Austen's novels depicted a small and ordinary world, but with exceptionally precise realism. Following Scott, many of Austen's earliest champions focused on her realism as the best evidence of her artistry.

Like her heroine Emma, Austen's own strengths and weaknesses were closely bound together. Her focus on a narrow series of problems within a tiny portion of society was what readers both loved and hated about her works. True, she was praised for her realism. But in her own time period, many critics and readers felt that high art should achieve something more than what one experiences in ordinary life. The best literature, they argued, evoked a depth of feeling stirred only by intense circumstances, like the murderous machinations of Shakespeare's *Hamlet*, or the pathos of Satan's fall in *Paradise Lost*. By this metric, books about everyday people's unremarkable lives could rarely evoke the same transcendent response. As a friend of the author Maria Edgeworth said in an 1814 letter about *Mansfield Park*: "It has not however that elevation of virtue, something beyond nature, that gives the greatest charm to a novel, but still it is real natural everyday life, and will amuse an idle hour very well in spite of its faults."

The fact that Austen never reached for this transcendence bothered many readers and critics. It would take decades before her novels achieved the same level of esteem as those by Walter Scott, who appreciated Austen's minute pictures but wrote in a grand style himself (which he charmingly called his "Big Bow-wow strain"). Yet Austen knew her own voice. The most important thing she did as an artist was maintain the discipline to be true to it. For instance, when the regent's librarian recommended that she write a historical novel about the royal House of Saxe-Coburg, she politely demurred. "No, I must keep to my own style and go on in my own way;

and though I may never succeed again in that, I am convinced that I should totally fail in any other." This was the confidence of Jane Austen that I admired so much.

Emma was the last novel that Austen saw published. In 1816, only five years after the publication of her first novel, she had begun to show signs of serious illness. Based on her symptoms, scholars have suggested she suffered from Addison's disease, which affects the adrenal glands, or possibly cancer, though we cannot be sure. She still worked on her novels, but her health continued to deteriorate and she died in July 1817. She was only forty-one.

The final two novels Austen completed, *Northanger Abbey* and *Persuasion*, were published together in four volumes a few months after her death in December 1817 (with the title page dated 1818). The edition numbered 1,750 copies. *Northanger Abbey* was Austen's phoenix, a revision of her first sold novel, *Susan*. After the publication of *Emma* in the spring of 1816, Jane had instructed Henry to purchase *Susan* back from the publisher, who had bought the manuscript for £10 in 1803. Upon accomplishing the errand, Henry "had the satisfaction of informing [the publisher] that the work which had been so lightly esteemed was by the author of 'Pride and Prejudice.'"

In *Northanger Abbey*, seventeen-year-old Catherine Morland experiences high society for the first time on a trip to Bath. She has lived a quiet life in the country and most of what she knows about the world comes from the books she reads. In Bath, Catherine quickly makes friends through a shared love of reading: with Isabella Thorpe, whose capricious taste is reflected in the books she reads, and with Henry Tilney, who appreciates a good novel himself, yet brings a cheerful mockery to both the books he reads and the world around him. (A number of critics have remarked upon Henry Tilney's similarity to Austen. In 1952 Marvin Mudrick joked that Tilney "closely resembles, except for a few details of dress and appearance, the author herself.") Still learning about the world around her, Catherine makes the mistake of expecting life to unfold like the plots in the gothic romances she reads—and gets into trouble when it doesn't. In 1818 the *British Critic* called it "one of the very best of Miss Austen's productions," though most critical attention upon publication was directed toward its companion, *Persuasion*.

Persuasion was Austen's final completed novel, begun in August 1815. The heroine Anne Elliot is the middle child of a proud genteel family whose money troubles instigate a move to Bath to lower expenses. When she was younger, Anne had become engaged to Frederick Wentworth, but ultimately broke off the connection at the advice of friends because he was without a similar family pedigree and had few prospects for building wealth. Eight years later, the still-heartbroken Anne and the now Captain Wentworth, made wealthy by a successful career in the Royal Navy, meet again. *Persuasion* is Austen's most mature novel; she examines not the flutter of young love, but the depths of feeling forged by the weight of years. According to one important review, published in 1821 anonymously by the *Quarterly Review*, *Persuasion* was perhaps "superior to all" of Austen's novels; "on the whole, it is one of the most elegant fictions of common life we ever remember to have met with."

The co-publication of *Northanger Abbey* and *Persuasion* was publicly announced as posthumous. In the first edition, Henry revealed Jane Austen's name as the author in print for the first time in a "Biographical Notice" added to the beginning of the production. Naturally, reviewers included an appraisal of Austen's life and work as a whole in their articles, and their remarks were largely ambivalent. The reputation we have of Jane Austen today as one of the greatest novelists in English took time to grow. She was respected, but most critics also considered her too limited. Austen wrote only what she knew; and that realism, for these readers, was both good and bad. A review in the March 1818 *British Critic* reads: "Her merit consists altogether in her remarkable talent for observation." A trait Sherlock Holmes would have appreciated, to be sure—but not sufficient to make up for her weaknesses. "In imagination, of all kinds, she appears to have been extremely deficient; not only her stories are utterly and entirely devoid of invention, but her characters, her incidence, her sentiments, are obviously all drawn exclusively from experience." At the time of her death, it was by no means clear that Austen's work would acquire the monumental reputation that it eventually achieved.

Austen's literary fate was now in the hands of her family. First Henry had revealed Austen's name in that fifteen-page "Biographical Notice" he added to the publication of *Northanger Abbey* and *Persuasion*. This grief-stricken eulogy for a beloved sister provided the foundation for our image of Austen for centuries to come. Because it is such an important document, its limitations are all the more frustrating. For instance, the modern scholar Emily Auerbach dissects Henry's love of the word "sweet": he "favored adjectives such as sweet, kind, happy, and tranquil. For example, we learn that his sister had an 'extremely sweet' voice and endowments that 'sweetened every hour' of her relatives' lives." This adjective also stuck out to me because every time someone has called me "sweet," I've thought: *Boy, you don't know me very well.* Henry gave us an angel, not the truth.

Besides Henry's "Biographical Notice," another major source of information about Austen's life comes from her letters. Henry selectively quoted some to emphasize her piety and, yes, sweetness. But he did quote one letter about her work, in which she compared it to "a little bit of ivory, two inches wide, on which I work with a brush so fine as to produce little effect after much labour." This single passage has been examined for centuries as a precious gem, revealing in Austen's own words how she viewed her style. For years it was one of the only statements we had from Austen herself on her writing because the bulk of her letters were not accessible to the public. Over time, our understanding of Austen would be revolutionized by the gradual publication of her surviving letters.

Austen's sister Cassandra took on the care of most of Jane's literary possessions after her death, including her manuscripts and letters. Unfortunately, to Cassandra this responsibility also entailed burning large masses of those letters. Burning the correspondence of the deceased was common practice, an act of privacy to ensure words not meant for public consumption remained that way. In fact, it was remarkable that Cassandra didn't burn them all. Nevertheless, I can't help but dream of what was in those that were destroyed. We have a tantalizing account by one of Francis's daughters of Cassandra returning to these letters to enjoy her sister's "triumphing over the married women of her acquaintance, and rejoicing in her own freedom from care." Because of Cassandra's cautionary conflagration, much of what we know directly about Jane Austen's life derives from accounts of her relatives, such as Henry's "Biographical Notice."

In the early 1830s, publishers began approaching the family to reprint Austen's books. Henry sold to publisher Richard Bentley the copyrights for all six previously published novels, now given life for another generation in Bentley's Standard Novels series. These books each contained an illustrated scene facing the title page, known as a frontispiece, making them the first illustrated editions of Austen's novels in English—readers' first view of Elizabeth Bennet, accosted by Fitzwilliam Darcy's aunt; and of Catherine Morland, suspecting Henry Tilney of using a secret passageway. These editions are in great demand by collectors, and I nab one for my rare book shop at every opportunity. From this point forward Austen's novels remained in circulation with readers through numerous popular reprints—as documented by another book collector, the scholar Janine Barchas, who hunted down cheap, beat-up, and well-marked copies of these humble and fascinating productions in *The Lost Books of Jane Austen* (2019).

Austen received less notice from critics in the decades immediately after her death, but she did have a few champions. The critic George Henry Lewes published multiple articles attempting to bring Austen the attention he felt she deserved, as in this opening to an 1859 essay: "For nearly half a century England has possessed an artist of the highest rank, whose works have been extensively circulated, whose merits have been keenly relished, and whose name is still unfamiliar in men's mouths." (Lewes's partner was one of the great novelists of the Victorian era, George Eliot, though she did not share his high opinion of Austen.) He also argued with Charlotte Brontë over Austen's merits. Inspired by Lewes's praise of *Pride and Prejudice*, Brontë gave it a try. She was not impressed, calling it "a carefully fenced, highly cultivated garden, with neat borders and delicate flowers; but [. . .] no open country, no fresh air, no blue hill, no bonny beck." In short: it had no spirit. Austen was too ordinary to be transcendent. In a follow-up

letter to Lewes, Brontë wondered, "Can there be a great artist without poetry?" Austen "maybe *is* sensible, real (more *real* than *true*), but she cannot
be great." Some read and loved Austen; others didn't. Nevertheless, she
kept being read. For the first few decades after Austen's death, her legacy
hovered between the two extremes of ascension and oblivion.

A major turning point in Austen's canonical rise occurred on her birthday, December 16, in 1869. Her nephew, James Edward Austen-Leigh,
published the first book-length biography of Austen. He was the son of
her oldest brother, James, and only eighteen years old when she died in
July 1817. The engaging *A Memoir of Jane Austen* (its title page dated 1870)
received significant attention in the press and occasioned a new appraisal
of Austen's novels. While it was limited in scope, based upon decades-old
memories and whatever documents her family kept, it nevertheless gave
critics important material to recontextualize her writing. I decided that I
would seek a copy of this book for my collection, an apt beginning to this
investigation.

Finding one was trickier than I thought, as it's quite scarce these days
on the antiquarian marketplace. I finally found one lying abandoned on
a pile of not-yet cataloged books at the bookshop of a friend of mine in
London. This multilevel shop specializes in nineteenth-century literature,
with only the first floor typically accessible to the public. I had picked this
volume up on a higher floor, the one dedicated to theater and nonfiction
(eighteenth-century literature floated to the top floor, while the Romantics shared a space with the back-of-house kitchenette). Because it wasn't
shelved in the main part of the shop, I feared it wouldn't be for sale. How
excruciating to get a long-sought book in your hands, then have to let it
go! Or, my friend could have quoted a price way above what I was willing
to pay. But he did give me a price, and a good one. Austen-Leigh came
home with me that trip (along with an 1820 gothic romance with a villain
modeled after Lord Byron—but that's a story for another time). Now this
book sits on my bookshelf, where its simple cloth binding, with minimal yet
elegant gilt tooling to the boards and spine, belies its central importance to
the story of how Jane Austen joined the canon.

Like Henry Austen's "Biographical Notice," Austen-Leigh's memoir focused on Austen's commitment to family and—once again—a "sweetness of temper that never failed." These were understandable observations from a teen nephew, but delivered in a way that placed Austen within the bounds of the ideal womanhood championed in Victorian England. This was the era of the "cult of domesticity": a conviction, espoused by no less than Queen Victoria herself, that women's "sphere" was the home. To Austen-Leigh, she was, literally, "my dear aunt Jane." But the symbolism of this idea appealed to his contemporary audience. One 1870 reviewer was so taken with this portrait that he ended his essay with the decision to call her "dear aunt Jane" himself. The image was eagerly embraced by her Victorian readers. It also took decades for commentators to wash out the more saccharine aspects of its influence. (Like me, however, a number of women questioned the "sweet" adjective. Of Austen's "sweetness of temper that never failed," the great writer of detective novels P. D. James observed in 2000: "On the contrary, it failed frequently, and if it hadn't we would not have had the six great novels.")

In 1871 Austen-Leigh published a second edition of the biography, expanded by request to include some of Austen's unpublished manuscripts. This is the edition of the book I read, accessed via Google Books on my laptop, over the course of a few grey mornings before I went to work. These manuscripts had been kept in Cassandra's charge until her death in 1845, and were then bequeathed to various family members. For this edition, Austen-Leigh arranged to include the first printing of *Lady Susan* and *The Watsons*, along with a summary of *Sanditon*, which he considered too fragmentary to publish. First editions of Austen's works were appearing in the 1870s! This is the kind of tidbit you often learn when collecting. You'd think that all of Austen's first editions were issued in her lifetime or just after it, but that's not the case. (One of her books of juvenilia, *Volume the Third*, did not see publication until 1951; as of this writing, copies of this Austen first edition can be had for only $25 to $100 from antiquarian booksellers. And yes, I have already nabbed one for myself.) By 1882, the *Memoir* itself had become part of the Austen must-haves: in that year the Bentley "Steventon

Edition" of her works included the *Memoir*, along with *Lady Susan* and *The Watsons*, in the set. Unsurprisingly, this edition is also quite collectible.

Austen-Leigh's *Memoir* was the catalyst for Austen's meteoric rise in the subsequent decades. Following its success, Austen's grand-nephew Edward, Lord Brabourne published the *Letters of Jane Austen* (1884) in two volumes, containing the ninety-four letters he had inherited from his mother, Fanny Knight, the oldest daughter of Austen's brother Edward. Brabourne broke from family tradition that held the letters should be kept private; together with Austen-Leigh's *Memoir*, the material published in the *Letters* ushered in a new generation of scholarship.

In the United States, too, Austen found champions. One was William Dean Howells, who wrote popular essays in *Harper's* magazine beginning in 1889 extolling her realism as "writing simply, honestly, [and] artistically." Also in 1889 the American Oscar Fay Adams published the earliest critical edition of Austen's novels, *Chapters from Jane Austen*. For years now the only copy of this book I've been able to track down is one on eBay for a very reasonable price—because it's covered in dampstaining (that is, evidence of exposure to some kind of moisture). I hold out hope for another. In 1891, Adams followed it with *The Story of Jane Austen's Life*, the first critical biography of Austen—based on original research and analysis, rather than family memories. I did buy a copy of this one via eBay, paying for upgraded shipping in hopes that the seller would pack it more carefully. This is a hazard of using marketplaces with unvetted sellers: they rarely pack professionally. I once wanted to weep at the sight of a signed first edition of an Ursula K. Le Guin book that had been wedged diagonally across the interior of a box it would not have normally fit into. But in this case, the book came packaged in a manner quite unusual for eBay—in what I call the Etsy treatment: not only was it carefully wrapped in tissue, but also entwined in a bright green ribbon from which a handwritten note dangled.

While Austen was enjoying a new generation of critical attention, her readership was quickly expanding. In Britain, the Elementary Education Act of 1870 and its subsequent incarnations transformed public schools, including making school for younger children compulsory. Austen became a favorite for teaching. This is one of the most powerful factors in many authors' ascent into the canon: when an entire generation is required to read the same texts, those texts become part of their shared vocabulary. One of Austen's biographers, Goldwin Smith, had complained in 1890 that her novels "are spoken of respectfully as classics, and as classics allowed to rest upon the shelf," i.e., unread—but by 1897, the American professor Arlo Bates listed Austen as a novelist "which it is taken for granted that every person of education has read."

Austen's novels were printed and reprinted. It wasn't only scholars and students who picked them up; everyday readers were enjoying them. The last years of the nineteenth century marked the first major wave of Austen fans. One of the most highly sought editions of *Pride and Prejudice* by collectors was issued in this period. Colloquially called the "Peacock" *Pride and Prejudice*, it features a gorgeous gilt peacock design on the emerald-green cloth cover. In fact, it was my familiarity with this edition of *Pride and Prejudice* that gave me confidence I could sell that row of emerald-green bindings that I purchased on the Georgetown house call, including Burney's *Evelina*. Those books were part of Macmillan's Cranford series, so named after the first book published in the group in 1891 by Victorian novelist Elizabeth Gaskell. Their extravagantly gilt designs, set off with the contrasting emerald background, were extremely popular and led to many imitations, like publisher George Allen's 1894 "Peacock" *Pride and Prejudice.*

I still remember a terrific coup a few years back in finding an underpriced copy of this edition. Scouring the new arrivals of bookseller websites, a weekly habit, I noticed one who had missed its importance and put it up for sale as a simple nineteenth-century reprint for about $100. I purchased it, then turned around and sold it to another bookseller for $1,000 a couple weeks later. That bookseller subsequently would have charged even more and certainly obtained it. A few years later, I myself was charging more than double that. Demand is so high for this edition that these prices are already far out of date: as of this writing, the price is closer to $5,000. Everyone knows this version because its cover is iconic. But this edition is a landmark in Austen studies for an additional reason. Its introduction, by the critic George Saintsbury, coins the term "Janite"—what we now spell as "Janeites," the popular fandom of Jane Austen.

These new fans were not content to leave Jane Austen to the critics. They began producing books themselves, such as Constance Hill and Ellen Hill's 1902 bestseller, *Jane Austen: Her Homes and Her Friends*, which chronicled their Austen "pilgrimage" to the important places in her life. This book's binding has a fetching embroidery pattern based upon one "from a muslin scarf that was satin-stitched by Austen herself," its design speaking to the theme of the book, Austen's home life. The sisters visited Steventon, Bath, Southampton, Chawton, Godmersham, and more. Given Chawton's role in the publication of Austen's novels, that house took on a special significance. In the 1930s, the Jane Austen Society was founded specifically to purchase Chawton cottage and turn it into "a national memorial to the novelist." Today it is a museum renovated to look as it might have during Austen's residence there, and Edward's neighboring Chawton estate has become a major research center for the study of women writers. A healthy fandom, a critical framework, and accessible reprints of her books: Austen now had everything she needed to become canon.

Austen's triumphant narrative continued its momentum, from the blossoming of academic studies after World War II, to the worldwide fame that came with the film and television adaptations of her novels, and the work of both collectors and fan organizations in preserving materials related to her life and context. When I first started reading Austen as a teenager, I thought I had come to her organically. It didn't occur to me that the reason it felt natural to pick up an Austen novel was because of these turning points in her legacy. Austen had begun as an anonymous author writing better-than-usual novels. But, generation by generation, she found champions who loved her work and encouraged others to give her a try: Walter Scott, George Henry Lewes, William Dean Howells, and more. The publication of Austen-Leigh's biography sparked a reassessment exactly at the right time, when Austen's style of realism was coming into critical favor. Her new readers then visited her hometown, formed fan clubs, collected her works, established museums, and published their own books.

I knew none of that when I was growing up. I had simply heard she was good—I don't even recall where—and thought I would give her a try. That foundation had been missing for the other women writers on my list. I hadn't even heard of Frances Burney until I became a professional in the rare book trade. It was time to find out why.

Chapter Two

FRANCES BURNEY
(1752-1840)

[...] if to PRIDE and PREJUDICE you owe your miseries, so wonderfully is good and evil balanced, that to PRIDE and PREJUDICE you will also owe their termination.

—Frances Burney, *Cecilia*, 1782

Frances Burney had a bad habit. One that compelled her to stay up late while the rest of her family slept. She tried to fight it for years, but she could never manage to stop. Until one day in 1767, just after her fifteenth birthday, she decided she must.

That bad habit? Burney had been writing a novel in secret. She felt terrible shame about it. Her father was out of the house, on a trip: now was her chance. She gathered up all the evidence, dumped it into an enormous pile in the garden, and burned it. Her little sister, the only one who knew her secret, watched the bonfire with tears streaming down her cheeks. The flames consumed all of Burney's manuscripts.

In that moment, Burney turned her back on writing for the honor of her family. This worked for a while. But Burney's mind soon again filled with words.

Here in the twenty-first century, I already knew how Burney's story would end. She kept writing. She published her first novel anonymously, but she did not remain anonymous for long. Over the years, she published three further novels, all eagerly sought by her reading public—including an aspiring author in the village of Steventon, Hampshire, named Jane Austen. In Austen's impassioned defense of novels in *Northanger Abbey*, she named as examples three novels "in which the greatest powers of the mind are displayed." Of those three, two were by Burney. But before them came Burney's first published novel: the one she could not bring herself to destroy. It was called *Evelina*.

Among Burney's four novels, *Evelina* was the most frequently published after her death. In the Victorian period, it was often praised as one of the greatest novels of the bygone Georgian era. In the twentieth-century, it was reprinted at least once a decade and attracted admirers like the book collector A. Edward Newton, who wrote about it in a now-classic of the field, *The Amenities of Book-Collecting* (1918). It was an early-twentieth-century copy of *Evelina* that had spurred my curiosity about Burney in the first place, the one in the emerald-green binding I had come across during the house call in Georgetown.

Evelina tells the story of an orphan who leaves her guardian's home in the country at seventeen to visit London for the first time. Through a series of letters to her guardian, Evelina chronicles her mistakes as she contends with a variety of suitors—especially the smooth, but dangerous, Sir Clement Willoughby and the kind Lord Orville.

The basic framework of the book follows an established form: a coming-of-age tale in which the protagonist undergoes various trials associated with growing up (and typically ending in marriage). Other examples include Samuel Richardson's *Pamela* (1740), which tells the story of a working-class girl who resists the advances of a rich suitor until he mends his ways and proposes to her; and Henry Fielding's *The History of Tom Jones, a Foundling* (1749), the story of another orphan who must find his way to happiness despite the obstacles created by his status as a bastard. I knew these two authors and I had read these books: Fielding and Richardson are always well covered in surveys of the English novel. But Burney's novel emphasized an important aspect of this story that their novels did not, one that she knew intimately. She vividly re-created her heroine's interior world. Evelina shone with an emotional complexity rarely seen in the new form of the novel. It made Burney's book into a literary sensation—and one of Austen's favorite novels.

There are several mentions of Burney's books in Austen's letters to family members and friends, so much so that familiarity with Burney's novels became a shorthand for taste (good or bad). In one letter to her sister, Austen uses *Evelina* to dismiss a new acquaintance: "he is a very Young Man, just entered of Oxford, wears Spectacles, & has heard that '*Evelina*' was written by Dr. Johnson." (In other words, he was one of those guys who argues today that Truman Capote *actually* wrote *To Kill a Mockingbird*.) In another, Austen invokes Burney's third novel, *Camilla* (1796), as a way to praise a friend: "There are two Traits in her Character which are pleasing; namely she admires Camilla, & drinks no cream in her Tea." Tea and books: a strong foundation for any friendship.

Once I started to look for examples of Burney's influence on Austen, I noticed evidence everywhere. I had already read that it was from Burney's second novel, *Cecilia* (1782), that Austen borrowed the phrase "pride and prejudice." Tracking down the full sentence in which the phrase appeared through a quick internet search, I was struck not just by the use of the phrase, but also the fine rhetorical balance of its expression: "if to PRIDE and PREJUDICE you owe your miseries, so wonderfully is good and evil balanced, that to PRIDE and PREJUDICE you will also owe their termination." Reading it sent goose bumps up and down my arms, as if a ghost had whispered in my ear. Despite knowing little about Burney herself, I realized that I had long been familiar with her work in its echoes.

So why did Burney's books, once so famous and so influential that they shaped the work of Jane Austen, disappear from bookshelves?

The first answer, the one that's easy to reach for, is that Burney's novels probably weren't good. This is one of the main reasons why a canon exists, right? We cannot possibly read everything, and we often seek the opinions of other trusted readers to help us determine what to prioritize. While I was not under any illusion that the critics shaping the canon were inherently objective judges, I was still open to the general idea that those books designated as "classics" have proven themselves, often over centuries, as works of high quality that remain relevant to readers in any era. Surely if Burney's novels didn't make those lists anymore, it was because they simply weren't good.

But there was evidence to the contrary: Austen's praise. If I loved Austen's books, and Austen loved Burney's, certainly these books were worth looking into. At the very least, my esteem for Austen suggested they deserved an honest chance. I had begun my investigation, and it was time to figure out what Austen saw in them. I downloaded a copy of *Evelina* onto my phone, ready to give it a try.

Then I left it unopened for months.

Even with Austen's recommendation, I struggled to find the motivation to commit to an eighteenth-century novel that, as far as I knew, had few modern readers. But I am excellent at productive procrastination. So instead I grabbed three biographies and read about how Burney came to write *Evelina*.

The first I read was Claire Harman's *Fanny Burney: A Biography* (2000), the most recent major biography meant for a wide audience. Reader and collector came together in this acquisition, as is often my habit; I bought a first edition of it, leaves already toning despite its relative youth, and proceeded to mark my way through it in pencil.

Did that last bit shock you? Most people assume that they should not be writing in their books—but book historians love it. One of the most difficult questions book historians seek to answer is: How did everyday readers respond to books? We often have access to printed professional reviews, but what everyday readers thought of a book is rarely recorded for posterity. So yes: I write in my books, for me and for future book historians. But, as in my book collecting, I maintain parameters. I always use pencil, since modern conservation best practice is not to do anything to a book that cannot be undone; and I only make notes in the books that could be considered "contemporary" to me, i.e., published within my lifetime. My books, my rules.

My collection grew. My next acquisition was a bit older: Margaret Anne Doody's *Frances Burney: The Life in the Works* (1988), which explored Burney's life through the lens of her writings; I hoped it would inspire me to start

Evelina. Despite Doody's brilliance, it didn't. Then came Joyce Hemlow's *The History of Fanny Burney* (1958), the most significant biography of Burney in the twentieth century: it was a turning point in launching modern academic interest in her. I bought a first edition in the original dust jacket. I began reading it after I conceded defeat to four o'clock insomnia one morning and slunk out of bed hours before my alarm. It kept me company in the weak light of sunrise, chronicling a life so interesting that I didn't regret losing sleep.

Frances Burney was born in 1752 in a port town about one hundred miles north of London. She was the third oldest among six children, and ultimately among eight when her father remarried a few years after her mother's death in 1762. When Burney was eight years old, the Burneys moved to London. There, the family flourished.

Frances, remembered as the most celebrated member of her family today, was once considered the dunce of the lot. The Burneys were like Salinger's Glass family, each member a special kind of genius. Her father Charles was a charismatic music master and published historian who counted among his closest friends David Garrick, the biggest theater star of the era; Joshua Reynolds, the influential artist who helped found the Royal Academy; and Hester Thrale (later Piozzi), a prominent and vivacious literary patron, who brought Charles into acquaintance with Samuel Johnson, the most acclaimed man of letters in his day. Her older brother James twice voyaged with Captain Cook, and later became the informal interpreter of Omai, a man from the Society Islands who traveled back with Cook on his first voyage and became the toast of London. Her older sister Esther was a musical child prodigy, lauded by royalty, the sensation of the scene before the next young savants appeared—Wolfgang Amadeus Mozart and Maria Anna Mozart, his sister. After a rambunctious youth, her other brother Charles Junior became the intellectual of the family, whose book collection would eventually be purchased by the British Library. And her younger sister Susan showed such promise that both she and Esther were sent abroad to be educated. Frances, who did not show such promise, was the only Burney child who did not receive a formal education. But she still absorbed something of a literary education because of her family environment; as Frances got older, she became an amanuensis for her father, writing out manuscript copies of Charles's books for publication. These works were, however, never fiction. Charles Burney only published nonfiction, and he owned only one novel in his entire library (Henry Fielding's *Amelia*).

The Burney family was active and tight-knit; they loved coming together for games, concerts, skits, and more. They built an elaborate series of inside jokes and neologisms with the kind of energy that brings to mind a pun competition. This was a joyful household, prizing wit as much as learning, and the talent to entertain as high as the impulse to create. But at night, Frances would sneak away, disappearing into a "closet up two pair of stairs" to write while the rest of her brilliant family slept. She never knew why she did this; she only knew she couldn't stop. That bonfire she made of her first efforts would ultimately be only a small setback. While she destroyed her manuscript about a woman named Caroline Evelyn, Burney could not shake the image of the heroine's daughter from her mind. Years later, that daughter's story would be told in *Evelina*.

In reading about Burney's childhood, I was struck by her belief that novel writing was a bad habit. Her sense of shame baffled me, especially in the context of her gifted family. I couldn't understand what Burney could possibly be concerned about since, today, the achievement of writing a book is generally greeted with celebration by one's friends and family (though how many will actually read it is a debut author's eternal disappointment). I realized I must have been thinking about this differently than an eighteenth-century aspiring novelist would.

One of the best ways to get a sense of the everyday currents of a given society is to swim about in its newspapers, literary magazines, and essays. It didn't take much investigating to learn that most novels in the eighteenth century were considered, well, bad for you. The eighteenth century is known for the rise of the novel in English, but that ascendancy also caused great alarm. Essays in literary journals and elsewhere labeled novels "dangerous," especially for their "extreme indecency." Conduct books, a popular genre of the era meant to educate young people (and especially young women) in propriety, etiquette, and taste, were particularly critical of them. One of the most-read commentators of the day, Hannah More, said in one of her conduct books that she believed "the corruption occasioned by these books has spread so wide, and descended so low, as to have become one of the most universal, as well as most pernicious, sources of corruption among us." (I found More's influence particularly haunting, as you'll see later.) Novels were "fatal poison," according to the Reverend James Fordyce in *Sermons to Young Women* (1766). Fordyce's work was one of the most popular conduct books of Burney's youth—read not only by Burney, but satirized by Jane Austen in *Pride and Prejudice*. As with many of Austen's literary references, her description of Fordyce's book helps communicate the personalities of her characters. Mr. Collins is invited by Mr. Bennet to read

aloud to the ladies. Mr. Collins readily assented, and a book was produced; but on beholding it [. . .] he started back, and, begging pardon, protested that he never read novels. —Kitty stared at him, and Lydia exclaimed. Other books were produced, and after some deliberation he chose Fordyce's Sermons. Lydia gaped as he opened the volume, and before he had, with very monotonous solemnity, read three pages, she interrupted him [. . .]

In his *Sermons*, Fordyce stated that the only kind of woman who would read any of the racier novels available at the time "must in her soul be a prostitute, let her reputation in life be what it will."

That is a real quote. From a book.

Fordyce continued to proclaim that those who read such novels "carry on their very forehead the mark of the beast." To Fordyce, novels might as well be a device for punishment found in a circle of Dante's Hell: they are an "infernal brood" that commit "rank treason against [. . .] Virtue" and are "a horrible violation of all decorum."

Less virulent critics simply complained of novels as "but a useless employment." Yes, the fact that novels were read for entertainment was itself a problem for some. "They excite a spirit of relaxation," explained Hannah More without a speck of irony. She was certain they made young women lazy, which in turn led to loose morals. Should that jump in logic seem unbelievable to modern readers, I offer receipts: More says that novels meant for amusement "nourish a vain and visionary indolence, which lays the mind open to error and the heart to seduction." One popular conduct book by Thomas Gisborne—a work we know Austen read—coyly says, "To indulge in a practice of reading [novels] is, in several other particulars, liable to produce mischievous effects." They're so entertaining that they're addictive, and "hence the mind is secretly corrupted."

Of course, everyone read novels, not just women, and not just younger women. But they were most often criticized as dangerous for that particular demographic, who were considered so impressionable that they were susceptible to imitating what they read. According to the modern Austen scholar Katie Halsey, because many girls did not receive a formal education in the eighteenth century, conduct book writers expected that young women would have to learn from their own informal reading. In 1761, the year Frances Burney turned nine, a gentlewoman named Sarah Pennington published a popular conduct book in the form of a letter to her daughters, in which she advised that novels "are apt to give a romantic Turn to the Mind, that is often productive of great Errors in Judgment, and fatal Mistakes in Conduct; of this I have seen frequent Instances, and therefore advise you never to meddle with this Tribe of Scribblers." In 1795, another conduct book writer named Ann Wingrove described a novel-reading girl who refused to marry because she was not meeting "such a lover as her romantic imagination had represented as absolutely necessary to render her happy in the marriage state."

The criticism of novel readers for wanting happy endings themselves had been argued for decades, as in a 1754 op-ed in *The World* that asserted "this doctrine of ideal happiness is calculated for the meridian of Bedlam." The writer bluntly attacked the "unreasonable" expectations that novels encouraged in women. "Believe me," he said, "I know several unmarried ladies, who in all probability had been long ago good wives and mothers, if their imaginations had not been early perverted with the chimerical ideas of romantic love." Yes, what an awful shame that would be: women refusing to settle because novels depicted men of higher standards. No wonder these commentators thought novels were so dangerous! They often encouraged women to choose a marriage partner based upon mutual esteem and proof of his good conduct, rather than prioritizing a match of families and finance that more typically made upper-class marriages in this era. "Bedlam" man above argued that "such men [. . .] never have existed." And yet, everyone kept reading novels.

Just as more and more women were reading, more and more women were writing, too. According to the modern scholar Judith Phillips Stanton, the number of women publishing increased "around 50 percent *every decade* starting in the 1760s." Yet most were dismissively called—and not just by Pennington—"scribblers," as opposed to authors. This new term was a catchall for low-quality writers, fundamentally associated with writing books for money. It rapidly attracted gendered connotations, referencing women writers whose work might be popular but was beneath serious consideration. Often, their books were novels. In fact, women wrote more than 50 percent of novels published.

In his conduct book, Fordyce allows one novelist as an exception, one man amid the many women "scribblers"—Samuel Richardson. Richardson alone deserved praise. Throughout the eighteenth century and beyond, Richardson's name was invoked to gatekeep: if you can't write as well as him (and, if you're a woman, you cannot), get out. The other novelist that habitually attracted praise was Henry Fielding. For instance, one essayist early in the novel boom wrote a literary magazine editor to "forbid your readers [. . .] even to attempt to open any novel, or romance, unlicensed by you; unless it should happen to be stamped *Richardson* or *Fielding*." This set the tone for critical commentary for over two centuries. Every so often later critics would add to this list a writer from the previous generation, Daniel Defoe, author of *Robinson Crusoe*. This is reflected in perhaps the most famous twentieth-century book on novels of this era, Ian Watt's *The Rise of the Novel: Studies in Defoe, Richardson, and Fielding* (1957). By the late eighteenth century the majority of novels were written by women, yet most critics chose to talk about one of these men.

After digging into eighteenth-century reactions, I was beginning to understand why Burney hid her writing. In this context, a young woman writing novels could only serve as an embarrassment. Burney later admitted, "So early was I impressed myself with ideas that fastened degradation to this class of composition, that at the age of adolescence, I struggled against the propensity which, even in childhood, even from the moment I could hold a pen, had impelled me." Many critics at the time assured their readers that novels were frivolous at best; at worst, they could endanger a woman's virtue—and even her eternal soul. And if some believed this of novel *readers*, to be a novel *writer* was a further disgrace. Beyond her own reputation, Burney was terrified that her novels would harm her family's position. The Burneys were upwardly mobile middle class, and her father had ambitions to rise still further. The potential of disappointing her father weighed heavier on Burney than disappointing herself. In a later memoir of her father, she wrote that "she considered it her duty to combat this writing passion as illaudable," burning her manuscripts "with the sincere intention to extinguish for ever in their ashes her scribbling propensity."

Yet Burney couldn't stop herself. Almost immediately after the burning of her manuscripts—a pile so big she "thought it prudent to consume it in the garden"—Burney began writing again. Her journal entries revealed the slow crumble of her determination. In one early entry, she wondered whether she should commit the journal itself "to the Flames" like her previous work; in the very next entry, she was already stealing moments to write more in it: "I have resolved, neck or nothing, to take the Pen once again in Hand!" She told herself it would be harmless this time because she was only writing in a private diary, rather than sharing her work with others: "to *whom* dare I reveal [. . .] my own hopes, fears, reflections, and dislikes?—Nobody." Later, after I had tracked down my own copy of her diaries, published posthumously in 1842 by her niece, I read this statement of loneliness that quickly turned into a resolution: "To Nobody, then, I will write my Journal!" Burney needed to write, and "Nobody" was a safe audience:

as her entry said, "From Nobody I have nothing to fear." (This earnest confession reminded me of another writer who was famously uncomfortable with the vulnerability that publication would bring: Emily Dickinson. One of Dickinson's poems begins "I'm nobody! Who are you? Are you nobody, too?")

Even so, Frances Burney was ambitious like the rest of her family. As she reached her twenties, her desire for an audience of somebodies grew. Yet Burney was already an anxious person by temperament, so silent and stiff in company that the family was calling her "the old lady" by age eleven. Even among the family Burney shrank from special attention. In one diary entry, she recorded "how *infinitely*, how *beyond measure* I was terrified" to be asked to play a small role at a tea table in a private family production of a play: "I looked like a most egregious fool," she recalled; "once, indeed, I made an attempt [. . .] to drink a little, but my Hand shook so violently, I was fain to put down the Cup instantly, in order to save my Gown."

Frances Burney may have been anxious, but she also believed in herself more than she admitted to others. Eventually, she took the bold step of seeking a publisher for her work. Her desire for publication proved her writing was more than a compulsion. Burney knew her work was good enough to share. Given the risks, both to herself and to her family, nothing short of a bone-deep confidence could have led her to this moment.

Ironically, it was because of her work as her father's secretary and amanuensis that she gained the knowledge needed to publish a book. Burney knew all about publishers, negotiations, proofs, and corrections. She submitted her manuscript of *Evelina* in a disguised hand, concerned that the printers would recognize her writing from the manuscripts of her father's productions. But she needed help in order to sell the book, so she confessed her secret to her siblings. The Burney children formed a family conspiracy to accomplish the task. Her brother Charles Junior, then only nineteen, disguised himself in clothes much too large and took on the persona of an older man with the totally-not-fake name of "Mr. King." Then "gaily, without reading a word of the work," he served as the agent to deliver Frances's manuscript to prospective publishers. The rights were sold to publisher Thomas Lowndes for a modest twenty guineas, which was about twenty-one pounds. (By way of comparison, another debut author named Henry Mackenzie received fifty guineas—about fifty-two pounds—for his surprise bestseller of the same decade, *The Man of Feeling*; and Jane Austen received only ten pounds for her first sold novel in 1803, *Susan*, which would later be published as *Northanger Abbey*.)

The contract arranged, *Evelina* was going to be published—and anonymously, as Burney required. Though it may seem counterintuitive today, anonymous authorship was a respected convention of this period, as well as of Austen's. Like the reasons for using anonymous avatars on the internet, there was a wide range of explanations why one would choose to publish work anonymously. One might do so in order to attack others (a common motive both in the 1700s and now). One might wish the work to stand on its own merits regardless of who wrote it, as with nobility who published then, or as when a famous author like Stephen King decides to publish under a pen name today. (Of his novel *Thinner* [1984], published under the name Richard Bachman, King once recounted a reader saying: "This is what Stephen King would write like if Stephen King could really write.")

Or one might wish to use anonymity as a shield for one's reputation. Anonymity allowed authors a genteel distance from the marketplace. Before the era of the Romantics, a kind of detachment between the writer and their work was often viewed as positive, no matter the gender of the author. But it was, of course, particularly appealing to women who wanted to contribute to the literary world. Women, encouraged to remain in the "private" sphere of life within the home, were often attacked for daring to enter the "public" sphere by publishing books. In fact, these women typically weren't criticized for publishing something deemed offensive; they were criticized for publishing *at all*, since that act was viewed as opening themselves up to the impropriety of public commentary. Many publishers accepted novels for anonymous publication.

Burney was elated that her book would see print, but the feeling soon morphed into dread. Even while maintaining anonymity, she realized that publishing a book meant people might actually read it. It was an "exceeding odd sensation," Burney admitted, "when I consider that it is now in the power of *any* and *every* body to read what I so carefully hoarded even from my best Friends." She felt suddenly exposed.

Perhaps because of that feeling, Burney added three different prefaces to the first edition of *Evelina*. The first was a poem dedicated to her father, whose name was printed only as blanks. In it, she desperately claimed her work was only a weak imitation of his own, and that she was writing anonymously because she "cannot raise, but would not sink, thy fame." Her next dedication was for the reviewers. Expecting they would read the book with "contempt," she straight-up pleaded for their "protection." Finally, she added a note from "the editor" tepidly defending the choice of a novel, which "may be read, if not with advantage, at least without injury." Burney knew her audience, noting that "in the republic of letters, there is no member of such inferior rank, or who is so much disdained by his brethren of the quill, as the humble Novelist." To the modern reader, these prefaces may seem a bit overwrought. But they are also moving. Because they are evidence of conflict raging within her—and proof that she conquered it.

By January 1778 Burney knew her novel was nearing publication, but she learned of the actual event by accident. Many years later, Burney still recalled the scene vividly: over the breakfast table, her stepmother was casually reading aloud notices from the newspaper, as she did every morning. One of them was an advertisement for *Evelina*. Her stepmother continued to read to everyone, amid the crinkle of turned pages and clink of teacups, unaware that Frances had begun blushing furiously. Her two youngest sisters, in on the secret, didn't even pretend to hide their smiles.

Burney fell sick soon after the book's publication with an inflammation of the lungs that required a long convalescence, so she missed the initial signs of *Evelina*'s ascent. She received her first inkling of the book's success from extended family: her sister reported that their aunt was reading *Evelina* aloud to their cousin while he was confined in bed. This news made Burney, finally on the mend, so physically ill that she excused herself from the day's plan to visit them. She waited, dreading "a thousand dangers of a discovery," as she recorded in her diary. But her sister returned from tea to confirm that her secret was still safe: "they had concluded it to be the work of a *man!*"

The next day, Burney felt relieved enough to restore the visit she had canceled earlier. She listened in apparent tranquility to her aunt, ignorant of the book's authorship, reading it aloud and describing it in glowing terms: "I must own I suffered great difficulty in refraining from laughing upon several occasions,—and several times, when they praised what they read, I was upon the point of saying, 'You are very good!' and so forth, and I could scarce keep myself from making acknowledgements, and bowing my head involuntarily."

Readers across London felt the same as Burney's unsuspecting family members. *Evelina* was a sensation, with four further editions published by the end of the following year. Instead of being "mauled" by reviewers as Burney feared, literary journals loved *Evelina* too: the *Monthly Review* called it "one of the most sprightly, entertaining & agreeable productions of this kind which has of late fallen under our Notice." Inevitably, readers were interested in the author's identity. Burney recorded in her journal a report she received from her sister of two family friends arguing whether the author was a man or a woman: "he must be a man of great abilities!" Burney triumphantly added to herself, "They little think how well they are already acquainted with the writer they so much honour!" Even though she still had no intention of revealing herself, she privately basked in their praise, her true thoughts known only to her siblings and her diary.

Evelina's success soon grew so wide that Burney was dismayed to realize discovery was a real possibility. Her dread built as one of her sisters begged to let their father in on the secret. In the meantime, multiple people had recommended the book to her stepmother. Rave reviews from readers and critics alike were gratifying, but she was still terrified of her parents' reaction. Having worked for decades to build a respectable reputation, her father's name could be destroyed in a moment by the knowledge that his daughter was a scribbler. Burney saw her inability to stop writing as a "conscious intellectual disgrace." As a modern biographer, Claire Harman, put it: "If she had conceived an illegitimate child she couldn't have tried harder to cover it up."

While Burney was away, her sisters gently let their father in on the family conspiracy, knowing the author herself wouldn't have been able to bear witnessing his reaction. Charles Burney did not immediately panic. The novel was being praised even by his famous patron Hester Thrale (whose own story is coming in chapter eight). But he was suddenly very nervous. He determined that he must read *Evelina* and see for himself. By his own account, he began to read the book "with fear and trembling." The first page he read was the dedication—which he realized was addressed to him. Scanning over the verses, he teared up. Gradually his nerves released as he read further. At the climax of the book, he actually "blubbered," lost in the moving scene his daughter had fashioned. He concluded, "it is, indeed, wrought up in a most extraordinary manner."

The single biggest wish Frances Burney nurtured in her heart was her father's approval of her writing. But she could not bring herself to believe he was capable of it. When her father wrote to tell her how much he loved the book, she was flabbergasted. "How little did I dream of ever being so much honoured! But the approbation of all the world put together would not bear any competition, in my estimation, with that of my beloved father." When they saw each other again, her relief was so powerful that it brought her to tears.

But the "approbation of all the world" had just begun. The politician and philosopher Edmund Burke and the painter Joshua Reynolds adored the novel. Hester Thrale insisted that Samuel Johnson read it. Johnson, the most respected literary critic of the day, could recite entire scenes from memory and concluded that "Henry Fielding never did anything equal" to the second part of *Evelina*. Even the king and queen read it. The scribbler became a superstar. "That a work, voluntarily consigned by its humble author, even from its birth, to oblivion, should rise," Burney reflected late in life, "seemed more like a romance [. . .] than anything in the book."

After the success of *Evelina* and her revelation of its authorship to her father, Burney had no more reason to keep her writing a secret. She embarked upon a literary career. But she confessed in her diary,

> **I have already, I fear, reached the pinnacle of my abilities, and therefore to stand still will be my best policy. But there is nothing under Heaven so difficult to do. Creatures who are formed for motion *must* move, however great their inducements to forebear.**

She still had no inkling that she would become so famous that people would want to read not just *Evelina*, but would also seek out her diary entries about how she came to write it. *Evelina* was published when Burney was twenty-six, but she lived to eighty-seven. This public and personal triumph was only the beginning of her remarkable career. She wrote more books, including three further novels, *Cecilia* (1782), *Camilla* (1796), and *The Wanderer* (1814); and a number of plays that are now enjoying revived critical attention. She entered into the service of King George III and Queen Charlotte, then married a titled officer-refugee of the French Revolution (hence her later name, Madame d'Arblay).

Burney learned courage, too: she underwent a mastectomy without anesthesia. Her description of that experience became a classic in the history of medical writing. In 1815, she navigated Brussels as a fugitive while the Battle of Waterloo raged nearby (her account of which Thackeray used in writing *Vanity Fair*). Through it all, she wrote. She had to. Burney's bad habit led her to become one of the most respected authors of her time, and one of Jane Austen's favorite writers.

The story of the unexpected success of *Evelina* seemed like a fairy tale. But somewhere between its happy ending and today, Burney's reputation began to falter. It was here that my book collecting slowly revealed evidence as to why. In looking for various editions of Burney's works and critical biographies of her, I started to mark the turning points in critical opinion over the centuries, volume by volume. As the books gradually lined up next to each other on my shelf, the evolution of her legacy became obvious. I could literally trace it from one book to the next.

In the late eighteenth century and early nineteenth century, Burney was praised as a realist writer whose satirical eye captured an impressively wide range of British society. As Joshua Reynolds joked at a party with Burney when the great historian Edward Gibbon proved a quiet guest, "He's terribly afraid you'll snatch at him for a character in your next book!" In 1810, Anna Laetitia Barbauld, the editor of a work called *The British Novelists*—the kind of anthology meant to define the canon—said that "Scarcely any name, if any, stands higher in the list of novel-writers than that of Miss Burney." Burney's final and highly anticipated novel, *The Wanderer* (1814), was panned, but in 1823 critics were still referring to Burney's novels as "monuments of genius," as one anonymous reviewer called them in the *Retrospective Review*.

As Austen's reputation began to rise—slowly in the middle of the nineteenth century, then quickly toward the turn of the twentieth—the books I sought revealed a different opinion of Burney. Because the two writers treated similar themes in similar settings, they were often compared. Yet over and over, Burney was invoked by Austen admirers in order to be dismissed by comparison. In fact, that's exactly what the *Retrospective Review* critic went on to do in that 1823 review: "Born in the same rank of life [to Burney], familiar with the same description of people, equally precocious, and equally possessed of a lively fancy, and an acute perception of character, with the single advantage of belonging to a later generation, [Austen] has produced works of much fresher verdure, much sweeter flavour, and much purer spirit."

While browsing a sharply kept antiquarian bookstore on the coast in the north of England, I had nabbed Thomas Macaulay's popular critical essays written for the *Edinburgh Review*—not a first edition, but one I couldn't resist. It was gorgeously bound, its spine so heavily stamped in gilt ornaments that I had difficulty distinguishing the tan of the leather underneath. Macaulay's essay on Burney, first published in 1843, became an influential analysis of her life and work. To Macaulay, *Evelina* was "extraordinary," and her second novel *Cecilia* was placed "among the classical novels of England." But he ended with an observation that two novelists had "surpassed" her: Jane Austen and Maria Edgeworth. Essays like this, however well meaning, provided the kinetic energy for one particular message. Burney was a watered-down version of Austen.

That criticism persisted. Many years later, in Ian Watt's foundational *The Rise of the Novel: Studies in Defoe, Richardson, and Fielding* (1957), he summarized Burney's entire career with the claim that "it was Jane Austen who completed the work that Fanny Burney had begun, and challenged masculine prerogative in a much more important matter." Much has changed since that book's publication, as scholars returned to Burney's writings and produced more nuanced academic work. But they first had to contend with the dominance of narratives formed by critics like Watt.

Foremost in this struggle among Watt's contemporaries was Joyce Hemlow, who published in 1958 one of the Burney biographies I'd read early on—and who "is more responsible than anyone else for the resurgence of Burney's reputation in our time," according to Burney Centre director Lars E. Troide. In some circles Burney's reputation had never deteriorated. But I wasn't part of those circles. My frankly more casual knowledge came from taking a few literature survey courses in college and reading "authoritative" overviews of the period like Watt's. I was not an academic. I read books meant for nonspecialists, like the *Critical Companion to Jane Austen* (2008), that maintained the opinion of Watt and his like. While acknowledging Burney's influence, that book still made clear there was no reason to *read* her novels: "Essentially then, Jane Austen admired and learned from the art of Fanny Burney," the entry stated. "However, 'it is only by reading Fanny Burney that one can realize how far' [. . .] superior Jane Austen's own artistic achievement is."

These kinds of statements use comparison to rank rather than to reveal. In her 1988 biography of Burney, Margaret Anne Doody said as much: "It is as if there were a quota for female fiction writers, preferably no more than one per century or at most per half-century. We have one already in Austen, the position is filled." Today we call this phenomenon "the Smurfette Principle," a phrase coined by the critic Katha Pollitt in 1991 in the *New York Times*. Pollitt observed how stories are often defined around an entirely male ensemble, "accented by a lone female, stereotypically defined." The Smurfette Principle has proven especially applicable in the formation of the Western literary canon. Between women writers, you have to beat the best or you don't get to play at all.

So it wasn't that Burney's novels weren't good—it's just that a few influential male critics, over many years, said she wasn't as good as Austen. More evidence appeared as I pursued my investigation, keeping my eyes out for appearances of Burney's books in the wilds of the rare book marketplace. As I read catalogs and browsed collections, I had a harder time locating copies of *Evelina* from after about 1850 until the 1890s. Around the middle of the nineteenth century, editions of Burney's novels were published less often. But I noticed that in their place came editions of her diary and letters. I, too, had gotten sidetracked from reading Burney's novels when I got sucked into the story of her life. I found the coincidence intriguing.

Burney and Austen were often mentioned together after their deaths as among the most esteemed novelists of their respective generations, with Austen beating Burney out as the better of the two. (Burney in fact lived longer than Austen, dying in 1840.) But in the Victorian period, Burney transformed from a novelist into a diarist. In 1842, two years after Burney's death, her niece Charlotte Barrett published a set of seven volumes of the *Diary and Letters of Madame d'Arblay, Author of Evelina, Cecilia, &c.* (which used her married name, Madame d'Arblay, alongside her traditional moniker for print, "author of *Evelina*"). This publication was met with great acclaim and turned Burney into "an iconic figure" of her era, according to the modern scholar Susan Civale. It was reprinted repeatedly in the following decades.

Sets of the *Diary* were produced in such high numbers that they remain common today, appearing in regional auctions of rare books with enough regularity that coming across them is like waving hello to a neighbor. Incomplete sets, lacking one volume or more, drift across antiquarian bookshops; complete sets will fetch a premium if they feature particularly elaborate bindings. A set of Madame d'Arblay's *Diary* would have been a classic addition to a late nineteenth-century library. It is easy to imagine them set high on shelves of dark wood, their gilt-stamped spines glittering in candlelight.

A copy of this set was too expensive for me to consider for my own shelves, but I absolutely wanted one for my rare book company to sell. Because it was so popular, and there were so many to choose from, I allowed myself to be picky when it came to selecting one. I passed up set after set, until one day, I came across one in crisp leather bindings. The price was surprisingly low. Clearly the dealer I purchased it from took one look at "Diary and Letters of Madame d'Arblay" on the spines and thought that nobody would be interested in reading it.

After I received the package, I unwrapped each individual volume with the energy of a twelve-year-old hoping for a cell phone. That's when I knew I had to keep this set for myself. But in doing so I broke one of my own rules: rare book dealers must be careful about defining boundaries between their inventory and what they keep for themselves. It's hard to stay in business if every sale feels like losing a prize from one's own collection. Though this may explain the notoriously curmudgeonly atmosphere of many rare book shops.

Once I claimed this set for my own, I took it home to inspect at leisure. When I examine a book, I read what's inside the pages, yes, but I also pay attention to how it's bound, printed, and sold. Studying this set of the *Diary and Letters of Madame d'Arblay*, I thought about how Burney's name has been variously identified in print over the centuries. In the larger context of what I had learned about Burney's shifting reputation, it became a clue that reflected the change in her reputation over the course of centuries. In letters to her family, Frances was called by her family nickname, "Fanny." When Burney's reputation as a diarist soared, readers saw those letters and happily embraced the diminutive, even though her name was stated as Madame d'Arblay on the title page.

Seeking out more books about Burney from the late nineteenth century, I noticed the nickname migrating. First, I picked up a popular biography of

Burney from 1890 by L. B. Seeley, bound in elegant blue cloth and stamped with a gilt frame, titled *Fanny Burney and Her Friends*. It was essentially an abridgement of her diaries and letters, with a few bits of editorializing to connect the cherry-picked stories. The choice of the diminutive in the title here seemed meant to convey the intimate content.

Later, I was amused by Austin Dobson's 1903 biography because it placed Burney in a series called the "English Men of Letters." But there was far more to that publication: the English Men of Letters series was meant to define and introduce classic authors—in other words, shape canon— and Burney was one of the first women included in it. (Austen was added to this series only a decade later, in 1913.) Further, Dobson's was the first book-length biography of Burney. Dobson was one of the most important critics who laid the groundwork for the revival in Burney studies that Joyce Hemlow and her colleagues would continue after World War II. He titled his historic biography *Fanny Burney (Madame d'Arblay)*, which helped solidify the nickname as the formal critical preference.

In the conclusion of this biography, Dobson also placed Burney's *Diary* "high above [her] efforts as a novelist," which did not exactly help his advocacy of Burney *as* a novelist. Nevertheless, that same year Dobson wrote the introduction to what would become a highly collectible edition of *Evelina*, illustrated by Hugh Thomson, the artist whose illustrations for the 1894 "Peacock" edition of *Pride and Prejudice* are now iconic. That edition of *Evelina* was the same one that started this whole project when I stumbled upon a copy on that house call in Georgetown, the one with the emerald-green binding. In the bottom corner of the front cover are gilt letters: "Evelina by Fanny Burney Illustrated by Hugh Thomson."

It was not until the 1980s that a few scholars began publicly questioning the appropriateness of the nickname and campaigned for a return to "Frances" Burney. The choice of name, they argued, carried consequences in how critics and readers interpreted the author's work. According to Doody, "'Fanny' is a patronizing diminutive. It makes the author sound the harmless, childish, priggish girl-woman that many critics want her to be." As she pointed out, there is no logical reason for continuing to use the diminutive, yet there are multiple reasons to bury it. First, it is anach-ronistic, since no writer of her time would have called her that in print. Next, it is not Burney's own stated preference. And finally, it's a double standard, since it's not "Harry" Fielding (as Johnson called Henry Fielding) or "Jemmy" Boswell (as Doody remarks of James Boswell).

"Let her have her adult name," proclaimed Doody in her 1988 biogra-phy (which I marked in pencil with an emphatic "YES!!!" in my own copy). And yet two major biographies of Burney since Doody's proclamation have named her "Fanny" Burney. The diminutive will not die. It's enough to make one want to call all authors by diminutive nicknames they would never want to be known by. "Chuck Darwin" and "Ernie Hemingway" do have their charm.

Now I knew part of the reason I was struggling to find the enthusi-asm to read *Evelina*. The gradual loss of Burney's hard-earned reputation, making her seem like a minor figure in English literary history today—a watered-down Austen, little "Fanny" Burney next to Samuel Richardson and Henry Fielding—had played a subtle, but powerful, part in my reluctance.

But there was one last, more personal, reason I had underestimated Burney for all those years. No matter how important it was, *Evelina* was also inescapably a courtship novel, a story about finding love and a happy ending. Today, we call these romance novels—and until my thirties, I did not like them. As a rule. My love for literary "classics" served me well when I first entered the rare book trade, but I also loved science fiction, fantasy, and mystery novels. This was thanks to the privilege, like Austen, of being raised in a bookish family whose habits I absorbed as naturally as breathing. I read many kinds of books. But not romance novels. I didn't think books like *those* were for me.

In retrospect, this is one of the most embarrassing admissions I can imagine putting into print. It was what one might call an overreaction. You see, I grew up as a tomboy in a socially conservative town in Idaho. Every week, I had to attend gender-segregated activities where the girls were taught how to apply makeup, bake brownies, and care for children, while the boys played basketball and got to go white-water rafting. I wanted to go white-water rafting. I chafed at the expectations that reflected so little of my natural temperament. The modern feminist scholar Sara Ahmed describes moments like these as when "we begin to experience gender as a restriction of possibility." That is what I felt. A specific kind of powerlessness, every day, endlessly varied in small ways.

However I might instinctively define myself, this world pressed its own image upon me. There were no choices of what to wear to church: it was dresses. I could ask to join the boys in white-water rafting, as of course I did, but I would simply be told no, as of course I was. So I fought back on the same terms, in countless small ways. These acts of resistance wrested back some feeling of control. I built armor for these battles in the form of opposition to anything labeled "feminine." I came to hate pink, and hearts, and baby pictures, and flower prints.

That's how I came to hate romance novels. Reading is, inescapably, personal. This genre came to represent to me the culture of my childhood, the one that wanted me, above all else, to become a wife. It was an ever-present pressure, the idea that marriage should be among a woman's principal aims in life. So I hacked books about women finding love from my reading list without distinction. Books like *Evelina*. (Austen, of course, was the exception. She was canon.)

But I was no longer that child. I set the terms of my life now. All this time I had assumed I hated romance novels . . . even though I had never even read one.

Centuries apart, here it was again: the "scribbler" problem.

I hadn't thought about the large, seemingly coincidental overlap between the fact that romance is the only major genre with a thoroughly feminine reputation and the fact that it has been, for many years, the most despised of all genre fiction. What a feminist I had been!

I considered my own hypocrisy. The most common criticisms thrown at romance today break down as soon as they are applied to genres that are not heavily associated with women writers and readers. For example, a favorite criticism of romances is that they are "formulaic." Romances do have a set formula, or at least a predetermined ending. In order to be considered romance in the eyes of American readers of the genre today, a book must primarily concern a romantic relationship and must end with a Happily Ever After (HEA). But as one who spends most of her professional hours launching between a fifteenth-century edition of Sophocles, a seventeenth-century edition of *A Midsummer Night's Dream*, and Edgar Allan Poe's *Tales* from 1845, I have examined loads of books demonstrating that such a criticism is a double standard completely lacking in historicity.

Plenty of genres are "formulaic." Sophocles's *Oedipus Rex* ends exactly in the tragedy that is promised from the beginning—that the king will kill his father and marry his mother—yet critics don't dismiss its plot of prophecy fulfillment as "limiting." Are Shakespeare's comedies inherently inferior because they always end in a marriage—a happy ending? A foregone conclusion is a bizarre means of judging romance in a literary culture that sings the praises of Sophocles and Shakespeare. It seems we have no problem with formulas. Except when it's romance.

The principle of "the journey, not the destination" is what guides modern popular romance. But it's also what guides modern popular mysteries. Edgar Allan Poe's "tales of ratiocination," considered by many to be early experiments in what would become the detective story, are an excellent example. In "The Purloined Letter," Poe's detective Auguste Dupin produces the stolen correspondence of the title's story for the police officer, effectively beginning with the ending, and only then proceeds to explain how he figured out where it had been hidden. Poe conceived of such stories as miniature puzzles, in which the reader was presented with the answer first, then must work out the conclusion through the story's progression. Poe's tales were not about the destination; they were about the journey. Most mysteries begin with a crime and end with it solved. Most romances begin with a spark and end with a happy relationship. It's the push and pull throughout the narrative that makes these genres enjoyable. Mysteries and romances both thrive on the gradual reveal.

I learned this myself only after I faced up to my prejudices and began reading modern romances. I read a lot of them before I finally opened their ancestor, the courtship novel *Evelina*. I read classics like Julie Garwood's

The Bride (1989), Loretta Chase's *Lord of Scoundrels* (1995), and Beverly Jenkins's *Indigo* (1996), as well as newer releases like Alyssa Cole's *An Extraordinary Union* (2017). In these I saw how romance's established structure often serves another valuable purpose: it allows an in-depth exploration of the complexities that exist within relationships. For example, in Cole's *An Extraordinary Union*, a historical romance set during the Civil War, the Black heroine is a spy in a Confederate household; her love interest is a white Pinkerton agent pretending to be a Confederate soldier. In maintaining an established structure for the arc of the book, the conventions of romance give Cole a firm foundation from which to tackle questions of power and consent, freedom and control, communication and intimacy. You know, many of the fundamentals of human experience that "great literature" is said to explore.

After having actually taken the time to read these books, other common objections to romance also began to feel like straw men fallacies. Perhaps most commonly, the Happy Ever After bothers critics of romance. Many of us don't like the idea that finding love is often presented as a requirement for happiness. I certainly felt that way. But if you look more closely, questions of love and marriage have historically been central to the fate of women's lives, legally and economically. I was slowly beginning to appreciate the implications of the disadvantaged legal status of women in England and the United States at the time of Frances Burney and Jane Austen. A story with a heroine who achieves a happy ending is a symbol of the heroine's complete victory, of getting both what she wants and what she deserves in a world that works very hard to take that choice from her. Remember, eighteenth-century critics of the novel thought it was dangerous specifically because it encouraged women to be picky about their romantic partners! A genre that celebrates the triumph of a woman's choice as its most recognizable trait—well, I can see how that might make some people uncomfortable.

Once I had read actual romances, I made up for lost time. I still don't like hearts, or most shades of pink. I will not wear any clothing with a flower print. But I love romance novels. Soon I started collecting copies of my favorites. Collecting has never let me down yet; I have always discovered something about the books I collect that I would never have learned otherwise. At one point I became obsessed with an indie press of the 1990s, Odyssey Books, that specialized in Black romance. In that era, small presses sprung up to meet the market demand for Black romances that major publishers were not meeting, and Odyssey Books was one of the most important. Odyssey issued books by industry veterans like Barbara Stephens and Sandra Kitt, but they also published the first books of a number of authors who went on to distinguished careers with major publishers—before those companies were willing to take them on. Among those whose first romance was published by Odyssey are Donna Hill, Eboni Snoe, and Francis Ray, all of whom would publish books with Arabesque, the first big press line dedicated to Black romances, upon its rollout in 1994.

Odyssey had been founded by Leticia Peoples in Silver Spring, Maryland, a suburb of Washington, D.C., and the very city where I lived and worked. Such an important indie press, in my own town! I wanted to collect all the books that Odyssey published. The trouble was that I didn't know how many it published, or even what all the titles were. There were no resources, online or in print, that came even close to a comprehensive accounting. So I figured it out through collecting. Through the lens of collecting, books can speak to you beyond their texts. Many paperback books include extra leaves at the beginning or end of the text that advertise other books by that publisher. I already knew the titles of a few Odyssey novels; once I acquired copies, I used the advertisements in their own pages to compile a record of Odyssey's list. It was great fun—and another reason to put off reading Burney. (I still was! At this point I couldn't even say why!)

In the process of collecting, I dug into the history of the postwar paperback industry for modern romances that functioned so differently from traditional publishing. Instead of selling hardcover books at bookstores on a seasonal basis, companies like Harlequin pioneered selling their slim paperbacks on grocery store racks. Their titles changed every few weeks, like magazines. Because of this, vintage romances seem more ubiquitous than they are; old Harlequin romances are overflowing in secondhand marketplaces, as any walk through a romance-friendly used bookstore will suggest. But, in fact, many of the individually important first editions are significantly more difficult to find than, say, a first edition of Hemingway's *The Old Man and the Sea*. For example, the first two titles that Harlequin contracted to publish from London-based romance specialists Mills & Boon were printed in trial runs of only one thousand copies. Today they are quite elusive in the first printing, particularly in fine condition.

I learned this the hard way, after I had begun work on a catalog for my business documenting my collection, placing modern romances—all those Harlequins, "bodice-rippers," and more—into historical context. For every beautiful, first printing copy I found, I turned away hundreds of other copies. Not that I minded. Walking the aisles of a secondhand bookstore, my eyes raking across spines, seeking that one right book . . . There is no better way to spend an afternoon. It was my hope one day to sell my collection to a university for research and teaching in special collections.

In the end, it was thanks to this separate project that I finally read *Evelina*. My romance collection had come up in conversation with an English professor at a university where I had been invited to deliver a lecture. To my surprise, she was delighted to hear about it. She was teaching a class for freshmen on the history of reading: Would I consider doing a workshop based on my romance collection while I was there? I had just heard the request every rare book collector dreams of hearing. *That niche project you're working on? The one that makes the eyes of your loved ones glaze over whenever it comes up? Come talk about it for hours in front of my captive audience, who will be graded according to their level of attention!*

I prepared for the workshop with glee. Only one aspect became troublesome: I needed an early example of modern romance's ancestor, the courtship novel. Jane Austen was the perfect choice, but the first edition of *Pride and Prejudice* I had was priced significantly over $100,000. I couldn't casually cart around a six-figure book for a workshop that was meant to be hands-on. I needed books that students wouldn't be afraid to touch. Studying a book as an object is a full sensory experience: paper from eighteenth-century England feels different between the fingers than paper used in a book from 2010. It is lush, thicker than most papers made today, with a texture almost like linen. This makes sense when you consider that paper in that era was made partly from recycled rags. Every book tells the story of the time and place of its creation. They can look different, feel different, even smell different than what we are used to. I wanted the students to have the chance to experience that with an actual book from the eighteenth century.

I took a second look at the shelves in my office, and I spied a copy of *Evelina*. A beautiful little copy in two volumes, bound in half calf with a gilt-stamped spine and plain paper boards. It wasn't that one with the emerald-green binding. It was an earlier edition, from the eighteenth century. I don't even remember where I first picked it up. But most important, it was not Jane Austen—which meant that, even though this copy was published in 1794, it cost only a few hundred dollars. Ironically, it was because Burney was so much less popular with collectors than Austen that I could even include her in the lecture.

So that's how I came back to *Evelina*. It wasn't because I nobly recognized my own internalized sexism. Even after I knew how large a part it played in my reluctance, after I read the biographies, after I had overcome my prejudice against romance novels, I still didn't rush to read it. In the end, it was because my pride wouldn't let me lecture a room full of college freshmen about a book I hadn't read.

Tucked between couch, cat, and blankets, I settled in to read a book that Austen had loved. Within pages, I became attached to the heroine. I was surprised by this because eighteenth-century heroines can be so virtuous they appear flat. (Richardson's own Pamela is famous for this.) I'm a twenty-first-century woman; pure and perfect heroines are more likely to inspire impatience than admiration. But Evelina, like her creator, is more complicated.

Evelina is morally upstanding, as she must be. Burney would never write a shady heroine when so many critics were railing against corrupt novels that "carry on their very foreheads the mark of the beast." Yet she is still far from perfect. She is constantly making mistakes, and they are the believable missteps of a seventeen-year-old. She writes to her mentor for advice—whether she should accept an invitation to a ball, or stand up to her grandmother—but his responses will only come days later by post. Evelina has to learn how to act independently, according to her own judgment. Some of her predicaments are genuinely funny. During an evening out when Evelina has lost her friends, she asks for help from two nearby women—whom she doesn't realize are prostitutes: "to be sure, they said, I should not want for friends, whilst I was with them." I laughed out loud at this. But I also felt for Evelina. As I continued reading this scene, I kept standing up from the couch and sitting down again, as if I wanted to intervene and help Evelina myself.

Evelina comes to life in part because Burney was able to bring her own experience to the character. Very like her heroine Evelina, Frances Burney had grown up in the country, then came to London. Biographer Claire Harman captures how Burney transformed elements of her own life into art:

> **Evelina's breathless letters to her guardian, Mr. Villars, catch the childish beguilement of the author herself experiencing the bustling, brightly-coloured, noisy, smelly and dangerous life of the capital for the first time when she arrived there in 1760, an open-minded, open-eyed and open-mouthed eight-year-old.**

Harman calls Evelina's letters "breathless," and she's right. Burney's writing has such power of animation that Evelina really does seem to breathe (even though, when she's embarrassed, she often forgets to).

When Evelina gets flustered, she becomes even more awkward, acting so meek that her friends wonder if she's quite well. You can practically see her trying to shrink herself into invisibility. It's all pulled off swimmingly by one who experienced this problem herself: "the old lady" here again. Burney records the time she once froze because of a question from King George III (a reminder that, yes, the king was a fan of *Evelina*):

Then coming up close to me, he said—

"But what?—what?—how was it?"

"Sir?"—cried I, not well understanding him.

"How came you—how happened it—what?—what?"

"I—I only wrote, sir, for my own amusement,—only in some odd, idle hours."

"But your publishing—your printing,—how was that?"

"That was only, sir—only because—"

I hesitated most abominably [. . .]

The *What!* was then repeated, with so earnest a look, that, forced to say something, I stammeringly answered—

"I thought—sir—it would look very well in print!"

I do really flatter myself this is the silliest speech I ever made!

That story from her own life illustrates how winning Burney's writing could be. She had a talent for replaying such moments realistically on the page. This knack was based partly in that Burney genius; like many of her siblings, she had a nearly photographic memory. She had a talent, too, for comedic timing. It was cultivated as she grew up in a family that loved word games and performance, including informal plays and musicals. An offhand comment by Charles Burney captures the native Burney environment: "We were merry, & laughed as loud as the Burneys always do."

This ebullient approach to life couldn't help but seep into *Evelina*. It was a quality that became central to the book's success: critics at the time lauded *Evelina*'s comic realism. After her authorship had been revealed, Burney was regularly invited over to dinner by the literary patron Hester Thrale along with Samuel Johnson. During one dinner, the perceptive Mrs. Thrale teased her, "Miss Burney looks so meek and so quiet, nobody would suspect what a comical girl she is." Burney then watched in shock as Johnson fairly roared over one of her satirical characters, an irritating suitor of Evelina: "'Oh, Mr. Smith, Mr. Smith is the Man!' cried he, laughing violently. 'Harry Fielding never drew so good a character!'" Still in-credibly bashful, Burney pulled an Evelina and shrunk in her chair, though silently she exulted.

The "comical girl" is also "so meek and so quiet": Burney was a glori-ously complex person. At the time, she shared her innermost thoughts only with intimate friends and family. But her personality is more visible to us today than nearly any other woman of her era because of the mountains of letters and journals she and her family kept. Only a fraction of these were printed in the Victorian set I had acquired; as I delved into various biographies of Burney, I learned that many more have been made available online via the Burney Centre at McGill University—a project begun by one of the great advocates for Burney in the twentieth century, the aforemen-tioned scholar Joyce Hemlow. One reason Burney's novels are so compel-ling is because they reflect these rich textures of her personality.

In *Evelina*, fear and anxiety shape the action as much as comedy. This is especially the case when Burney's protagonists confront the behavior of problematic men. For Evelina, fear of sexual predators is very real. In fact, it drives much of the plot. Evelina's difficulty is that she is both incredibly beautiful and apparently of low birth, an appealing combination for un-principled rich gentlemen looking for a mistress. Add to that her "air of in-experience and innocency," and she becomes an obvious target to men who look for victims they can more easily isolate and manage. Throughout the book, Evelina is dogged by a baronet whose goal is to make her his mistress. The baronet, Sir Clement Willoughby, takes her refusals as a challenge. At one party, she rejects Sir Clement with an impromptu lie that he makes her regret. She says that she already has a partner for the next dance, but

I suppose my consciousness betrayed my artifice, for he looked at me as if incredulous; and, instead of being satisfied with my answer and leaving me, according to my expectation, he walked at my side, and, with the greatest ease imaginable, began a conversation in the free style which only belongs to an old and intimate acquaintance.

In just a few sentences, Burney efficiently summed up some of the most common methods of men who don't like to be told no. Don't believe you can ever be rejected. If rejected, don't take the woman who rejects you at her word. Force the conversation into more intimate territory. And do not leave her alone. I was amazed at how clearly Burney had captured what it feels like for a woman to be in a situation like this, even in the twenty-first century. This wasn't watered-down Austen.

Throughout that night, Evelina continues to state her feelings in no uncertain terms. Sir Clement plays innocent while she begs, "you have but to leave me—and O how I wish you would!" He laughs off her feelings as uneducated and declares, "you will hereafter be quite charmed with me." When Evelina retorts, "I hope I shall never—" Sir Clement cuts her off. At that point, Evelina records that "my spirits quite failed me, and I burst into tears" in front of the entire party. In response, "They all seemed shocked and amazed." It is Evelina who comes off as the unreasonable one.

Separated by hundreds of years, I lived the night of this ball like it had only just happened. Because it has happened, to me, in countless little iterations that made me question my own judgment as well. Once, a boy took me on a first date to see *Zoolander*, which I found funny and he did not. We did not go out again. When he saw me at a party with another boy weeks later, he yelled, "I want my money back, bitch." Then there was the time a different boy asked me to go to the movies, which I agreed to with the stipulation that we didn't choose a horror film—only to find myself "surprised" in the seats when I learned that he had steered me to a horror film I had never heard of (with an explanation that I could "hold on to him if I got scared"). These two experiences occurred when I was seventeen, the same age as Evelina. In each case, my upset was met with a wall of disbelief. I was the one making a big deal out of it. They just wanted to have a good time. They "all seemed shocked and amazed."

This is why we continue to read books centuries after they were first published: not because they have reached some subjective standard of "perfection," as some critics like to suggest, but because they still have something to say that is meaningful to us. I have many more of these stories. So does

Evelina. It's easy to assume that, before the modern feminist movement, women were not always as vocal about their difficulties *as women*. But it doesn't take too much reading to discover otherwise. Burney, for instance, is never evasive in expressing Evelina's fears. Hundreds of years ago, Burney gave a voice to concerns we are still attempting to overcome today. For all their similarities, there is nothing quite like this direct confrontation with fear in Austen's novels. It was this aspect of *Evelina* that I responded most strongly to. I had felt what Evelina had felt. I read it and knew I wasn't alone.

In *Evelina*, the only man who consistently recognizes the heroine's discomfort is a man named Lord Orville. More than that, he attempts to alleviate it, and he calls out others for their gross behavior. Some critics have called Lord Orville too flawless to be believable. Yet there are times in the novel when he shows jealousy, narrow-mindedness, coldness, and plenty of other flaws. Like Mr. Darcy, he is the hero *and* he is imperfect. It is almost as if what these critics mean is that he isn't realistic because, despite those flaws, he is a kind and thoughtful man.

Spoiler: Evelina and Lord Orville fall in love. More than that, the story of a woman like Evelina finding true love is also the story of her learning to trust her own judgment. Evelina wins when she stands up for her right to choose her *own* happily ever after. In *Evelina*, Burney explores power from a woman's perspective.

————

Burney, like me, struggled against the gendered expectations of marriage in her own life. Before she published her first novel, she caused a serious quarrel within the family over the question of "true love." An otherwise amiable young man had proposed to her after falling in love in a single meeting. Burney sensibly turned him down. The rejection sparked an uproar in the family, who began conspiring to change her mind. Her own mentor, Samuel Crisp, criticized her choice by outlining the very real fears of economic vulnerability that women faced: "Suppose You to lose yr Father—take in all Chances. Consider the situation of an unprotected, unprovided Woman." When she learned her father had joined the rest of the family in opposition to her, she "wept like an Infant." Burney adored the people who were now urging her to change her mind: her lively father, her spirited younger sisters, her beloved mentor. Yet she refused. Hester Thrale might call her meek, but Burney also had mettle. Many years later, she fell in love with a titled refugee of the French Revolution who had lost everything, Alexandre d'Arblay. After she became Madame d'Arblay, they purchased their first house as newlyweds from the earnings of her third novel, *Camilla* (1796).

I should say that Burney was incredibly conservative by temperament. Politically, she was not a feminist, either by the standards of our time or her own. But she believed in the importance of granting a voice—and therefore authority—for women to talk about oppressive circumstances that can determine the course of one's life. I learned this not by reading about Burney, or even by reading Burney's diaries and letters, but by finally sitting down and reading *Evelina*.

I loved it. In fact, I could now voice a heresy with my full heart: I enjoyed *Evelina* more than many of Austen's novels. And I desperately wanted a first edition of *Evelina* for my collection. Over the years I'd handled first editions of Richardson's *Pamela* and Fielding's *Tom Jones*; surely *Evelina* could not be any trickier to track down. I have "a very particular set of skills," to quote someone totally unlike me. I started doing some research.

In 1778, *Evelina* had been issued as a set in three volumes by a publisher who considered it something of a risk; he printed only five hundred copies. This is a phenomenon rare book collectors see time and again. We are surprised that a famous book like *Harry Potter and the Philosopher's Stone* was first released in only five hundred copies in hardcover because we have the benefit of retrospect—but Harry Potter was not a worldwide phenomenon when the publisher issued the first book. Further, the number of copies printed in a first edition run does not always help us predict the rate of survival (about three hundred copies of the *Philosopher's Stone* went to libraries, which skewed the survival rate even lower: poor library books). Nevertheless, very low runs like these do tend to express themselves in scarcity on the rare book marketplace.

A first edition set of *Evelina* had only appeared at auction twice in the entire twenty-first century. The last time it appeared, it sold for £10,000. Gulp. I knew what this meant. If it did appear at auction again, it would fetch at least that amount, but probably much more. If another bookseller found a copy, they would certainly price it at least that high . . . and likely a lot higher. I didn't have the funds to add a book like this to my personal collection. If it did appear, I'd have to decide whether to purchase it as a business decision, for resale through my rare book company. But the possibility of even being able to make that choice now felt remote.

I looked for a year before I got my first chance. A copy of the first edition of *Evelina* was coming up for sale at auction. When I first saw the listing, my pulse jumped: this was the opportunity I had been waiting for. The auction was a smaller one—not quite as small as what we call a "regional" auction, which focuses on locally sourced material and a nearby audience—but not big enough that it was known for special expertise in rare books. For this reason, I knew there might also be fewer eyes on the lot, and therefore fewer bidders. A strong price at auction is like a ballroom dance performance: it takes at least two people to realize its potential. Perhaps I could sneak away with a prize that no one else was looking for.

But my hopes crashed just as quickly when I saw the phrase "rare in any condition." This is a euphemistic idiom that we use in rare books when the current copy is a goddamn mess. A copy pulled from the bowels of a flooded building abandoned for a decade? "Rare in any condition." Sprouting mushrooms from the rear board? "Rare in any condition." Lacking the title page? "Rare in any condition." This copy of *Evelina*, it turns out, was lacking title pages for two of the three volumes. "Sold with all faults," the listing concluded. That's another common euphemistic idiom, sometimes abbreviated to "w.a.f.," to the consternation of new collectors who didn't realize rare book descriptions use as many acronyms as a government agency. I couldn't bring myself to bid. The estimate—what the auctioneer expected it to fetch—for this "rare in any condition" copy was $2,000 to $3,000; it sold for $630. I don't regret it.

I would find another edition that was meaningful to me. And I knew just the one. I thought back to that glittering gold spectacle that had so struck me from that house call to a retired bookseller's home in George-town, the 1903 edition with the introduction by Austin Dobson. That Georgetown buy had been an important beginning for me. However, I had dutifully cataloged and sold that copy, the fate of most every book I buy for the business (if I'm doing it right). I began eyeing opportunities for ac-quiring another. I searched regularly at book fairs, auctions, and online, weighing the condition of individual copies against the price of acquisition. I found one, finally, online at a shop in the UK that fit my taste: not a fine copy, as I was not prepared to pay the premium for that, but a very good one, priced modestly for its condition. I felt like that book had been waiting for me. A patient thing, looking for me to catch it.

By now, I did love *Evelina*, just as Jane Austen did. My greatest dis-covery in reading *Evelina* was seeing firsthand why Austen appreciated her work so much. Austen has rightfully earned the title of the queen of romance, and her dominance is unassailable: I do still prefer *Pride and Prej-udice* over *Evelina*. But reading *Evelina*, I kept seeing characteristics of the genre that I had thought originated with Austen. That delicious push and pull that has me yelling at characters in triumph or frustration—oh, they have a moment; oh, they have a misunderstanding—is one of Austen's greatest talents. In *Pride and Prejudice* the first meeting of Elizabeth Bennet and Mr. Darcy occurs at a ball, where Elizabeth overhears him refuse to dance because there is no "woman in the room whom it would not be a punishment to me to stand up with." In *Evelina*, published thirty-five years before, these same dynamics play out between the potential lovers. In one of its earliest scenes, also at a ball, Lord Orville misjudges Evelina's lack of experience and calls her "a poor weak girl"—a comment overheard by a friend of Evelina, who completes the mortification by sharing it with her. If this scene hadn't been published decades before Austen's first pub-lished novel, *Sense and Sensibility* (1811), I would have said it was straight out of Jane Austen.

Just the opposite turned out to be true. The first-ever appearance of Jane Austen's name in print wasn't in one of her own books, but in one of Burney's. In June 1796, Burney's third novel *Camilla* was published by subscription: subscribers paid in advance for a book in order to defray its publication costs or more directly benefit the author, much like our modern crowdsourced projects. And just as in many of today's productions, those who contributed saw their name recorded in print. Austen's name appears as "Miss J. Austen, Steventon" in the list of subscribers included in *Camilla's* first edition. Mere months later, in October 1796, Austen started drafting *First Impressions*. Soon after, Austen's father wrote to offer *First Impressions* to one of the publishers of Burney's *Camilla*, pitching it as "a Manuscript Novel, comprised in 3 Vols. About the length of Miss Burney's *Evelina*." Though rejected then, this was the novel that would eventually be published as *Pride and Prejudice*. According to Harman, who has published books on both Burney and Austen, *Pride and Prejudice* "has so many resonances with *Camilla* as to constitute a form of elaborate homage."

Burney's name shows up in Austen's novels, too. In *Northanger Abbey*, Austen uses appreciation of Burney's novels as an indicator of which characters have taste. *Northanger Abbey* follows Catherine Morland, a book-obsessed teen from the country who visits Bath and enters high society for the first time. The oafish John Thorpe, in attempting to court Catherine, doesn't realize he's damning himself: "I never read novels; I have something else to do." Catherine feels "humbled and ashamed, and was going to apologize," but Thorpe cuts her off—just as Sir Clement had done to Evelina. While he is trying to remember a novel he has read—"I was thinking of that other stupid book"—Catherine realizes he's talking about Burney's *Camilla*. "I took up the first volume once and looked it over, but I soon found it would not do; indeed, I guessed what sort of stuff it must be before I saw it." In that last line, I recognized my former self with a shudder.

I knew better now. And my collection kept growing. After spending an equally needless and satisfying amount of time looking for the right copy, I had settled on a modern reprint of *Northanger Abbey* that featured a cover design by one of my favorite modern artists in that field, Coralie Bickford-Smith. It has a rough cloth texture that provides friction for the hands, the boards of the binding a little scritch against one's palms while reading, and a brazen hot-pink pattern of keys against a somber tan background. This inexpensive twenty-first-century edition, covered with my opinionated pencil annotations, sits on the same shelf as that elaborately bound Victorian set of Burney's diaries and letters. They each bear their own histories; together, they tell a new story.

Side by side, each of the books I added to my collection reconstructed the narrative of Burney's rise and fall as a novelist, then her second rise and fall as a diarist, and finally, her slow rise again as a major eighteenth-century British novelist. The set of her *Diary and Letters* (1842–46) published by her niece embodied the turning point of her new reputation in nonfiction. The 1890 remix of her *Diary, Fanny Burney and Her Friends*, was designed as a gift book—in vivid blue—and marked her popular transformation into "Fanny" Burney. It sits next to Dobson's important turn-of-the-century biography in a less exuberant rust-colored cloth binding, *Fanny Burney* (1903), which includes Dobson's wonder about the "irony" of Burney receiving so much money for her final novel, *The Wanderer* (1814), when Austen's *Mansfield Park* had been published the same year—a mark of the turning point between Burney's falling reputation and Austen's rising one.

Then there is the book that sparkles in the light, my gilt-and-green 1903 copy of *Evelina*, the one I specially tracked down after selling the Georgetown copy. It is followed by the staider productions of the mid-twentieth century, like a first edition of Joyce Hemlow's biography, *The History of Fanny Burney* (1958). An Oxford University Press book in navy cloth and a black-and-white portrait of Burney on the dust jacket's front panel, it ushered in a quiet revolution in the critical reassessment of her life and works. I had gathered the evidence. I laid it out across my bookshelves.

I already knew that Austen was the queen of romance. Now I had come to see that Frances Burney could very well be considered the queen mother. In collecting these books about Burney's life and literary reputation, one fact became undeniable: Austen didn't write in a vacuum.

Modern critics, including even infamously male-centric authorities from Ian Watt to Harold Bloom, regularly cite Austen as one of the best writers in the English language. In a duel for canonical status, Austen would be a crack shot. But we seem to force these competitions only upon those who don't fit the "default" of the Western canon: white women novelists, LGBTQ+ writers, authors of color. I haven't read a single critic or historian proclaiming no one should read Richardson because his novels weren't as good as Austen's. Yet Burney is inevitably thrown into a duel with Austen. When Burney loses, that's it: she's off those canonical reading lists. Meanwhile Richardson, never asked to duel in the first place, could remain unchallenged on those same lists.

So I decided to put Burney on a list of my own. Thanks to a few rare book connections in England, I tracked down a set of the first edition of *Camilla*—the one that includes the original subscribers' list marking the first time Austen's name appeared in print. It was a stunning set, five volumes in calf bindings with raised bands on the spine and red goatskin spine labels lettered in gilt. The red spine labels were by no means unusual, as it has long been a common practice to choose a bright contrasting color against leather bindings that are often various shades of brown; binders are artists, and they want to ensure the title pops when the book is resting on its shelf. The leaves were crisp and thick, thanks to the high-quality handmade paper. They elicited a sharp scraping sound as I turned them. But I didn't keep this set. I had other plans for it.

I added *Camilla* to its rightful place in that collection I was building to trace the literary ancestry of modern romance. When I finished the collection, I wrote a catalog documenting it and sent it to a rare book librarian whom I knew was equally excited about the subject. As a result, this collection is now held at the renowned Lilly Library at Indiana University, accessible to scholars for research, to professors for teaching, to students for discovery—and, according to Lilly Library policy, to anyone who takes the time to put in a request to see the books, for any reason at all. I simultaneously produced a hardcover edition of the catalog that we sell as a reference book to private collectors and rare book institutions across the country, including the special collections at Harvard, NYU, Stanford, and the University of Pennsylvania. No one can continue to deny the importance of romance in the history of the English novel after seeing all the rare books systematically laid out in that collection. It is one of my proudest accomplishments to date as a rare book dealer.

Although I sold that collection, I keep buying Burney's books whenever I see them. (My latest, an 1888 copy of *Evelina* bound in cherry-red cloth, was part of a publisher series known as Cassell's Red Library—and it still prints Burney's first name as "Frances.") Reading *Evelina*, I learned that a comparison of similar authors can be useful without turning reading into a contest. As one point of comparison, Austen is certainly more subtle than Burney—but Burney is no less satirical. In fact, Austen's brand of subtle satire has its drawbacks next to writing like Burney's. Austen's disinclination for straight talk can result in a lack of engagement with many issues that Burney chooses to face unflinchingly, like catcalling.

Burney's work also includes comedic scenes that are much more violent than Austen's. While these aren't always to modern taste, bringing in the notes of violence is a conscious choice, and it creates effects that Austen's work doesn't. Such scenes capture how quickly a dubious character can become actually dangerous, conveying the unfortunate truth that real-life stakes are much higher than a gentleman simply leaving in a huff, as they often do in Austen. That's not a criticism of Austen; it's a compliment to Burney.

When approached with curiosity, these kinds of comparisons can start conversations instead of ending them. In both her letters and novels, Austen does not speak highly of those who dismiss Burney without having read her. When I finally practiced Sherlock Holmes's philosophy—to *observe*, not just to see—I understood what Austen had been telling us this whole time: Austen never viewed herself as the lone great woman writer of her era. And she wasn't.

Chapter Three

ANN RADCLIFFE
(1764-1823)

"[. . .] while I have Udolpho to read, I feel as if nobody could
make me miserable."

—Catherine Morland in *Northanger Abbey*

Northanger Abbey is rarely an Austen reader's favorite, but it is mine. After all,
I work in books: I love how the heroine Catherine's bookishness drives the
plot. As the story begins, Catherine is reading a gothic romance called *The
Mysteries of Udolpho* by Ann Radcliffe. Her fellow novel-loving friend asks
Catherine about her first impressions of the book:

"But, my dearest Catherine, what have you been doing with
yourself all this morning?—Have you gone on with *Udolpho*?"

"Yes; I have been reading it ever since I woke; and I am got
to the black veil."

"Are you, indeed? How delightful! Oh! I would not tell you
what is behind the black veil for the world! Are you not wild
to know?"

"Oh! yes, quite; what can it be?—But do not tell me—I
would not be told upon any account. I know it must be a skeleton; I am sure it is Laurentina's skeleton. Oh I am delighted
with the book! I should like to spend my whole life in reading

it. I assure you, if it had not been to meet you, I would not have
come away from it for all the world."

Catherine knows the rewards of finding a great book. "While I have
Udolpho to read," she says, "I feel as if nobody could make me miserable." On the other hand, *Northanger Abbey*'s most obnoxious character, John
Thorpe, refuses to read it. But our hero, Henry Tilney, states without a hint
of embarrassment that "when I had once begun it, I could not lay down
again;—I remember finishing it in two days—my hair standing on end the
whole time."

The main characters in *Northanger Abbey* love *Udolpho*. I loved *Northanger
Abbey*. By some kind of transitive property, I *should* love *Udolpho*. Yet I hadn't
ever considered reading it.

In *The Jane Austen Book Club* by Karen Joy Fowler (2004), the modern
characters in this "all-Jane-Austen-all-the-time book club" hadn't read it
either. When it's time to discuss *Northanger Abbey*, only one member of the
group has done so:

> "You've read *The Mysteries of Udolpho*?" Allegra asked.
>
> "Black veils and Laurentina's skeleton? You bet. Didn't
> you think it sounded good?"
>
> We had not. We'd thought it sounded overheated, overdone,
> old-fashionedly lurid. We'd thought it sounded ridiculous.
>
> Actually it hadn't occurred to any of us to read it. Some of
> us hadn't even realized it was a real book.

On the one hand, I knew it was a real book. I even knew it was "important." *Udolpho* usually appears in one sentence of literary surveys, in which
they briefly pause to name-check a couple of gothics, the genre that *Udolpho*
made popular (more on that later). But I confess, none of those drive-by
mentions had ever moved me to consider investigating the book myself.
The word I associated with it: melodramatic.

In the eighteenth century, readers and critics alike considered *Udolpho* a masterpiece. The hero in Austen's *Northanger Abbey* rushes through the book with his "hair standing on end." Yet two hundred years later, Karen Joy Fowler's twenty-first-century characters assumed it was "overheated, overdone, old-fashionedly lurid." Who was right? Fresh off the pleasure of being wrong about Burney, I decided Radcliffe would be the next author whose books I'd add to my shelf.

———————

Ann Radcliffe was born in London in 1764, making her about twelve years younger than Burney and eleven years older than Austen. Few details about Radcliffe's life have come down to us, but what we do know is compelling. Whether by eighteenth-century standards or twenty-first-century ones, young Ann's education was unconventional. While she was barred from an extensive classical program more commonly granted to boys of the genteel class into which she was born, she did receive training that few of her generation could match. As a child, Ann became the ward of her uncle Thomas Bentley during a period when her father transitioned careers. Bentley was famous for partnering with Josiah Wedgwood, whose innovations in ceramics made him a leading producer of fine china and other dishware. Bentley was both well traveled and well educated, bringing much of the artistic inspiration to Wedgwood ceramics. One of Radcliffe's major modern biographers, Rictor Norton, summarized the company roles as "Wedgwood supplied the science, while Bentley provided the taste." Even today collectors seek examples with the "Wedgwood & Bentley" mark. Through this career Bentley became a kind of art historian, collecting books and prints to study ancient art, then working with artists to adapt his findings to modern preferences. Right after young Ann came to live with him, he began researching Gothic architecture for an exhibition.

The house became filled with every obtainable book and engraving on the subject, in addition to original commissions from artists: visions of towering churches and ruins of the late Middle Ages. These images were often precise down to tiny ornamental details, from the floral designs gracing the top of a pillar to the slender, spindly frame of a side window. At the age of ten, little Ann skipped about the house surrounded by the Gothic, watching her uncle systematically describe and catalog examples. It's easy to imagine a wide-eyed girl roving among the old books and hand-colored engravings, perhaps even then making up stories about other little girls lost in the soaring landscapes she saw depicted in them. There are very few children in the world, then or now, who have been exposed to such an art history education. Naturally her later descriptions of ancient castles and abbeys would be compelling: she knew their intricacies from childhood.

In 1787 when she was twenty-three, Ann married William Radcliffe, who was trying to establish a career as a parliamentary reporter. William would watch members of Parliament debate matters of state, whether they were minor questions of law or major proposals like ending Britain's involvement in the slave trade, then return to his office on the Strand to summarize events for the morning papers. A publisher from this era described the newspaper printers on this thoroughfare as the "hot-bed" of literary London: "During the sitting of Parliament, and when warmly-contested party questions are under discussion, the activity and excitement in this region are only to be compared to a hive of bees, at the time of swarming." Reporters like William would remain at the office late into the night, where the lights of the buildings blazed and the "continued rattle and noise" of the presses carried through the otherwise quiet streets.

Meanwhile, Ann Radcliffe remained at home alone. She was bored. According to her first biographer, Thomas Talfourd, she took up writing in order to pass the evenings by herself. She wrote of deserted abbeys as shelter for people on the run, and of those in pursuit, just out of sight. She wrote of a fragmentary manuscript left by one who died in captivity. She wrote of a foreboding dream of a dead man's blood overflowing within his coffin to spill through the room. When William returned home, Ann would ask him to read her compositions. It would seem an odd hobby to some, a young woman writing horror-inducing scenes while home alone late at night. Such people would wonder later if the habit had twisted her mind. Talfourd, who worked with her husband on his biography of Ann Radcliffe, dismissed the suspicion with an evocative picture: "So far was she from being subjected to her own terrors, that she often laughingly presented to Mr. Radcliffe chapters, which he could not read alone without shuddering." I like to imagine Radcliffe waiting with a grin, knowing that what she had written was good. That it was terrifying.

Radcliffe soon found a publisher and anonymously issued her first book, *The Castles of Athlin and Dunbayne* (1789). As I've mentioned, works of fiction in this period were often published anonymously, no matter the author's gender. This suited Radcliffe just fine, since she loved to write but hated drawing attention to herself. *The Castles of Athlin and Dunbayne* received only a little notice, though at least one reviewer attributed the anonymous book to a man.

It was her second book, *A Sicilian Romance* (1790), that "attracted in no ordinary degree the attention of the public," recalled the Scottish writer Walter Scott in his 1824 sketch of Radcliffe's life: "Adventures heaped on adventures, in quick and brilliant succession, with all the hair-breadth charms of escape or capture." Her third novel, *The Romance of the Forest* (1791), decisively established her fame. In it, the orphaned heroine Adeline seeks refuge with a couple on the run in a dilapidated, abandoned abbey that the locals believe is haunted. Maria Edgeworth, soon to become a famous novelist herself—and another favorite of Austen's—wrote to her cousin about it. "It has been the fashionable novel here," she said, "everybody read and talked of it." Perhaps most important, it achieved a level of popularity that gave Radcliffe the confidence to publish under her own name, beginning with the novel's second edition that followed quickly after the first.

Romance of the Forest wasn't a courtship novel, despite its title. This is an important distinction because how Radcliffe's novels were categorized by critics played a major role in shaping her legacy. In the European Middle Ages, the term "romance" developed to account for original works in vernacular languages (i.e., not Latin), and progressed into a label for writings not based in historical fact: think of "Arthurian romance." Before the eighteenth century, a "romance" could be any work with fantastical elements, like Shakespeare's *A Midsummer Night's Dream*. It could be set in an unknowable time or place, like the "long time ago in a galaxy far, far away" of *Star Wars*. Or it could just be a story of everyday people whose lives weren't seen as significant enough to appear in history books. This verbal lineage is still visible in languages like French and Italian, where *roman* and *romanzo* translate to our modern English "novel."

As the English novel developed, the term "novel" was used initially as a specific kind of story within the larger category of "romances." The "novel" was then defined as a story of current events. (It shares the same root as the word "news.") By the late 1780s when Radcliffe first started to publish, "romances" were no longer the larger category *for* "novels," but a distinct category *from* "novels." Clara Reeve, a novelist herself, published an important piece of criticism at this time called *The Progress of Romance* (1785), defining romances as "a heroic fable, which treats of fabulous persons and things." A novel, on the other hand, is "a picture of real life and manners, and of the times in which it is written." In other words: romances depicted fantasy, while novels strove for realism. So when one contemporary critic called Radcliffe "the Shakespeare of Romance Writers," that had nothing to do with her writing about love.

The development of these terms reflects how rapidly this new literary form was changing in the eighteenth century. The definitions continued to evolve, actually inverting from their origins: the term "novel" became the universal term to mean any kind of fiction, with "romances" becoming a subgenre of the novel. Thus the "romances" of Radcliffe's time were somewhat like what we call "genre fiction," especially speculative fiction like science fiction, fantasy, and horror: still novels, but of a particular kind. By the eighteenth-century definition, The Lord of the Rings, *Dracula*, and *War of the Worlds* are all romances—and in fact, H. G. Wells's works in this vein were called "scientific romances." Like modern genre fiction, the romances of Radcliffe's day were simultaneously widely read as page-turners and freely condemned as inferior in quality. That disconnect is tied intimately to the story of Radcliffe's fall from favor.

But that would come later. For now, Radcliffe's career soared with the two-hit combo of *Sicilian Romance* and *Romance of the Forest*. These were stories of adventure set in the distant past, quite different from the contemporary courtship novels popularized by Burney and others. Playwrights adapted her books for the stage, reaching ever greater audiences. Imitations of Radcliffe, and "romances" generally, started to shift the marketplace: in 1794, one of the biggest literary magazines of the era expanded its Monthly Catalogue of "Novels" into "Novels and Romances." Radcliffe was inspiring an entire generation of writers, and especially women writers who followed in her footsteps.

When she sold the manuscript of *The Mysteries of Udolpho* (1794), Radcliffe negotiated the sale for £500, more than double the previous record paid to a British woman. (The previous record was held by none other than Frances Burney, £200 for her second novel, *Cecilia*.) When one of Burney's publishers, Cadell, heard the amount, he was so sure it was an exaggeration that he wagered £10 against it. He not only lost that bet, but then went on to pay even more himself for the rights to Radcliffe's next novel. Burney had proved that women could write novels just as good as those of Richardson or Fielding. Now Radcliffe was proving that women could ask for more money for their work. She soon made significantly more money than her husband who, to his credit, was by all accounts relentlessly supportive of her literary career.

She was worth the investment. Readers reported staying up all night to finish *Udolpho*. Poets printed odes inspired by it. All of Radcliffe's books received acclaim in her lifetime, but none was more lauded than *The Mysteries of Udolpho*. In the year *Udolpho* was published, one reviewer called it "the most interesting novel in the English language." This was the book that established Radcliffe not only as a celebrity but as a genius. I had to read it.

It took a few weeks to pick up a copy of *Udolpho* because, of course, I couldn't read just any copy. I was collecting, so I wanted a copy that had some historical interest. I scoured online marketplaces to get a sense of the options and price points. Looking for books online sounds simple, but the wonderful accessibility also brings some challenges. Chief among them is *too* much accessibility: carefully cataloged listings by professionals will appear right next to those of amateurs, who often misuse technical terms, have less experience to contextualize rarity, and clumsily over- or under-represent condition issues. Learning to recognize the difference between expertise and opportunism is an important skill for the book collector, and one that is learned only by practice. But that's part of the appeal. More than once over the course of researching this book I sat down to write and instead got distracted by hunting online for my collection. Then my kids would run into the room, or my alarm would go off (an alarm I keep specifically for this purpose)—and I would find myself blinking away from the laptop's glow, realizing that hours had passed.

Eventually, I found my copy. I chose an elegant little two-volume pocket edition printed in 1931 by the Everyman's Library. This was one of the most successful twentieth-century reprint series of "world's classics," as the publisher termed them. I liked that they acknowledged Radcliffe as a "classic," and I liked that it was meant for everyday readers, not for specialists. Besides, this was a score that any rare book dealer would appreciate because the original red dust jackets were intact, a rarity for the 1930s volumes of the series. This particular edition was bound in a brilliant red cloth, rough to the touch, with red patterned endpapers to match.

I read the first page, then the second. It didn't take me long to realize that Henry Tilney, that smug, darling man, was right. *Udolpho* turned out to be one of the best reading experiences I have ever had. I kept putting off sleep to read just one more chapter. On a day off from work, I didn't even bother showering or changing clothes; I read. Another morning, I was so involved in reading that I poured water into the wrong compartment of the coffee maker, where it spread damningly across the counter, unnoticed.

The Mysteries of Udolpho was another "romance," by the eighteenth-century definition, but specifically a subcategory of it that we now call a "gothic": its prevailing atmosphere is one of terror. The plot follows the fate of heroine Emily as she comes of age, beginning with a picturesque journey through the South of France with her father, then briefly to living with her aunt in Venice after her father's death. Newly orphaned and an heiress, Emily is taken to the ominous Castle Udolpho by the villain, her uncle Signor Montoni, where she is effectively imprisoned until she signs over her inheritance to him. There Emily faces increasingly dangerous situations that heighten the thrill of the mysteries for which the book is so famous, primary among them the "black veil" mentioned by the characters in Austen's *Northanger Abbey*. Already under threat, Emily stumbles upon a room with some *thing*, enormous and unmoving, covered by that black veil. When she peeks under the veil, what she sees is so terrifying that she faints. The reader is not told what she saw under the veil until the end of the novel.

That summary does not begin to capture how very fun *Udolpho* is to read. There is no way to appreciate that except by reading it. Radcliffe crafts a terror that is architectural: built slowly, carefully, stone by stone. To a modern reader, the pace is nearly too slow—nearly. And that makes it exactly the right pace. Radcliffe has you begging for another glimpse, another turn, another risk. Her chapter-ending cliff-hangers still compel the reader to turn to the next page, two hundred years after she wrote them.

Radcliffe teases by degrees. She allows a startling glimpse of what's next, then yanks the reader back into the dark. She uses tropes that I'd seen repeatedly in later classics: a sudden, unexplained sound in the silence—Lovecraft's *At the Mountains of Madness*; a lurking shadow that may or may not be waiting to do harm—Shelley's *Frankenstein*; exploring deserted rooms as if in a dream—Stoker's *Dracula*. (And did my earlier reference to the image of a room filling with blood put you in mind, perhaps, of *The Shining?*) I knew these tropes, yet I found myself responding to Radcliffe's particular use of them. My pulse quickened; my breath caught; my body stiffened. I was thrown down the long galleries and cavernous staircases of that ancient castle.

Readers of Radcliffe's own time experienced much the same thing. The first major critical assessment of Radcliffe's work, John Dunlop's *The History of Fiction* (1814), captures her power: "in the hands of Mrs Radcliffe, not merely the trampling of a steed, and the pauses of the wind, but, in certain circumstances, even common footsteps and the shutting of a door become sublime and terrible." Radcliffe's architecture of terror is compelling in a way few authors can hope to achieve, whether modern, historical, or canonical. In fact, authors like Charles Dickens read Radcliffe's books as manuals, studying them for their pacing, their use of cliff-hangers, their cultivation of atmosphere. Radcliffe was the teacher to whom subsequent authors turned for instruction.

It's difficult to discuss *Udolpho* for long without veering into spoilers, but that's a challenge I willingly accept. When it comes to reprints of older works, modern forewords tend to talk about the work without concern that they've just revealed the entire plot to some unsuspecting reader. But I refuse to ruin the ending here. As Catherine's friend teases, in *Northanger Abbey*, "Are you not wild to know?" Yes—I was wild to know what was behind that black veil. At one point, I broke my own rule about marginalia and literally wrote in pencil in the margin of my copy from 1931: "Eeee what did she seeeeeee!" All I will admit is that the terrors in Radcliffe's books all have explanations that are logical rather than fantastical. The term for this is "the explained supernatural," and it became one of the most divisive aspects of her books. Some readers argued that the gravest sin of a book driven by hidden terrors is to resolve that darkness with clear-eyed, rational explanations. They felt it was jarring that Radcliffe, the "enchantress," had snapped her fingers to lift the spell. In 1814, Dunlop complained about this using a metaphor reminiscent of Radcliffe's own Gothic architecture: he called them "passages that lead to nothing."

After reading the book myself, I disagreed. Such a heavy focus on one aspect of the ending diminishes most of the reading experience— and the exquisite feeling of terror it inspires. For Radcliffe, the atmosphere is the point. That's clear even looking at a copy of the book. Modern paperback editions tend to run a bit over five hundred pages; the answers to the big mysteries take up perhaps the last five. Radcliffe's aim was to stir fear in the hearts of her readers, then let them soak in it. *Udolpho* is a book that makes you slow down. The more you try to rush to the action, the less satisfying it is. Don't force anything: just embrace it. (It is interesting to consider this idea as a kind of life lesson that several of Austen's heroines could have benefited from—most obviously Emma, but also, quite appropriately, Catherine from *Northanger Abbey*.)

Udolpho is certainly one of the best reading experiences I've had, but I don't mean to suggest that it is a perfect novel. I struggled with the fact that landscapes are described, at length, throughout the novel. The first part of the book, the picturesque journey of Emily and her father through the South of France, was far too long for my taste. (If you want to pick up *Udolpho*, do not give up before getting to the castle!) Yet plenty of readers from Radcliffe's generation adored that part of the book, praising her extended descriptions of cliffs, rivers, valleys, and shade as "gorgeous"; one reviewer stated that the scenes of Venice were "some of the most finished pictures that are to be found in any language." Radcliffe was so good at this that her contemporaries confidently stated that she had visited the glamorous scenes of France and Italy in person—when in fact she had never left the country before. In other words, this particular complaint was perhaps a question of personal, or even generational, taste. More to the point: such a quibble didn't undermine the affection that grew in my heart for *Udolpho*. I've read many books that I consider technically perfect, yet have left me cold. *Udolpho* has flaws—and—it moved me far more than those seemingly flawless books. It had that very quality of transcendence sought by Austen's early critics, like Charlotte Brontë.

Now that I had read and loved *Udolpho*, I wanted more. And so did the public of the 1790s. In the wake of Radcliffe's unprecedented success, gothics became one of the biggest trends in fiction in the country. Radcliffe didn't invent the gothic, but she's the one who made it big.

The gothic boom led by Radcliffe was the culmination of three major literary movements of the eighteenth century. First, critics laid important groundwork with a rise in appreciation for "the sublime." Second, the singular championing of Shakespeare as England's greatest writer played a part. Finally, the novel found its footing in the rapidly maturing marketplace for printed books as its own genre of literature, distinct from the epics, folktales, and "romances" of yore. I had already investigated the rapid growth of the novel while wondering about Burney's anxiety over publishing, but the first two points deserve some brief context to appreciate Radcliffe's place in the literary landscape, and in my collection.

In 1757, politician and philosopher Edmund Burke helped launch an interest in the sublime in Great Britain with his book *A Philosophical Enquiry into the Origin of Our Ideas of the Sublime and Beautiful*. Burke praised the sublime as a specific kind of emotional reaction: the thrill you experience when afraid. It is that delicious dread you feel when staring down a vast cliff or looking out at a roiling sea. In one chapter, Burke used stories of "ghosts and goblins" as examples of that sublime feeling. Whether it's being awestruck in nature or spooked in the confines of our own home, he outlined various ways we enjoy being scared. As Great Britain marched into Romanticism, away from the detached logical perfections of neoclassicism and toward a celebration of individual emotional experience, Burke's celebration of the sublime provided the intellectual framework for embracing the dark, the wild, and the terrifying.

At the same time, Shakespeare's plays were attracting more critical praise than ever. Upon his death in 1616, Shakespeare had a stellar reputation as a playwright, but it was by no means a foregone conclusion that he would one day develop into England's "national poet." In the century of his death, four major collections of his work were published. The first, issued in 1623, is now called the First Folio; when it appears on the rare book marketplace today, it sells for millions and always makes headlines. (I've sold copies of the Second Folio from 1632 and the Fourth Folio from 1685, but not yet a First Folio: that one's for the bucket list.) These collections kept his reputation alive and provided the access necessary to keep his plays on the stage through the eighteenth century, when he developed into an icon, the best English literature has to offer. As with most significant turning points, this occurred both because of shifts in the wider cultural context and because of individuals who took action at exactly the right time.

Those shifts in the wider cultural context began to form in early-eighteenth-century England, what we call the Augustan age. Writers then were simultaneously inspired and intimidated by the great classical traditions of ancient Greece and Rome. The Augustan poet Alexander Pope not only took inspiration from classical authors like Horace and Virgil, but enjoyed commercial success with his translation of Homer's *Iliad* (1715–20) and *Odyssey* (1725–26) into English. The British literati wanted to establish a formidable tradition of their own, one to match those of ancient Greece and Rome—and also that of modern France. The French celebrated their great playwrights like Corneille and Racine; the British looked to their own playwrights to compete. Over the course of the eighteenth century, Shakespeare's reputation soared within this culture war with France.

Among the leaders of this movement was the Burney family's friend David Garrick, the most celebrated actor of his day and later a manager of one of the three authorized theaters in London. Garrick partly owed his own rise as an actor to Shakespeare, having first achieved success playing the Bard's Richard III. He drove the effort to sanctify Shakespeare as a national hero alongside the critics who exalted his plays as works of genius. Shakespeare's rise created a fertile climate for writers like Radcliffe because his tragedies were often cited as ideal examples of the sublime in literature. What is more sublime than Macbeth confessing that his "Present fears / Are less than horrible imaginings"?

Along with the rise of the novel as a form, these two trends sparked something new and exciting in English fiction: the gothic. Writers became interested in exploring the sublime through fiction, and Shakespeare was one of the first authors these authors turned to for inspiration. A case in point is the book that traditionally has the honor of the label "the first gothic," Horace Walpole's *The Castle of Otranto* (1764). Walpole subtitled it *A Gothic Story* because it took place in the Middle Ages, after the Goths sacked Rome. Not coincidentally, Walpole modeled *The Castle of Otranto* on Shakespeare.

In *Otranto*, the lord of a castle ignores ghostly portents in order to secure his kingdom, with the result that (spoilers, which I don't mind giving for this one) his own heirs are tragically murdered. By the end the true heir, a knight with a humble background, is revealed. The fight over succession brings to mind *King Lear* and *Macbeth*; the accidental death of the lord's daughter *Romeo and Juliet*; the ghostly portents *Hamlet*. Walpole admitted that he had used Shakespearean imitation as a cover for his experiment with the concept of the sublime, confessing that he hoped "to shelter my own daring under the canon of the brightest genius this country, at least, has produced." While his gothic experiment was just that—an artistic caprice, not some grand attempt to begin a new genre—it included many of the later hallmarks that would inform the gothic tradition: a large estate, ghostly apparitions, secret passageways.

A little over a decade after *The Castle of Otranto* appeared, Clara Reeve would take the next big step forward in the gothic by publishing *The Old English Baron* (1778). *The Old English Baron* was a significant evolution from the oddity of Shakespearean fanfic that was *Otranto*, giving the gothic a more palatable structure. In her introduction, Reeve explained that she hoped to "unite the most attractive and interesting circumstances of the ancient Romance and the modern Novel." Her plot was set like *Otranto* in the Middle Ages and also focused on a virtuous orphan's recovery of an estate lost through treachery—but it was paced more like a typical novel than a play, and it was far more grounded (no gigantic swords).

Walpole and Reeve focused primarily on the heroic conflicts of their male characters; next, Sophia Lee brought heroines into focus in *The Recess* (1783–85), the story of two noble sisters from the Elizabethan era—secret daughters of Mary, Queen of Scots—amid ruins, caves, and underground passageways. (Sophia Lee was also a subscriber to Burney's *Camilla* alongside Jane Austen.) Finally, a year before Radcliffe's first book was published, another popular novel took the gothic a step further: Charlotte Smith's *Emmeline* (1788). *Emmeline* brought gothic elements into the Burney-esque courtship novel. It began in a gothic setting—with an orphan heroine growing up in a largely abandoned castle—but quickly moved on, with most of the book taking place in the drawing rooms of elegant households. When Radcliffe took up the form, she held on to the elegant heroines of this tradition, but she also perfected the terrifying settings of the gothic: an abandoned abbey, an isolated castle, a room filled with hints of past violence. The architecture of terror became a trademark of the gothic, and no one did it better than Radcliffe.

Thanks to Radcliffe's success, gothics exploded. Only a handful were published after *Otranto*; after Radcliffe, imitators sprang up so fast that they soon represented at least one-third of the entire fiction market. These novels started appearing right when higher literacy rates and the development of circulating libraries magnified the size of the English reading public. The gothic takeover was "a most singular revolution," according to the *Gentleman's Magazine* in 1798. One publisher, the Minerva Press, devoted more than a third of its entire business just to publishing gothics.

Udolpho had made an entire marketplace. When I read the book myself, I could see why. I had been mistaken for believing in its reputation as "overheated, overdone, old-fashionedly lurid." After my experience of misjudging *Evelina*, this didn't shock me. I was wrong again. But in a different way this time. I didn't ever think Radcliffe was an inferior version of Austen. I had accepted that she was inferior, period.

I kept investigating: enjoying Radcliffe's novels, reading biographies and critical analyses, and collecting her books. What I found was both fascinating and infuriating. Fascinating because I could directly observe the changing tone of critics over more than one hundred years. Infuriating because, well, you'll see.

——————

The seeds of Radcliffe's fall were first sewn in 1797. That year her fifth novel, *The Italian*, appeared. It featured Radcliffe's most compelling villain, Father Schedoni, a priest with a dark past who attempts to prevent the marriage of the hero and heroine. Reviews at the time were a bit mixed (one of the reviewers preferred *Udolpho*, for which he cannot be blamed), but readers loved it. This was the book that inspired one author in 1798 to call Radcliffe "the Shakespeare of Romance Writers." After a rather large first print run of two thousand copies, *The Italian* went into another edition only a few months later. Once again, everyone was talking about Radcliffe's books.

Then, without explanation, she simply stopped publishing.

At first, many assumed Radcliffe must have died. My favorite example of this comes from the French, who also loved her. Reporters in France mistook an English notice of her mother-in-law's death in 1809 as an obituary for the author herself. Her French admirers mourned her extravagantly in a very nineteenth-century fashion: by publishing a heap of fake "posthumous" works under her name. I first learned about these books' existence thanks to Norton's modern biography of Radcliffe. Then, I tracked down Deborah D. Rogers's *Ann Radcliffe: A Bio-Bibliography*, which has an appendix of "Spurious Attributions" that include publication information. Now I had to find them. The next time I went to Paris to scout for books, I made it a point at antiquarian bookshops to ask for books by Radcliffe before her actual death date, 1823. No luck. Even though they were not really by Radcliffe, these early-nineteenth-century publications are quite rare, so (much to my anguish) I still haven't been able to acquire one. But one day I will accomplish my dual aims of leaving with a bag of pirated books from the late Napoleonic era and gaining a reputation across the city as "cette étrange femme qui cherche Radcliffe." Book collecting is one of those areas in which being a bit odd is an advantage.

Reports of Radcliffe's death, in France and beyond, were widely believed because the public could not comprehend her silence. Why would such a successful author retire? Radcliffe could have been basking in the spotlight, sparkling at the tables of London hostesses who managed to snag her as a guest for a dinner party. Instead, it turns out, Radcliffe took her well-earned money and bought a house in the English countryside. As soon as they had enough funds, she and her husband began to travel, not only to various regions of England but also abroad, to Germany, Holland, and beyond. She kept journals of these trips, filled with passages about those grand and terrible landscapes that she continued to capture with the eye of an artist: "In a high window of the tower a light. Why is it so sublime to stand at the foot of a dark tower, and look up its height to the sky and the stars?"

Even during select visits to London, Radcliffe disliked attention and avoided it. For instance, though she loved to attend the theater, Radcliffe always sat in the orchestra so that she was less visible from the general seats. When in society, she sought to be invisible. Until finally everyone thought she had disappeared.

Part of the confusion about Radcliffe's disappearance arose from the fact that the public knew very little about her in the first place. For such a major author, the known biographical details about Radcliffe are frustratingly scarce. Radcliffe's aversion to attention ensured few personal details appeared in print during her lifetime, and most of her letters, diaries, and other unpublished writings were lost or destroyed before later generations could bring them to print.

This created problems for those who came to be interested in her many years later. The great Victorian poet Christina Rossetti, who had loved Radcliffe's works since she was a teenager, attempted to write a biography of her idol in the 1880s, "altho' I know next to nothing about her." She visited the archives at the British Museum, consulted with historians and literary scholars, and finally placed an open call in a magazine to solicit previously unknown material. Rossetti's excitement dimmed as she realized how little information had survived. She finally conceded to her editor: "I despair and withdraw."

Failures like this had significant implications for Radcliffe's posthumous legacy. At a time when Radcliffe's place in the canon was waning, a biography by one of the most respected authors of the Victorian period could have brought Radcliffe back to life for another generation. It was, after all, James Edward Austen-Leigh's 1869 *Memoir* of his aunt that launched the first major revival of interest in Austen: the modern scholar B. C. Southam argued that it was responsible for "awakening public interest in an author virtually forgotten." But a similar biography of Radcliffe never happened because Rossetti couldn't find the material.

A few years after Radcliffe stopped publishing, and many thought she was dead, a different rumor began to circulate: she had gone mad. Perhaps, critics speculated, the terrors she had created on the page had wreaked havoc in her own mind. These rumormongers took their worst fears of what novel reading would do to their bookish daughters and projected them onto the most visible target, Radcliffe herself. The gossip culminated in 1810, when a pompous but well-connected poet named Charles Wheelwright published a book with this rumor stated as fact. In one of his poems he referenced Radcliffe, then included an unsubstantiated footnote: "Mrs. Ann Radcliffe, the ingenious authoress [. . .] is reported to have died under that species of mental derangement, known by the name of *the horrors.*" Those italics are original; "the horrors" was an actual medical term in the era, meaning "a fit of depression or fright as occurs with mental delirium" (according to *Merriam-Webster*). In other words, said this printed gossip, Radcliffe had died of madness.

While the literary world speculated on her death and derangement, Radcliffe was taking walks in the park with her dog and complaining about hotel service on vacations with her husband. Still very much alive and sane when these rumors first appeared, Radcliffe didn't know how to react. Was she supposed to write into the newspapers and say, "No, I'm not actually mad?" That would never do. Even the thought of such an inelegant letter gave her shivers—more shivers than writing her own "horrors." So she did nothing.

Upon her actual death in 1823, Radcliffe's husband authorized a short biography by the lawyer and writer Thomas Talfourd in the hopes of restoring her reputation and ensuring her legacy. This was the first extended account of Radcliffe's life and intended by her widower to be the official one. In it, Talfourd dismissed all suspicion of madness. Instead, he chronicled Radcliffe's retirement activities like sitting in the orchestra and taking walks in the woods. He also included excerpts from Radcliffe's travel journals to prove that she retained her gift for writing, even if she didn't choose to continue monetizing it.

But Talfourd's illuminating biography came too late for her contemporaries. He and Radcliffe's widower discovered to their dismay that the charge of madness was not to be countered so easily. Like Radcliffe's own "explained supernatural" endings in her books, they were bringing logic to an emotional argument. The idea of her madness felt poetic, appropriate to her image. Radcliffe helped so many readers feel mind-bending terror that it made some sort of sense that her own mind must have been warped in the process. The brilliant Radcliffe couldn't simply be a woman who liked walks more than people. This iconification happens to most public figures, not just those who reach fame at the level of Radcliffe. (Was it a surprise when I, the rare book dealer, mentioned downloading e-books?)

The public's embrace of the madness narrative also reminded me of something Burke had said when he laid out his theory of the sublime for the eighteenth-century British public. He identified obscurity as the source of the sublime's power, that we fear things more when we can't see them clearly. "When we know the full extent of any danger, when we can accustom our eyes to it, a great deal of the apprehension vanishes." Applied to the world of gossip, this principle holds: when we lack information, our heads tend to fill holes with the worst-case possibilities rather than the most likely ones. This is one explanation for what happened to Radcliffe's legacy. When Radcliffe retreated from the public eye, she left an absence of information behind her. And, boy, did it get filled. Radcliffe evoked our deepest fears by lingering in the unexplained; her readers rushed to resolve it. Rumors of death could be countered with fact. But madness? The idea of a madwoman in the attic was appealing to Englishmen long before *Jane Eyre*.

Yet this couldn't account entirely for Radcliffe's fall from grace. The problem is that, typically, madness isn't enough to destroy an artist's reputation. On the contrary, we love a touch of madness in our creatives: Van Gogh, William Blake, Hunter S. Thompson . . . Our creative men, I should say.

I began collecting examples of these rumors and their counterclaims in print so that I could track them as they transformed over time. I acted quickly to obtain a copy of Wheelwright's book with the infamous rumor that (the still-living) Radcliffe had died of *"the horrors."* Across all my connections, I found only one copy of this book on the market and—I must add with pleasure—for a fraction of the price of any of Radcliffe's first editions. The high end of the collectible book market, which has traditionally been dominated by male collectors, hasn't always valued women authors as much as their male counterparts. In this context, it really was a statement that this guy's first edition could be picked up for a song, even in a solid leather binding contemporary to its era.

Next, I grabbed the first publication of Talfourd's memoir of Ann Radcliffe, the one authorized by her widower immediately after her death. This one ended up taking up more space on my shelf than anticipated because it was published as the preface to Radcliffe's posthumous final novel, *Gaston de Blondeville* (1826), in four volumes. But with their raised bands—that series of little horizontal ridges you see on the spines of older leather bindings— and gilt-stamped ornaments to the compartments in between, I welcomed them. I wasn't running out of room on my shelf. Yet.

My collection was beginning to tell the story of Radcliffe's afterlife. While she was alive, some gossiped that she was mad. After her death, I noticed the emergence of a new rumor: critics began to say that her writing was bad. But I had read her books and no longer believed that line. So I searched for the evidence on how it slowly became accepted as the truth. There were more books to add to my shelf.

One of the most important I sought was Dunlop's *History of Fiction* (1814), which I had already referenced as a major early critical assessment of her work. After the era of her contemporary reviewers—who were publishing only short pieces in literary magazines as each book came out— Dunlop's treatment was the first extended overview of Radcliffe's work as a whole. It was published while Radcliffe was still alive, and it was highly complimentary. Dunlop was one of the critics who compared Radcliffe to Shakespeare, arguing that her brand of terror "is that which is raised by a delineation of guilt, horror, and remorse, which, if Shakespeare has equaled, he has not surpassed."

I found a copy of Dunlop's book on the website of a fellow dealer that I circled around for months, trying to reconcile myself to what I would have to spend in order to obtain it. Then one summer I received a modest honorarium for teaching at a seminar for aspiring rare book dealers. As far as I was concerned, this was bonus money. I gave in and used it to order the Dunlop first edition. Some people splurge on handbags, or concert tickets, or weekend getaways. I have done these things too . . . but I'm most likely to splurge on a first edition.

Dunlop's book represented a positive turning point in Radcliffe's career. It had, after all, compared her to Shakespeare. Radcliffe's association with

Shakespeare stemmed from their mutual talent in invoking the sublime. In fact, she showed such a precise application of aesthetic theories—recall her singular art history education—that she was more likely to be paired with poets like Milton than with fellow novelists like Walpole in literary criticism of the time. Poets were artists; novelists were rarely considered such. "That her genius was poetical, is proved by the beautiful and sublime descriptions of scenery with which her romances abound," argued the editor of an 1815 unauthorized compilation of poetry that had been excerpted from her novels. It was partly because her writing was considered "poetical" that critics felt comfortable crowning her with laurels at a time when novelists as a whole were still very much dubious characters, charged with corrupting the minds of young women across the country (that "mark of the beast" line). While Radcliffe was alive, her writing remained "sublime," like Shakespeare, Milton, and Dante. After her death, critics with agendas of their own decided she was only a writer of "romances."

Romances: not stories of love, but stories of imagination. It became important in my investigation to remember that, by Radcliffe's time, a "novel" was becoming the umbrella term for fictional prose narratives—and "romances" were a *subset* of the novel. A book would be labeled a romance if it had unrealistic traits or storylines like what we might label today "speculative fiction." (A critic would often refer to such a work as both a "novel" and a "romance" in the same review.) Radcliffe wrote romances that elicited terror in the reader: what we call gothics today. While reading and collecting, I kept noticing that critics might praise individual novels, but they were almost universally derisive of romances as a category. I considered whether Radcliffe's fall from the canon might have more to do with her books' genre than their plots.

Reading critics of the era, it is clear this kind of fiction was always considered a "lower" form. Ann Radcliffe's name was inextricably tied with that genre. In 1797, when Radcliffe published *The Italian*, one of the major reviews used it as an opportunity to spell out this hierarchy between genres. Sure, the *Monthly Review* affirmed, Radcliffe was "distinguished" among romance writers. But it went out of its way to stress that romance was simply inferior to realist novels: "the most excellent, but at the same time the most difficult, species of novel-writing," the reviewer argued, "consists in the accurate and interesting representation of such manners and characters as society presents." Even while critics praised Radcliffe, they could not praise her genre.

This perspective was common because gothic romances attracted two associations loathed by many male tastemakers: broad commercial appeal and artistic dominance by women. A letter to the editor of a Bristol-based magazine from 1796 complained, "it has been the fashion to make Terror the order of the day, by confining the heroes and heroines in gloomy castles, full of Spectres, apparitions, ghosts and dead men's bones." Perhaps most famously, the aforementioned Minerva Press was notorious for flooding the market with imitations of whatever was selling, and critics viewed this distastefully as prioritizing profits over art. According to a pioneering study of Minerva Press by Dorothy Blakey in 1939, "So closely identified with cheap fiction was the famous publishing house [. . .] that to nineteenth-century critics the name Minerva meant little more than a convenient epithet of contempt." Thanks to Radcliffe, gothic romances were what was selling. The "contemptible" Minerva Press published an avalanche of them. In 1798 the *Critical Review* complained of the "vapid and servile imitations" that were appearing due to the "creative genius and the descriptive powers of Mrs. Radcliffe."

Then there was the dominance of women in the field. In the period when Radcliffe, Burney, and Austen were publishing, more women published novels than men. Many published gothic romances in the style of Radcliffe. Women drove that genre: the majority of gothics were written by women, about women, for women. Skeptics who questioned the usefulness of novels as a literary form felt even stronger about its dubious subgenre, the gothic romance. In their view, books read by young women should communicate strong morals—yet gothics were more focused on providing a good time than offering models of virtue. Indeed, gothics were a symbol of emotion over reason.

Further, the very fact that women were finding success writing such books was resented. Some readers may object that I'm overstepping when I state that attacks on gothic romances were specifically gendered, but this wasn't a conclusion I had to infer. A number of critics outright said it. One reviewer, in panning Charlotte Dacre's 1806 gothic *Zofloya*, complained about the gothic elements, adding that "the *grossest* and *most immoral* novelists of the present day, are *women!*" [italics are, in fact, *sic*]. Another writer tsked, "when female invention will employ itself in images of the grosser sort, it is a fatal prediction of relaxed morals, and a species of—at least—LITERARY PROSTITUTION" [*sic!*]. Better yet, this comment came from the preface of the writer's own gothic romance. For him, gothics were only bad when women wrote them.

Radcliffe's reputation was so strong that it held even under these kinds of attacks—for a time. Just before he condemned all women who wrote gothics, the same writer who called gothic writing by women "literary prostitution" also admitted that his love of the genre was "caught from an enthusiastic admiration of *Udolpho*'s unrivalled Foundress." In her lifetime, Radcliffe was always the exception. Remember, she was "poetical." Critics hailed traits in her work that were similar to her male peers in order to distance Radcliffe, whom they liked, from the scribbling women following her in the gothic genre, whom they didn't.

But there comes a time when every "not like the others" girl learns that being more like the boys doesn't, in fact, save you. Radcliffe was acclaimed for her "poetical" writing until some of the most celebrated poets of the upcoming generation—who later became known as the Romantics—turned against her. They were artists who also prized an emotional appreciation of nature and presented an evocative picture of the past. A number of the most influential Romantics took inspiration from Radcliffe's work, as Radcliffe's modern biographer Rictor Norton has painstakingly documented. "Many 'serious' male poets borrowed the poetic phrases and techniques of her novels," Norton stated, "while doing their best to cover the traces of her influence."

Percy Shelley loved her novels unabashedly. Lord Byron was so taken with Radcliffe's description of Venice that he plagiarized it in his 1812–18 poem *Childe Harold:* in one example, her Venetian buildings, "called up from the ocean by the wand of an enchanter" become Bryon's buildings that "rise / as from the stroke of the enchanter's wand." Samuel Taylor Coleridge's *Christabel,* John Keats's "Ode to a Nightingale," and many of the most respected poems of the Romantics were clearly informed by their authors' readings of Radcliffe. William Wordsworth was especially influenced by her novel *The Romance of the Forest*—but wrote acerbically about gothics as a genre.

In Wordsworth's famous preface to the 1800 edition of *Lyrical Ballads,* often considered the manifesto of Romanticism, he raged about readers' "degrading thirst" for "frantic novels." (Remember that word, "degrading"; we'll see it again.) In 1815, while critics like Dunlop continued to praise her, Wordsworth was dismissing writers of the "Radcliffe school" as universally suffering from a "want of taste." This was a subtle but powerful shift: instead of Radcliffe being the *best* of a genre, she became *representative* of the entire genre. Wordsworth was pulling a sleight of hand on the "mighty magician of *Udolpho,*" and it would have profound implications. For now, it was a private argument; Wordsworth wrote it in a letter to another writer, Robert Pearse Gillies. But it would not remain so.

The campaign from respected literary men continued after Radcliffe's death in 1823. One turning point came in Walter Scott's 1824 biography of Radcliffe, perhaps the most influential of the nineteenth century, which seesawed between brusque criticisms and backhanded compliments. The riveting reading experience of *Udolpho,* for instance, Scott compared to "the use of opiates": "baneful, when habitually and constantly resorted to, but of most blessed power in those moments of pain and of languor, when the whole head is sore, and the whole heart sick." As for the reason Radcliffe stopped publishing, he mused that "she may have been disgusted at seeing the mode of composition, which she had brought into fashion, prophaned by a host of servile imitators, who could only copy and render more prominent her defects, without aspiring to her merits." (For months I've had a tab open on my computer with a bookseller's listing for a copy of this, but it's just a bit more than I want to spend. Write to me and tell me to buy it.)

The seesaw of compliments and attacks, modeled among the Romantics and Scott, continued in the generations after her death. As I hunted for first editions that talked about Radcliffe and her work, I came across an essay from 1839 by George Moir, a professor at the University of Edinburgh who wrote the description of "modern romance" for the *Encyclopaedia Britannica*. He argued that the gothic romance "was probably carried to its perfection by Mrs. Radcliffe," and in that genre she "has never been excelled"—yet he attacked her preference for the "explained supernatural" and argued that, to be "fully enjoyed, the Romances of Mrs. Radcliffe must be perused in youth." With such commentary, Radcliffe was simultaneously acknowledged for her genius and categorically dismissed from the canon that included only "serious" literary work.

Meanwhile, Wordsworth's collapse of distinction between Radcliffe and her imitators in the "Radcliffe school" became public. In 1851, his private correspondent Robert Pearse Gillies published *Memoirs of a Literary Veteran*, printing a number of Wordsworth's letters—including the one that spoke so disdainfully of the "Radcliffe school." This, too, was a major turning point. Once I began collecting books about Radcliffe's legacy, I discovered that Wordsworth's framing—the "Radcliffe school"—became something of a virus. Another book I acquired, a literary history in a green cloth binding from 1871 called *The Novels and Novelists of the 18th Century*, took the phrase to its logical conclusion in its discussion of Radcliffe: "the gloomy horrors of the Radcliffe school"—Radcliffe here placed at the head of her imitators—could be safely passed over.

But Radcliffe was too good to disappear from critical discussions without argument, and other critics defended her. In her 1882 *Literary History of England*, the popular Scottish novelist Margaret Oliphant says that Radcliffe is a "name everybody knows, but whose works [. . .] are less known now than their merit deserves." In 1894, Professor William Minto at the University of Aberdeen declared attacks on her "explained supernatural" a mere "affectation" and blamed Scott for starting "the fashion of objecting to Radcliffe's explanations." In 1898, Edmund Gosse admitted that gothic authors like Radcliffe were both "widely appreciated" and influential on the poets of the Romantic era—but summarized them as "crude romance-writers" and quickly moved on.

The main fields of battle occurred in these two areas: her use of the "explained supernatural" and her status as the icon of a derided genre. This put her reputation in a similar détente as Austen's had been before the publication of Austen-Leigh's *Memoir* in 1869: champions on both sides, and a reputation teetering between ascension and oblivion. But Radcliffe did not get a *Memoir.* The paucity of biographical information left behind meant that critics like poet Christina Rossetti, who hoped to raise her reputation again, did not have enough material to work with.

As I added each new first edition to my shelf, this one in blue cloth, that one in green cloth, I traced the fight between Radcliffe's admirers and her detractors through the remainder of the nineteenth century. Jumping from argument to argument, across decades and centuries, my shelf proved that there was no objective reading of Radcliffe. She had become a polarizing figure: either a genius of her genre, or the leader of an inferior kind of novel. It wasn't simply that her style didn't appeal to modern readers. Critics shaped that change in taste. In each subsequent generation, her position in the canon was questioned anew, and each detractor seemed to knock her further from the top of the list of England's finest writers. My shelf was becoming a centuries-long eulogy to Radcliffe's reputation.

By the early twentieth century, Radcliffe's work was no longer considered a requirement in canonical surveys. For example, she was left out of the English Men of Letters series (begun in 1878) that had kept in Burney and eventually added Austen—perhaps, again, due to lack of sufficient biographical information. In the United States, Henry Cabot Lodge's Best of the World's Classics series (1909) included a volume of British and Irish authors from 1740 to 1881 that contained excerpts from Scott, Coleridge, Lamb, Hazlitt, Byron, Percy Shelley, and De Quincey—all of whom were deeply influenced by their reading of Radcliffe—but nothing by Radcliffe herself. (Jane Austen wasn't there, either, though George Eliot was one of the two women who were. The other was Charlotte Brontë, whose sole contribution was an essay about the superiority of Thackeray.) Lodge was an American politician with a PhD in history from Harvard. He wasn't an English professor or a literary scholar. But as the editor of a reprint series meant to make works from previous generations accessible to a new generation, he claimed authority to create a canonical reading list in the US. This is how canons are sculpted in each generation—and how some authors are removed from it. The individual choices of tastemakers matter.

By the twentieth century, the narrative that gothics were inferior had won. Gothics were still studied—but typically distinct from "higher" literature. A separate tradition of gothic studies grew, beginning in the 1920s and '30s with pioneers like Edith Birkhead's *The Tale of Terror* (1921), Eino Railo's *The Haunted Castle* (1927), and Montague Summers's *The Gothic Quest* (1938). (I've been trying to add these to my shelf as well, but it's been slow work: they're tricky to find in the original dust jackets.) Yet even some of the literary critics interested in gothics accepted their inferiority as a whole: J. M. S. Tompkins, who published an entire book in 1932 on the popular novels during the late eighteenth century—when gothics reigned— described her subject as "tenth-rate fiction." Tompkins, like many before her, had nothing but praise for Radcliffe herself: "Others had paddled toyboats in the edge of the perilous seas; her great ship takes the tide with its flags floating and its mistress aboard." Yet Tompkins began her work with "two chief facts" about the novel of the late eighteenth century: "its popularity as a form of entertainment and its inferiority as a form of art."

Meanwhile, influential scholars taking a broader approach like Ian Watt in *The Rise of the Novel* (1957) simply repeated versions of Wordsworth's old insult. Wordsworth had described the "degrading thirst" for these novels; Watt dismissed the astounding explosion of novels by women of Radcliffe's era with the phrase "literary degradation." For Watt, who preferred realism, this was the justification to skip nearly half a century of writing as if it never happened.

Radcliffe could not escape her own role in the rise of the gothic. Interestingly, Austen worked in a similarly belittled genre—courtship novels, or what we now call romance, meaning a story about love with a happy ending. But even scholars who are happy to demean the entire genre of romance still allow Austen into the ranks of "higher" literature. She is the best. Radcliffe was the best of her genre, too. It was Wordsworth's sleight of hand that changed her from "best" to "representative," thus dismissing her.

Ironically, Austen's own parody of Radcliffe's work stuck around much longer than Radcliffe's did. Because Austen remained canonical, I had known about *Udolpho* from reading its comic imitation, *Northanger Abbey*. But that may have been part of my problem. Judging Radcliffe by those she influenced is like judging *The Godfather* only from the mob movies that have followed, without ever seeing the source material. So now I wondered: Despite her praise of *Udolpho*, did Austen herself have a hand in guiding the changing opinions of Radcliffe? Now that I had read *Udolpho*, it was time to return to *Northanger Abbey*.

In my earlier readings of *Northanger Abbey*, I understood the book simply as a satire of gothics like Radcliffe's. I recognized that the absurd mistakes Catherine Morland made during the plot occurred when she was inspired by scenes from these gothics. But this time, I read *Northanger Abbey* differently. I was arrested by lines like the hero Henry Tilney's familiar remark on *Udolpho*: "when I had once begun it, I could not lay down again. I remember finishing it in two days—my hair standing on end the whole time." I had done the same! I was positively gleeful to read her characters' lavish praise of *Udolpho*, as if I had just made new friends over a shared favorite book.

The balance of satire and sincerity in this text is often lost when we talk about *Northanger Abbey*. I'm not the only one who accepted *Northanger Abbey* simply as a satire of gothics. A quick internet search for the novel brings up countless articles describing it as such from sources like the *Encyclopaedia Britannica* and PBS. But Austen had a more complex view.

Like Burney and Radcliffe, Austen grew up hearing that novels create an "imbecility of the mind"—and that this was especially a problem for "weak and youthful minds," i.e., unmarried women. This misconception is what *Northanger Abbey* is really satirizing: the belief that novels have such unmitigated power over the minds of unmarried women. In a startling break in form within *Northanger Abbey*, Austen switches to the first person to explain exactly what she thinks of people who denigrate novels:

> **I cannot approve of it. Let us leave it to the reviewers to abuse such effusions of fancy at their leisure, and over every new novel to talk in threadbare strains of the trash with which the press now groans. [. . .] Although our productions have afforded more extensive and unaffected pleasure than those of any other literary corporation in the world, no species of composition has been so much decried. From pride, ignorance, or fashion, our foes are almost as many as our readers.**

To summarize *Northanger Abbey* only as a satire requires the reader to ignore entire passages like this one. The way some scholars achieve that is to bring back that old argument about genre: novels vs. gothics. One modern biographer of Austen, John Halperin, goes as far as to argue that "*Northanger Abbey* may attack gothic fiction, but it also goes out of its way to defend the *genre* of the novel" [emphasis original]. He uses a line from Henry Tilney in support of his argument: "The person, be it gentleman or lady, who has not pleasure in a good novel, must be intolerably stupid." The problem is that, to make this distinction, Halperin has to selectively quote the text. He leaves out Tilney's very next lines—in which the hero talks rapturously about reading Radcliffe, *the queen of gothics*. Austen clearly included Radcliffe's gothics in her praise of novels; yet critics have tried to make it seem like she didn't.

Northanger Abbey does contain satire; Austen's love of parodying the world around her is evident in all her books. But it communicates so much more than that. The young heroine Catherine reads (and loves) *Udolpho*. She is only seventeen and new to society, much like Emily in *Udolpho*. She is thrilled to visit the hero's historic house, Northanger Abbey, because it's so much like the locations in the gothics she reads. Then she gets a little too caught up in the similarities of setting and jumps to a very wrong conclusion about her hosts—specifically, the hero's father, General Tilney.

The chambers where the general's late wife slept, and eventually died, have been shut up; Catherine imagines that his wife was shut *in* those chambers before her death, just like Emily's aunt in *Udolpho*. This is one of the parts critics focus on when they dismiss *Udolpho*. But after she realizes her mistake, Catherine is horribly embarrassed. She changes her behavior toward the general immediately. Yet, while all this is happening, the general is jumping to his own very wrong conclusion about Catherine. He isn't naive enough to believe the storylines of gothics—but he does take the known oaf John Thorpe at his word when Thorpe gossips about Catherine, at first bragging about her (nonexistent) fortune, then claiming she is a fortune hunter after she rejects him.

In the end, it's not Catherine's credulity that wreaks havoc upon her life. It is the general's. The general, however, can't place the blame for his error on novels. Catherine is inexperienced in the world; the general is not. There is no accounting for the general's behavior except that he is an ass. Catherine, on the other hand, is simply a teenager. A novel may have influenced her perception, but observation corrects it. An error of naivete is contrasted here with an error of experienced judgment. Within this very plot twist, Austen challenges the common criticism of novels at that time and lays the foundation for a major message of *Northanger Abbey*: We all make mistakes, but how do we react when we've made them?

Northanger Abbey is a classic in part because its themes remain relevant to readers—as do many themes in *Udolpho*. Since I had finally read the book, I had learned this firsthand. One theme that rings out in Radcliffe's novel is the question of women's autonomy. The entire plot of *Udolpho* could be said to be about the loss of, and the fight to regain, a woman's control over her own life. Emily is rarely allowed to make her own choices, even before they reach Castle Udolpho. In Venice, a wealthy and titled man offers for her hand. Emily refuses. Her uncle soon begins to threaten her. She must marry, or else. When Emily turns to her aunt for help, Madame Montoni replies: "I [. . .] think Signor Montoni right in enforcing, by any means, your consent."

This tension animates the book's plot. When Emily's persistent suitor follows her to Castle Udolpho, he says: "Yes, I will leave the castle; but it shall not be alone. I have trifled too long. Since my prayers and my sufferings cannot prevail, force shall." Any woman who has experienced the advances of a man who considers "no" a challenge might have predicted this turn of events. What's scary about a man taking "no" badly is not having to reject him; it's how often rejection leads to escalation. Radcliffe understood this, and in *Udolpho*, she used the full power of the gothic to explore what it felt like to live through it.

When Emily reaches Castle Udolpho, she literally becomes her uncle's prisoner. As Emily's captivity lengthens, the reader experiences how this fear affects her. "Long suffering had made her spirits peculiarly sensible to terror, and liable to be affected by the illusions of superstition." Emily starts questioning what she thinks, what she feels, even what she sees. Many of us know too well today that this self-doubt is the result of others consistently dismissing our perceptions. We have given it a name: gaslighting. The further I read, the more I found myself relating to a woman who was losing her mind.

Beyond Emily's struggles, there are a number of subplots and anecdotes in *Udolpho* involving otherwise privileged women who fight for their autonomy. Ghosts, dark halls, banditti, sword fights (multiple!), kidnappings (also multiple!), and poisoning are all thrilling—but it is these constant battles for autonomy that ultimately propel the story forward.

Once I realized that *Udolpho*'s central theme is that of a woman who lacks control over her own life, it also explained the one characteristic that lived up to its bad—sorry, melodramatic—reputation. Emily has a tendency to faint. A lot. I began marking every time Emily lost her senses, and it soon started to feel like a drinking game. I rolled my eyes at the idea that an otherwise abled woman might be so overcome, so frequently. (Austen did too. In her teenage satire *Love and Freindship* [*sic*], she makes fun of how easily women faint in novels. One of her characters writes in a letter, "It was too pathetic for the feelings of Sophia and myself—We fainted alternately on a sofa.")

At this point, I respected Radcliffe as an artist, so I wouldn't dismiss an aspect of her storytelling without investigating it. I knew Emily was at the mercy of many of the book's other characters, but why couldn't she ever seem to catch her breath? A little investigation brought me to the first obvious answer: corsets. In the eighteenth century, these were a common accessory for women. In practice, corsets were rarely tightened to the extreme extent we see in period films today, with actors clinging to tables and gasping as someone yanks on the ties behind. But in her book *The Corset: A Cultural History*, Valerie Steele explained that "even a moderately laced corset" creates difficulty breathing: "Corseted women must rely on the accessory respiratory muscles, resulting in shallow upper-diaphragmatic (or costal) breathing." Because I kept thinking about Jane Austen when reading *Udolpho*—Austen, who published in the Regency era of flowing Empire-waist gowns and looser supportive garments—the restrictions of corsets hadn't even occurred to me. Radcliffe was writing what she knew.

More important, the fainting stereotype also developed in part from the belief, very much in fashion in eighteenth-century England, that women have categorically weaker constitutions than men. And this "weaker" constitution of Radcliffe's time was more complex than physics alone. It was popularly believed that women had more "delicate taste" than men too. This sensitivity to emotion was known as "sensibility." Both men and women of the era viewed sensibility as a special virtue in women, especially useful in attracting a partner. (This is part of what Austen dissects in the "sensibility" of *Sense and Sensibility*.) Radcliffe's heroine acts like the ideal woman of an eighteenth-century conduct book when she is moved by a beautiful landscape or transported by a song.

But there is another major reason, beyond corsets and sensibility, why fainting proliferated in novels of this period. Modern scholarship has demonstrated that women tend to faint in novels when what they're really trying to do is to say no. They swoon when a man attempts to assault them, as in Samuel Richardson's *Pamela*. They swoon when they realize they're trapped by someone who wants to harm them, as in Radcliffe's *Udolpho*. In each of these cases, a modern woman is more likely to flip the bird than swoon (which is not necessarily, ah, safer). But propriety meant a respectable Englishwoman in the 1700s couldn't do that, or act out in another way, without social consequences. Pamela cannot forcibly shove her predator away. Instead, she plays dead like an opossum. Emily does grandly talk back to her uncle on a few occasions, but at other times, as after she has literally been running for her life, she faints. As soon as she gets a moment to rest, her body shuts down. It can't process her terror. In *Udolpho*, Emily's tendency to faint represents fear that she is unable to express. The manners of that era—"propriety"—forbid her. Today, we talk about "fight, flight, or freeze." When eighteenth-century heroines can't fight or flee, they faint.

While I was tracing the various sallies in the critical battle over Radcliffe's reputation, I noticed the most derisive twentieth-century comments often focused on Emily's excessive sensibility. Since it strikes such dissonance with our tastes today, this aspect of Radcliffe's writing can't be ignored. But it can, and should, be contextualized. The passages about fainting bothered me significantly less after I started reading them as symbols of Emily's lack of agency. When there's nothing else in her power she can do, her body protects her mind by fainting. Yet some modern critics have approached this trait without any curiosity as to its function; it's easier to believe that eighteenth-century readers had bad taste. For instance, a review in *Time* magazine for a 1966 reissue of *Udolpho* begins by acknowledging Radcliffe's strengths and the importance of her influence on later writers, then strikes: "Yet if in 1794 her virginal vaporings came on as symptoms of high sensibility, in 1966 they come off as conventions of high comedy. All unintentionally, *Udolpho* is one of the funniest books ever written, a travesty of the romantic ethos."

The publisher of the 1966 reprint that occasioned this review must have hoped to reignite interest in *Udolpho*. The publication was, after all, part of a groundbreaking Oxford English Novels series of reprints making important early novels available for a new generation. It's difficult for a book to remain a "classic" if no one can read it. Yet such a vicious review in a famous magazine would have been a serious blow to that momentum. Scholars in academic circles could, and would, continue to write articles and dissertations exploring the complexities of Radcliffe's rich texts, but the influence of one review in a popular magazine can do lasting damage.

Watch it: in the 1987 biography of Jane Austen often called "definitive," Park Honan appears to be referencing this review in his single line dismissing *Udolpho*. Emily, he says, "weeps on every other page with unintendedly comic pathos." That's not a description by someone who has read this book. (Emily cries a lot, but not *that* much.) It's closer to a paraphrase of someone else's opinion—such as the 1966 *Time* reviewer's. It was the same effect I had recognized in Wordsworth's "Radcliffe school": a turn of phrase by a prominent commentator becomes an accepted fact. Critics echo critics, passing opinions down as received wisdom, without going back to the source and judging for themselves.

The canon is supposed to be about relevance: good books become "classics" because they still have something to offer to modern readers. But how can a critic know if that's the case when he hasn't read the book? In *Udolpho*, I felt it, that closeness when I connect with an author through their books. What Radcliffe had to say mattered to me. For women in the eighteenth century and in the twenty-first, the fight for autonomy is one of the most important themes we explore. After reading Burney and Radcliffe, I was beginning to understand how many plots about marriage and wealth came back to that single idea. I started to wonder: How many other novels by women had I skipped over that beat with this subtly subversive heart?

There was more to discover, and to read. But for now, I focused on Radcliffe. I understood why I had previously assumed Radcliffe would be "overheated, overdone, old-fashionedly lurid"; that she would be "melodramatic" rather than "sublime"; that she would be bad. Over the centuries, we made her "representative" rather than "superior." We stopped reading Radcliffe and only read about her. Like so many others, I had simply taken Wordsworth and his followers at their word. They were wrong. *Udolpho* is a fantastic book.

That had been my mistake. My expectation of reading *Udolpho*, shaped by those literary authorities, was so different than my experience. I had imagined it to be a chore; instead it was a pleasure. Whenever I put the book down, I was waking from a dream, with an accompanying rush of the senses: suddenly noticing the pillow crumpled under me on the couch, hearing again the cars passing outside, adjusting to the unnatural light of my cell phone. It is the perfect volume to curl up with, cradling a cup of tea, while the rain sweeps down the windowpanes outside. In fact, that's the atmosphere I associated with reading Jane Austen. And now it was what I imagined it felt like when Austen herself read *Udolpho*.

It has never been so fun to be wrong. Many modern scholars feel the same, and they have come back to the high opinion that Radcliffe's contemporaries had of her. What began academically in the 1920s as a small but important strain of attention to the gothic—a back alley of literary scholarship—continued to gain momentum over the course of the twentieth century. Today such scholars try to be professional about Radcliffe's removal from the canon. But they're incensed, and they are fighting back. The first and last chapters of Rictor Norton's 1999 biography of Radcliffe are filled with punch after punch against the literary establishment that pushed her down to bear themselves up. He's not afraid to stake his ground: "Radcliffe has been ejected from her rightful position among the Romantic poets, but that she no longer figures largely in the history of the English novel is less forgivable."

As my conviction in Radcliffe's importance grew, I began to think of my collection as a small way that I could contribute to the restoration of her reputation. That shelf was not a eulogy, but an argument. I wanted to fight back against Wordsworth and Scott too. I was a Sherlockian at heart, an investigator, and I valued evidence. Critics used their words; I used my shelves.

I combed through printed catalogs, seemingly endless online listings, book fair showcases under squint-inducing spotlights, and shops' shelves for more rare books about Radcliffe. As I did so, I kept coming across surprises. At one point, I tracked down the full reference from Wordsworth about the "Radcliffe school" suffering from "want of taste." When I had first come across this line, it had been quoted in various pieces of modern scholarship as an excerpt from a much longer letter. Then I finally got a copy of Gillies's *Memoirs* into my hands. I leafed through to find the right letter and learned with surprise that Wordsworth's derogatory remarks about the

"Radcliffe school" were actually directed at a novel of Walter Scott's! He had just finished Scott's second novel, *Guy Mannering* (1815), and felt that it showed a "want of taste, which is universal among modern novels of the Radcliffe school."

Now that I could read the letter in full, not just read *about* the letter, I better understood Scott's ambivalence toward Radcliffe. She was an enormous influence on him, but her increasingly tarnished reputation required that he publicly distance himself from her if he didn't want to get dragged down alongside her. So, yes, while Scott absolutely did contribute to the demise of one of his own literary models, the wider context of his remarks revealed much more. Scott saw what was happening to Radcliffe's legacy and was taking steps to defend himself from similar attacks. I would have missed this if I hadn't gone back to the source in its original context.

I've become a tireless advocate for Radcliffe. There is a strong case to be made that Radcliffe is the most influential woman novelist in the English language—even more than Austen. I love books like *Frankenstein* and *Dracula*; in *Udolpho*, I kept coming across scenes that felt familiar. In reading Radcliffe, I began to understand why there were so many long passages of atmospheric landscapes in *Frankenstein*. Emily's nervousness when approaching her uncle's castle was repeated in *Dracula*, when the fellow passengers in the hero's carriage become more agitated as they approach Dracula's castle: "[. . .] on each side the passengers, craning over the edge of the coach, peered eagerly into the darkness. It was evident that something very exciting was either happening or expected, but though I asked each passenger, no one would give me the slightest explanation."

Of *course* one of the greatest of all gothics would contain the seeds that grew into *Frankenstein* and *Dracula*. I understood that theoretically; even "geniuses" look to others as models as part of their artistic process. But seeing how the tendrils took root has been especially gratifying. Even if you don't care for Radcliffe, you've likely enjoyed a novel by one of her literary descendants. After reading *Udolpho*, I've developed a better appreciation for that central element of the gothic, the allure of landscape as character.

Radcliffe showed me how a writer can shape the reader's mood by including atmospheric descriptions of landscapes and architecture that often expose the feelings of the characters. *Wuthering Heights* feels reborn. H. P. Lovecraft has an entirely new dimension. Most surprising of all, I think of Tolkien's Lord of the Rings trilogy in a different way. Middle Earth is famous as a world of total immersion. The reader takes each step of Frodo's sublime and picturesque journey along with him. Tolkien's tendency to linger in the landscape was baffling to me when I first read it. Now I want to return to Middle Earth with Radcliffean eyes. I bet that I'll love those scenes.

In the meantime, if you think I haven't already hunted down a copy of the 1932 book that called novels of Radcliffe's era "tenth-rate fiction," you don't know me at all. The copy I acquired was once owned by the former director of collection development at the British Library; in other words, the person who decided which books were important enough to be included in a venerable institution like the British Library had acquired a study calling these novels subpar. Each book I added to my shelf provided new insight to Radcliffe's afterlife.

It has also led to more discoveries. I plan to continue my search for all those French books falsely attributed to Radcliffe, and one more: I learned the inimitable fact that there is a French novel, from 1875, featuring Radcliffe as the leader of a group of vampire hunters. It's called *La Ville-Vampire*. I still haven't found a copy, but I've begged one of my friends who lives on a boat on the Thames and specializes in such niche areas as nineteenth-century vampire literature that he must tell me if he sees one. Although if he does, I wouldn't blame him if he decided to keep it for himself.

A work can be imperfect, so long as it moves you. I devoured *Udolpho*, despite its flaws, because Radcliffe is so deft at building tension and atmosphere. I was taken in by the spell that she patiently cast around me. In her time, critics and casual readers alike called Radcliffe a "genius," "unrivalled," and "the great enchantress"—because her books function like sorcery upon their readers. Contemporaries associated her with Homer, Virgil, Milton, and Shakespeare. And Radcliffe would go on to influence many writers, beyond Austen. There's Coleridge, Byron, and Keats; Mary Shelley, Emily Brontë, and Bram Stoker; Hawthorne, Melville, and Poe. *A Christmas Carol*, *The Hound of the Baskervilles*, and *Jekyll and Hyde*.

In the end, investigating the arc of her afterlife led to more than I had imagined. Not only did I come to understand the turning points that shaped her legacy, but I found a new favorite author. In my estimation, at least, she's back in the stars where she belongs.

Chapter Four

CHARLOTTE LENNOX
(C. 1729-1804)

Female Quixotte [*sic*] [...] now makes our evening amusement; to me a very high one, as I find the work quite equal to what I remembered it.

—Letter from Jane Austen to Cassandra Austen,
January 7–8, 1807

Charlotte Lennox was next on my list of women writers to investigate. By now the mechanics of how these writers had dropped from the canon were becoming clear, and here again I would find evidence as to why those mechanics were so effective. But I had also begun to fall in love with these women and their work. So when I turned to Lennox, I was ready to fall in love again. What I did not expect was that, of all the women to whom Austen had introduced me, I came to love Charlotte Lennox most of all.

"To say the truth, I am not without some little ambition," Charlotte Lennox once admitted in a letter to an eminent friend, the Earl of Orrery. Writing to another famous acquaintance, David Garrick, she ruefully conceded her "reputation for candor." Few letters by Lennox survive, but as I made my way through a modern scholarly collection of them, I felt I had met someone with traits I especially admired: she was witty and bold.

What I also admired was that, unlike many of her literary peers, Lennox actually had to work for a living. When you study the world of eighteenth-century women writers, you often focus on the economically secure. Austen herself is a case in point: thanks to the support of her male family members, she never needed the money she made from her writing. Further, "poverty" in her class would have meant not having enough money to hire a servant. By that definition, I was poor. So was Lennox. She did not come from a stable financial background and had no economic fallback. Nevertheless, she was always taking risks, catching the door with her foot, before she put her shoulder against it and burst it open.

Yet as her letters to friends suggested, not everyone appreciated her boldness and wit as I did. She had "ambition" rather than deference; "candor" rather than constraint. This was Georgian-era London, and a woman using these traits to pursue a career was bound to make enemies. Did these qualities ultimately help her—or hinder her?

Charlotte Lennox was born between 1729 and 1730 as Charlotte Ramsay, in Gibraltar. Her Irish mother moved there with her Scottish father, who was then serving in a British regiment. With a growing family and no inherited wealth to draw upon, Charlotte's father accepted a more lucrative position in the British colony of New York, and the family relocated. Charlotte's experiences growing up in the American colonies were to prove formative in her career. Both her first novel, *The Life of Harriot Stuart* (1751), and her penultimate novel, *Euphemia* (1790), take place partly in pre-Revolution New York. Before the likes of Washington Irving, James Fenimore Cooper, and Susanna Rowson (whose 1791 novel *Charlotte Temple* was the first American bestseller), Charlotte Lennox would become the most famous author who wrote stories about the British American colonies. But before that, she had to learn how to survive.

When Charlotte was thirteen, her parents decided to send her to England to live in the care of a wealthy aunt, an arrangement not unlike that in Austen's *Mansfield Park*. They placed Charlotte with a single female companion on a ship to England, where Charlotte had never been, to live with that aunt, whom she had never met. Upon arrival, Charlotte was greeted with the news that her aunt had died. Soon after, Charlotte's father in the colonies also died. This was much worse than an Austen novel.

The timing of these events changed the trajectory of her entire life. Charlotte needed to figure out how to live on her own. She had no money. But she had her wit.

Although young, Charlotte had already made a reputation for herself as a precocious poet, composing verses that were received with astonishment in literary circles. These verses came to the notice of Lady Isabella Finch, an unmarried woman of aristocratic birth who was first lady of the bedchamber to a princess. Lady Isabella took young Charlotte in. Known as the only woman at court with her own library, she fancied the idea of becoming a literary prodigy's patron. At fourteen, Charlotte learned that her skill with words would give her the best chance of survival. When she published her first book a few years later, *Poems on Several Occasions* (1747), she dedicated it to Lady Isabella Finch.

Charlotte spent her teen years dependent upon aristocratic patrons. They were generous, certainly, but her writings reveal how she chafed at the treatment she often received because of her lower class. The plot of *Harriot Stuart* (1751), Lennox's first novel and considered by many of her contemporaries to be her "own history," speaks to this complicated relationship. In it, the heroine Harriot also sails from New York to England with a single female companion, only to learn that the aunt with whom she was to stay is dying; as a result, she is taken in by "a lady of great distinction at court, remarkable for the brilliancy of her wit"—about whom one character notes, "I have heard of a number of people, who have had an entire dependance upon her." Harriot observes, "I did not, at that time, take any notice of the sarcastic turn of these words."

Harriot's time with the lady of letters turns disastrous, with the lady obstructing Harriot's advancement, while claiming she's looking after the young woman's interests. This unflattering portrait of a character clearly modeled on Lady Isabella infuriated some of her aristocratic friends, like Lady Mary Wortley Montagu, who called it a "monstrous abuse of one of the very few women I have real value for." It was quite a daring move by

Lennox to humiliate a known benefactor so publicly; it could easily make future potential benefactors wary of supporting her. But then again, she was always bold.

When she was around eighteen, Charlotte married Alexander Lennox in 1747, the year her first book of *Poems* was published. We don't know much about how they met, except that Charlotte was on the literary scene in London, and Alexander worked for the publisher William Strahan. I admit, a courtship amid printing presses and cases of type does sound rather romantic to me. Even more fascinating, the most successful poem from that first book was "The Art of Coquetry," which played on the negative stereotype of the coquette, or the "flirt." It's a delightfully subversive celebration of the power that a young woman with wit can wield. "Let a soft sigh steal out, as if by chance," Lennox advises, "Then cautious turn, and steal another glance. / Caught by these arts, with pride and hope elate / The destin'd victim rushes on his fate." Calculated to scandalize—the classicist Elizabeth Carter complained that it was "intolerably provoking to see people who really appear to have a genius, apply it to such idle unprofitable purposes"—the poem was reprinted continuously.

Many readers appreciated the poetic prowess mixed with a fresh, youthful iconoclasm. Lennox claimed the dubious title of "coquette," then proceeded to compose perfectly structured lines of verse in celebration of it: "Who o'er mankind a haughty rule maintains, / Whose wit can manage what her beauty gains." The whole piece feels like a dare: you can try to dismiss me as a "coquette," but you can't write better than I can.

After *Poems*, Lennox's fame began to spread. Her name appeared with regularity in the popular literary review the *Gentleman's Magazine*. One poem published there in honor of her work claimed "Not *Sappho* more the yielding soul could move." Over the next fifty years, Lennox would regularly be identified as a "Muse" or a "Sappho" of Britain. Good thing, because she needed her reputation to grow: her new husband also had no fortune but what "consisted wholly in hopes and expectations." In other words, they were broke.

Lennox set about building a career as a writer. In the mid-eighteenth century, more writers than ever were attempting to make a living by their pens. One of Lennox's earliest allies was Samuel Johnson, the literary critic and essayist who was then still working on the *Dictionary* that would be his crowning achievement. Johnson and Lennox had much in common: both had first come to London young, impoverished, and brandishing their genius like a weapon. As Johnson later said to a mutual friend, "I was miserably poor, and I thought to fight my way by my literature and my wit." He saw in Lennox a kindred spirit.

Like Johnson, Lennox relied on a combination of patronage from rich friends and admirers alongside income from writing. Before the maturation of the print marketplace, authors often found support via patronage, as Lennox had with Lady Isabella Finch. As London's print culture began to thrive in the eighteenth century, the idea of a professional author was only just beginning to become achievable—one where you might make a living by income from writing alone. Johnson and Lennox were working in a painful transition phase where it was technically possible to make a career this way, but only just. Both were constantly in financial straits.

On the eve of the publication of *Harriot Stuart* in 1751, Johnson threw a party in Lennox's honor, crowning her with laurels and requesting a "magnificent hot apple-pye" specially ornamented with bay leaves to represent her poetic prowess. The party, hosted at a place called "the Devil tavern," began at eight in the evening and lasted until eight in the morning. Though Lennox's husband and another woman were in attendance, the rest of the guest list consisted of literary men.

How different Lennox was from the rest of the women whose works I was reading thus far. Not one of them would have dared to pull an all-nighter with nearly twenty men in celebration of a book publication. Frances Burney would have shrunk from an event so unrespectable for a woman, while Ann Radcliffe likely would have done anything possible to avoid that level of attention. Austen also would probably have turned down any such invitation, as she once did an opportunity to meet novelist Madame Germaine de Staël, author of *Delphine* (1802) and *Corinne* (1807) and "the period's icon of empowered feminine genius." But Lennox needed work. The men she made professional connections with at events such as these were to prove invaluable to her career. She desperately needed to succeed. So she kept doing what she was good at: acting with boldness and wit.

These two traits came naturally to Lennox, and evidence of them can be found across her writing. In "The Art of Coquetry," she had teased readers with the adage that "What's won by beauty, must be kept by art." Advising young women to manipulate men's feelings by feminine wiles was quite an audacious move as a career opener. Then, in *Harriot Stuart*, a ship captain attempts to rape the heroine—so she draws *his own sword* and stabs him with it. Radcliffe's and Burney's heroines would never!

For Lennox, these two traits were inextricably connected; it was her skill in wit that helped her get away with such boldness. In fact, a character in *Harriot Stuart* suggests as much: "These ladies that are distinguished for their wit [. . .] may say and do any thing. Methinks there is something very new and agreeable in this gallant way of breaking through the little rules, that custom and decency have imposed on our sex."

Lennox's talent as a writer was often described by her contemporaries specifically in terms of wit. One 1762 poem argued that she was as good as (or even better than) any of the celebrated ancient poets: "If Wit into the scale is thrown, / [we] Can boast a LENOX of our own." The term "wit" in this period meant much the same as it does today—a clever facility with words—but with a slightly stronger emphasis on the artistic craft of language. I learned this because when I kept seeing Lennox referred to as a "wit," I decided I had better make sure I knew what exactly that meant in the mid-eighteenth century. So one day while at work in the shop, I swung down the enormous volume that made her friend famous: Samuel Johnson's own 1755 *Dictionary of the English Language*, volume II.

This book is a monument of the English language, one of the most important works ever printed in the field. After seven years of work, Johnson brought it to print in two volumes in folio format. Each are over sixteen inches high and ten inches wide, and more than five hundred pages long. It could certainly be the cause of an Edward Gorey–esque accidental death for any rare book dealer who has made the mistake of shelving it high above their heads. (When we had acquired it a few months earlier, I had initially shelved it this way. After a couple harrowing experiences, I decided to move the volumes to a waist-height shelf.)

The leather binding on this book was spectacular: full calf contemporary to the period of the book's publication. The calf was speckled, a subtle decorative technique of tiny black spots that add depth to the leather's tone. It also betrayed hints of its past lives, with a few dark scratches that were perhaps incurred from others who struggled to pull the enormous volume off the shelves over the centuries. The spines, however, told a different story. Only a few decades ago a celebrated bookbinder was commissioned to re-back the volumes "to style," replacing the worn-out spines with new ones to match the bookbinding fashion of the mid-eighteenth century. They were exceptional work, those new spines, decorated with elaborate ornaments stamped in gilt. The irony was, of course, that a dictionary is meant for hard use. This modern spine may have matched the style of some of the fancier eighteenth-century bindings, but it was vastly more spectacular than it should have been for what was technically a reference book. The simple calf boards spoke to its original purpose. The new spine, on the other hand, reflected our modern opinion of this book: that Johnson's *Dictionary* is now a treasure, not to use, but to value.

I was going to use it anyway. I had managed the lift, but my work was far from complete. Even turning the leaves of these mighty volumes feels like an athletic event. To avoid the same kind of strain on the spine that led to its replacement, I had to hold the front board of the binding carefully with my left hand while I used my right hand to handle the leaves. I flipped through the volume, my left arm beginning to tremor from the weight. Finally, I found it: "Wit." Johnson listed eight meanings, but I was primarily interested in the first few. "1. The powers of the mind; the mental faculties; the intellects. This is the original signification. [. . .] 2. Imagination; quickness of fancy. [. . .] 3. Sentiments produced by quickness of fancy. [. . .] 4. A man of fancy. [. . .] 5. A man of genius." I had my definition: Lennox, a woman notwithstanding, was an author of imagination and genius.

The work for which Lennox is most celebrated, her second novel *The Female Quixote* (1752), is also her wittiest. This was the book mentioned by Austen in her letters that inspired me to add Lennox to my shelf. It is based on Cervantes's *Don Quixote*, but set in eighteenth-century England. Its heroine Arabella grows up isolated in the country, where she reads romances of early-modern Europe to learn about the world. These romances followed the same codes of chivalry that led Don Quixote to tilt at windmills; here, they lead Arabella to assume that every man who doesn't act like a knight must be planning to kidnap her. Lennox maintains the premise in countless clever ways, as in this editorial aside about a simple trip from Bath to London:

> **Nothing very remarkable happen'd during this Journey, so we shall not trouble our Readers with several small Mistakes of Arabella's, such as her supposing a neat Country Girl who was riding behind a Man, to be some Lady or Princess in Disguise, forc'd away by a Lover she hated, and intreating Mr. Glanville [the hero] to attempt her Rescue.**

The Female Quixote is a comic riff on chivalric romances, while also satirizing the critics who feared that young women would be endangered by novels because they couldn't tell the difference between stories and reality. Sounds a lot like . . . Oh, right: *Northanger Abbey*.

Even though they were published sixty-five years apart, the parallels between these two books are obvious. The naive young heroine of *The Female Quixote* (1752) loves novels, just like the naive young heroine of *Northanger Abbey* (1817). The main difference is that, instead of reading the older chivalric romances that Arabella likes, Catherine prefers the gothic romances that were popular at the time of *Northanger Abbey*'s first composition and original sale (as *Susan*) in the 1790s and early 1800s. In other words, Austen took the central joke of *The Female Quixote*—a young woman learns how the real world differs from her novel-inspired fantasies—and updated it for her generation.

The similarity in plot wasn't a coincidence. We know that Austen read

The Female Quixote more than once, and that she loved it. In 1807, Austen wrote to Cassandra that she picked up Lennox's book to reread after trying a different book and disliking it: "we changed it for the 'Female Quixotte [*sic*],' which now makes our evening amusement; to me a very high one, as I find the work quite equal to what I remembered it."

Austen must have first read *The Female Quixote* when she was very young. There are scenes in her story *Love and Freindship* [*sic*] dated 1790, when she was only fifteen, that echo Lennox's book. At one point the two novel-reading girls convince their friend Janetta that her suitor is a poor match. Their reasons? He hasn't read the popular novel *The Sorrows of Young Werther* (1774), about a tragically lovelorn young man—and even more objection-ably, he does not physically resemble a hero type. Others "said he was Sen-sible, well-informed, and Agreable; we did not pretend to Judge of such trifles, but as we were convinced he had no soul, that he had never read the sorrows of Werter, and that his Hair bore not the least resemblance to au-burn, we were certain that Janetta could feel no affection for him" [*sic all*].

When Austen revisited Lennox's novel in 1807, seventeen years later, she was more than twice the age as when she first read it. She found it every bit as good. It was to Austen what Austen's novels are to many readers today: a book you know will live up to your warm memory of it. I could appreciate that, having just come off a reread myself of *Northanger Abbey*, which I did find every bit as good. But the book hit new notes after I read *Udolpho*. And of course it did. That's how rereads work.

On the one hand, we come back to certain books because we want to experience, again, the feelings they first sparked. But books inevitably change with us. We notice new aspects of old favorites because our lives are different. Books are not static things. I've said that one reason I love reading is that I can examine the emotions it stirs safely from a distance, at my own pace. When I'm rereading, I'm doing that, and more. I'm remembering the emotions of the last read. I am remembering my past self. Simultaneously, I'm noticing the emotions of this read. I am marking the outlines of my current self. In that way, reading is not a separate act from the rest of my life. It is central to it.

————————

The Female Quixote would become an early triumph for Lennox, so successful that people like Austen would be reading and rereading it over fifty years later. But the book almost didn't make it to print at all. In 1751, printer Andrew Millar had agreed to read Lennox's manuscript. He had initially been keen to consider it for publication. But then he handed it to a few trusted "outside" readers—we know of a Mr. Gray and a Mr. Seymour—and their opinions cooled Millar's interest considerably. Mr. Gray took issue with a scene about a young woman who has a child out of wedlock, which he insisted "will not be printed." Novels were fast becoming the moral battleground that Burney faced with trepidation; the idea that one of these books would depict a character who had broken the moral code for genteel women of the eighteenth century—sex before marriage—was not easy to accept. We don't know many more particulars of what Mr. Gray found to criticize, but it was apparently so much that, as Lennox recounted with pique, they would "make it necessary to write a new Book if I would please him."

Now Millar seemed to be hesitating about taking on the book. But Lennox was counting on him to publish it. To do so, he would pay for the "right to copy" (an early kind of copyright) up front, and Lennox needed the money to survive.

In response, she called upon her heavyweight literary friends, not only Johnson but Samuel Richardson too. Richardson was the most celebrated novelist of the era, thanks to books like *Pamela* and *Clarissa*. Johnson and Richardson had read *The Female Quixote* and thought it was brilliant, with the heroine Arabella captivating her audience; Richardson wrote to Lennox that "I am quite charm'd with the lovely Visionary's Absurdity." Johnson enlisted the influential Earl of Orrery, a well-known literary patron who had been a friend to both Swift and Pope, to read it as well. The three of them each praised it to Millar.

The Female Quixote was indeed published by Andrew Millar in 1752.

Yet this success story behind the publication of her best book demonstrates a fundamental fact of Lennox's career. It was constantly limited by male authority or given a chance to succeed by male mediation. I don't mean that as a pointed attack on men so much as an acknowledgment that the move from patronage to profession made this gendered power dynamic stronger. Patronage could come from wealthy women as well as men, as in Lady Isabella Finch's early support of Lennox. But a literary *profession* meant navigating a publishing trade run primarily by men.

Before Richardson became an influential champion of her novel, Lennox had to ask Samuel Johnson to introduce them. Johnson took Lennox to Richardson's house in order to do so. But when it came time to knock on the door, Lennox suddenly asked Johnson to leave: she was determined to do this herself. She needed the men in positions of authority to walk her to the door, but she chafed at the necessity and, when she reached the threshold, looked for ways to walk through it herself.

Lennox's wit and boldness, in writing and in life, was so refreshing to me. Austen had wit, too—but she was nowhere near as bold. This has been a persistent source of my dislike about how we talk about Austen's novels, that their unassailability is why they are classics. Her novels are indeed perfect, or nearly so. But it's because she refines; she doesn't reach. I know, I know: heresy. One of my favorite Victorian poets, Elizabeth Barrett Browning, had a similar reaction in 1855 to Austen and her characters, who "struck me as wanting souls [. . .] The novels are perfect as far as they go—that's certain. Only they don't go far, I think." I was drawn to Lennox because, even with her career on the line, she reached.

In the 1750s, Lennox needed that boldness to get her foot in the door. Once she was in, she proved her place through her wit. Her books, like *Harriot Stuart* and *The Female Quixote*, are simply *fun* to read. This was as true in her time—Henry Fielding called *The Female Quixote* a work of "true Humour"—as it is today. One of the strengths of *The Female Quixote* is that it never takes itself too seriously: one chapter begins with "some historical Anecdotes, the Truth of which may possibly be doubted, as they are not to be found in any of the Historians."

The heroine of *The Female Quixote* is a particularly delightful example of how Lennox combined boldness and wit. Arabella is far more than she seems. She may mistake the age of chivalry with modern society, but she is also the smartest person in the book. Other characters recognize this throughout, as when her uncle says with awe, "you speak like an Orator." Arabella often sees to the core of the issue at hand. In most of her conversations about novels, Arabella appears to be talking nonsense about brave heroes and virtuous heroines, but she actually uses them to explore ideas of morality and truth, responsibility and knowledge. Lennox made heavy philosophical topics interesting by weaving them into a satirical adventure novel.

The brilliant but sheltered Arabella begins to accept the realities of the world around her only when someone else is finally able to speak to her in terms she appreciates: in the language of romances. A learned lady—who has a similar taste in books and "no Superior in Wit, Elegance, and Ease"—makes Arabella's acquaintance and helps her begin to reconcile the inconsistencies between the world of the romances and modern society. But then something odd happens. The learned lady is called away in the middle of the book, never to return. Instead, the penultimate chapter of the second (and final) volume introduces a series of conversations with a "divine," that is, a pastor and doctor, which would have been read as an eighteenth-century shorthand for a wise man. He quickly finishes the work that the learned lady started.

Lennox had considered writing another volume to conclude the book. But in the end, she had to wrap up the story in two volumes, instead of three, in order to make the calendar for the current publishing season. This abrupt ending speaks to a tension in how novels are crafted—they are, after all, both works of art and commercial products. In London publishing of this era, most novels were published from the fall to the spring, with the summer serving as a break. Lennox worked to ensure *The Female Quixote* would be published in February of 1752, as her financial situation was too precarious to wait. In fact, she hoped that the book would be popular enough to merit a second edition in the next season so that she could get paid again as soon as possible. In this, Lennox was always at a disadvantage next to many of her peers.

The rushed wrap-up of *The Female Quixote* was a disappointment to me, and I can't help but want a different ending, one where the learned lady returns. Perhaps that's what Lennox had intended in the unrealized third volume. But instead of composing solely at her own discretion and on her own timeline, Lennox had to make artistic choices according to what she could afford.

Naturally, I had to track down a first edition. The first time I tried, lounging on my couch with computer on my lap, I let out a bark of dismay that startled my cat when I realized that, just a few months earlier, I had missed the first copy at auction in five years. I kept searching.

One of my first stops when researching books printed in London before 1801 is a monumental work of bibliography known as the English Short-Title Catalogue, commonly called ESTC, available online via the British Library. I went straight to its homepage. Thanks to the ESTC I had confirmed that *The Female Quixote* went into a second edition the same year as the first (1752), as Lennox had hoped. It continued to appear in new editions a number of times in the eighteenth century, including at least three translations abroad. It can sometimes be difficult to pin down just how successful a book was hundreds of years ago, but a book going into that many editions was evidence that it was widely purchased; booksellers don't print new editions of books they don't think will sell.

The Female Quixote was also well received by critics. In the spring of 1752, the novelist Henry Fielding published a lengthy review of it in his literary journal, putting it on par with Cervantes's work. In a "fair and balanced" approach, he listed four points where Cervantes was superior, observations on where they were equal, and five points where Lennox was superior. (Lennox wins! Take that, Cervantes.) Fielding especially found Arabella "endearing" as a character—and she absolutely is. "I do very earnestly recommend it," he concluded, "as a most extraordinary and most excellent Performance." For years Lennox would trade on this book's success, putting "by the author of *The Female Quixote*" on the title pages of future books instead of her own name. "The Art of Coquetry" had introduced Lennox's status as a wit; *The Female Quixote* cemented it.

Today, we celebrate Austen as a wit. The distinguished rare book institution in New York, the Morgan Library & Museum, held an exhibition titled "A Woman's Wit: Jane Austen's Life and Legacy" in 2009 to 2010. On the TED-Ed website—"TED's youth and education initiative"—a video by Iseult Gillespie on "The Wicked Wit of Jane Austen" has over 1.7 million views. But when Austen's contemporaries praised her, it wasn't for her wit. Rather, they tended to remark on how "naturally drawn" her characters were. In Walter Scott's review of *Emma* in 1815, which was named by twentieth-century scholar B. C. Southam as the "first major critical notice" of Austen, Scott emphasized her talent for realism, not her humor: her characters are "finished up to nature, and with a precision which delights the reader." What readers then thought most remarkable about Austen was how well she re-created the everyday, the recognizable, the ordinary lives of women.

Those who knew her best, Austen's own family, did praise her wit. But it was also minimized, as if to reassure others that even though she was smart, she was still ladylike. A woman could be witty—just not *too* witty. In her brother Henry's "Biographical Notice" about her, printed in late 1817, he does describe Austen's "keenest relish for wit"—right alongside her "perfect placidity of temper." Remember: to Henry, she was "sweet."

The idea of a demure Austen, as forwarded by her family, lasted through the Victorian era. Her nephew Austen-Leigh's *A Memoir of Jane Austen* characterized her as domestic, kind, unambitious: "'Aunt Jane' was the delight of all her nephews and nieces. We did not think of her as being clever [. . .] but we valued her as one always kind." The allure of this matronly vision proved great. To most people throughout the nineteenth century, Austen was charming and even had a "subtle humor," but she was not especially witty.

That changed in the twentieth century, when critics began recognizing the steady undertone of irony and sarcasm in Austen's novels. Some of them seemed shocked to discover it. One biographer commented about Austen's juvenilia that "If it is unusual to find an eleven- or twelve-year-old girl spending much of her time writing so determinedly, it is even more unusual to find her, at so tender an age, already a confirmed parodist and cynic." As the mother of a preteen girl at the time I read this, I found his surprise *hilarious*.

A number of Austen's heroines, perhaps especially Elizabeth Bennet in *Pride and Prejudice*, cast a sharp eye on their surroundings and never miss the opportunity for a dry line. Elizabeth once jokingly admits this to Mr. Darcy: "We are each of us [. . .] unwilling to speak, unless we expect to say something that will amaze the whole room, and be handed down to posterity with all the éclat of a proverb." Around the middle of the century, the scholar Margaret Kennedy put forth the argument that Austen was a "comic novelist"; following on her heels was Marvin Mudrick's *Jane Austen: Irony as Defense and Discovery* (1952), which became a turning point in Austen studies. Mudrick started by distancing Austen from "the tide of feminine sensibility in novels of the time." That's what opened up the possibility to consider Austen as a master of irony. In this book, Mudrick argued of *Emma* that it has "wit, irony, light laughter shining in a triumph of surface." Finally Austen could be witty.

It did not escape me that, in Mudrick's view, Austen could only have "wit" now that she wasn't writing "feminine" novels. Wit is a kind of humor, and there's a complicated relationship between women and humor. In the twenty-first century, we are still filming documentaries investigating (ironically) why "Women Aren't Funny." The truth that women are funny—self-evident to most women—has been questioned by men for centuries. In part, this is because comedy has a well-earned association with being transgressive. Over centuries, comedians have mastered the strategy of pushing boundaries to shock their audiences into laughter. The element of surprise has been identified as a tool of humor at least since Aristotle. Yet "pushing boundaries" will mean something different depending on who does it. In the culture of eighteenth-century Britain, women were limited by many more boundaries (legal, social, financial) than men—and they faced much harsher penalties for stepping out of line.

For a woman in Lennox's position, it took guts to be transgressive. *The Female Quixote* was nearly pulled from publication because of her audacious decision to include a woman with a child out of wedlock. But earlier in her career, during the formative months when she first achieved literary fame, Lennox learned that combining her boldness with wit could bring her success: that was why everyone loved "The Art of Coquetry" so much. Lennox's wit was indeed recognized by her contemporaries. But tied with her boldness, it also made her enemies. Years after Elizabeth Carter first wrote to a friend to complain about "The Art of Coquetry," she was still making derogatory references to "Mrs Lenox's [*sic*] sort of coquetry" in her letters. For every two supporters Lennox cultivated, she managed to attract at least one critic. Over her career, that math meant that she gained quite a reputation: for her wit (with supporters like Lady Isabella, Samuel Johnson, Samuel Richardson, the Earl of Orrery, and Henry Fielding)—and for her boldness (with critics like Mr. Gray, Mr. Seymour, and Elizabeth Carter).

While I can value Lennox's boldness because it's a trait I admire, I have nevertheless struggled to celebrate it in myself. One of my mother's favorite stories about me that has, over time, become something like family lore, takes place when I was in preschool. She attended a parent-teacher conference in which the teacher remarked, with a tactful pause, that I was a "strong leader." My mother responded, "Oh, you mean she's bossy?" The teacher agreed. They laughed together. Even in my own lifetime, this trait in a girl carried a whiff of negativity. Reading about similar instances in the life of another woman, hundreds of years before me, gave me a little bit of comfort—and confidence. Because Lennox found the courage to stay true to herself despite her critics.

Not all of Lennox's own friends appreciated her boldness. One advised her to compose "graceful nothing[s]" to make a living. She didn't listen. Instead, she formed an ambitious plan for a work on the ultimate subject of the era: Shakespeare. Her next book after *The Female Quixote* was *Shakespear Illustrated* (1753). (This variant of Shakespeare's name was common in this era, incidentally; it's not that Lennox was a bad speller.) It wasn't a novel, but a work of criticism—and it was an iconoclastic tour de force.

The cult of the Bard had reached unprecedented heights in the eighteenth-century thanks in part to the influence of Shakespeare popularizers like Alexander Pope, the famous Augustan poet who edited a collection of Shakespeare's plays (1723–25) on the heels of his celebrated translations of Homer's epics *Iliad* and *Odyssey* (1715–20); and like David Garrick, who achieved fame as an actor in the 1740s for his Shakespearean roles, then led further stage revivals of Shakespeare's plays at Drury Lane Theatre when he took over its management in 1747. Remember, this was the era that saw Shakespeare's transformation into England's "national poet." Lennox, being Lennox, threw a grenade into the middle of the party.

Shakespear Illustrated was the first-ever book-length investigation of Shakespeare's sources, the earlier works that provided inspiration for many of his play's plots. According to the scholar Norma Clarke, it was also "probably the first study by a feminist critic of an already canonical author," and Lennox certainly hoped it would establish her as an author-itative voice in English criticism. Her friend Johnson made his living, after all, more on his criticism than the other genres he attempted. In this book, Lennox retrieved and collected, for the first time, the original sources for many of Shakespeare's plays from the French, Italian, and German. She published them in translation alongside commentary that compared and contrasted how Shakespeare handled the material next to his predecessors.

It was a historic production, and provocative too—in Lennox's anal-ysis, Shakespeare was far from perfect. In fact, she argued that in many cases his sources were superior. *Much Ado About Nothing*, for instance, uses a story from Ariosto's great Renaissance epic *Orlando Furioso* (1516–32) that is "mangled and defaced" by Shakespeare, "full of Inconsistencies, Contra-dictions, and Blunders." Lennox adds an observation that would destroy any lesser writer than Shakespeare: he "borrowed just enough to shew his Poverty of Invention, and added enough to prove his want of Judgment."

Those were fighting words. Samuel Johnson wrote Lennox with glee just before the book's publication that Shakespeare would be "demolished" by the work. Then he gave Lennox a compliment that I would be delighted to receive as a writer: "you are a bird of Prey," he gushed. For her next work, he proposed that "I will fly you at Milton." But that didn't happen. *Shakespear Illustrated*, which one of the most respected literary critics of the day assumed would be a triumph, became one of Lennox's largest professional missteps.

The problem was simple. She had dared to treat Shakespeare as an author with flaws, not as England's inimitable genius. She had been bold; she had transgressed a boundary. Her friend Orrery anticipated the difficulty when he himself considered writing a book on Shakespeare. He—an Earl—was too fearful of the response from the Bard's champions, "who seemed to think Shakespear was the Sanctum Sanctorum where they only were sufficiently holy to enter." But Lennox had pushed on, betting on her wit to buttress her boldness.

Unfortunately, she had underestimated critics' ability to read a book for its logical arguments. David Garrick was publicly outspoken against *Shakespear Illustrated* when it was issued. In a private letter to Lennox, he admitted his criticisms "were perhaps stronger Proofs of my Zeal for Shakespear, than of my Judgment." But he stuck by his claim: her method was "unjustifiable, when us'd against so great and so Excellent an Author." In this, modern critics would side with Lennox; we do not think greatness should mean immunity to criticism. But Lennox's contemporaries did not necessarily feel the same. Even though the book sold well—her publisher asked her to write an additional volume on the strength of sales—Lennox's gamble would haunt her for years to come. After the publication of *Shakespear Illustrated*, the literary establishment began to turn against Lennox—including friends who once praised her genius.

Among them was Johnson. Although Johnson had encouraged Lennox at first, the response of Garrick and others must have shaken him. When he proposed his own book on Shakespeare three years later, he left Lennox's work conspicuously off the list of those that had tackled the subject in recent memory. This was an especially damning choice, considering that Johnson had *written the dedication* for Lennox's *Shakespear Illustrated*. Now he wouldn't even name it, still the most comprehensive book on the subject of Shakespeare's sources published to date.

That wasn't all. Lennox's modern biographer Susan Carlile ferreted out a passage where Johnson used an interpretation borrowed from *Shake-*

spear Illustrated, then attributed it to "an anonymous critick." Initially, I read that phrase—"an anonymous critick"—as Carlile did: a betrayal. That was his friend!

But a new perspective occurred to me after I tracked down a copy of the first edition of *Shakespear Illustrated* from a dealer in England. It came cushioned in enough tape and bubble wrap to withstand a hurricane, as nearly all packages from UK-based rare book dealers do. It was a painstaking task to remove layer after layer, since opening a package with rare books takes delicate work, especially if you have to use something sharp, like a box cutter, to slice through its packaging.

As with every book from this era that I acquire, the first thing I did when I had finally unwrapped the volumes of *Shakespear Illustrated* was to collate them. Collating is the process of checking to ensure that all the leaves of the book are still present. It involves knowledge of how the book was constructed—an octavo, in gatherings of eight leaves; a quarto, in gatherings of four; and so on. What it really means is counting a staggering number of pages. (After having been interrupted and losing track of her count one too many times, one of my colleagues created a special sign she puts up when collating. It reads: "Don't bother me: I'm counting.")

As you count, you examine. Collating a book demands your full attention. It requires looking at every single leaf. Nothing should stay hidden during a proper collation. This is the moment a rare book dealer discovers handwritten notes in the margins and tea stains tracing the edges. Have you ever turned the page of an old book to discover a flower, hundreds of years old, pressed between pages? It's a bit of magic, a spell murmured across time. For me, it's also an antidote to the relentlessly disembodied experience of our digital lives. Collating a book gives me a moment to slow down, to become aware of my physical surroundings again, to appreciate their materiality. I am not only my avatar on the screen; I am a person, sitting at a desk, turning the pages of a book, one that another person wrote, and other people printed, and still other people read. I am real. They are real.

When I picked up *Shakespear Illustrated* to collate it, I realized that Charlotte Lennox's name was not on the title page. It was a piece of evidence that I hadn't considered before. Instead, the work was attributed to "the author of *The Female Quixote*." Lennox's name did not explicitly appear on the title page of *Shakespear Illustrated* until 1809, in an edition published five years after her death. Lennox had been following the convention of publishing a book "anonymously," wink wink, in which everyone knew who the author was, but the work itself didn't advertise it. (Burney kept it up for every one of her novels; by the time of her fourth and final novel, *The Wanderer* [1814], this led to the somewhat inelegant naming of every prior book on the title page: "by the author of *Evelina*; *Cecilia*; and *Camilla*.")

Before this, I had of course known that Lennox published *Shakespear Illustrated* anonymously. Because anonymous authorship was so common in this era, I had read about this fact multiple times. But that was all in theory. I hadn't considered the practical implications of it until I found myself staring at that title page. While Johnson could have (and should have) referenced Lennox's book itself in his list of recent works on Shakespeare, it's also likely that his use of the phrase "an anonymous critick" in the text was not a betrayal, but an act of loyalty. He was respecting Lennox's choice of formal anonymity in print. He was well placed to understand this, since he himself wrote many works anonymously or pseudonymously. (A favorite pastime of Johnsonians—yes, there are Johnsonians just as there are Janeites—has been trying to identify all the works that Johnson authored anonymously.)

Johnson also respected Lennox's "anonymity" in his most lasting work, the 1755 *Dictionary*. He quoted Lennox in the *Dictionary* over a dozen times, more than any other woman author. She was also the youngest author cited in the *Dictionary*. But none of those references ever include her name. For example, the word for "talent" included examples from Shakespeare, Dryden, and Swift, authors all explicitly named—alongside only "Female Quixote" for Lennox's contribution. For what it's worth, the inclusion was a spectacular one: "Persons who possess the true talent of raillery are like comets; they are seldom seen, and all at once admired and feared." (I had to look up "raillery" too: it means "Slight satire; satirical merriment.") Imagine the dinner party guest Lennox must have been, with a line like that.

Lennox's combination of boldness and wit was her strength as a writer. But when she transgressed too far, the literary establishment would knock her back, as they had with her *Shakespear Illustrated*. Yet to be conventional has rarely been the path to building an enduring legacy, as her contributions to Johnson's *Dictionary* demonstrate.

Lennox was conventional when she followed the tradition of anonymity, and that led her actual name to be unrecorded in one of the most influential works in English.

Not so for Johnson. While he wrote an enormous amount of material anonymously or pseudonymously, his most lasting work—the *Dictionary*—proclaimed his full name on the title page.

It's worth comparing Lennox's legacy with Johnson's, both then and now. Both of them enjoyed something of a turbulent reputation (Lennox as too bold, Johnson as too caustic) while also being hailed as geniuses. In his time, Johnson's writing was also celebrated for its wit. Johnson maintained his "classic" status and his books are still read today. *The Female Quixote* continued to be read and enjoyed decades after its publication: it was a classic. The novel was included in Anna Laetitia Barbauld's *The British Novelists* anthology (1810; reprinted 1820), meaning it was still making canonical lists after Lennox's death in 1804. By 1820 it had been printed at least nineteen times, including translations in German, Danish, French, Italian, and Spanish. But it did not survive the Victorian era, falling suddenly out of reprints and literary tastemakers' essays after 1820. Austen seems almost to have predicted this when she joked in an 1816 piece that the ideal heroine in a novel should have "not the least Wit."

In 1774, the year before Austen was born, a conduct book specifically aimed at young women argued that "Wit is the most dangerous talent you can possess. [. . .] Wit is perfectly consistent with softness and delicacy; yet they are seldom found united." The rejection or approval of women's wit balances on a knife edge, as Lennox and Austen both experienced. Even in print, they had to contend with it. A contemporary review of *Pride and Prejudice* demonstrates the delicate balance Austen had to create in her wittiest heroine, Elizabeth Bennet: she has a "well-timed sprightliness" and an "in-

dependence of character, which is kept within the proper line of decorum."
She is witty—but not too witty. Why is wit so fraught for women?

Eighteenth-century men were ready with an answer. As George Lyttelton, 1st Baron Lyttelton, advised "a lady" in 1731: "wit, like wine, intoxicates the brain, / Too strong for feeble women to sustain." It feels relevant
here to mention that not only was Lord Lyttelton a high-ranking politician
during the period of Lennox's greatest literary productivity, but he was also
an important patron of the arts. Henry Fielding's book *Tom Jones* was dedicated to him, and he arranged jobs and pensions for many of his literary
friends (Lennox was not among them).

Naturally not all men (#notallmen) held views like Lord Lyttelton's,
as is clear from the many male champions of Lennox's work. But lest the
Baron appear an isolated case, I present an excerpt from a 1786 treatise by
a French doctor—yes, doctor—and politician: "Because of their natural
weakness, greater brain activity in women would exhaust all other organs
and thus disrupt their proper functioning. Above all, however, it would be
the generative organs which would be the most fatigued and endangered
through the over exertion of the female brain." Modern translation: women
who use their heads may become infertile. I came across this quote in Susan
Carlile's excellent 2018 biography of Charlotte Lennox, which now boasts
a large scribble in the margin where my hand, poised with a pencil to take
notes, instead spasmed in rage.

In her lifetime, perhaps the biggest retort Lennox could offer to this
kind of criticism was her exemplary life as a wife and (later) a mother. There
were no implications, even from people who really disliked Lennox, of her
acting with impropriety in her personal life. This meant more than it might
seem, as wit, if acknowledged in a woman, was often tied to bawdiness.
In the generations before Lennox, a number of witty women writers were
attacked along these lines, including Aphra Behn, Delarivier Manley, and
Eliza Haywood. These three women were all famous in their own day, but
quickly condemned for their personal lives by their critics. In a 1709 collection, one author published an (admittedly catchy) line calling Aphra Behn
a prostitute ("punk"): "*Punk* and *Poetess* agree so pat. / You cannot well be

this and not be *that*." As the modern scholar Jane Spencer points out, such critics were "able to seize on the view that selling one's work was like selling oneself." Lord Lyttelton's verse on wit makes a similar connection between women writers and promiscuity: "Of those who claim it, more than half have none, / And half of those who have it, are undone." By "undone," he meant lacking in sexual "virtue," which for a woman meant either celibacy or monogamy within marriage.

Keeping her personal life as unremarkable as possible helped Lennox professionally. This should not have to be true, but it was. She needed any advantage she could get. Lennox was constantly coming up with new projects to make money. After the rough reception of *Shakespear Illustrated*, she turned to translation in hopes of securing a steadier income. *Shakespear Illustrated* had itself already required a significant amount of translation work to make sources from Italian, French, and more available to English speakers, so she understood the labor and expertise involved.

Her first major translation was the *Memoirs of Maximilian de Bethune, Duke of Sully* (1756), the autobiography of the minister and advisor to the French king, Henry IV. According to Susan Carlile, it was "an instant classic." The translation appeared during the time when the English literary scene was transitioning from the patronage system into the trade publishing business, and Lennox balanced both sides of that system in this publication. She dedicated the work to the Duke of Newcastle, who was then a powerful political figure. As a result, he offered to put in a request for the Crown to set up a pension for Lennox, a form of royal patronage via an annual payment granted to a writer of literary merit. (Johnson, who assisted his friend again for this book by writing the dedication, would himself receive a royal pension of £300 a year in 1762.) But Lennox turned it down, requesting a different favor: that the duke find a steady job for her husband. This he eventually achieved, setting up Alexander in a government position at the Customs House.

In the meantime, Lennox kept working. She had to. As a 1783 biography put it, "the duke's promise not immediately taking effect, she was obliged to engage in a new and laborious work." With *Sully* she entered her most productive period. From 1756 to 1769, she published six translations, three novels, started her own periodical, and more. She had another hit in the courtship novel *Henrietta* (1758), about an orphan girl who comes to London to make her way in the world. It saw a Dublin edition, three editions of a French translation, and a second London edition in just a few years. Her translation of a work on ancient Greek theater, *The Greek Theatre of Father Brumoy* (1759), would also have a far-reaching impact by making a large body of ancient Greek tragedies available in a single collection in English for the first time.

Not content to publish solely in genres where women writers were more accepted, such as poetry, novels, and translations, Lennox also decided to try her hand at becoming a playwright. In 1769, she wrote a play called *The Sister*, which was based on her successful novel *Henrietta*. Opening night was much more crowded than other plays that season. This wasn't because a crowd showed up to support Lennox. They showed up to sabotage her. By "hissing"—the eighteenth-century equivalent of booing and heckling—this group of theatergoers sought to make it impossible for the play to go on. And it worked. There was so much commotion that they stopped the show.

Lennox laid the blame for the disruption on another playwright, Richard Cumberland, who was known for such tactics. He feared that Lennox would encourage more women writers to stage plays, and that would mean fewer opportunities for him. He wasn't wrong: there were a limited number of patents, or licenses, to stage plays in London in this period. He didn't want more competition for the few spots available. This is the bigotry of the small-minded; in a scarcity environment, Cumberland wanted to win by ensuring he and his friends were the only players, not because they produced the best work.

While Lennox accused Cumberland, there may have been others in the crowd who plotted against her. According to one account, *The Sister*'s opening night was crashed by a group of theatergoers still angry about Lennox's harsh treatment of Shakespeare many years before. Johnson's friend James Boswell records one account that a man "at the Club" had been telling people to go to the play "and hiss it, because she had attacked Shakespeare."

It was at this point in Lennox's biography that I became overwhelmed with frustration. How difficult it must have been to write boundary-pushing work, to publish to acclaim, and to make enough money to survive when your fate depends on such fickle crowds!

Lennox's experiences with such bad faith arguments—Cumberland attacking for fear of the competition, or Garrick and those theatergoers taking it personally when she looked at Shakespeare critically—have plenty of parallels today. A teacher advocates reading more works by contemporary people of color in classrooms, and some parent inevitably Cumberlands all over that: "If we read more books by contemporary people of color, when will we ever read the important dead white men?" they say, while somehow missing that the syllabus is still well populated with those very authors.

It is true that we have limited time to read among so many choices, and many defend the canon because it's the "best" that literature has to offer. But the more authors I sought from Austen's bookshelf—these women whom tastemakers removed, replaced, and effaced—the more I became convinced that there is no one book that "everyone" should read. If I had focused only on what we currently label "canonical" works, I would never have made it to *The Female Quixote*, or to *The Mysteries of Udolpho*, books that I adored. Rather, I was coming to appreciate the canon more as a starting point. It was Austen who brought me to Lennox, after all. I had always enjoyed Austen's wit, and now I was enjoying the wit of her predecessors. To my surprise, I found that *The Female Quixote* was far wittier than any of Austen's novels. The "best" book is not necessarily the canonical one. What ultimately matters is finding books that are meaningful for you. Read those books.

I had started this investigation thinking that I would simply be reading a lot of mediocre eighteenth- and early-nineteenth-century novels. Then I actually read them, and they surprised me, challenged me, and delighted me. Why had I assumed, again, that they would be mediocre? Where did I pick up that lie? What began as doubts about their removal from the canon changed to suspicion. In seeking copies of these novels published over centuries in various forms—an unobtainable first edition, a fifth edition published only a few years later, an anthologized edition a generation later—I had gathered evidence of how the canon is formed. Burney, Radcliffe, and Lennox had all enjoyed popular and critical success in their lifetimes. Their books were considered classics for generations. But they didn't remain so.

As I researched each of these women, and the ones that follow in these chapters, I tried to identify moments when this happened, the turning points. Sometimes, it happened suddenly; other times, by degrees. But in each case, these writers went from the spotlight—acclaimed as geniuses, as good as Sappho, better than Fielding—to the shadows.

For Lennox, one such moment came in 1843, nearly one hundred years after the publication of *The Female Quixote*. This was the year an article in the *Gentleman's Magazine* first claimed that the second-to-last chapter of Lennox's most celebrated book was written not by Lennox, but by Samuel Johnson. There had not been any evidence of such an idea earlier. In Johnson's lifetime, no one among his friends nor among his multiple biographers (who all knew Lennox personally) had suggested it. The assertion was made "on internal evidence" such as "style," and because Johnson had written the preface. But the fact that he contributed the preface was already well known in their lifetimes, and thus hardly supports the theretofore unmentioned argument that the penultimate chapter was too. After this claim first appeared in the nineteenth century, it was repeated with increasing regularity by critics. In the twentieth century, literary scholars were looking at "both sides" and seriously weighing the possibility that Johnson wrote a chapter of *The Female Quixote* because, well, hopes and dreams?

Some critics argued for the Johnsonian attribution because they considered that chapter the most philosophical of the book. But those critics seemed to ignore other major facts about the novel and its publication. First, philosophical debates occur throughout the entire work. Further, that chapter was composed under very specific circumstances. As I mentioned, *The Female Quixote* was issued in two volumes, even though Lennox had initially hoped to extend the denouement for another volume. Under the duress of economic necessity, she finished it so the printer could publish it before the end of the season. Lennox composed that chapter as a quick resolution to the narrative, thus making it more packed—again, by economic necessity—with all the ideas she had intended to convey in the previously planned third volume.

Beyond that, there's actual proof. The Beinecke Rare Book and Manuscript Library at Yale University holds a letter documenting Lennox's authorship of the chapter. The letter, written by Lennox to Johnson just before the publication of the book, describes her sending him a copy of *The Female Quixote* and asking "if you do me the favour to read over the latter part of the second Voll. [*sic*] which you have not yet seen." Citing this letter and other arguments, an article by O. M. Brack Jr. and Susan Carlile in 2003 definitively told the rest of the literary world to cut it out: there was no evidence, nor had there ever been evidence, that the famous chapter of Lennox's best-known book was written by Johnson.

Just to review: for over 150 years, scholars earnestly argued that part of a woman writer's most important book must have been written by a male friend of hers, because of . . . reasons. Because someone who loved Johnson suggested it, and others were willing to consider it because they too loved Johnson. Because *The Female Quixote* was a great book, and Johnson a great writer.

These critics did get one thing right. *The Female Quixote* was a great book. I still wanted to hunt down an eighteenth-century copy for myself. It was printed numerous times in the eighteenth century, so despite my miss at that cursed auction, I held out hope for any eighteenth-century edition. In searching, I came across a second edition, listed for $350 by a dealer who is a fellow member of the Antiquarian Booksellers' Association of America (ABAA), the nation's most important trade organization for rare book dealers. Members of this organization are supposed to demonstrate the highest standards in research, cataloging, and professionalism in the rare book trade. My colleague's description for *The Female Quixote* included this line: "Lennox's mentor Samuel Johnson is believed to have written the dedication as well as the penultimate chapter." No citation. Just a simple assertion that was proved wrong decades ago, in the listing of a $350 book by a well-established rare book dealer.

I understand how he got there. Johnsonians have a long and fervent history of book collecting. Adding more about Johnson would make the book more appealing to Johnsonians who are, quite frankly, a larger lot than Lennoxians. (I am not actually sure there are Lennoxians, but I would join that club.) Yet surely my colleague might have hit that selling point by limiting his description to the dedication by Johnson, which has the benefit of noting his involvement while also being, you know, true.

I am, despite current appearances, sympathetic to these kinds of errors. Another reason an experienced and respected dealer might commit a gaffe like this can be traced back to old-school rare book cataloging practices. Rare book dealers are magpies of knowledge; we gather bits and bobs of facts about a wide range of authors to assess the books we acquire. To accomplish this, we love a standard reference work. Any experienced dealer knows that a good reference work pays for itself: sometimes it offers exactly the sentence you need about a book's importance to justify changing the price from $400 to $500.

The reference library at our shop contains thousands of titles. Much of this information is still in copyright, yet too niche to attract an e-book edition, so it sits in an uncanny valley where buckram-bound tomes are the only way to access it. Further, to many rare book dealers, the proliferation of online articles without peer review and the problems of internet ephemerality (like link rot, when hyperlinks do not remain active long term) make them skeptical of online resources for research. These dealers—and I often count myself among them—believe the most efficient *and* trustworthy way to learn about a subject is to consult an authoritative reference work.

This is why you'll see more references to the *Oxford Dictionary of National Biography* (*ODNB*), first published in 2004, in a single rare book dealer's catalog than you're likely to see anywhere else in your entire lifetime. Dealers in the ABAA enjoy subscription access to the *ODNB* online as one of their member benefits. Many look up an author in a work like that, summarize the relevant information in their catalog description, and call it a day. But this is where a dealer can also go wrong. Here's a sentence from the *ODNB*'s entry on Lennox: "as a person, she is perhaps most human when she boasts her hand at making gooseberry tarts and apple dumplings."

That quote gets to the heart of the problem. In an article written to convey her professional accomplishments, Lennox's reputation is discussed in terms of baking. These massive reference works routinely omit, or otherwise marginalize, writers outside of dominant power structures: women writers, writers of color, LGBTQ+ writers. Because women's accomplishments are less often included in standard reference works, or summarized in condescending terms when they are (most human when making gooseberry tarts?), it's easy to consult many standard books for rare book cataloging and arrive at flawed conclusions. Lennox had received only oblique credit in Johnson's *Dictionary*, the ultimate reference work of the eighteenth century; now a major reference work of the twenty-first century concluded with a comment on her baking rather than writing. While collecting, I kept running into these kinds of texts that are adjacent to the canon, but buttress it. In practice, they are received as objective reference works. They are just . . . not.

So this dealer had engaged in some lazy cataloging. He should have double-checked modern Lennox scholarship. But I understood immediately why he hadn't. $350 may sound like a lot, but it's not for a rare book dealer. He had covered his bases and moved on to the next book because time is money. However, that certainly could not have been the case for another dealer's error that I came across as I looked for an eighteenth-century copy of *The Female Quixote* to add to my personal collection.

I saw this one in a description for a first edition of the *Memoirs of Maximilian* [. . .] *Duke of Sully* (1757), which was one of Lennox's most critically acclaimed translations. This copy was listed for $1,000, bound in beautiful subtly purple boards, contrasting against their tan leather spines— what we describe as "quarter" when only that portion is leather. It was gorgeous. Yet the dealer struggled to attribute the translator. "The ESTC notes that the translator may have been Samuel Johnson, but the book itself (as well as later editions) credits Charlotte Lennox." The "ESTC" referred to here is the same standard reference work I had just used when looking up first editions of *The Female Quixote*. The dealer seemed to realize that this Johnsonian attribution was silly; Lennox was duly credited as the translator on the title page: "Translated from the French, by the Author of the *Female Quixote*." Yet this dealer likely included the possibility that she wasn't anyway because more people collect books by Samuel Johnson.

Another description for this same book, but from an entirely different dealer, didn't even mention Lennox's name at all—yet it did make sure to note that "Samuel Johnson wrote the dedication." The conventional wisdom of the rare book trade is that this book has a better chance of selling if connected to Johnson, who has long been highly sought in book collecting circles. These dealers are pragmatists, not feminists.

And thus, in the face of every logical argument and documented evidence, questions of authorship over Lennox's works continue, reminding us at every turn that her biggest value to the modern collector is her relationship with Samuel Johnson. Lennox and Johnson were friends and peers. Throughout her career, Johnson was her vocal champion. But Johnson's own canonical status has made it harder for modern collectors to recognize Lennox's books as worthy on their own terms. Even in her afterlife, connections to famous literary men both helped and hindered her legacy.

Johnson's influence on Lennox has long been established, but Lennox's influence on Johnson has only been truly appreciated in this century. Because many scholars came to Lennox after studying Johnson, their commentary often reflected an assumption of his superiority, even when it made little sense. For example, in 1935 Miriam Rossiter Small published a major biography of Lennox. She argued that the penultimate chapter of *The Female Quixote* in 1752 was written by Johnson in part because a passage in his 1759 work, *Rasselas*, contains a similar sentiment to one in *The Female Quixote*—even though Lennox's novel was published seven years earlier. It didn't seem to have crossed this scholar's mind that it is more likely Lennox influenced Johnson in this case, not the other way around. But such a conclusion would be a stretch for someone who opened her biography of Lennox arguing that "the most important single fact in Mrs. Lennox's literary life" was that "she received the warm approval and assistance of Samuel

Johnson." It was an important fact, no doubt. But I still think that Lennox's financial circumstances, her wit, and her boldness were the most important facts in her literary life. Not until 2018 did a biography of Lennox appear that analyzed in detail how she influenced Johnson: Susan Carlile's tremendous *Charlotte Lennox: An Independent Mind*. In this context, Carlile's subtitle feels like a pointed commentary on the long history of Johnsonian condescension.

This widening of perspective on Lennox and Johnson's mutually beneficial literary friendship was built over the course of decades of work by multiple scholars. How to reflect that in my collection? I wanted to. I mapped the arc of Lennox's life, and afterlife, and charted the turning points. It wasn't an eighteenth-century edition of *The Female Quixote* I needed; it was a twentieth-century one.

Let me explain. Today much eighteenth-century material is digitized and available for free online. When I came across that reference to *The Female Quixote* in Austen's letter as "very high" entertainment, I searched for an e-copy of Lennox's book, downloaded it onto an app, and started reading. But before 1970, there had been no new edition of *The Female Quixote* in the entirety of the twentieth century—and no internet to access digitized copies. So if an Austen reader like me had run across that same reference, she would perhaps have been curious about the novel, but she would have had a hard time tracking it down. *The Female Quixote* wouldn't have been on the shelves in her local bookshop, or even in the vast majority of secondhand bookshops. Nor was it likely to be accessible in a public library system—and in 1970 one could not go to special collections libraries and simply ask to read one of their novels printed in 1752 because Jane Austen wrote a similar novel. For that reader, the trail would have gone cold. She would never have met Arabella, like Austen did, like I did. She would never have come to love Lennox like Austen did, like I did.

In 1970, *The Female Quixote* became available to a new generation of readers. Edited and introduced by the scholar Margaret Dalziel, it was part of a larger series called the Oxford English Novels, which had already published twenty-eight other novels (of which ten were by women, including

Burney, Radcliffe, Edgeworth, and Inchbald—not a bad showing). I decided I must track down a copy of this edition. After all, it marked the moment when *The Female Quixote* was reintroduced to a twentieth-century readership. From this point forward, reprints of *The Female Quixote* were issued regularly once again, often in inexpensive paperback editions as a "classic."

The 1970 edition was a hardcover, with a bright dust jacket in coral, on which the title was embellished in blue. When I tracked down a copy and placed it on my bookshelf, it stood out cheerfully next to the quieter leatherbound volumes from centuries before, but it nevertheless belonged. It was evidence not of how Lennox fell from the canon, but how she has begun to make her way back to it. From that publication forward, any Janeite who stumbled upon the reference in Austen's letter could find and read a copy of *The Female Quixote* by Charlotte Lennox.

Chapter Five

HANNAH MORE
(1745-1833)

**Of course I shall be delighted when I read it, like other people,
but till I do, I dislike it.**

—Jane Austen, on Hannah More's novel,
Coelebs in Search of a Wife

Hannah More had a reputation, and Austen didn't consider it a good one. When Austen's sister Cassandra wrote praising More's wildly successful novel *Coelebs in Search of a Wife* (1809), Austen replied, "You have by no means raised my curiosity about Caleb [*sic*];—My disinclination for it before was affected but now it is real [. . .] Of course I shall be delighted when I read it, like other people, but till I do, I dislike it." Austen was admitting to a major bibliophilic sin: judging a book before having read it. But her reluctance is understandable considering how outspoken against novels Hannah More had been before she wrote her own. It had been commentary like More's—that novels "nourish a vain and visionary indolence, which lays the mind open to error and the heart to seduction"—that had given Austen's beloved Frances Burney so much anxiety. More sounded judgy, hypocritical, and sanctimonious. It is hard to imagine how those qualities would lead to a fun novel.

Coelebs (probably best pronounced "see-libs"; and yeah, I know) combined the plot of courtship novels by authors like Frances Burney with the morals of a conduct book. The hero is ready to get married, but he's having a hard time finding a woman who lives up to his standards. He assesses and discards various young ladies for their perceived moral failures. Along the way, he meets many other people whose own flaws and virtues offer lessons for the reader. Perhaps this is an unfair summary of the book. I'm not entirely sure, as I couldn't finish it. Over the course of years, I started and stopped, started and stopped.

Nevertheless, the work was a phenomenon in More's (and Austen's) time, going into a whopping twelve editions in the first year alone, as well as crossing overseas to sell tens of thousands of copies in the US over the next decade. Some modern critics even argue that its massive popularity was a turning point in the history of the novel, finally making that literary form "respectable" and therefore paving the way for novelists like Scott and Dickens to become bestsellers. Austen, too, admitted she'd probably like it once she did read it, since everyone did—but she didn't *want* to like it. It seems Hannah More's reputation as a self-righteous moralist was known to Austen; in one of her unfinished works, Austen introduced an annoyingly prim aunt who advises her misbehaving niece: "I had hoped to see you respectable and good [. . .] I bought you Blair's *Sermons* and *Coelebs in Search of a Wife*." Given that the book choices of Austen's characters reflect their personalities, this recommendation did not speak well of Hannah More's work.

Well into my investigation now, I decided to include Hannah More in my collection as something of a foil. *Coelebs* was a novel that enjoyed a moment of triumph—but was, perhaps, more justly removed from the canon than the others. Maybe Austen's criticism of More would reveal something that Austen's praise for other authors did not. I thought it was such a clever idea: read something Austen specifically didn't want to! Well, that backfired.

————

Coelebs didn't sound fun, and it turned out not to be fun. It really does read like a collection of sermons in novel form. I typically have a high tolerance for books that others call "boring," a word readers often use for works from previous centuries that have a style different from our modern tastes. But in many cases, the effort is worth the payoff. As recently as reading *The Mysteries of Udolpho*, I had found myself struggling as I followed the first part of the heroine's journey before she reached the Castle Udolpho—and in the end, I was glad I persisted. Yet when I started the first chapter of *Coelebs*, I could barely get through a paragraph without huffing in annoyance at some sanctimonious comment. The story begins with a pages-long defense of "conjugal obedience." The hero, you see, describes the concept of a wife being submissive to her husband as "woman's highest honour."

I stalled.

I needed a new plan. I pivoted instead to reading books *about* Hannah More, not *by* Hannah More. This felt like a good idea, since I had found the lives of the other women I'd researched so far fascinating. First, there was the riveting story of how Burney secretly pursued publication of *Evelina*. Then I had read, with the sympathy of an introvert, how Radcliffe simply wanted to be left alone. Most recently, I had fallen in love with the bold and witty Lennox. And I enjoyed their works more after I understood the context that informed their writing. So I began to look for biographies of More.

I checked out Anne Stott's indispensable *Hannah More: The First Victorian* (2003) from my local public university library. I read the first few chapters, put it down, and looked for another. My second choice was much shorter, a slim paperback copy of Mary Anne Phemister's *Hannah More: The Artist as Reformer* (2014). I got stuck in that one, too, and moved on to Patricia Demers's *The World of Hannah More* (1996), which incorporated much more literary analysis. No go. Next I tried the earliest authoritative biography, William Roberts's *Memoirs of the Life and Correspondence of Mrs. Hannah More* (1834), which I pulled up as a digital copy online. My already plodding progress slowed even further, until I finally set that one aside too. Perhaps a middle ground: Mary Alden Hopkins's *Hannah More and Her Circle* (1947) seemed more accessible, since it described the other people who populated More's life. Nope. Okay. What about the very academic *Hannah More: A Critical Biography* (1996) by Charles Howard Ford, which might give me a lot of material to chew on? Alas.

I just didn't like Hannah More.

My desk became littered with half a dozen biographies of More, each caught with a bookmark halfway through. I had already known that Jane Austen was not particularly inclined to like Hannah More. I had foolishly taken that as a challenge, rather than a warning. It wasn't just *Coelebs*; her life and works were filled with that same sanctimonious judgment.

I was beginning to think that Hannah More simply wasn't for me. I asked myself if I should even include her in this project. Did it make sense to explore how More fell from the canon if I agreed with her fate? Yet whenever that question surfaced, I'd open a biography, read a bit more, and determine that I needed to persist. Because even though I didn't like her, she interested me. There was always some detail, some action, some turn of phrase, that would not let me simplify her like I wanted to. I had to admire her ambition when she wrote a letter to a famous theater manager, hoping to suggest ideas to him for plays she could write. She earned my respect by taking action to effect meaningful change in the world: supporting the education of women and working-class children, or composing abolitionist poetry to drum up popular support while Parliament debated ending the slave trade. I did not like Hannah More. But I couldn't quit her.

It was for that reason I decided I should include Hannah More in this book. I was curious why her name doesn't make canonical lists anymore. But I was most interested in understanding my mixed-up feelings about her. That became the driving question.

I dove back into the story of her life, hoping I would find the answers.

Hannah More was born in 1745 to an upper-middle-class family in a suburb of Bristol. More's father was a schoolmaster; his five daughters, none of whom ever married, all followed him into the profession. Hannah and her sisters received an unusually thorough education, but Hannah truly distinguished herself. She was brilliant. As a three-year-old, she listened so closely to her older sisters' lessons that she had largely figured out how to read before her mother thought to teach her. Her father, regaling her as an eight-year-old with tales from classical authors like Plutarch, soon got more than he bargained for. As one of her earliest major biographers, William Roberts, put it: "Mr. More, who was remarked for his strong dislike of female pedantry, having nevertheless begun to instruct his daughter in the rudiments of the Latin language, and mathematics, was soon frightened at his own success." Her mother, however, was thrilled. Mother and daughter often worked together to convince her father to continue her studies. As a child, More wished only that "she might one day be rich enough to have a whole quire [of paper] to herself."

Hannah had a facility for language that her elder sisters, who ran the girls' boarding school she later attended, noticed and cultivated. As a teenager, she became known across Bristol for her talent as both a playwright and a poet. A play she wrote at the age of sixteen for performance at the girls' boarding school, *The Search After Happiness*, enjoyed enough popularity that it was soon published and reprinted multiple times, a success unusual even for more established writers.

This play centers on four young women who visit a wise shepherdess to learn the secret to happiness. More's wise shepherdess advises, "*Woman shines but in her proper sphere* [. . .] By yielding she obtains the noblest sway, / And reigns securely when she seems t'obey." It was the exact opposite of Charlotte Lennox's rebellious "The Art of Coquetry": as the verse suggests, More had a conservative view of women's roles in society. The market rewarded her for it, with teachers across the country eager to take up a work that instilled traditional values using such skillful language. Over the next few years her play sold more than ten thousand copies, with many copies circulated for performance at other girls' schools.

More became a teacher after graduation, like her sisters. It looked as if the rest of her life would progress like her sisters' too. Then, when she was in her early twenties, she became engaged to "a gentleman of fortune, more than twenty years older than herself" named William Turner. This was one of three key events in her life that set More on a different path than what she had expected. Had all gone to plan with the engagement, More may never have gone on to the extraordinary life she did.

In advance of the wedding, More quit her job and began "preparing and fitting herself out to be the wife of a man of that condition." She and Turner set a date for marriage. He postponed it. They set another date. He postponed it again. After six years, when More was nearing thirty, her friends finally stepped in: this could not continue. In response, Turner proposed settling her with an annuity, a structured annual payment, in lieu of the marriage—what he and her friends would have seen as something akin to damages for what they called "the robbery he had committed upon her time." More refused the annuity, but some of her friends (all of them male, and therefore able to accomplish it legally without her) worked with Turner to arrange the annuity without her knowledge. After the fact, she accepted it.

The sum that Turner settled on More was £200 per year, which was judged as the amount necessary for her "to devote herself to her literary pursuits." She wouldn't have to teach again. She could do anything she wanted.

It was not surprising that the question of money kept appearing as an important aspect in each of the careers of the literary women I had researched until now. Jane Austen, Frances Burney, and Ann Radcliffe had financial support from the men in their lives before they achieved success as authors. Charlotte Lennox, on the other hand, was constantly in need of money, which often limited her choice of what to publish, and when; she wrote what she hoped would pay her bills. Now here was Hannah More, not yet thirty, with enough financial security to write whatever she pleased, independent of the support of—or need to care for—a family or husband. After her experience with Turner, More resolved never to consider marriage again. Perhaps this decision came from the heartache of the prolonged and finally broken engagement. But it also meant that More was never in danger of seeing her newly achieved economic independence turned into dependence, by law, on a husband. She was legally and financially free.

The next year, in 1774, Hannah More flexed her newfound freedom by taking a trip to London. Soon she met the actor, influential theater manager, and indefatigable champion of Shakespeare, David Garrick—yes, him again—who was then at the peak of his fame. David Garrick and his wife, the Viennese dancer Eva Marie Veigel, soon became intimate friends with More. Her well-connected friends circulated More's poetry in manuscript form, raising her reputation across literary communities in London. The first time she met the eminent literary critic and lexicographer Samuel Johnson—yes, Johnson again too—at the painter Sir Joshua Reynolds's house, Johnson quoted one of More's own poems to her. Soon, Garrick had begun calling More by the nickname of "Nine," claiming she was all nine muses of ancient Greece, the goddesses that inspired the arts and sciences, rolled into one.

More's poetry also brought her to the attention of Elizabeth Montagu, then a London celebrity who was part literary patron, part hostess, part scholar. Hannah More excitedly summed up Montagu after her first dinner invitation as "not only the finest genius, but the finest lady I ever saw." She was "the Queen of the Blues," a nickname that referred to her social group's moniker, the Bluestockings, a tight-knit circle of upper-class women who prided themselves on their love of wit, learning, propriety, and quality tea.

The larger Bluestocking group included Elizabeth Carter, whose translation of the ancient Greek Stoic philosopher Epictetus brought her acclaim (and who was so irritated by Charlotte Lennox); Sarah Scott, a fine novelist and Montagu's sister; Frances Boscawen and Elizabeth Vesey, whose salons were the envy of the town; and Frances Burney (who was first invited after the success of *Evelina*). According to Burney, they were called Bluestockings after a legendary quip of Elizabeth Vesey when one of the men often invited, Benjamin Stillingfleet, initially refused an invitation because he wasn't properly dressed. She replied, "don't mind dress! Come in your blue stockings!" referring to a type of wool stocking more common of lower-class fashions. She wanted his company, not the white silk stockings expected at formal parties—so he appeared accordingly. "Bluestockings" became an inside joke, reflecting the open-minded atmosphere of these gatherings, where both men and women engaged in intellectual debate.

More was warmly welcomed among them. The Bluestockings formed strong friendships—and they were aces at throwing parties. The events of the Bluestockings were so bursting with talent that the most famous intellectuals of the day who attended were simply considered another dinner companion. And they were particularly supportive of More's authorship. More's schoolgirl play *The Search After Happiness* had been her first publication in 1773. The year she came to London, she published another play titled *The Inflexible Captive* (1774), and in 1776, she published her first book of poetry to acclaim.

In this new work, two of More's extended narrative poems were collected in one volume called *Sir Eldred of the Bower and the Bleeding Rock*. Both poems were a mix of popular entertainment and moral instruction, a strategy More would favor for most of her life. "Sir Eldred of the Bower" was based upon a popular ballad about a married couple that ends in tragedy when the husband suspects his wife of infidelity. "The Bleeding Rock," too, was a riff on a known tale. It retold a piece of folklore about a tragic love in the style of Ovid's tales in *The Metamorphoses*. It features a forlorn heroine who begs to be transformed into a rock when she is forsaken by a lover to whom she committed too quickly. Montagu, the Queen of the Blues, wrote to More to say that "you are doing so much honour to your sex in general by your works."

More's entrance into these circles, alongside her friendship with the Garricks and Johnson, laid out the path of where her literary career could go—all the way to the top—if she so chose. For a time, she did. In 1777, she composed a tragedy called *Percy*, which debuted at the famed Covent Garden theater. A tale of love thwarted during the Crusades, it went on to become one of the most successful original tragedies of the eighteenth century. Garrick gave it his seal of approval by composing its prologue and epilogue, short pieces in verse that contextualized the play. In Garrick's prologue, delivered by a woman, More's theatrical debut was celebrated as equal to her male colleagues: "I'll prove, ye fair, that let us have our swing, / We can, as well as men, do any thing."

Percy's success had me curious enough to give it a try. It was, after all, significantly shorter than a novel or a biography. It immediately struck me

that Garrick's endorsement was fitting far beyond any potential obligation
out of friendship; *Percy* reminded me of Shakespeare's tragedies. In fact, it
read much like an alternate universe *Romeo and Juliet*, recounting the completely different tragedy that would have ensued if Juliet had married her
parents' choice, Count Paris, instead of Romeo. After its debut, Montagu
triumphantly wrote to More that she was "the pride of your friends and
the humiliation of your enemies." (A year or so after reading it, I spotted a
first edition of *Percy* in a bookshop in London. Seeing the slim little volume
reminded me of that magnificent quote from Montagu, and I knew then I
would buy it for my collection.)

With the success of *Percy*, More received more dinner invitations than
ever. Rather than buoy her, this development fatigued her. Even before the
sudden increase in her popularity, there were signs of More's ambivalence
to London high life. In one letter, she made it clear that she didn't actually
enjoy most outings: "I find my dislike of what are called public diversions
greater than ever, except a play." In another letter she complained, "There
are so few people I meet with in this good town to whom one can venture to
recommend sermons." Ah, there it is. That judgy streak. Additionally, she
and Montagu were "the only two monsters in the creation who never touch
a card," as they both never gambled at parties, a common pastime among
the London elite (that did in fact lead to people losing astounding amounts
of money). More began refusing most invitations, unless from good friends
like the Garricks and Montagu.

During these years, More managed to spend six months at a time in
London before retreating to the home she shared with her sisters in Bristol,
or retiring to the Garricks' country house as a guest. She wanted the respect
of the literary community, but she disliked what she saw as the immorality
of that same circle. These conflicting desires come up again and again in
her correspondence. One day she would write a letter about a party at
Montagu's lasting until one in the morning, and the next spend an entire
letter ruminating on what she hated about London fashion: "Again I am
annoyed by the foolish absurdity of the present mode of dress. Some ladies
carry on their heads a large quantity of fruit, and yet they would despise a

poor useful member of society, who carried it there for the purpose of selling it for bread." Most of her criticisms revolved around what she viewed as the questionable morality of the social scene. And she itched to say more about it.

The same year as *Percy* debuted, More published her thoughts in *Essays on Various Subjects, Principally Designed for Young Ladies* (1777). It was a conduct book, an entry in that popular genre meant to educate young people (and especially young women) in propriety, etiquette, and taste. These were the kinds of books that fueled Frances Burney's shame about novel writing, and which Austen mocked when Mr. Collins chooses one to read aloud to the Bennet girls. Conduct books were useful cudgels for managing the thoughts and actions of young women. More was well-suited to the genre; it was an ideal format to vent the frustrations first recorded in her letters.

Essays on Various Subjects hinted at the shift to come in More's career. Dedicated to her dear friend Montagu, whom she called a model of "life and manners," the book was nevertheless not quite so well received in her own circles. One of the Bluestocking hostesses wrote to More that a mutual friend

> **has been reading your Essays, and likes them, (especially that on Education) as much as I promised her she would; but on the threshold she stumbled, and wrote me word that Lady Denbigh and she were in the greatest wrath against you for allowing the men so much the superiority [. . .] Indeed I cannot help thinking that in one part of your Introduction you *do* give up our cause too much; and where shall we find a champion, if you, (armed at all points) desert us?**

In the introduction referred to in this letter, More argued in favor of an idea she would support her entire life: that there were God-ordained separate spheres for men and women, one public and one private. According to More, "each sex has its respective, appropriated qualifications" that "Nature, propriety, and custom" kept bounded: "the female mind," for instance, "does not appear capable of attaining so high a degree of perfection in science as the male," but women have "other qualities much better calculated to answer their particular purposes." More's Bluestocking friends were disappointed by this use of her talents—and it must have seemed an additional hypocrisy to see More denigrating the capability of "the female mind" in the public sphere while pursuing a literary career herself. But More's conservative view on matters of gender and religion would only strengthen.

Hannah More was now the author of acclaimed works across multiple genres. The first key event of More's life, the annuity, had granted her financial independence. She used that opportunity to pursue her talent as a writer and had reached the highest circles of literary London. But her successes only served to intensify her dissatisfaction. She longed for purpose. In her first conduct book, More was trying to find it. Yet at the same time, she loved the theater and had enjoyed writing *Percy*, a tragedy full of violence and emotional excess—the villain of *Percy* says at one point about the woman who was forced to marry him, "I feast upon her terrors." She did not know yet who she should become. A second key event would help her decide.

———

In all those biographies I had started and stopped, this is most commonly where I placed my bookmark to languish. It was the moment before More committed to her role as an imperious moral leader. I didn't like what she became. I didn't want to see it happen.

But I'm stubborn. I'm one of those readers who struggles to stop reading a book even when I dislike it. Logically, I know this is absurd. But emotionally, it makes me feel like a quitter. This commitment to follow through is how I finished James Joyce's *Ulysses*, even though I think I understood only about 35 percent of what I was reading. Joyce hadn't defeated me. Hannah More was not going to defeat me either.

The second key event in More's life was the death of David Garrick in 1779. After his death, his widow Eva largely retired to their country house

in Hampton. She and More spent long months there together, away from
the bustle of London. In one letter from this time More remarked, "We
never see a human face but each other's. Though in such deep retirement,
I am never dull, because I am not reduced to the fatigue of entertaining
dunces, or of being obliged to listen to *them*."

Having largely left high society, More realized that she did not miss it.
Moreover, that distance had confirmed her instinct that it was corrupt. Her
next major work signaled the transition brought on by this retirement. In
Sacred Dramas (1782), More told stories from the Bible in the format of popular plays, mixing entertainment with instruction. She was moving toward
what would soon become her central mission: education and reform.

But Hannah More didn't just publish; she practiced. She began to
use her literary connections in the service of her charitable ideals. Before,
More had kept true to her morals without imposing them too directly
upon others. For instance, she declined to take part in many social gatherings on Sundays, but didn't fight with her friends who attended them.
Now, however, More was feeling more confident in committing to her
moral voice.

An important conflict in More's life that highlights this shift is her patronage of Ann Yearsley, the Bristol-born milkmaid poet. In 1784, Hannah
More met "a Milker of Cows, and a feeder of Hogs, who has never even
seen a Dictionary," yet whose favorite poetry was Virgil's *Georgics*, the lesser-
known pastoral poems of the great ancient Roman author of the *Aeneid*.
Yearsley was an untaught genius whose own poems showed an instinctive
ear that amazed More and her Bluestocking friends. Together with Montagu, More arranged for the publication of a book of Yearsley's poems by
subscription, as Burney would later do with *Camilla*. Because of her reputation and excellent contacts, Burney made far more money this way than
by the typical style of publication. Charlotte Lennox also tried to publish
books in this manner, hoping to reap rewards like Burney's, but failed without sufficient support.

On her own, Yearsley could never have mustered the kind of Rolodex
necessary to fund such a publication. Now she had two of the most famous

and well-connected intellectuals of the era to champion it. The subscrib-
ers' list of her poems, printed in 1785, runs fifteen pages long and has
been described by one More biographer as "a roster of the Bas Bleu [the
Bluestockings] and their friends." Name after name begins with titles like
"Marquis," "Her Grace the Duchess," "Earl," "Right Honourable Lord,"
"Countess," and more.

Poems, on Several Occasions (1785) became the success everyone had
hoped. More paid all the other expenses involved, with the result that
£370 was earned on Yearsley's behalf. This was a life-changing amount
of money. Years earlier, Yearsley had married her husband because he
"had an Estate of near Six *pounds* a year, and the marriage was thought
too advantageous to be refused." Her book of poetry had brought more
than sixty times that.

But More didn't simply hand the money over to Yearsley, even though
it legally belonged to the newly published poet. She persuaded—or, by
some perspectives, pressured—Yearsley into putting the money into what
was known as a "5 percent" fund. These funds were essentially government
bonds, offering a steady 5 percent in interest back annually. More invested
£350 into a five percent fund, which would provide the Yearsleys with a
little less than eighteen pounds a year to live on with her six children—not a
lot, but triple the estate of Yearsley's husband. More gave her the remaining
twenty pounds "to cloathe her family and furnish her House."

This created friction between Yearsley and her benefactor. In order to
invest the funds on Yearsley's behalf, More had to arrange for a deed of
trust. While Yearsley did consent to the process, almost from the beginning she expressed concerns. Yet More bristled when Yearsley requested
a copy of the deed of trust. For her part, Yearsley had somehow gotten
into ten pounds of debt, which More paid on her behalf, but with great
annoyance. Soon after, during a dinner at More's house, Yearsley openly
accused More of attempting to defraud her of the money. More wrote in a
bewildered and defensive tone to Montagu about it. She ended this letter, "I
hear she [Yearsley] wears very fine Gauze Bonnets, long lappets, gold Pins
etc. Is such a Woman to be trusted with the poor Children's Money?" More

clearly had opinions on how Yearsley should be spending her earnings. More's friend, the splendidly wealthy Montagu, could wear gold pins—but if Ann Yearsley did, that made her morally questionable (and also, therefore, a terrible mother).

Living comfortably on £200 a year, More didn't quite grasp Yearsley's perspective. The fact was: £18 a year was not enough for Ann Yearsley, the genius milkwoman poet, to transcend above the working-class life into which she was born. Yearsley did not want to continue milking cows. She had talent. At her best, her verses have something of Emily Dickinson in them. One reads "For mine's a stubborn and a savage will; / No customs, manners or lost arts I boast, / On my rough soul your nicest rules are lost." Yearsley wanted more, and she felt that she could achieve it. But Hannah More did not encourage class mobility, believing one's station was predetermined by God. In her mind, Ann Yearsley was a milkwoman, and she would always be a milkwoman. As she said in a letter to Montagu, "I am *utterly* against taking her out of her station."

Eventually, Yearsley would wrest her money free from the trust set up on her behalf. She invested a large part of the funds into buying an apprenticeship for one of her sons with an engraver, establishing him in a profession. With another portion she started her own business, a circulating library. Before the movement for free libraries, circulating libraries gave subscription-based access to books that allowed middle- and lower-class readers to read at a much greater rate than they would have been able to achieve if they had needed to buy each book individually. (Recall that Jane Austen, who never had a substantial library of her own, relied not only upon the libraries of her father and brothers, but also upon circulating libraries for access to books.) With both endeavors, Yearsley showed she very much wanted to be out of her station.

The public rift with Yearsley had the effect of pushing More further to the margins of the literary world—and into another space altogether. More began to embrace the growing evangelical movement in England, a sort of religious revival within the Anglican church that encouraged its members, among other things, to pursue charitable causes. More devoted herself more and more to these large philanthropic projects. Around this time, she became particularly active in the anti-slavery movement.

In the 1780s she developed what would become a tremendously consequential friendship with fellow evangelical William Wilberforce, one of the main players in Parliament who worked to eliminate the British slave trade (finally succeeding in 1807). While her friends worked within the government to push for reform, More (who could not hold office) used her talents to sway public opinion. As surprising as it may seem today, she did this by writing poetry.

One of her most influential poems, *Slavery* (1788), was published during the period of the first Parliamentary petition to investigate the horrors of the slave trade. In it More said the country's participation in the abominable practice meant that Britain "raves of mercy, while she deals out death." She refused to stand by while England perpetuated these atrocities. More's work increasingly focused on concrete actions to bring about societal change aligned with her religious values.

In 1789, the third key event in More's life occurred, one that would complete her transition to charitable work as her calling. While visiting the More sisters in their country home, their friend Wilberforce took a day trip to Cheddar Gorge, near the town of the same name and known for its cheese making. It was intended as a leisurely hike to appreciate the beauty of the cliffs, but Wilberforce returned to the cottage that night utterly demoralized. Cheddar was poverty stricken. At dinner, Wilberforce told More, "something must be done for Cheddar [. . .] If you will be at the trouble, *I* will be at the expense." The funds accounted for, Hannah More and her sisters took up the idea with a speed, organization, and energy that had become a trademark of the family. Hannah and her youngest sister Patty took the lead with the Cheddar project, which began with the creation of a Sunday school.

Sunday schools were a relatively new phenomenon, established with the goal of teaching poor and working-class children their letters so that they could read the Bible, alongside lessons in moral behavior and individual responsibility. The proposition was a delicate one: many of the wealthy and powerful people in the neighborhood believed that educating laborers encouraged brazen ideas like not being content with their "place" in society (at the bottom). More and her sisters used their rhetorical skills to convince these opponents that proactive moral and religious instruction would instead help their employees act more piously and lawfully.

They often succeeded in their persuasions—primarily because they agreed with their listeners about the dangers of working-class people seeking to rise above their God-given social station. In a defensive letter sent to one detractor, More stressed "that my plan for instructing the poor is very limited and strict. They learn [. . .] such coarse works as may fit them for servants. I allow of no writing. My object has not been to teach dogmas and opinions, but to form the lower class to habits of industry and virtue." This was the hidden dagger behind all of the More sisters' charitable work: well-funded, well-connected, and well-educated, they offered tremendous help to people in need—so long as those people were content to live as their "betters" desired them to.

The Sunday school was voluntary, which meant its success required a great deal of coaxing. While many working-class parents were happy to have someone else watch their young children for an afternoon every Sunday, they were less keen to send their older children, who were another pair of hands. Some mothers even argued that it was they who should be paid to have their children attend, considering the loss of labor it would incur. So the Sunday schools as enacted by the More sisters functioned on a reward system to incentivize attendance and good behavior. Attending four Sundays in a row meant receiving a penny, and children in good standing also received new clothing each year. The Cheddar School was the first of many Sunday schools that the Mores opened across the countryside with the financial support of Wilberforce and his friends.

But even as the schools grew, larger world events added a new kind of cultural pressure. The French Revolution was well underway, and across England many of the conservatives in the upper classes feared that the French movement for a class-based revolution would bleed into their country. This anxiety was heightened by people like Thomas Paine, the radical who had moved to the American colonies in the 1770s and penned *Common Sense*, a pamphlet that built popular support for total independence from Great Britain. Now in 1791, Paine published another pamphlet called *Rights of Man*, arguing that citizens should be able to overthrow a government if that government was not protecting their natural rights. One mid-twentieth century biographer, Mary Alden Hopkins, explains how this affected the More sisters' Sunday school work: "though the leaders designed the instruction to teach the working class to be obedient to their betters, it is not clear that this was the result. Children who could read the Bible could later read Tom Paine [. . .] and many did."

More was once again approached by wealthy male friends asking her to do something to allay this growing anxiety. In response, More developed the Cheap Repository Tracts, a series that would exponentially outsell any of the works published by any of the other authors discussed in this book outside of Jane Austen herself, well into the millions of copies. These Tracts were short, cheaply printed, tiny productions, each containing a story that conveyed a moral lesson. I've sold a number of these in my career, which I often acquire tucked within larger collections of chapbooks. Their similarity to other chapbooks was their brilliance: they mimicked the form of popular media used for bawdy ballads, vicious tales of crime, and devil-may-care pranks—but exchanged this "vulgar" content for moral lessons in the same straightforward storytelling mode.

The Tracts are petite things, fitting in the palm of one's hand, often held together by a stitched thread. They're illustrated with simplistic woodcuts and printed on low-quality paper, which is by now almost always browned and stained with age and exposure. Thousands upon thousands were printed and circulated across the English countryside, primarily by upper-class leaders such as clergy, landowners, politicians, and philanthropists like the More sisters. Now living in Bath, Hannah More oversaw the execution of the project, in addition to writing more than half of the stories that comprise the Tracts.

The stories themselves described simple scenes of everyday life that their audience would recognize, but told so as to offer a practical model of moral behavior. For example, appearances and morality were always connected in More's mind, especially when it came to women. In one of the most well-known tracts, *The Shepherd of Salisbury Plain* (1795), More writes,

> **If I meet with a laborer, hedging, ditching, or mending the highways, with his stockings and shirt tight and whole [. . .] I have seldom failed, on visiting his cottage, to find that also clean and well ordered, and his wife notable, and worthy of encouragement. Whereas, a poor woman, who will be lying a-bed, or gossiping with her neighbors when she ought to be fitting out her husband in a cleanly manner, will seldom be found to be very good in other respects.**

Hannah More worked tirelessly on this and other charitable pursuits through the 1790s, so much so that her friends often worried for her. In a letter to a mutual friend after More had dropped everything to help someone in need, Horace Walpole—recall he was the author of the first gothic, *The Castle of Otranto* (1764)—remarked in his characteristically witty way that "Good Hannah More is killing herself by a new fit of benevolence." But by the early 1800s she was moving into her sixties, and she gradually began retiring from her most physically taxing charitable pursuits. Her mind, however, remained strong, and soon she would publish what would become one of the most successful novels of her time.

Here we are, back again at the novel neither Austen nor I wanted to read: *Coelebs in Search of a Wife* (1809). It was a new format for More—she had, after all, been attacking novels for a good part of her career—but in this case, she used the same strategy as she had with the Tracts, mimicking a popular format as a point of entry for readers who wouldn't otherwise sit through a sermon.

Coelebs was incredibly successful; in the first year alone, More made a staggering £2,000 from the publication. She had commandeered the popular courtship novel format and turned it into a blatant moral lesson. Of course, many novelists of More's time ensured that their heroines acted with perfect propriety in order to avoid the eager criticism of the genre's detractors, but there was satire in Burney's novels, and thrills in Radcliffe's, and wit in Lennox's. More's novel didn't even try to be anything other than a conduct book in novel form.

The success of *Coelebs* ensured that More's renown would continue in her twilight years. Over the course of her life, More became one of the most famous women writers in England. People would even make pilgrimages to her home. When they arrived at the More sisters' house, her youngest sister Patty would often walk into the room and announce, "I'm not Hannah More!" Another sister would follow, and Patty would add, "She's not Hannah More either!"

More became even more religious as she grew older and, after her four sisters died in quick succession, she became more reclusive too. When she died in 1833, she left an estate of £30,000, the biggest fortune ever amassed by an English woman writer to that point. She gave tremendous amounts of her estate away to anti-slavery initiatives. In the Victorian era, her reputation soared as the ideal pious woman. One of the most common ways I've seen this on the shelves as a rare book dealer is in books for children: the Victorians loved a good compendium of Famous Historical Figures whose lives served as a moral for young people. Hannah More is often one of the only women included in these anthologies of exemplary leaders.

But More was a controversial figure, both in her lifetime and after. During an 1802 dispute at one of her Sunday schools, one man wrote a two-hundred-plus-page hit piece on More under the pen name "the Reverend Sir Archibald MacSarcasm." Even while she became the darling of decorous Victorian biographers, others called her "one of the most detestable writers that ever held a pen." The man who said that, a late nineteenth-century commentator named Augustine Birrell, described her as "like a huge conger-eel in an ocean of dingy morality"—I don't even know where to start with that phrase—and merrily recounted digging a hole in his own garden to bury a nineteen-volume leather-bound set of her works. Hannah More has always been both loved and hated.

My response to More was an unfortunate reminder of how personal reading can be. I was struggling with her steady progression into that severe and powerful moral authority because it stirred memories from my own life. Growing up in a conservative religious community, I knew people like More. They helped to enforce an elaborate system of behaviors in the name of "what was best for me." This system governed my world in ways big and small. I've shared some of this before: in the culture of my childhood, I was barred from white-water rafting in favor of baking, and I was told that becoming a wife was central to my identity rather than one facet of it. These people, like More, were certain they knew better than I. And these people, like More, meant well. I knew that, so I believed them for a long time. But in doing all I could to follow their rules, I had to ignore the voice inside myself. Hannah More felt like a specter from the past I had escaped.

Yet if this were simply the story of one woman becoming more conservative with age, I don't think I would have kept coming back to More. Had that been the case, I would have concluded that she was not for me and moved on. But she resisted simplification at nearly every turn. When More fully embraced her role as guardian of conservative morals, she didn't just play the part of patriarchy's puppet. She also took up the cause of abolition, publishing and persuading on behalf of the anti-slavery cause. She established schools across the countryside where poor children had never before enjoyed access to any kind of formal education. She worked tirelessly among those communities to ensure resources were arranged so that parents could—and wanted—to send their kids to school.

At the same time, she taught these lower-class children that they should be happy with their place and believed strongly in a "God-given" social class structure that must be respected. She gave and raised enormous sums for charities, but also recommended funds only be given to "virtuous" poor people (as determined, naturally, by her own values). She was eager to use her talents to reward those like her, while righteously withholding her tremendous resources from those she deemed unfit.

On the other *other* hand, More was consistent in her critical eye across

classes: the conduct book that some of her fellow Bluestockings had objected to was filled with valid criticisms of upper-class society. Over the
course of her career, Hannah More managed to write something that upset
just about every kind of potential reader. Including me.

As I continued my research into the life and works of Hannah More,
I realized that I had started listening to Tori Amos again. Specifically, I
kept playing *Under the Pink,* her second solo record and the one that I had
become obsessed with as a freshman at Brigham Young University (BYU). I
would say that I had chosen to attend but, as a seventeen-year-old applying
to colleges, I didn't think that places like MIT, Brown, or Harvard would
want a girl like me, raised in Idaho and Las Vegas, sporting a strong but undistinguished academic record. So when I scored high enough on my ACT
to qualify for a full-tuition scholarship at BYU, the decision was obvious. I
didn't even apply anywhere else.

The Church's university would take me because I was one of their
own. I had followed the rules. I had earned their scholarship because I met
their intellectual standards and could maintain their moral ones. No sex,
no alcohol, no coffee, no boys in my room, no skirts above the knee; weekly
church attendance, daily prayer, nightly scripture study, respect for priest-
hood authority. I would have been a star student in one of Hannah More's
charitable projects.

I continued meeting the standards to keep my scholarship. I not only
had to maintain a high grade point average, but I was tested regularly by
the strict moral guidelines of the university. One such requirement was an
annual "ecclesiastical endorsement": each student had to undergo an interview with their religious leader to demonstrate they were in good standing.
This meant, in practice, that attendance to the three hours of church every
Sunday was mandatory, or else one's bishop could withhold his endorsement. I was reminded of these uncomfortable interviews—in which older
men asked blunt questions not only about my religious beliefs, but also
about other intimate topics like my sexual conduct—when reading a letter
by Hannah More. In it, she recounted with pride an annual festival they
had established for "the children and poor women":

> **As the morals of my own sex are the great object of my re-
> gard, I have made it a standing rule at these anniversaries,
> that every young woman bred in my school, and belonging
> to the club, who has been married during the preceding year,
> and can produce a testimonial of her good conduct from the
> parish minister and schoolmistress, is presented by me with
> a public reward, consisting of a crown-piece, a pair of white
> stockings of my own knitting, and a handsome Bible.**

More had just described almost the exact same system that I had ad-
hered to in order to maintain my scholarship. A bachelor's degree was my
crown piece, white stockings, and handsome Bible. I was proud of it because I had earned it. But there was a cost.

Hannah More's interpretation of religion required constant effort to
"humble the sinner and exalt the Saviour." Just as Hannah More taught
her students, my experience at that university felt like an epic battle of good
vs. evil. When I read Hannah More describing raunchy popular ballads as
"poison for the soul," it reminded me of my own Sunday school teachers
asserting that the music I liked would "drive the Spirit away." When More
wrote approvingly of a Sunday school organizer refusing to grant a job to
an otherwise qualified woman because "she used to send her children to
the shop on Sundays," I recalled a time working at a departmental library,
when a professor refused to hand me the papers I needed after she saw that
a sliver of my midriff had been revealed while reaching up to a high shelf to
grab a book. When I read More's tract describing the virtuous shepherd's
wife patching her husband's clothing, I was taken back to the moment when
another professor advised me that if I couldn't find "modest" clothing at
stores, I should sew my own.

As I read about the incredible system of education and charitable organizations that Hannah More and her sisters had built across the countryside, I kept seeing traces of the community I had once belonged to and
left. Yet it wasn't only the bad memories. In the clubs the More sisters organized for women, where each member would contribute funds that helped

care for the needs of other women in distress, I saw the clipboard calendar passed around at my church. We used it to sign up for making meals for the neighbor who'd just had a baby. I worked hard to follow the rules not because I was meek or weak-willed, but because I earnestly *wanted* to be good. I saw how being good could help others. My community taught me that.

But while I did these things, I ached for some reason I couldn't name. The people who cared about me had said that these rules would lead me to happiness and I believed them. But I can still remember a persistent, gnawing void lurking within me as I walked home from a late class during the Utah winter at night, the mountains looming so high in the background. Treading through the dark and snow, listening to the songs of Tori Amos, I could imagine someone truer than the person I was projecting on campus. It was the person I had been fighting for when I was that tomboy kid, clumsily rebelling by turning against pink, flowers, and romance novels. I hadn't yet won that battle as a college student, and fighting it was a daily effort. Tori Amos was my comfort while I struggled with that contradiction. These were the same songs that I instinctively reached for now when I thought about More.

Every time I had picked up a biography of More—and in the end, I read half a dozen—I stopped after Garrick's death. I hadn't wanted to keep reading. Because I knew what was coming. While More would remain close friends with the Bluestocking circle, her interests were taking her deeper into questions of morality. I had already read plenty of her writings from this period: I had known what Hannah More thought about things like novels. And I had recognized the philosophy behind her value system because I had grown up with it.

Experiencing it again was wretched. I found myself sitting for ten minutes at a time with a Hannah More biography in my lap, staring at nothing. This, too, is part of reading. What we feel when we read does not remain on the page. We take it with us. We absorb it. It doesn't have to change us, exactly (though it can), but it does affect us. It becomes part of the accumulation of all the little moments that make up our lives. Whether you read for education, for understanding, for a challenge, for fun, for relaxation, for escape, for another reason, or any combination of these, those hours have meaning. Reading is a solitary act that nevertheless connects you to others. It sets your interiority ablaze with ideas, connections, disagreements, or pleasures. In the process, you also learn to recognize—and to value—the world inside your own mind.

So More's most famous writing kept reminding me of all the voices around me as I grew up. So what? I had ultimately rejected them because I had learned that all my efforts trying to please others had only led to a fractured self. I say this matter-of-factly now. But that process was agonizing: to learn how to stop listening to others, and instead to look within myself for the answers. I loved the community I was born in. I loved much of what they taught me. Many of the personality traits that I'm most proud of—my capacity for hard work, my dedication to charitable projects and community building—were shaped by that world. I did not want to leave it. But I had to. It was the only way to survive. More: it was the only way I felt I could live a moral life. I could not be of much help to others while I lied to myself.

I broke from my community long ago. This many years later, I really thought I had made my peace with it. But reading about Hannah More had taken me back to that time, and there those feelings were again. So here I was, picking up, then setting down each More biography, letting them pile one on top of the other.

It was at this point that the serendipity of book collecting showed me the way forward, as it often does. A book can pull you back to the past, but it can also reveal a bridge to the future. The cofounder of my rare book company and I had been called to Florida in the middle of summer to look at a collection of children's books. I would normally not choose to visit Florida in August, but these were excellent copies of first editions, primarily picture books written or illustrated by major artists like Maurice Sendak. It included a shelf full of books illustrated by Leo and Diane Dillon, whose rising reputation deserves to soar higher still; and even signed limited editions of the children's books written by Madonna.

There were over one thousand books, and even though they were mostly picture-book thin, they filled about eighty banker's boxes. (Banker's boxes, made of cardboard with handles on the side and engineered to hold weight securely without tape, are an antiquarian book dealer's beloved tool of the trade. We measure in banker's boxes: "How big was the collection?" "Oh, it was twenty-five banker's boxes.") After a steaming morning packing books at an outside storage unit, among all those banker's boxes we hauled away at the end of the week was one upon which the seller had scribbled in Sharpie a single word: "Early." It was a bit of a grab bag situation; we had no idea what was in there, only that it was filled with books from before 1900.

Back in the office after U-Hauling those banker's boxes nearly one thousand miles, I finally dug into that one marked "Early." Most of what I found in it were chapbooks, the format of Hannah More's Cheap Repository Tracts: those palm-sized booklets, generally containing only eight or sixteen pages, illustrated with crude woodcuts. But what caught my eye was a book about the size of a trade paperback, hardbound in full sheepskin.

The leather of the binding was cracked and rubbed, not uncommon for sheep, which takes wear much harder than calfskin or goatskin. Yet this book also had large patches of scraping along the boards that I could not account for. A trained eye can often tell the cause of damage on a book: the path of a bookworm, the tidemark of moisture exposure, the chemical impurities in bleached paper that blossom into brownish spots called foxing. But here, sections of the binding had been gouged away, as if someone had angrily scratched it. Or maybe that was me projecting, knowing that this book contained the assertion that reading novels for amusement will "nourish a vain and visionary indolence, which lays the mind open to error and the heart to seduction." I had in my hands More's *Strictures on the Modern System of Female Education.*

This copy was published in Boston in 1802. Three years earlier, in 1799, the first edition was issued in London at arguably the height of Hannah More's influence as a public moralist. I hadn't gone looking for a copy of this. But now it was here, I could no longer ignore it. The season was finally turning, and I prepared myself to read. I pulled out wool socks and a quilted blanket. I made chai, listening to Tori Amos as I ground the green cardamom pods and star anise, macerated the ginger, steeped the tea leaves. Curled up in my armchair, I opened the ragged book to the first leaves, the blank ones that were added as part of the binding process in this period.

I always look for signs of previous readers in the books I handle, what is called their provenance, and these blank leaves are the most common spot for ownership markings. Just as we do today, readers going back hundreds of years in Western culture would write their name on the leaf at the beginning of their book to claim ownership. But so many books pass from hand to hand anonymously. We don't know where they've been. For all I know, I may have held books that Hannah More herself actually owned.

For this reason, I love when a book has clear marks of ownership. They reveal a bit of the mystery in that book's life: where it has been, whose lives it has possibly changed. This book had multiple names in it, dated between 1803 and 1830, all women. I wondered if it was one of them who had scratched the binding.

When reading a book from the nineteenth century, an awareness of its physicality never leaves you. These leaves had mellowed into a deep brown because of the cheap quality of paper. Many people think paper goes brown because of age, but only poorly made paper does: expensive books with handmade paper often look stunning white even after hundreds of years. This was not one of those books. It was a deep tan with only a touch of creaminess. The book also smelled, though not with that welcome hint of aged vanilla that comes from lignin, a compound found in paper from about 1850 onward. This book smelled like dust and deterioration. It smelled like I should wash my hands before touching anything else. The typeface, too, spoke to the book's era. The printer had chosen one that included the long *s*, a now defunct stylistic choice that modern readers often mistake for an *f*—although they can be distinguished by the fact that the crossbar of the long *s* doesn't go all the way through, and is printed only on the left side of the vertical line.

These factors, along with countless other tiny details, changed how it felt to be reading this book. It's not that it felt more important or meaning-ful. But it did feel like an event. I knew that I would remember the color of the paper, that particular smell, the strain I felt as I took in the typeface.

I started to read, and immediately, I was unnerved. The first paragraph of *Strictures on the Modern System of Female Education* was so unsettling because it was so right. It began, "It is a singular injustice which is often exercised towards women, first to give them a very defective education, and then to expect from them the most undeviating purity of conduct;—to train them in such a manner as shall lay them open to the most dangerous faults, and then to censure them for not proving faultless." Based upon what I knew of More, I had not expected her to express such empathy for those she was criticizing.

Because she had a track record of upholding patriarchal power struc-tures, such as her insistence that the domestic was women's proper sphere, I had viewed More as something of an anti-feminist. Yet this opening read remarkably like arguments in Mary Wollstonecraft's *A Vindication of the Rights of Women* (1792), which is widely considered one of the most influen-tial proto-feminist works in English.

But Hannah More had been writing specifically to *counter* works like Wollstonecraft's, I'd thought. Wollstonecraft's book had been in dialogue with Thomas Paine's *Rights of Man*; she was a known Jacobin, that is, some-one who supported the values of the French Revolution. Hannah More was her political opposite. Yet here was Hannah More, opening her book by pointing out the hypocrisy of neglecting women's education, then at-tacking women for living up to the very standards of shallowness that were encouraged for success on the marriage market. Mary Wollstonecraft made these same arguments throughout *Vindication*, criticizing conduct books for saying "that the minds of women are enfeebled by false refinement" while also directing them that marriage is their primary objective.

This wasn't the only time I agreed with More. In fact, a number of More's points about the education of young women made sense to me. For one, she encouraged the act of study because gaining knowledge takes "time and industry." Learning how to apply oneself is an impor-tant skill taught in schools today to all students, but it opposed a common eighteenth-century philosophy of educating genteel women, where the focus was on surface-level achievement of skills—just enough to prepare them for the marriage market. Once again, Mary Wollstonecraft made this same argument, stating that women

> **are still reckoned a frivolous sex, and ridiculed or pitied by the writers who endeavour by satire or instruction to improve them. It is acknowledged that they spend many of the first years of their lives in acquiring a smattering of accomplishments; meanwhile strength of body and mind are sacrificed to libertine notions of beauty, to the desire of establishing themselves,—the only way women can rise in the world,—by marriage.**

Wollstonecraft says here that girls are raised to learn the basics of accomplishments that will help them get married, but with none of the knowledge of healthy habits that would benefit their minds and bodies beyond that. More makes the same point in *Strictures*. In fact, a thorough reading of *A Vindication of Rights of Women* might surprise many modern readers who have only heard of it as the bastion of early feminist thought. Like More did after her, Wollstonecraft criticized "the women who are amused by the reveries of the stupid novelists" who write books that "equally tend to corrupt the taste, and draw the heart aside from its daily duties."

Both More and Wollstonecraft tackled the philosophy behind the current education of young women, and in this they found a common enemy. Is the enemy of one's enemy a friend? Actually, no: More wrote to a friend of *Vindication* that "there is something fantastic and absurd in the very title [. . .] there is perhaps no animal so much indebted to subordination for its good behaviour, as woman." They remained politically opposed on this, and many, fronts. But the fact that they could agree on this subject felt important to me. Not because I wanted to like Hannah More—I disagreed with them both in the case of novel reading—but because I wanted to understand her. She deserved an acknowledgment of her own complexity. A recognition of her accomplishments, without excusing her faults.

In the same chapter that Hannah More argued for young women to learn how to study, she also described novels as a "corruption." I'd first read *that* passage when I had been trying to understand Frances Burney. But when I read it this time, in this worn sheepskin copy from 1802, that particular section was marked by a single leaf that had been pressed between the pages. The leaf had lived there so long that a shadow of its form had marked the paper. Perhaps it meant nothing. But as I worked to make peace with Hannah More, I saw significance in it for myself. Another reader, long ago, had stopped on this page too.

Strictures remains on my shelf.

———

There is some evidence that Austen may have read and made use of *Strictures*, too. Scholars have noted traces of More's educational philosophy particularly in *Mansfield Park*. The heroine Fanny Price, something of a famous stick-in-the-mud herself, "embodies the lesson in Hannah More's *Strictures* [. . .] that a woman needs studies which avoid display but which 'will lead her to think,'" observed the modern Austen biographer Park Honan: "Hannah More is at the centre of *Mansfield Park*."

But bringing the shadow of Hannah More into Austen's novel is dangerous business; Austen is still her own person, and this is her book. *Mansfield Park* is a "subtle, dark, and difficult book," in which Austen ultimately diverges from More artistically. Austen didn't take up novel writing as a necessary evil, in the way More did with her novel *Coelebs*. Austen took up novel writing because she loved novel reading, and she enjoyed composing in the same format as her favorite books. We know Austen didn't wholeheartedly agree with More's worldview; in telling her sister Cassandra why she didn't want to read *Coelebs*, she said simply "I do not like the Evangelicals." Austen could use the form to agree with More in some instances, and to dispute with her in others.

When we flatten people from history into icons—Hannah More, the self-righteous moral authority; Mary Wollstonecraft, the rebellious feminist; Jane Austen, the quiet literary genius; Ann Radcliffe, the mad artist—it is so much harder to recognize their humanity, which is where their artistry ultimately lies. Austen's male relatives tried to simplify her into the nineteenth-century ideal of the sweet, nurturing "Aunt Jane." But the real Austen couldn't even remain consistent with herself: in 1809 she had asserted to Cassandra that she didn't like Evangelicals—yet five years later she wrote to her niece that "I am by no means convinced that we ought not all to be Evangelicals." Those contradictory statements made her much more human to me than that unnervingly anodyne vision of Aunt Jane.

I couldn't simplify More either. And, finally, I didn't want to. In this long process of reading, of beginning and stopping, returning and reexamining, I was coming to appreciate all the mixed-up feelings she inspired in me. By acknowledging these feelings for what they were, it gradually became easier to let them go. I could give Tori Amos a rest and let Hannah More just . . . be.

I decided then that I would give her novel *Coelebs* another try. It had been the novel that neither Austen nor I wanted to read. But the time I had spent investigating More's other works had been so productive that I felt maybe I too would "be delighted" with it, when I had actually read it.

Well, no. It turns out that I wasn't. In *Coelebs*, Hannah More puts her opinions about a proper wife into the mouth of her hero, thus finding an even more efficient way than letters, or poetry, or chapbooks to make her judgment unbearable. With every new conversation begun by *Coelebs*, my heart rate accelerated, my body responding as if I was preparing for a fight. It was not relaxing, or enjoyable, or satisfying, or even educational. It was not at all delightful. It just made me mad.

I had initially challenged myself to continue reading Hannah More despite disliking her. Then I kept feeling guilty giving up on her novel so soon. But one can take an idea too far. It's not Hannah More, or Jane Austen, or literary critics, or my parents, or my friends, or my community that determine how I spend my time. I do. I wanted to read Hannah More's books. And then I didn't. So I stopped. In that way, *Coelebs* was the most liberating reading experience I had yet.

Chapter Six

CHARLOTTE SMITH
(1749-1806)

> "You have read Mrs Smith's Novels, I suppose?" said she to her Companion—. "Oh! Yes," replied the other, "and I am quite delighted with them—They are the sweetest things in the world."
>
> —Jane Austen, *Catharine, or the Bower*

Charlotte Smith was one of the most popular and prolific novelists of her time, but most of those novels never became classics. They weren't meant to be: she wrote them to meet her most immediate need, for money. Who cares about legacy when creditors are knocking at your door?

In 1797, Smith wrote to a friend and patron about her financial distress. She already enjoyed a stellar reputation as a poet and created a solid writing career from the publication of her very first novel, *Emmeline* (1788)—a favorite of Austen's—but she still had not achieved financial stability. "I imagine I shall die in a prison," Charlotte Smith said in this grim letter to the poet William Hayley. Smith had been counting on a payment of £100 from her father-in-law's estate, legally due via his will and granted by the will's trustees. But the trustees seem to have changed their minds about how the payment should be executed, and delayed payment in full. Smith received only £10. Bankers began calling in her debts, and Smith was in real danger of going to prison.

Yes, in eighteenth-century England one could be imprisoned for debt.

Lenders could work with a judge to issue a warrant for the debtor's arrest, then the debtor would remain in prison until he paid off the loan (often through manual labor) or came to a new agreement with his creditors. Most debtors were men, but not all. In fact, Smith had already spent time with her husband in debtor's prison. And only a few years before she wrote that letter to Hayley, she herself had been briefly returned to debtor's prison for an alleged breach of contract with a publisher, a kind of debt.

Smith had four of her eight living children still counting on her, dependent upon her earnings. Waiting on the whim of the will's trustees was "so disagreeable & indeed dreadful where there is a large family to support," as she wrote to her publisher. She knew she must continue to work. Her husband had failed her; her father's and father-in-law's well-intentioned wills had failed her; the legal system had failed her. But she would not fail her children. In 1797, the year of that grim letter, Smith went on to publish one of her most acclaimed and important sonnets, "On Being Cautioned Against Walking on an Headland," and her publisher agreed to purchase her tenth novel.

I might have been tempted to read this as a triumphant narrative. Smith, ennobled through her suffering, produced great works of art. But in that letter to Hayley, she dismissed any such interpretation: "It is rather despair than fortitude that carries me on." Like Charlotte Lennox before her, Smith wrote to survive. That need would alter the trajectory of Smith's literary career—and have far-reaching consequences as to her place (or lack thereof) in the canon. What might her legacy looked like if she had been able to dedicate herself entirely to her poetic genius?

———

Young Charlotte's life had been shaped by tragedy. Though she was born into a genteel family, her mother died when she was three years old, and Charlotte and her siblings were raised by her aunt. But she had an excellent education arranged by her father and, according to her sister, she quickly developed a reputation for genius: "She had read more than any one in the school, and was continually composing verses." It was a comfortable life in many ways—until her father remarried when Charlotte was fifteen.

Charlotte and her stepmother, a woman with "a considerable fortune," got along poorly. So much so that her stepmother soon began working with her father to get Charlotte married off. For her part, Charlotte was also keen for a solution. If her father were to die before her new stepmother, she would be completely at the whim of a woman who despised her.

Just a few months before her sixteenth birthday, Charlotte married Benjamin Smith, the son of a rich London merchant. But the speed of this resolution gave Charlotte, then a teenager, little time to get to know her fiancé before marriage. Many years later, Charlotte would conclude that her father and aunt "thought it a prodigious stroke of domestic policy to sell me like a Southdown sheep." Her marriage was handled like a market transaction, without much consideration of the consequences. And it was a disaster.

Charlotte and Benjamin were poorly suited. She was a highly educated woman of sensibility, whose poems later in life would be so influential as to redefine the English sonnet and inspire other Romantic poets like Wordsworth and Coleridge. He was a high-stakes gambler, incapable of holding a job, who almost immediately took up mistresses after their marriage. But if only their worst conflicts had been ones of personality.

Benjamin lied, he cheated, he constantly breached contracts, he spent every cent that came into his possession, and he beat her. All the while he kept getting her pregnant: she bore ten children in the first twelve years of their marriage.

In 1783, after eighteen years of a miserable marriage, Benjamin was arrested and thrown into debtor's prison for the first time. Charlotte lived with him there on and off, working while away to arrange deals with his creditors and otherwise find the means to pay off the debts. On one of the occasions when she spent the night there, some prisoners attempted to escape by "blowing up the walls of the house." She described the scene with terror: "watching at the window, and expecting every moment to [. . .] perhaps be overwhelmed by the projected explosion."

During the day, the once genteel woman of sensibility found herself in the humiliating position of begging lawyers, merchants, and moneylenders for a compromise. According to Mary Hays, one of her earliest biographers (and friend of Mary Wollstonecraft), this was the period when Charlotte first learned "the chicanery of law." She struggled against it all while caring for yet another infant: she had born her eleventh child just the year before. During the period when Charlotte stayed in the prison with Benjamin, he got her pregnant for the twelfth time.

Over the years, Smith had composed poetry purely for her own pleasure. But after Benjamin's imprisonment, she decided to try to sell a volume of her sonnets as a way to make money to pay his debts. The publisher at first blithely informed her that he would publish it, but without payment because "for such things there was no sale," as "the public had been satiated with shepherds and shepherdesses." The bucolic verses of yore that Smith wrote were not in. Determined nonetheless, Smith secured a famous patron, the poet William Hayley, for the dedication—and the publisher now agreed to take it. Smith would only receive payment, however, by royalties from the book's sales.

Elegiac Sonnets (1784) was a hit, going almost immediately into a second edition. Mary Hays called these poems "exquisite," observing that "their melody, feeling, and pathos touch the heart." Smith was an extraordinary poet. Throughout her lifetime, *Elegiac Sonnets* would continue to be the most successful of her works, with nine editions and an additional volume added over the next sixteen years. But poetry doesn't pay *that* well, not even in the eighteenth century. The royalties allowed Smith to pay the rent and feed her children while her husband was in prison, but they weren't enough to get him released.

Nevertheless, Charlotte kept negotiating with Benjamin's creditors and they finally reached a compromise. The creditors required the removal of Benjamin as an executor of his father's will, which had made lavish provisions for other family members that Benjamin had not followed as required in that role. They agreed to this stipulation, and Benjamin came home.

It was a short-lived victory. Benjamin stayed in England only a few weeks before running from his creditors to France. Benjamin didn't speak French.

Her husband summoned Charlotte a few months later in October 1784, insisting that the family follow him despite the difficulties of moving an entire household, including nine children, just before winter, to another country. At least Charlotte did speak French.

Charlotte oversaw the voyage alone across the channel with their children, "so many little beings clinging about me (the youngest, whom I bore in my arms, scarce two years old)." Also, she was beginning the third trimester of the twelfth pregnancy. Benjamin, meanwhile, had invested in canaries. As her modern biographer Loraine Fletcher put it in a deadpan I couldn't help but admire, he was planning "to recover a fortune through breeding them; his concern for these birds had prevented him from meeting his wife and children." When they arrived at the harbor with no sign of the family patriarch, Charlotte arranged for last-minute transportation by carriage and paid the correspondingly extravagant fees.

Benjamin had rented an isolated, disused castle on the recommendation of some gambling friends. It was unprepared for habitation, especially by young children, and Charlotte was about to give birth. They had difficulty obtaining fuel to keep warm. The market was miles away, as was the closest midwife, who had to reach her through the snow using a farm cart. This was her twelfth labor but, according to her sister's account, Smith told her she had "forebodings that she should not survive the birth of her child."

She did survive the labor, but it was her last. Sometime during this harrowing experience in the winter of 1784, Smith finally decided she could not continue this way of life. She had first become a published author with the *Elegiac Sonnets*, but at that time she didn't intend to continue publishing. Her decision to begin a career as an author began in that isolated, disused castle. She wrote more poems, planning to add them to the upcoming new edition of *Elegiac Sonnets*, and started translating French books she had been reading to pass the time. As soon as the weather cleared, she returned to England with her children.

Back home, Smith found that her fame as a poet had continued to rise—*Elegiac Sonnets* would go through its fourth edition by 1786—and she worked on publishing her translations. Thanks in part to her growing reputation, Smith was able to negotiate new terms with her husband's creditors, and Benjamin too came home. But even while she looked after Benjamin's interests, Charlotte began thinking of ways to take care of herself and her children without him. She was planning to leave him. Yet if she managed it, she would have to forfeit part of her inheritance, a legal reality that the classicist Elizabeth Carter would later describe as having to "purchase her freedom from a vile husband." She would have to make more money.

Charlotte Smith was no longer a gentlewoman who published poems under difficult circumstances, written for her own pleasure. Now she approached her publishers as a businesswoman, looking to establish regular work beyond her preferred genre. She published her first novel, *Emmeline*, the year after her separation from Benjamin in 1788.

Upon her marriage, Smith had become a *femme couverte*, a "protected woman." This was the legal name for the status of women after they married and came under the "protection" of their husbands, known as coverture. It sounds nice on the surface. But coverture also meant that husbands had complete legal control over their wives—and it still applied to Charlotte after she separated from Benjamin. William Blackstone, who published an authoritative survey of British common law the same year as the Smiths' marriage in 1765, described the philosophy underlying this status: "the very being or legal existence of the woman is suspended during the marriage, or at least is incorporated and consolidated into that of the husband." Blackstone considered this a suitable measure, as it meant that a married woman could not, for instance, be imprisoned for debt. Except that's not how it worked out in practice. Once when Charlotte turned in two volumes instead of the three stipulated in her contract, the publisher had her arrested, not Benjamin.

Coverture affected all aspects of a woman's life, as Smith knew only too well. In eighteenth-century England, married women could not own property apart from their husbands. Even if they technically had funds separate from their husbands, male relatives or representatives still had control over their access to those funds. When she petitioned for money legally due to her from the interest on her own dowry or the inheritance from her father, she had to approach the male trustees of her father's estate. She had no "legal existence."

In practice, this meant that if any of those men did not approve of her reason for wanting the money (say, because she left her husband), were too busy dealing with other matters, or simply did not like her, then Smith would not receive any money. That happened often. In one letter, she remarked bitterly that instead of sending the funds legally owed to her, one trustee had sardonically advised her to use "<u>my admirable talents</u>" [*sic*] and earn the money she needed by writing more. She did. She also spent decades fighting these men in court. She had to. All the children chose to remain with Charlotte after the separation, living on a fraction of the annual income they had been brought up to expect. Benjamin contributed nothing to their financial support.

Even the funds she earned from her writing were not entirely in her control. As a *femme couverte*, any of Charlotte's earnings were legally her husband's. She learned early that Benjamin would forcibly take them. The month before the publication of *Emmeline* in 1788, Benjamin returned from hiding (again) in France to collect the semiannual interest payment of his father's estate. Charlotte and eight of their children, ages two to eighteen, were living quietly in a cottage in Surrey. Benjamin asked to meet and Charlotte agreed, to "convince him I had no malice against him." Benjamin used the opportunity to take "possession of [the house] & treated me with his more than usual brutality—threatening to sell the furniture, the Books, and every necessary which I have twice saved from the rapacity of his Creditors."

These intimate details are known today because she recorded them in a letter to her publisher (and Burney's), Thomas Cadell Sr., as context for her warning that Benjamin would come to him in London next. She recommended that Cadell immediately remove the funds owed to her from his premises—either "pay it into the hands of your own Banker or any confidential friend"—so that Cadell wouldn't have to hand the funds to Benjamin if he showed up. Of course, just because the funds weren't on his premises didn't mean Cadell wouldn't have to pay Benjamin in the end if he pressed. However, in that case Benjamin would have to specially petition for them—a trickier endeavor for someone temporarily in town and on the run from creditors. Charlotte ended the letter requesting to her publisher that "if he calls at your shop as I find he has already done, you will give him no information whatever As to the Sonnets or any thing else."

Legally, he was justified. Charlotte was his wife, even now. The house, the belongings, and the profits were his property. In this instance, as in many others referred to in Smith's letters, we don't know exactly how these situations ended. But we do know that such events left Smith feeling hounded. In another letter over a decade later, Smith described renewed hopes that she would receive a "proper distribution" of funds owed her, but "Alas! No—Mr Smith himself is come from Scotland to oppose it. He wants to take not only my fortune but all that his Father left his Children to his own use [. . .] What we are now to do I have no guess, & yet I cannot escape from the misery of being worried with it all."

The original justification for coverture was that it granted legal protection to powerless women. Often, it provided legal protection to ill-behaving men. The law did not just put a wife's property into the hands of her husband; it made *her* property too. Stripped of a legal existence, wives had little recourse if they had the misfortune to marry an abusive husband. As long as Benjamin lived, Charlotte was legally under his power.

Separation was Smith's best solution in an impossible situation, and it was still an imperfect one. Divorce was out of the question. Not only would Smith lose the funds bequeathed to her by her father-in-law, but she would also seriously jeopardize her father-in-law's bequests to her children—funds she spent her entire lifetime fighting to keep safe. The law did not look kindly upon divorced mothers, and Smith would not give up the little advantages she had.

When Elizabeth Carter said that Smith had to "purchase her freedom from a vile husband," the purchase price was something like half of Smith's own inheritance. She accepted this in large part because she felt that she couldn't stay with her abusive, profligate, adulterous husband any longer, who had a temper "so capricious and often so cruel that my life was not safe."

Smith's sister, Catherine Ann Dorset, noted in a posthumous biography that many considered Smith's quick separation "injudicious" because "she should have insisted on legal arrangements, and secured herself the enjoyment of her own fortune." But Dorset, who had a much more intimate understanding of her sister's situation, disagreed. Smith's decision was made "with the entire approbation of her most dispassionate and judicious friends" and was "perhaps, under the then existing circumstances, unavoidable." Dorset added that "those who knew [. . .] could only regret the measure had not been adopted years before." Half her inheritance to escape Benjamin was, apparently, an acceptable price to pay. But it was a heavy one. "[I]t really is almost too much for me," she wrote to a friend after publishing her second novel to great success in 1789, "to be compelled to live only to write & write only to live."

More disastrously, Smith's children found themselves vulnerable despite her efforts to shield them. Charlotte's father-in-law, Richard Smith, had settled a large portion of his wealth onto his grandchildren. But he knew his son well, and he took elaborate steps in his will to keep Benjamin from suborning his wishes. Unfortunately, he developed those elaborate steps without the help of a lawyer. The resulting will was both confusing and, in some places, contradictory. And even though Richard had made Charlotte an "executrix to his will," alongside Benjamin and his widow, her legal status as a *femme couverte* "rendered [it] ineffectual."

Richard's will had also provided £200 a year for Charlotte, "the magic sum necessary," biographer Loraine Fletcher says, "for freedom from want and a small measure of independence"—and, indeed, the same amount that had provided independence for Hannah More after her suspended engagement. But Smith never received it because of disputes over the will's wording with the male trustees. Intra-family fights about how to execute the will would last beyond both Charlotte's and Benjamin's lifetimes. According to the modern scholar Judith Phillips Stanton, the value of the estate at the time of Richard's death in 1776 was £36,000—but by 1813, when the children finally got their settlement, "decades of delay and litigation had reduced the estate's value to about £4,000."

Amid these setbacks, Smith still tried to raise her children in an environment that matched her own upbringing as a gentlewoman. She sought marriages for her daughters befitting the dowry expectations of their inheritance and set her sons up in careers appropriate to their status. In another instance, Smith used funds from her writing and, with the help of wealthy friends, purchased her son Charles a commission in the military. Later in life, she felt she had made a mistake in trying to maintain this upper-class lifestyle; whenever tragedies befell her children, she felt her lack of cash keenly. During the same year of the release of Smith's now most acclaimed novel, *The Old Manor House* (1793), Charles was wounded in battle. When his leg was amputated after, he again became financially dependent upon his mother. A few months later, her son Lionel decided to take up Charles's commission—in large part because Smith could no longer afford his tuition at Oxford. Lamenting that she was "denied the means" of keeping him out of the military, she wrote to a friend about her fears that he would suffer a similar fate as his brother, or worse: "I shall probably never see him again." She kept writing. In 1794, she published two novels, *The Wanderings of Warwick* and *The Banished Man*.

Smith's financial distress continued to have a direct impact on how her career as an author evolved. Over the course of the 1790s, she published eight novels, three children's books, and another book of poetry (in addition to composing further sonnets for new editions of *Elegiac Sonnets*). When it came to the novels, Charlotte was paid by the volume, so she wrote most of them to be as long as she could: in three, four, or even five volumes. More volumes, more money. We like to believe an artist creates whatever they are inspired to create. But they are subject to the same forces the rest of us are: gravity, time, the need for money to purchase food and shelter. As in the case of Lennox's rushed publication of *The Female Quixote*, the financial realities of an author's life can often have a direct effect on what they produce. Similar to Smith, Charles Dickens was often paid by the installment, and thus he wrote epic novels spread across hundreds of pages. But Smith didn't want to write novels at all. She did so because they brought the most consistent and manageable stream of income for an author at that time.

If she hadn't needed to earn money, her reputation over the generations might have been different. She might even have kept the fame she enjoyed in her lifetime and become part of the canon—as a poet.

Her poetry belongs in the same breath as that of Wordsworth and Coleridge. If she had been able to dedicate herself entirely to that kind of writing, maybe we would include her name when we speak of theirs. Nevertheless, she influenced them both in formative ways. Young Wordsworth looked up to Smith ever since his grammar school teacher lent him a copy of *Elegiac Sonnets*. The very first poem he published, the 1787 "Sonnet on Seeing Miss Helen Maria Williams Weep," imitates Smith's style. He returned to her sonnets throughout his life, as when his sister recorded his Christmas Eve activity in 1802, "turning over the leaves of Charlotte Smith's sonnets." Wordsworth recognized his own debt to her in describing Smith as "a lady to whom English verse is under greater obligations than are likely to be either acknowledged or remembered."

Nor was her poetry some eccentric side interest of Wordsworth's. Critics, too, were naming Charlotte Smith one of the main poets who revived the English sonnet. This form of poetry, embraced by such greats as Milton in the seventeenth century, had fallen out of fashion by the early eighteenth century. The publication of *Elegiac Sonnets* in 1784 marked its resurrection. By 1796, Coleridge put together a pamphlet of sonnets that celebrated the form in which he lavishly praised Smith alongside his own favorite, William Lisle Bowles, as "they who first made the Sonnet popular among the present English." Bowles, for his part, wrote poetry so similar to Smith's in form that critics did not fail to point them out as imitations of hers. Coleridge also composed sonnets that, according to the modern critic Daniel Robinson, "followed directly Charlotte Smith's lead."

Smith's style was so well known that other poets even satirized her, like William Beckford's 1797 "Elegiac Sonnet to a Mopstick," which is definitely the eighteenth-century sign that you've made it. By 1802, the *Critical Review* was stating with confidence that the "sonnet has been revived by Charlotte Smith: her sonnets are assuredly the most popular in the language, and deservedly so."

When I first thought of collecting works by Smith, I had assumed I'd be searching for her novels. But as I read more about Smith, about her life and her work, I decided to look for a copy of her first book of poetry.

———————

One of our funny quirks as humans is that we attach meaning to objects that don't inherently carry it. Whether it's a beloved stuffed animal from childhood or a wedding ring, we are moved by symbolism: what an object represents to us beyond the cotton fabric or the gold band. The word for this is cathexis, and book collectors are particularly susceptible to it. I know I am.

I liked the idea of hunting down the book that first gave Smith the hope that writing might free her from her husband. Its ongoing success helped her feed and clothe her children. As I was reading about each subsequent edition of *Elegiac Sonnets* published, the book became a symbol to me of that hope. It was also the book that represented all the different potential paths of Smith's career. There are quantum parallel universes out there in which Smith did not need to write to live and instead could dedicate herself entirely to poetry. Considering how much she influenced the course of English poetry from the limited circumstances under which she did write, imagine what the result could have been if she had been able to embrace it as fully as Wordsworth and Coleridge were able to.

Yet there's another quantum parallel universe in which Smith might not be remembered at all. Smith had decided to publish *Elegiac Sonnets* in the first place with the goal of obtaining funds to release her husband from debtor's prison. If Smith's life had gone according to plan, she may never have published *Elegiac Sonnets*, or any book. If her mother lived, or her father not remarried; if she never met Benjamin Smith, or his father properly consulted lawyers when writing his will; if she had legal control over her own inheritance, or that of her children; if the men in her life weren't wielding their power so unjustly, Charlotte Smith may never have needed to publish. If, if, if.

I was fascinated by the pivotal role *Elegiac Sonnets* played in Smith's life and career. It was not just the mechanism for Smith taking control of her own life, but it also symbolized the path of another life, a poet's life, that she had wanted and never quite obtained. I wanted that for her. She has finally begun to achieve that, in a way, in modern scholarship: Charlotte Smith's critical revival in the last few decades has focused largely on her poetry. Today, academics like Jacqueline M. Labbe put her poetry next to Wordsworth's and argue for "Smith's centrality to [. . .] the culture we call Romanticism." When Smith was creating work as a novelist, it was for money. When she was creating work as a poet, it was for art. But the real world intervened in her dreams; she had to prioritize her professional work over her true love, poetry. I could honor that in my collection.

Having set my sights on the *Elegiac Sonnets*, I started tracking copies. I combed through a series of specialist databases of bibliographic information. One such database is WorldCat, an online resource that brings together the catalog records of library holdings across the US and (somewhat) internationally. It's not perfect—in such large-scale aggregation many little errors abound, such as a microfilm copy accidentally getting marked as a true first edition copy—but rare book dealers like myself use it daily to get a sense of how many copies of a particular edition are documented in libraries. Another is Library Hub, a similar online database of library catalogs that I use in conjunction with WorldCat because it has more comprehensive records within its focus, UK and Irish libraries. These databases revealed that there were only about eight known copies of the 1784 first edition held in rare book libraries across the English-speaking world. I found a record of one more copy that appeared at auction in 2013, but no others at all, going back decades. By way of comparison, there are 235 known copies of the famed Shakespeare First Folio (1623), the first printed collection of his plays. The first edition of Smith's *Elegiac Sonnets* is a very rare book.

Its scarcity made sense. Recall that the publisher first attempted to dissuade Smith from publishing it at all, remarking that poetry didn't sell. A first print run testing the waters was very likely a small one, something in the low hundreds. Upon its success, a second—and larger—edition was printed the same year. The number of copies in a first print run isn't a surefire way to gauge how many copies of a book may survive today, but it's helpful context.

I had to admit that I wasn't going to find a first edition of this book anytime soon. I might still be holding out for that first edition of Burney's *Evelina*, printed in a run of five hundred copies, since that felt somewhat possible—even if not terribly probable, like jumping out of a second-story window without injury. But looking for a first edition of Smith's *Elegiac Sonnets* was more like jumping out of a plane without a parachute. I like a challenge, but I'm not a masochist. (See: Hannah More.)

That didn't mean giving up on finding a copy of *Elegiac Sonnets*. I just had to change my strategy. Smith kept writing sonnets as the years went by, sometimes even including them in the text of her novels. She would frequently add these to later editions of *Elegiac Sonnets*, just as Walt Whitman's "O Captain! My Captain!" did not appear in the 1855 first edition of *Leaves of Grass*, but was added to the 1867 edition, after it was composed in response to Lincoln's assassination in 1865.

These kinds of situations speak to why book collecting isn't only about seeking first editions. Rather, it's about seeking a particular copy of a book for a particular reason. First editions offer a compelling reason: they represent the first time the public would have been able to read the book. But there are other compelling reasons to seek other editions. If "O Captain! My Captain!" is your favorite Whitman poem, you want the 1867 edition of *Leaves of Grass*, and not the 1855 first edition. I had realized that I wanted a 1970 edition of *The Female Quixote*, after all.

So I wasn't too disappointed that I wouldn't be able to obtain a first edition of *Elegiac Sonnets*. I liked the idea of seeing Smith's progress. An expanded edition would include the poems of the first edition next to compositions from later years, showing side by side how her style matured over time. I kept seeking the right copy. I would know it when I saw it.

I love this part. I love the looking. I love the notifications for new auctions, the announcements for new dealer catalogs, the emails to our company inbox offering private collections for sale, the out-of-the-blue phone calls when a scout wants to come by to sell us some of their finds. If I didn't love this kind of thing, I would make a terrible rare book dealer. It's tough to work in a retail business where you can't manufacture your product. You have to find it.

This is also one reason why the job can be so frustrating. I keep what we call "want lists" for institutions and collectors: imagine that you have a $10,000 sale waiting, or even a $100,000 sale, if you could just *find that thing*! For years I knew a collector who wanted an original leaf from the Gutenberg Bible (circa 1455), the first substantial book printed with moveable type in Europe. But she only wanted a leaf from the New Testament, while most that appear on the marketplace come from the Old Testament. Because a couple incomplete copies were famously broken up in the twentieth century, individual leaves are indeed obtainable—I have sold a number of them—yet it took me years to find the right leaf for her. It required a great deal of patience, but this is also one reason why the job can be so satisfying. My job is knowing how to find the unfindable, and my success depends on my wits. (It's no wonder the lives of writers like Lennox and Smith appealed to me.)

One day, perhaps two years into searching, I was browsing the listings of a friend and colleague in San Francisco when something caught my eye. His company is somewhat unusual in the US rare book trade: since 1915 it had lived through multiple generations of owners, passed down not to family but to successive booksellers who had worked there. Unusual, too, was the kind of service it provided. The company is of an old-school type that has mostly disappeared in the US, a general antiquarian bookshop open for browsing but with niche specialties depending on the interests of the shop's owner at the time. The last time I visited, I had a twenty-minute conversation about the Victorian fad for the "language of flowers," in which different species of flowers were used to symbolize very specific concepts, almost like a botanical code. (Today we still associate roses with love, but that's only the beginning: bluebells meant kindness, rosemary meant remembrance, and rhododendrons meant danger.)

In many ways, the current owner and the shop fit all the stereotypes of the rare book dealer. Except one. He may look straight out of central casting—he was once featured in the *New York Times* fashion section for his tweed suit—but he does not play the role of curmudgeonly bookseller. In fact, he is a lovely man. For many bibliophiles, and especially for those new to book collecting, walking into a rare book shop can feel both magical and intimidating. But at his shop, he makes sure that it feels only magical. He allays any of his visitors' fears with an easy demeanor and sincere attention. No matter the question you ask, he answers it with care, taking a moment to give it real consideration before he begins to answer.

What's more, this owner has an unusually strong record of researching, buying, and selling the works of women writers. This should not be a remarkable statement. But in the traditionally masculine environment of the US rare book trade—even today, membership in our most elite trade organization is less than 20 percent women—it is. It also gets him my business.

This time, I purchased a book from him sight unseen, without even any pictures. It was a copy of *Elegiac Sonnets,* and his description of the condition was highly favorable. He had called it a fine copy, "fine" here meaning the highest condition grade possible. For a book from the eighteenth century, that doesn't mean it will be flawless; but it means that it is about the nicest you can expect to see. Since I know and trust him, I took him at his word.

I emailed to ask whether I could trouble him to have it sent with an invoice. This is one of the great traditions of the trade among colleagues: the "courtesy" extended to a fellow professional of not requiring payment up front. It is a mark of trust, but it has a practical purpose. Remember, we cannot manufacture our product. You never know where the book you've been seeking will turn up, so traditions like this position dealers to make the most of opportunities. For instance, if I see a copy of a book from one of my collectors' want lists in the shop of another dealer, I will ask them to send it to me "with an invoice" that I will pay once I've offered it to the collector and finalized the deal. A great portion of the trade runs this way; I've literally driven away from bookshops with tens of thousands of dollars' worth of rare books in my trunk and nothing but an IOU to pay for them in a few weeks.

The owner's response in this case was characteristically good humored: "Could you trouble me?? Of course, trouble me all you want. Ms. Smith will be on her way to [you] by sunset."

When it arrived, I dug through the blank newsprint, which had been crumpled up and used as padding for the package. (Always a sign of a traditionally trained dealer, the blank newsprint stuffing. You need cushioning material that is inexpensive, but won't lead to incidental damage; a less experienced dealer might use actual newsprint, a grave mistake when you realize how easily its ink rubs off onto your hands.) I carefully pulled apart the wrapping around the book itself. (Another sign of a traditionally trained dealer, using more of that blank newsprint to wrap the book like a present, which is then typically swathed in bubble wrap to prevent incidental dings, rubbing, or other damage in transit.)

I unfurled two volumes in eighteenth-century bindings. But not just any bindings: tree calf bindings. To create this style, binders add a solution to the surface of the calfskin and sweep outward, creating graceful arcs from a central pillar that often look like branches on a tree. A gilt border had been ruled across the edges of the boards. The spines sprouted leaves and florets in a geometric pattern, interrupted near the top only by red spine labels. The endpapers were marbled, as I had expected for such a beautifully bound book; I immediately noted their swirling pattern in blues and reds across the opening leaves. The paper was a touch musty, but still bright. The entire production was stately and elegant. And it needed to be, for its price of half a guinea (ten shillings, six pence). The typical range for a book of sonnets then would have been two to three shillings. When it first appeared, this edition was more expensive than any other version of Smith's *Elegiac Sonnets*.

These volumes were from the fifth edition, printed in 1789. It was the first subscription edition and the first illustrated edition, ornamented with copperplate engravings, all compelling reasons to consider adding it to my collection. It was an ambitious production for Smith, funded by subscribers who would pay up front for a project and see their names printed in the final product—that same method More used for Ann Yearsley's poetry in 1785 and that Burney would use for *Camilla* seven years later, in 1796 (in which Austen became a subscriber).

The subscription model functioned as high risk, high reward for the author rather than for a publisher. An author might not be able to attract enough subscribers to pay for the production and be forced to cancel it, as happened to Charlotte Lennox at least three separate times over the course of her career: proposals for subscription editions survive for (1) her collected poetry in 1752; (2) a collection of her "original works" (e.g., not translations) in 1775; and (3) a new edition of *Shakespear Illustrated* in 1793. None of these came to fruition.

As Lennox's failed efforts suggest, attracting subscribers was not simple. Books were expensive, rarely purchased outright by those outside of the upper classes due to their cost. Novels in this period were priced on average at three shillings a volume, and most novels were, like Smith's, published in multiple volumes. That meant a three-volume novel cost more than a week's wages for the typical laborer. To make a book a success on the subscription model, the author would need to rely upon an extensive network of wealthy friends. If an author had such a network, it was an appealing option; authors could typically charge more for the subscription edition and reap the financial benefits of the sales directly, as opposed to contracting much of the profits out to the publisher as in a typical publication.

Smith, a gentlewoman with wealthy friends and a well-established reputation for writing some of the best poetry then being composed in England, had no trouble attracting a large group of subscribers for her deluxe edition. The names listed after this edition's new preface were some of the best known in England: General Burgoyne (who had surrendered to the American colonists at Saratoga a decade before); our own Frances Burney; the classicist and Bluestocking Elizabeth Carter (who so disliked Lennox's poetry); the painter George Romney; the gothic originator Horace Walpole; Hannah More's abolitionist friend William Wilberforce; and more. Many subscribed for multiple copies. I couldn't help but be moved as I scanned the names: here were so many people who stepped forward to support her art. This edition, according to the modern scholar Bethan Roberts, "marked the high point of Smith's sonnet success."

The subscription edition made Smith about £180, the most by far she had ever made on a single edition of the *Elegiac Sonnets*. In the meantime, her four- and five-volume novels paid a steady fifty pounds per volume—thanks to the precedent, as Smith described it, of the "price Miss Burney obtain'd, & the fix'd price for works whose Authors are <u>known.</u>" (She was speaking here of Burney's second novel, *Cecilia*; the record-breaking numbers of Radcliffe and Burney's *Camilla* were still to come.) Smith therefore typically received £200 to £250 for each novel, plus an additional payment if they went into another edition. With Smith's steady popularity, nearly every one did. So instead of focusing exclusively on her poetry, Smith wrote novels to earn the money she needed to support her children. As she wrote of selling the copyright to her novel *Celestina* (1791), "it is my poverty and not my will that has forced me to do it."

Considering that Smith could not pursue poetry with the same determination, it's impressive how much influence she did have. But her novels had profound impact, too. They would go on to influence one of the greatest novelists in the English language.

One year before that fifth edition of *Elegiac Sonnets*, Charlotte Smith published her first novel, *Emmeline* (1788). Jane Austen read it as a teenager. We know this because Austen was already writing her own original compositions then, and she referenced this novel in more than one of them. In *Catharine, or the Bower* (1792), an unfinished novel written when Austen was sixteen, her characters talk about "Mrs Smith's Novels": "I am quite delighted with them—They are the sweetest things in the world," one character notes, adding that she prefers *Emmeline* over "any of the others." The modern scholar Jacqueline M. Labbe, who has written multiple books on Smith, calls her "pivotal in Austen's development as a writer." Academics and casual readers alike have noticed the influence of *Emmeline* throughout Austen's early original compositions, as well as in all six of her published novels. I saw it when I read *Emmeline* myself.

———

Emmeline, the Orphan of the Castle is the story of an orphan girl who grows up neglected on a crumbling estate—an evocative setting that made it one of the precursors to Radcliffe's gothics. Her bittersweet solitude is interrupted when her uncle decides to visit the estate for a holiday and brings his son, Delamere. Delamere is spoiled, brash, and ebullient. Naturally he falls in love with Emmeline against everyone's wishes. Including Emmeline's. Delamere chases Emmeline all across England and France, begging for her favor. At one point, Emmeline feels honor bound to become engaged to him. Though the marriage does not happen, it was one that the young Austen eagerly wanted to occur: in her juvenile *History of England* she compares Elizabeth I's "torment of Essex" (in not marrying him) to that of "Emmeline of Delamere." (In fact, Emmeline gets a real happy ending with a man she actually loves.)

Intriguingly, one of Emmeline's most important companions through these travels is a woman whose life story is similar to Charlotte Smith's own. This character, Mrs. Stafford, is married to a man who had a "temper growing more irritable in proportion as his difficulties encreased [*sic*]." She "had been married to him at fifteen"—the same age as Charlotte when she married Benjamin—"[so] had long been unconscious of his weakness: and when time and her own excellent understanding pressed the fatal conviction too forcibly upon her, she still, but fruitlessly, attempted to hide from others what she saw too evidently herself."

At first, I questioned this autobiographical reading of Mr. and Mrs. Stafford; surely this kind of relationship dynamic is common. Then I reached the passage where Mrs. Stafford arrives at a town in France to meet her husband. He "had been prevented meeting her, by the necessity he fancied himself under to watch the early nests of his canary birds, of which he had now made a large collection, and whose encrease [*sic*] he attended to with greater solicitude than the arrival of his family." Canaries! That's the kind of detail you don't forget. I wondered if I had gotten mixed up in my reading and had assumed a scene from her novel was in fact a scene from Smith's life. I climbed the stairs to my room and pulled Loraine Fletcher's 1998 biography of Charlotte Smith from my bookshelf. No, no: it was there too. I hadn't been wrong. Now, as I read about Mrs. Stafford and her marriage, these lines spoke to deeper truths: "Others have, in their husbands, protectors and friends; mine, not only throws on me the burthen of affairs which he has himself embroiled, but adds to their weight by cruelty and oppression."

I was spellbound by the novel, reading its five-hundred-plus pages over the course of two dreamlike days.

Smith's experience as a young wife profoundly shaped her perspective on marriage. In the story of Emmeline and her friends, one particular argument breaks through: that young women should not get married quickly.

To make this case, *Emmeline* broke form in the tradition of courtship novels. Fletcher notes that, typically, "a virtuous heroine must marry the first person she seriously considers as a husband." Most of the novels I had read thus far followed this principle. In Lennox's *Female Quixote* (1752), Arabella turns down the first proposal of Glanville, but accepts him in the end; in Burney's *Evelina* (1778), the heroine eventually marries her first crush, Lord Orville; Radcliffe's *Mysteries of Udolpho* (1794) would not be published for another six years, but in it too, Emily's commitment to her first suitor never wavers. Emmeline does not marry Delamere. Teenage Austen registered her disappointment in that Elizabeth I comparison in her *History of England*, but in her later novels, she shows more appreciation for it. In *Sense and Sensibility*, Marianne Dashwood does not, in the end, marry her first suitor, Willoughby—who is, much like Smith's Delamere, spoiled, brash, and ebullient.

It is in *Persuasion* (1817), however, where the example of Emmeline's delayed marriage brings out a touching complexity. Before the action of the novel begins, Austen's heroine Anne Elliot has already rejected the first proposal of her love, Frederick Wentworth, on the advice of an older and wiser friend, because he "had nothing but himself to recommend him, and no hopes of attaining affluence, but in the chances of a most uncertain profession." In other words, her friend feared he could not provide for Anne financially. Eight years later, the now Captain Wentworth's fortunes have changed dramatically. They meet again. Having lost him once, Anne Elliot bears the pain of her past choice quietly until the two are finally reconciled. (The letter in which Captain Wentworth confesses he is still in love with her contains some of the most moving and most quoted of all the lines in Austen's novels: "I am half agony, half hope.")

Yet even after accepting him this time, Anne remains at peace with her decision as a younger woman. She tells her fiancé, "I was right in submitting to her," speaking of her friend's advice not to marry the first time around; "if I had done otherwise, I should have suffered more in continuing the engagement than I did even in giving it up, because I should have suffered in my conscience." This part of *Persuasion* is often glossed over by readers who want to believe Anne's first refusal was a mistake. Anne doesn't see it that way. In this novel—the last Austen completed—it's as if Austen fulfills her childhood desire to see Emmeline and Delamere end up together, but in a manner that stays true to Smith's argument: that rushing into marriage is foolhardy. As Labbe argues, Austen "reads *Emmeline* and revisits it, pleasurably, by rewriting it."

Before I started my research, I had assumed that Frances Burney and Maria Edgeworth were the most influential women writers on Austen's work. I had read, long ago now, that passage in *Northanger Abbey* where Austen names their novels as works "in which the greatest powers of the mind are displayed." Certainly they did inspire her, both through their books and through their choices, as models of what the life of a women writer could look like. For Austen, as for any artist, these strands of influence wove together into an entirely new style that was uniquely hers. As I read Smith's works, I began to appreciate yet another strand.

The question of influence got a lot more complicated when I picked up Smith's fifth novel, *The Old Manor House* (1793), about a young man whose inheritance of the titular estate is jeopardized when his wealthy aunt disapproves of his choice of wife, a woman below his class. This was the single novel of Smith's that became a classic: it was included in Anna Laetitia Barbauld's 1810 set *The British Novelists*, which created the "first novelistic-canon" in English. While reading, I was surprised to discover that the phrase "pride and prejudice" appears in *The Old Manor House*, just as it does in Burney's *Cecilia* (1782).

Now this was fun. Finding that phrase in a new place complicated things. In *Cecilia*, the phrase comes up twice at the end of the book: "if to PRIDE and PREJUDICE you owe your miseries, so wonderfully is good and evil balanced, that to PRIDE and PREJUDICE you will also owe their termination." In *The Old Manor House*, it appears as "these fits of half repentance, originating in pride and prejudice"; and nearly such as "Why has she invincible pride, and obstinate prejudice?" In both cases, haughty relatives object to the main characters' love match on the basis of either class or money. In *Pride and Prejudice*, Darcy's aunt objects for both reasons.

I had a new question to answer. Did Austen borrow that phrase from Burney, or from Smith? She certainly read both novels. Austen of course immortalized *Cecilia* in *Northanger Abbey*; meanwhile, Darcy's aunt, Lady Catherine de Bourgh, shares much in common with the hero's aunt in *The Old Manor House*, the haughty Mrs. Rayland, who owns the eponymous estate (and is one of the best-drawn characters of any novel I had read in this investigation thus far, including Austen's). Across editions, across generations, I followed the evidence. I might not ever know the true answer to the source of Austen's phrase, but the investigation itself thrilled me.

There were more strands of Smith's influence to unravel in Austen's books. One of the most interesting is how well Smith captured the moral ambiguity of her world, which is an oft-praised feature of Austen's novels. In both authors' books, the heroine may get her happy ending, but that doesn't always mean that the bad guy suffers. Remember, Smith wrote novels to support herself and her children while the legal system of England—in this case, coverture—delayed, limited, or obstructed access to her rightfully inherited funds. These experiences made their way into her fiction, giving many of Smith's plots a political edge, as they criticized the government, the law, and how these systems treat women. In *Emmeline*, for instance, a family of lawyers attempts to keep the heroine from claiming property legally willed to her because they stand to gain much more from their patron, who currently runs the property, than her. While they don't succeed, what's most telling is that they also don't suffer for their evil deeds. They simply continue onto their next morally bankrupt scheme.

This kind of realism—that the bad guys don't always pay—is also a hallmark of Austen's books. In *Persuasion* the two biggest frauds, Mr. Elliot and Mrs. Clay, don't succeed in their initial schemes—so they simply run away together. Meanwhile, Anne Elliot's immediate family members, who have treated her poorly for the entire novel, are left only pleasantly surprised by her good fortune. No moral comeuppance required.

As time went on, Smith became more direct about the politics in her novels. In 1792, she received a rejection from her usual publisher for a novel she desperately needed to sell. *Desmond* was set in the then-ongoing French Revolution and told the story of an Englishman in France, Desmond, hoping distance will cure him of his doomed love for Geraldine, who is trapped in a marriage with a profligate husband and sympathizer to the French Crown (in other words, an anti-revolutionary). Desmond is a supporter of the political ideals of the Revolution, which had occurred with relatively little bloodshed before the Reign of Terror still to come in 1793. Smith was one of the few English writers to set a novel amid the French Revolution while it was happening.

Over the course of the novel, the hero Desmond has an affair in France with a different unhappily married woman, Josephine. In the end, Desmond and Geraldine are able to marry, and they bring up Desmond's illegitimate child from this previous affair as their own. Josephine also gets a happy ending, reuniting with a former lover after the death of her own awful husband. It sounds like the kind of plot Mary Wollstonecraft would come up with (and should, therefore, be a strong reminder that Wollstonecraft wasn't the only woman with liberal politics publishing at this time). *Desmond* was, as Fletcher argues, Smith's "most overtly feminist novel." It was all a bit too much for her regular publisher, who turned it down. Smith turned right around and sold it to another publisher who had liberal politics, George Robinson. Well, technically, *Benjamin* sold it to Robinson: coverture meant that legal contracts were still supposed to go through Charlotte's husband, no matter their separation.

Desmond was a more overt example, but all Smith's novels reflected her politics. More than any other political theme, her books drew attention to the unjust legal system that limited the rights of the *femme couverte*. Her own story was well known at the time not because it was singular—many women across Great Britain lived in similar circumstances—but because she spoke about it, even in her very first novel, *Emmeline*. She begins the book with a poem addressed "To My Children." It describes her need to work to provide for them: "Must my exhausted spirit struggle yet? / Yes! robb'd myself of all that Fortune gave, / Of every hope—but shelter in the grave; / Still shall the plaintive lyre essay its powers, / And dress the cave of Care, with Fancy's flowers."

Smith had always been frank about her troubles to explain why she kept asking for advances, kept looking for work, and kept publishing against her own inclination. In a 1792 letter to her publisher Cadell, Smith detailed some of her latest financial problems—while "Mr Smith [. . .] lives upon the interest of my fortune with a Woman he keeps, leaving me to support as well as I can his seven Children who are in England." This was coverture in a nutshell, as the poet Elizabeth Thomas once quipped earlier in the century: "The man may range from his unhappy wife, / But woman's made a property for life." Yet Smith's comments were never just included to bemoan her situation; they are always accompanied by some plan or action she was taking to alleviate it. In this same letter Smith was trying to sell Cadell her sixth edition of the *Elegiac Sonnets*, explaining why she kept connecting her personal problems to professional efforts: "to shew you that I cannot afford to lose the smallest profit that may arise from my exertions which, but for these difficulties, I should never make." She hoped to assure her publisher that she had a vested interest in producing work that would sell.

As her reputation grew with the success of each book, Smith began to use the prefaces of her publication to talk directly about these issues, and not just obliquely through poetic discourse, or distantly through the acts of "fictional" predatory lawyers in her novels. In 1792, in the preface to that sixth edition of the *Elegiac Sonnets*, Smith began making some details of her story public in print for the first time. She briefly described the controversy over her father-in-law's estate and its effect on her life. About these constant legal disappointments, she quoted Proverbs, "still I am condemned to feel the 'hope delayed that maketh the heart sick.'"

A month later, Smith's novel *Desmond* was published. It also included a preface in which she elaborated further upon her legal problems. Since *Desmond* concerned the ongoing French Revolution, she addressed that up front: "women it is said have no business in politics." Those who argued this, Smith explained, thought women should focus instead on "domestic virtues." To such people she responded, "I however may safely say, that it was in the *observance*, not in the *breach* of duty, *I* became an Author." She had stepped out of the domestic sphere and into public life *in order to* care for her children. Her career became a necessity because the men with the legal power in her life had acted unjustly: "the affairs of my family, being most unhappily in the power of men who seem to [act] with impunity, I am become an Author by profession."

By publicly tying her legal struggles to her career, Smith was critiquing the philosophy underlying her status as *femme couverte*: that its so-called "protection" only held so long as the husband decided to maintain it. With an irresponsible and profligate husband like Benjamin, Charlotte Smith saw very little benefit from that protection. On the contrary, coverture largely harmed her and her children. Many women across the British legal system had similar experiences. The difference was that Charlotte Smith, through necessity, had built herself a platform to talk about it. So she did. She wrote about it in letters. She used it as a prologue in her novels, and she wove it into her plots. She advocated for the many women who could not.

She also advocated for her daughters. Many years later, Smith supported one daughter's match with a financially destitute refugee of the French Revolution because the two were deeply in love. But she also fought the marriage of another daughter, Lucy, to a medical student on the grounds that it was not a devoted match. She suspected Lucy might repeat her mistakes. And that's exactly what happened. That daughter married and was "abused, poor, and often pregnant," just like Smith had been. This was not because she and her daughter were so alike in temperament, but because such a fate was common. Coverture gave such behavior fertile ground. And because it was legally condoned thanks to coverture, married women had little recourse.

When her abusive son-in-law died, Smith took on the support of Lucy and her three grandchildren. As she wrote in a letter from 1805, the year before she died, "Of course I cannot see her want while I can supply her by denying myself or by my labour." She would rather keep writing or go without than see her children struggle.

In Jane Austen's class, a good match did not necessarily mean a love match. Genuine feeling between a couple was nice, and certainly to be hoped for, but optional. On the other hand, financial compatibility was a requirement. As the modern scholar Deborah Kaplan notes, "Even the most enthusiastic advocates of domesticity generally disapproved of marrying into affection-filled poverty." A conversation between two women in Maria Edgeworth's novel *Patronage*, published in 1814, the same year as *Mansfield Park*, glibly summarizes the common sentiment among the gentry: "'allow me to ask, what you mean by happily married?' 'What do I mean? Just what you mean . . . what every body means at the bottom of their hearts—in the first place, married to men who have some fortune.'" But Charlotte Smith knew that wasn't always the case. She experienced it firsthand. Across her novels, she counters that same common sentiment. Instead she makes another claim, again and again, against the wisdom of her class: marrying for financial security is riskier than marrying for love.

For many upper-class women in eighteenth-century England, refusing to marry at all was not an option. Socially, it could be suicide. At one point in *Emmeline*, the heroine becomes financially stable enough that she states it is her intention "never to marry at all"; in response, her friend "Lord Westhaven, at the solemnity and gravity with which she pronounced these words, began to laugh so immoderately, and to treat her resolution with ridicule so pointed, that he first made her almost angry, and then obliged her to laugh too."

More practically, there were few ways that genteel women could support themselves financially, and any inherited money was often socked away in their dowry, incentivizing them to marry simply to access it. (It's noteworthy that Hannah More, who didn't marry, had enough independent funds that she could choose not to marry.) In this context, women who chose husbands based on mutual respect and affection were rebelling against the pressure of marrying for money and status. They were putting their own safety first, acknowledging that a man's character made far more of a difference in their lives than his income.

Novels like Smith's used storytelling to warn women against the dangers that the status of the *femme couverte* created. It is natural that novels about women in this era would focus on the most critical point in a woman's life, one of the few moments where she exercised power: the question of marriage. Those who denigrate courtship novels rarely consider these plots with the law of coverture in mind. When a man has that much control over your life and your children's lives, the kind of man you marry can literally be a question of life or death. The history of English courtship novels is a literary history of women's protest against the *femme couverte*.

Jane Austen's novels and letters demonstrate how seriously she thought about the consequences of marriage. There is certainly heart-stirring love in Austen's novels. There is also a cynical assessment of marriage as a means of social or financial benefit. In *Emma*, the titular character nearly destroys her best friend's life by trying to convince her to marry a well-off man rather than the farmer whom she loves; in *Persuasion*, Anne Elliot agrees to break her engagement with the man she loves because her friend worries that he can't financially support her. Austen's novels are a conscious contribution to this larger tradition.

I had wanted a copy of the *Elegiac Sonnets* on my shelf as a symbol of Charlotte Smith's hope for freedom. Now I wanted one of Smith's novels on my shelf as a symbol of that literary history. While Jane Austen was growing up, attending balls and still considering the possibility of a husband, she was reading Charlotte Smith's novels, and thinking about the status of a married woman in the eighteenth-century English legal system.

I know now that she was thinking about a topic as specific as that because that's a large part of what Smith's courtship novels are about, as are Burney's, and Radcliffe's, and Lennox's, and Austen's own. These novels reflected real-life stakes, like the poverty, abuse, and lack of legal protection that Smith suffered her entire married life. Novel to novel, these women were sending messages to each other: the law will not protect you, so take steps to protect yourself.

But which of Smith's novels should I add to my collection? I liked every Smith novel I read, so in my collecting I was content to be guided by chance. Once again, it rewarded me. First, I ran into a first edition copy of *The Old Manor House* while searching for books online. But the spines were cracked and worn, which would have made it difficult to handle the volumes without weakening them further. And I wanted to handle them, to turn the leaves and read about the heroine in eighteenth-century type. So I let that copy go.

I had long ago learned that patience pays off, as when I searched years for the right leaf from the Gutenberg Bible. It did here too. A year passed, then another and another. Finally, I came across a listing for a first edition copy of *Emmeline* on a London shop's website. My partner and I had already been planning to visit that very shop in a few months. This part was tricky: I couldn't ask them to hold it for months before I saw it in person, but I wouldn't know if I wanted it until I did. I had to take a chance that no one else would snatch it up before my visit. Sometimes I have waited and returned from these visits devastated when the book that I had coveted already sold. (An inscribed book by the science fiction author Leigh Brackett still makes my heart pang.)

When I'm weighing the risks between buying something immediately and regretting it or waiting and potentially losing the copy, I try to imagine how Future Rebecca would feel if she visited the shop and found it gone. If the thought fills me with dread, I usually give in and buy the book immediately. If I'm at peace with the fact that it might go to someone else, I wait. In the case of Charlotte Smith, I had already been waiting for years to acquire the right copy. In the end, I split the difference. I did wait a couple of months.

But a few weeks before my visit, I emailed friends at the shop to ask if they would hold it for my visit. It was still available. They put it aside for me.

This rare book firm was one of the oldest in London, established in the mid-nineteenth century. It had moved to a new location in Bloomsbury just before the pandemic, so this was my first visit to its new space. Our hosts apologized about the August "heat" (which we had been enjoying as a respite from the humidity of Washington, D.C.) and offered us tea. No, thank you: straight to the books, please. Like other Charlotte Smith novels I had been inspecting, this four-volume set of *Emmeline* betrayed some damage from its journey across hundreds of years through the hands of many owners; a few of the labels on the spines were missing. But once I opened the first volume to the title page, I knew this was the one.

On that page, a sloppy cursive hand had recorded, "M. Hill's copy." The people at this rare book company are professionals: they had already done the research to identify whose signature that might be, and they had included this information in their description. In addition to the brief overview of the book's history and importance, they documented the unique physical traits of that copy, including its condition and provenance (this owner inscription). This set of *Emmeline* had been owned by Mary Hill (née Sandys), Marchioness of Downshire, later Baroness Sandys. She was twenty-three when the book was published in 1788, and had already been married for two years. Marriage at twenty-one seems young to us, but Charlotte Smith and Mrs. Stafford in *Emmeline* were married at fifteen. Mary Hill was older, even, than Emmeline at the time of her wedding.

Mary Hill loved books, and added many new works to the family library over the years. According to the bookseller's catalog, "as her resources grew so did her appetite; with a remarkable consistency she favoured works written by women." Her library included four others by Smith in addition to this one. Now it would be mine. I was ecstatic to acquire a Charlotte Smith novel that had been owned by a woman who actively collected the novels of other women writers, just like I was. This acquisition connected the two of us as collectors in a dialogue across time. Yes, we both agreed: this book belonged on our shelves.

In their description, the bookseller had also noted that the marchioness was a subscriber to the 1789 edition of *Elegiac Sonnets*, the same edition I had picked up from that dealer in San Francisco a year or so earlier. One of the first things I did when I returned home from this trip was to retrieve my copy of the deluxe edition of the *Elegiac Sonnets*. I leafed back to the subscribers list, scanning the names of all the people who had paid extra up front in order to help Charlotte Smith publish it. There she was: "Mrs. Hill," a subscriber.

That copy of *Emmeline* now sits on my bookshelf next to the *Elegiac Sonnets*. Early in *Emmeline*, the narrator takes a moment to describe the heroine's determination that keeps her from "sinking under the pressure of those evils which overwhelm." Emmeline does faint frequently throughout the course of the book, as a proper eighteenth-century heroine of sensibility. But she also acts. "Instead therefore of giving way to tears and exclamations, she considered how she should best perform all she now could do." Just like her author. As much as I wanted a different life for her, with a different canonical fate, these books were evidence of a more important truth in Charlotte Smith's life. That she wrote herself free.

Chapter Seven

ELIZABETH INCHBALD
(1753-1821)

"Lovers Vows! [...] How came it never to be thought of before? It strikes me as if it would do exactly."

—Tom Bertram, speaking of an
Inchbald play in *Mansfield Park*

At thirteen, a farmgirl named Elizabeth pronounced that "she would rather die, than live any longer without seeing the world." She had a burning ambition to live a different kind of life. At eighteen, she secretly left her rural birthplace in Suffolk for London, unchaperoned. In a farewell note to her widowed mother, she wrote: "By the time you receive this I shall have left [...] and perhaps for ever." This dramatic move suggests a kind of rashness on her part—but Elizabeth always put in the work after she committed to a course of action. Her efforts would pay off through sheer determination.

This unschooled farmer's daughter would become one of the most renowned writers of her time. After achieving her first dream of becoming a professional actress, she wrote, revised, submitted, and wrote again until she became a successful playwright, with such hits as *I'll Tell You What* (1785) and *Such Things Are* (1787). From there she continued to push herself, dusting off and entirely reworking a novel that had been rejected years earlier, *A Simple Story* (1791), that became one of the most acclaimed novels of the eighteenth century. She would be the "Celebrated Mrs. Inchbald," "one of the most important [English] writers of the years 1784–1808," and "the cleverest self-educated woman that ever lived." Yet today we remember her primarily as the author of a single play—because that play sets up the plot in Austen's novel *Mansfield Park.*

When I began researching Elizabeth Inchbald, I had expected to read several biographies of a staid, unremarkable author and a stack of out-of-date comedies. What I found was a writer who constantly elicited that rare reaction in readers: I kept laughing aloud at her genuinely funny jokes. Elizabeth Inchbald is, simply, great. Radcliffe's transcendent gothic excesses may not be to your taste, and Smith's brilliant novels may be too long for you—but, if you like Austen's novels, you'll find much to appreciate in Inchbald's. How had a writer this fresh and entertaining fallen out of favor?

———————

Elizabeth was born in 1753, four years after Charlotte Smith. By all accounts, she was not only ambitious but strikingly beautiful. She also had a speech impediment, a stutter that made her shy in company. Yet she adored the theater. She wanted to become a player in an acting company, like her eldest brother George. When she was sixteen, Elizabeth secretly wrote to the manager of the local Norwich theater company in hopes of finding similar work. While he was kind and encouraging, the manager had not forgotten she was a minor and gently put her off. But she wouldn't be put off forever.

It wasn't just Elizabeth and George; the entire family adored the theater. They attended plays frequently and made the acquaintance of many professional actors. During this time Elizabeth met Joseph Inchbald, who was acting in the company Elizabeth had attempted to join. Joseph was smitten with her and proposed. Elizabeth, then eighteen, declined his offer. She explained to him in a gentle rejection letter that she was not ready for marriage: "In spite of your eloquent pen, matrimony still appears to me with less charms than terrors." (Does she sound like one of Charlotte Smith's characters? I think so.) Joseph accepted this answer in good grace and they remained friends . . . for now.

The love of theater in Elizabeth's family did not stop at viewing professional performances. As many families did in this period, they staged dramatic readings at home for entertainment. (Austen's family also did this a generation later.) Elizabeth struggled to participate because of her stutter, but she worked hard to do it anyway. According to James Boaden, her first major biographer in 1833, "She wrote out all the words with which she had much difficulty [and] carried them constantly about her." Despite the rejection from the local Norwich theater company, Elizabeth began to prepare for auditions. She memorized the parts of major Shakespearean roles for women, like Cordelia in *King Lear*, to prove to theater managers that she had the standard repertoire down. Practicing her elocution, writing theater managers, mastering the repertoire, all by seventeen: if she failed, it would not be for lack of effort. Step by step, play by play, year by year, Elizabeth Inchbald built the life that she wanted.

But those triumphs were still many years away. The teenage Elizabeth wanted nothing more than to act onstage, even though her mother wasn't supportive of her daughter entering the profession. So she ran away to London. She did have something of a plan: distant family friends had a home there, and she knew they would take her in while she figured out her next steps. Nor was she unfamiliar with the city; a number of her elder sisters had married and moved there, and she had visited them before. This time, like a heroine in a Georgette Heyer novel, Elizabeth arrived alone via stagecoach. She rented a room at the charmingly named Rose and Crown, but soon ran into trouble when she learned that those family friends she had hoped to meet had moved away.

A teenage girl staying alone and entirely unchaperoned in an inn was exactly the kind of scenario to draw attention, either in the suspicion of well-meaning bystanders, or the interest of shadier characters. Elizabeth left for another lodging, explaining her presence to the innkeeper by claiming to be a milliner's apprentice. After she was followed home one day by a stranger, Elizabeth moved to yet another public house with yet another fib, this time pretending to be a disappointed traveler who had sought a place on the already full coach to York. She was not yet ready to give up. She had moved three times and called on two different men who handled casting in theater troupes. She doggedly pursued her singular goal: to find work as an actress.

It was not going as expected. Elizabeth found herself in an increasingly desperate situation. She was still staying alone in public lodgings, with no work. What's more, she had started receiving letters from a strange man who had taken unnervingly close notice of her comings and goings. Elizabeth finally wrote to one of her sisters who lived in town. The sisters acted immediately to step in and assist their younger sibling. One of her brothers-in-law gave her a lecture so vivid that Elizabeth would later recall his skill in "frightening you to death, to have the pleasure of recovering you." It took a few days, but her family managed to convince her to stay with one of her sisters. Elizabeth was willing to amend her plan for a safe place to stay, but that did not mean she would give up her ambition to become an actor.

Only a few weeks after she moved to London, an old acquaintance came to town and began calling on her at her sister's house. It was Joseph Inchbald, the man whose marriage proposal Elizabeth had turned down about six months earlier, citing her own fear of getting married. He was seventeen years older than her and already had two children. But now she was beginning to view Joseph in a different light. Elizabeth was still being turned away by every acting company she approached. Joseph was a fine actor, experienced and well connected. Soon she was asking for his advice. He was happy to offer it.

But finding work in the field was not easy—and carried risks for a beautiful young woman with no experience. It was during these early months in London that Elizabeth experienced the first of more than one recorded assault during her career. The manager of the Bristol Theatre, James Dodd, was in town, and Elizabeth called on him looking for work. He met with her multiple times, but his behavior during these visits began to leave Elizabeth "rather frightened." Dodd was coming on to her, and he became more aggressive with each visit. Elizabeth, still a teenager, didn't know how to respond, becoming "terrified and vexed beyond measure at his behavior." At one point she had to physically defend herself, grabbing the nearest item at hand—a basin of hot water—and throwing it in his face. Yet he was one of the only theater managers considering her for a job, so soon after, she wrote a note attempting to reconcile. Dodd declined.

Around this time, Joseph renewed his proposal, and this time Elizabeth accepted. They were married two months after Elizabeth ran away to London. Thanks to his help, Elizabeth secured her first acting position in the same company that employed him. The night of their wedding, Joseph still "tread the boards," appearing in a play ironically titled *The Jealous Wife*. It was an emblematic beginning to the marriage. Despite disagreements and jealousies, the strength of their relationship grew from their shared love for the theater.

When they married in 1772, Elizabeth was eighteen. Joseph was thirty-seven. From a twenty-first-century perspective, that age gap brings up serious questions about motives, as well as the power imbalance in such a dynamic. Commentators as far back as the 1830s were skeptical of it, reading their relationship as something of a marriage of convenience. James Boaden, not only Inchbald's first major biographer but also a playwright himself, emphasized the practical uses of such an arrangement: "her husband might consider that her rising talent and most lovely person would, by steady perseverance, secure to them [. . .] many lucrative engagements." But it was more complicated than that, as indeed most relationships are.

Elizabeth kept a thin but regular pocketbook diary for more than fifty years; stray comments from the earliest one that survives, from 1776, hint to what their marriage was like. It included many nights of arguments, as on January 11, 1776: "Mr. Inchbald came home we had High Words about what he said to me in the Green room &c&." But their marriage included many days of productive conversation, such as Joseph helping Elizabeth study her lines and eliminate her stutter during performance (January 8, 1776: "while my Hair was dressing Mr Inchbald heard me my part"). They worked side by side, playing *King Lear* together in Ireland (she, Cordelia; he, Lear) and *Othello* in Edinburgh (she, Desdemona; he, Othello). Elizabeth's independent streak persisted: only a few years into their marriage, they argued when Elizabeth asked for a "parting" of their salaries, i.e., that she be paid for her acting work separately from his own. In the end, he agreed. It was not simply that Elizabeth wanted to spend her money how she liked. Quite the opposite; she was frugal by temperament. She spent as little as possible of her own money so that she could send it back to her family, with whom she remained close despite her dramatic departure from the farm.

The chosen life of Elizabeth and Joseph required absolute dedication to their craft and unremitting support of each other. Traveling theatrical companies like theirs were tight-knit; the actors lived and worked in close proximity, rehearsing in the morning, performing in the evening, and memorizing lines whenever they could squeeze in the time. Nor were the rewards for their efforts certain. This life was precarious: on the way back from a stay in Paris, they were so short on funds that they regularly skipped meals and, in one case, foraged in the field for a dinner of turnips. According to Annibel Jenkins, who published Inchbald's most recent book-length biography (2003), no matter how their relationship started, it "became a love match." Over time, by virtue of their shared love of the theater and the demands of their chosen work, they drew closer.

Elizabeth might have spent the rest of her life on the road with Joseph. In 1779, they enjoyed a productive spring in Leeds. Joseph appeared in Shakespeare's *Henry V* and Elizabeth in the recent comedy *School for Lovers*. Then they took a short holiday with friends from the theater company in the nearby town of Halifax. The day after they returned, Joseph died suddenly in Elizabeth's arms, apparently of a heart attack. They had been married for seven years. For the following months Mrs. Inchbald, as she would be known for the rest of her life, grieved her loss. And, because she always had, and she always would, she kept working to build the life she wanted.

While Joseph was alive, Elizabeth's theatrical ambitions were both achieved with his assistance and limited by his presence. Of the two, he was the better established, so they went where his career took them, not where she might hope her career could go. She did develop a strong reputation as an actress, but it was for her reliability more than for her talent. A theater manager once wrote to ask her to play a small but important bit part because "I cannot depend on any other person's attention or punctuality with safety to the welfare of the theatre."

Her fate was once again entirely in her own hands. Before Joseph's death, she had written about one hundred pages of a novel; in the months after his death, she finished the draft and submitted it to a publisher. It was rejected. But that didn't stop her. After all, she had been put off before.

Inchbald continued to look for better acting opportunities. She may have been widowed, but by now she was firmly ensconced in the world of the theater. In 1780, after working relentlessly through the contacts she had made over the years with a traveling company, Inchbald secured an acting position at the pinnacle of her profession: in London at Covent Garden.

In eighteenth-century England, the government controlled the London theaters. At the beginning of the English Civil Wars in 1642, the new Puritan-controlled Parliament had objected to them on moral grounds and closed them all. When Charles II came to the throne in the Restoration of 1660, he opened them again—but he granted only two patents for London theaters to perform plays in order to keep a close eye on what was performed. Every play had to be reviewed by the Lord Chamberlain before it could be authorized for show. By Inchbald's time, one more theater had received a royal license, bringing the total to three: Covent Garden; Drury Lane; and the latecomer in 1766, the Haymarket. Covent Garden and Drury Lane were rivals, fighting to get the same celebrated actors, the most exciting new plays, and of course the biggest paying audiences. The Haymarket was active only during the summer when the other two theaters were closed.

With so few theaters and so many aspiring actors, only the best were welcomed onto these stages. Only the best of the best were well paid. If you weren't a star, actors received "take what you can get" wages. To accept the position at Covent Garden, Inchbald had to take a pay cut. But she was more than willing to endure a short-term setback if it would benefit her in the long term.

With an "excessively interesting" countenance and eyelashes the color of sand, Inchbald had the beauty of a star—but never the natural talent of one. One fellow actress described Inchbald's roles later at the Haymarket, where she also acted in the summers beginning in 1782, as "those parts that no person cared whether they were well or ill performed." Inchbald made up for it with dedication. According to Boaden, she passed "all her evenings in the theatre, whether she act[ed] or not." Yet she was still seeking something she could be truly great at. She wanted not just to act in the theater, but to write for it.

Her pocketbook diary from 1780 shows that she was already trying her hand at playwriting. The earliest surviving entries speak of a "farce," a kind of play that was usually shorter in form and lighter in content than a typical comedy. In January, she recorded working on it "all the afternoon and Evening"; in July, she skipped Sunday service to work on it: "did not go to Prayers but read my Farce"; in December, a friend visited and they "went through all my Farce." I loved the way these spare entries stacked up, like bricks, into the life Inchbald was building. (Ever since I read about her pocketbook diaries, I had returned to my old journaling habit too.)

Long experience with the practical ins and outs of acting gave Inchbald a significant advantage compared to other aspiring playwrights. By memorizing the parts of major Shakespearean roles as a teen, she developed an early ear for dialogue. By spending years on the road with a theater company, she knew what made a script easy to work with. For eight years she had been fully immersed in the workings of this world: watching other actors, negotiating with managers, observing audience reactions. It trained her in a sense of the pace and structure necessary for each act—and an instinct for what would excite audience applause.

But because there were only three licensed theaters, very few new plays were accepted. The theater managers were inundated with submissions and ignored most of them. Inchbald tried to use the connections and working relationships she had already developed as an actress. But one play was rejected. Then a second. And a third.

Inchbald continued to live on the meager wages from her unremarkable roles, saving money where she could. She would often eat at the house of a friend, but there were plenty of occasions "when she did not happen to be invited there, she just did not dine at all." She wrote again to the theater managers. She submitted more plays. She revised the drafts. She asked for critical remarks from friends. She revised the drafts again.

In 1784, four years after she started her first acting job in London, Inchbald's first play was accepted by George Colman the Elder at the Haymarket. *The Mogul Tale* was a farce that followed a group of Londoners in a hot-air balloon who have been blown off course and into the territory of a Middle Eastern ruler. Colman gave her editorial feedback on the play and assured her "with a little care, I think it can't fail." In reworking the play, then developing the production, Inchbald participated like a playwright—but secretly. She was also cast in the play, so to everyone else she was just an actor with a small part (the Mogul's former favorite concubine). She was not named as the playwright because she and Colman had strategically agreed to keep the work anonymous.

Anonymous authorship was a smart move for her first play. Just as in the cases of Burney, Lennox, and Radcliffe, there were practical reasons why a woman writer might prefer anonymous authorship. This was especially true in Inchbald's field, the theater. Even while some women novelists gained respect in social circles, actresses rarely did. Actresses came into frequent, close contact with men. What could they be up to, behind the scenes? The exploits of some actresses were well known. In 1761, the famous courtesan Ann Elliot (who counted the king's brother as one of her conquests) had first tread the boards in a play at Drury Lane written by her lover, the playwright Arthur Murphy (and a close friend of Burney's). Women playwrights moved in these same circles and might find themselves in such questionable situations (according to the double standards of British society: male playwrights suffered no damage to their reputations for extramarital relationships).

On top of that, women playwrights had to risk their feminine reputations in that most masculine of spheres, business. One couldn't sell a play without talking about money, and the idea of a woman negotiating a fee was generally looked upon with distaste. (Charlotte Smith did this herself by necessity; most of the other women writers I had been researching relied upon male relatives to serve as intercessors.) Colman knew the audience would be thinking all these things, and more, if they knew that the farce had been written by a woman. He wanted Inchbald's play to succeed and believed it would. So he advised her to keep her authorship anonymous until they knew how the play was received on its own merits. Inchbald agreed. If the farce did poorly, no one had to know she was the author. She could continue to submit other plays anonymously, without the risk that one bad reception would dispose audiences against her future work.

But Inchbald nearly gave herself away. In one rehearsal, she stepped in to correct another actress's delivery. That woman took offense to the presumption and commented snippily upon Inchbald's "great agitation." Then, early in the first performance, Inchbald's nerves uncharacteristically got the better of her and she nearly missed her cue. She stuttered through her line, "Hyde Park Corner." There was a breath during which the audience prepared to turn against the play—but when Inchbald laughed aloud at her fumble, the audience joined her.

In the end, the debut was a grand success. Forgetting herself once again, Inchbald ran into the greenroom where the actors had retired, her joy astonishing her colleagues. One was so confused by her conduct that she wondered whether Inchbald "had an affection of the brain and this was a paroxysm." Another asked her why she was so happy: "was it some great aunt who had died, and left her a large fortune? or was she about to be *married*? Or had she captivated the heart of some dear swain?" Insanity, love, or fortune were the only reasons they could imagine for Inchbald's behavior. But the real reason was better. Inchbald, a farmer's daughter, had run away to London to make a name for herself in the theater. Now, after years of work, she had achieved something tremendous. With pride, she owned her accomplishment: "No, Sir, it is none of the circumstances you mention, but what I prize far more—*I* am the authoress of the farce you have just played."

The Mogul Tale ran for ten days in the summer of 1784, which was

considered a terrific run for a new play in that season, and it earned Inchbald one hundred guineas. She paid off her debts, then gave the rest of the
money to relatives. (For her entire life, whenever Inchbald had spare funds,
she would send enormous sums to family members.) Her newfound celebrity also earned her a raise as an actress of an additional one pound a week.
But soon she would make more money in a month as a playwright than she
could ever have hoped to achieve as an actress in a year.

After her first play's success, Inchbald nudged Colman about another
play she had submitted before *The Mogul Tale*. It had been languishing on
his desk, and now he finally read it. He believed he had another hit on his
hands. He was right.

Inchbald's next play, a full-length comedy titled *I'll Tell You What*,
opened with a prologue written by Colman that, this time, drew attention
to Inchbald's gender: "The Muses, Ladies Regent of the Pen, / Grant
Women Skill, and Force, to write like Men." Colman recounted the success
of *The Mogul Tale* as proof of her skill, then set up the beginning of the
play: "But hold—I say too much—I quite forgot— / And so I'll tell you—
No—SHE'LL *tell you what*." (I am obsessed with that line. It fills me with
glee every time I read it.) This comedy tells the story of a married woman
caught in an affair, her subsequent divorce and marriage to her lover, and
the new couple's ultimate unhappiness with each other. It ran for a total of
twenty-eight nights at the Haymarket the summer of 1785, an unquestion-
able coup.

That September, Inchbald used her earnings to buy £400 in stock, a
common strategy for those who received large but inconsistent payments.
This strategy allowed investors to receive annual payments, as interest, from
their invested funds. If the amount invested was large enough, that interest could be used to cover everyday expenses. Hannah More had invested
Ann Yearsley's profits this way, and that had been what led to their dispute,
since it left Yearsley with only a fraction of her total wealth—the interest—
to spend when and how she wanted. Austen herself invested a substantial
part of her earnings in a similar way, buying the "Navy Fives" stock that
was popular during the Napoleonic Wars. (Like government bonds today,

"Navy Fives" worked by supplying funds to the navy, often in active en-gagement during this period, at a 5 percent rate. Austen had brothers in the navy, so this was both a logical and sentimental way to handle her money.) By resisting the urge to spend rather than save, Inchbald bought long-term stability with her success.

After a somewhat undistinguished career as an actress, Inchbald achieved renown in an even more exceptional role, as a playwright. I'm not sure whether Inchbald pursued all this for money, for fame, or simply for a love of the theater. I only know that she was smart, and she was driven, and she succeeded. As another actress concluded of Inchbald's rise, it "plainly shews that if a comet is ordained to consume the world, however long it may remain unseen and unnoticed, that, when least expected, it will shine forth with additional lustre."

After the triumph of her second play, Inchbald prepared another farce, *Appearance Is Against Them*, in which a valuable shawl is stolen and nearly every member of the cast is, at one point or another, accused of being the thief. Colman refused it—but Inchbald turned right around and offered it to the manager of Covent Garden, Thomas Harris, who happily accepted it for the fall 1785 season. This was the first of several of Inchbald's plays for which King George III, a fan of comedies, requested a special perfor-mance.

From 1784 to 1794, Inchbald saw fifteen of her original or adapted plays produced on the stage. Her greatest success was *Such Things Are*, about the social infighting of expat Englishmen in the British colony at Sumatra. It brought her an astonishing £900; other hits brought her as much as £600 or £700. Remember that £200 a year was the amount an indepen-dent genteel woman needed to live comfortably, as in the annuity Hannah More received and the unfulfilled bequest of Charlotte Smith's father-in-law. In 1786, a colonel had proposed to Inchbald with an accompanying offer of £500 a year; she declined. A year later, when *Such Things Are* pre-miered, Inchbald's annual payments from her investments reached that magic number of £200 a year. The farmer's daughter had risen far above her station. (Hannah More probably would not have approved.)

Inchbald was a star on the London theater scene. During this time, the biographer Boaden described how she balanced her work and her celebrity: "She had the happiness now of having her door eternally besieged, and a large majority of her callers determined to see her, if she was within; so that she was obliged to lock herself rigidly up when she had any business of either composition or transcription to get through." Inchbald had gone from snatching every opportunity to turning down engagements.

By the summer of 1789, Inchbald resigned her acting position at Covent Garden. She was a writer now. It was during this summer that she returned to her novel, *A Simple Story*, about a charismatic young woman in love with her guardian—a Catholic priest. Inchbald had set aside the manuscript when she had first failed to find a publisher in 1779. Now she brought the skills that she had honed writing plays over the last decade to its revision: the ability to write realistic dialogue, to communicate depth of emotion by a simple gesture, to evoke a laugh with a single line.

In the process of revision, Inchbald decided to combine *A Simple Story* with another novel she had been writing about a young woman who seeks to reconcile with her estranged father. The book became a two-part novel about different generations of a single family. Boaden loved pointing out moments like these in his 1833 biography, examples of when Inchbald succeeded through work and will; he joked that this decision "was productive of more labour; but she laughed at the toil of common mortals, and successfully combined them." This time the manuscript was accepted by George Robinson for £200. It was published in February of 1791, the same year as Radcliffe's breakout gothic, *The Romance of the Forest*.

The first part of *A Simple Story* centers on Miss Milner, a recently orphaned but spirited seventeen-year-old heiress. Miss Milner falls in love with her guardian, Mr. Dorriforth, who cannot marry because he is a priest. However, Dorriforth is released by the Vatican from his vows when he himself becomes heir to a large estate. In this era, the Catholic Church especially encouraged English Catholics in landed or titled positions to marry and raise children, as Catholics (like Inchbald herself) lived in Protestant England in a distinctly precarious détente; this shored up more power in an environment that could quickly turn hostile. The first part ends with the two happily wed as Lord and Lady Elmwood, having overcome all obstacles and the meddling of the hero's advisor, Sandford.

Much has changed when the second part of the novel opens seventeen years later. Lady Elmwood has had an affair while Lord Elmwood has been away for years managing "a very large estate in the West Indies." (References to such estates in fiction of this period, both here and in Austen's *Mansfield Park*, are rarely described as run on the forced labor of enslaved people, but that fact plays an important role in the critical interpretation of both novels.) Upon his return, Lady Elmwood flees their estate in guilt. Lord Elmwood righteously cuts off all contact with her—and betrays their own daughter Matilda in the process, refusing even to be in the same room with her. "[H]e vowed in the deep torments of his revenge, not to be reminded of [Lady Elmwood] by one individual object; much less by one so nearly allied to her as her child." The second part, though ostensibly still a romance that leads to Matilda's engagement to a worthy young man named Rushbrook, hinges on Lord Elmwood's reconciliation with his daughter; only after Lord Elmwood finally acknowledges Matilda as his daughter can the pair be wed with the assurance of financial stability.

A Simple Story was a triumph. It went into a second edition less than a month after the first, with laudatory reviews following each. The *Critical Review* praised its realism and novelty: "the incidents are natural; and, what is more extraordinary in the present state of novel-writing, they are new." The *Monthly Review* similarly complimented it for that balance—"though probability is not violated, surprize is constantly awakened"—and highlighted its superiority of style: "A vein of elegant simplicity runs through the whole."

Already famous for her plays, "the Celebrated Mrs. Inchbald" watched her literary reputation ascend even higher. Her pocketbook diaries recorded visits with some of the most prominent literary and political elite of London, including King George III and his daughters the princesses. In the next few years, she would also make friends with both Charlotte Smith and Ann Radcliffe, who issued novels with Inchbald's publisher, Robinson (*Desmond* in 1792 and *Udolpho* in 1794, respectively).

A Simple Story was praised for its witty dialogue and its economy of prose, hallmarks of all of Inchbald's plays. This connection to her experience in the theater was not lost on contemporary reviewers, who noted for instance that the "secret charm, that gives a grace to the whole, is the art with which Mrs Inchbald has made her work completely dramatic. The business is, in a great measure, carried on in dialogue." In some scenes, Inchbald didn't even need dialogue to convey the characters' deep feelings for each other; with the experience of an actor, she used gestures. In one scene, Dorriforth enters the room and Miss Milner says nothing, but starts making mistakes in her card game.

And her characters: the people in Inchbald's book didn't read like *characters*. They felt alive. This is what struck the writer Maria Edgeworth after reading *A Simple Story* for the fourth time, as she wrote in an effusive letter to Inchbald many years later. Hoping to assess it "as an author, to try to find out the secret of its peculiar pathos," her professional eye instead gave way to the readerly pleasure of following these characters' lives. "I never read any novel that affected me so strongly, or that so completely possessed me with the belief in the real existence of all the people it represents," she wrote. "I am glad I have never met with a Dorriforth, for I must inevitably have fallen desperately in love with him."

Today most people have never heard of *A Simple Story*. Yet those who have are extravagant in their praise. In 1986 the scholar Terry Castle, who specializes in the history of the novel—and knows the eighteenth-century canonical favorites like Richardson and Fielding better than just about anyone—called it not only "the most elegant English fiction of the century," but also "one of the finest novels of any period." How was a book described like that no longer recognized as a classic?

I needed to read *A Simple Story*.

Now I was fudging the parameters of my investigation a bit. We have no concrete evidence that Austen read this novel. But circumstantial evidence strongly suggests she did. We know Austen was familiar with at least some of Inchbald's work, since Inchbald's play *Lovers' Vows* (1798) is rehearsed by the characters in *Mansfield Park*. And though Austen is technically considered an author of the Regency period (which formally began in 1811), she was just as much an author of the 1790s. That was the era of Radcliffe's *Romance of the Forest* (1791) and *Udolpho* (1794); of Charlotte Smith's most productive work, including her grand novel *The Old Manor House* (1793); and of Burney's *Camilla* (1796), which printed Austen's name among the subscribers. While Austen published *Sense and Sensibility* in 1811 and *Pride and Prejudice* in 1813, she wrote the first drafts of these novels in the 1790s. Inchbald's *A Simple Story* was published in 1791, and went on to be hailed as one of the most acclaimed novels during Austen's formative years as a writer.

We know too that Austen paid close attention to the most praised and popular books of the time. I hadn't forgotten that Austen wrote she would read Hannah More's *Coelebs in Search of a Wife* not because she wanted to, but because so many other people had read and enjoyed it. In this context, the idea of Austen ignoring *A Simple Story* would be like a musician of her time paying close attention to Haydn but never listening to Mozart. (Incidentally, Austen enjoyed playing piano and copied out pieces by both these composers for her own use.)

I decided that I wanted to find a copy of *A Simple Story* that I could dog-ear, write in, and leave splayed upside down on my nightstand to hold my place. I wanted a copy in which I could leave my own mark. I found a beat-up old copy on a secondhand website and ordered it. It was printed in 1988—I was still (mostly) following my rule for only marking up books (in pencil) published within my lifetime. Designed for students, it was one of the Oxford University Press paperbacks in the World's Classics series with an introduction by a modern scholar, Jane Spencer, and explanatory footnotes. Editions like this indicated that *A Simple Story* was still being read by the 1980s, though *who* was doing the reading is notable: a university press reprint aims for an audience of college students, as opposed to the broader audience that a modern Penguin paperback hopes to capture with, say, its Austen editions today.

When it arrived, this copy came with a huge barcode sticker on the spine that I fussily peeled off. Many enormous internet-only bookselling corporations use this sticker system to keep track of and retrieve the literally thousands of books they sell in a day, much to the bane of those like me who collect humble paperbacks. Removing the sticker can be tricky: if you move too quickly, you risk damaging the book. Depending on the recalcitrance of the sticker, I may first break out my hair dryer to loosen the grip of the adhesive through the application of heat. In this case, the sticker peeled away easily, leaving only a patch of stickiness that I rubbed away, grumbling.

I was glad I bought this copy. Turn to the fore-edge now and the number of dog-ears give it the uneven look of a city skyline. *A Simple Story* was the first eighteenth-century novel I've ever been tempted to quote on social media. Many of my favorite passages featured repartee between Milner and Sandford, Dorriforth's priggish advisor who opposes the match. Like this passage, marked with my pencil, in which Sandford has just accused Milner of lying and receives a wicked response:

> **"Deceit," cried Miss Milner, "in what am I deceitful? did I ever pretend sir, I had an esteem for you?"**
>
> **"That had not been deceit, madam, but merely good manners."**
>
> **"I never, Mr. Sandford, sacrificed truth to politeness."**

Inchbald's wit isn't limited only to dialogue. I kept noticing clever lines that hinted to the personality of the omniscient narrator, very much like what one sees in the novels of Austen. At one point, Sandford argues that Milner is too obstinate to listen to advice, and Milner upends her plans simply because she knows it will make Sandford look bad: "Miss Milner with apparent satisfaction adjusted the plan of her journey, (like those persons who behave well, not so much to please themselves as to vex their enemies).” Or when Milner's rival, Miss Fenton, shows up and sees Milner frustrated: “'I am sorry to see you so uneasy, Miss Milner,' said Miss Fenton, with the most perfect unconcern.” As the modern scholar Jane Spencer notes in the introduction to my paperback edition, “Inchbald's concise, ironic style anticipates Austen.”

I was riveted by these moments in the first part of the book. Like so many others before me, I was struck by Inchbald's humor and, like Edgeworth, by the vivacity of her characters. The reviews by contemporary critics had suggested that these were talents Inchbald had translated from her work in the theater. Now I wanted to read her plays, too.

I chose the work that fit into my investigation's original parameters: *Lovers' Vows*, the play that the characters in *Mansfield Park* decided to stage at home for fun. First performed at Covent Garden in 1798, it was adapted by Inchbald from a German play by August von Kotzebue called *Das Kind der Liebe* (“The Love Child,” i.e., a child born out of wedlock). Inchbald didn't read German, but the theater manager Harris didn't see this as a problem. In this period, most theater managers prioritized popular taste over perfect fidelity in their productions—even David Garrick famously played a *King Lear* with a happy ending after the audience rejected the tragic one. Harris wasn't asking Inchbald for an exact re-creation of the German play in English. He already had a literal translation of it. He wanted her to interpret it with their English audience in mind. As a result, *Lovers' Vows* differs from *Das Kind der Liebe* in major respects—even the personalities of the characters differ—while the overall plot remains the same. Inchbald's adaptation was somewhat more like a modern film reboot.

Initially, I thought that I'd hunt down *Lovers' Vows* in the formative twenty-five-volume anthology *The British Theatre* (1808), a production that set the terms for what was considered part of the canon at the turn of the century. In 1806, the publisher had approached Inchbald about writing introductions to a new edition of the long-standing series, which was first begun in 1775. She didn't choose the plays included—they didn't want her participation *that* far—but they wanted her name, which they displayed prominently on the title page of every book in the set. Those title pages were evidence Inchbald was famous enough that publishers wanted to use her reputation to boost sales.

The plays for which Inchbald wrote introductions included her own. It's so rare, even now, for women writers to be included in a canon-forming production like this, let alone to be sought out for their reputation to market it. It felt like an especially fitting addition for my collection. But it's hard to keep twenty-five volumes together over two centuries. The only complete set I found was accompanied by a description that spent more than half its word count talking about the "eminent lawyer" who owned it, and none on why Inchbald would have been asked to headline it. I decided not to buy it. I didn't want to give my money to someone who couldn't be bothered to show any curiosity about the person whose name was on every title page. If I was patient, I'd find another set.

In the meantime, I pulled up a digitized copy and read the play on my laptop. *Lovers' Vows* features a titled young man who once loved and then left his lowborn childhood sweetheart. The action begins a generation later, when that woman's son from the union returns from war to hear that his mother is destitute and in poor health. His father, now a baron, has also just returned to Germany after becoming widowed. Through a series of dramatic scenes, all the characters' respective relationships with each other are revealed and reconciled. Woven into this plot of family reconciliation is the illicit love story of the baron's daughter, Amelia, and her poor tutor, Anhalt. That all sounds complicated—but even on a screen, I breezed through *Lovers' Vows*. At least twice I barked out a laugh so strong that I had to take an extra moment to breathe, reminding me of theater manager and dramatist George Colman the Younger's remark to Inchbald that "you have often made people *laugh till they cry*." It's easy to imagine that reaction in a packed house at Covent Garden when an insufferable count attempts to flirt with the baron's daughter, Amelia:

Count. I have travelled, and seen much of the world, and yet I
can positively admire you.

Amelia. I am sorry I have not seen the world.

Count. Wherefore?

Amelia. Because I might then, perhaps, admire you.

This exchange is not in Kotzebue's original; it is wholly Inchbald's
invention. She was an expert at these efficient annihilations. With the
long experience of an actress, Inchbald knew that an audience's approval
could be lost in a moment, so she learned how to ensure her shots would
hit their mark.

When the characters in *Mansfield Park* are brainstorming which play to
perform as a neighborhood event, it is the frankness of the scenes between
Amelia and her tutor (and real crush), Anhalt, that raise eyebrows in the
more virtuous-minded participants. Even those in favor of the play, like
Miss Crawford, admit that Amelia is "a forward young lady" and that some
editing might be needed. But the situation especially worries Austen's heroine, Fanny Price, the poor relative of the owner of the titular estate.

Fanny, brought up with—yet apart from—her wealthy cousins, is pain-
fully aware of her inferior place in the house. Not that her family lets her
forget it; when Fanny declines a part in the play, Mrs. Norris snaps, "I shall
think her a very obstinate, ungrateful girl, if she does not do what her Aunt,
and Cousins wish her—very ungrateful indeed, considering who and what
she is." Fanny makes every effort not to upset or offend those around her.
Knowing she has done just that by rejecting a role in the play, Fanny finds
that Mrs. Norris's comments haunt her as she tries to sleep that night, "her
spirits sinking."

Fanny's concern about acting in a privately performed play may have
also grown from warnings in popular conduct books of the era, like Gisborne's *An Enquiry into the Duties of the Female Sex* (1797). Gisborne, whose
dislike of novels I've already mentioned, was also a friend of Hannah
More. In *Enquiry*, he cautions that "the custom of acting plays in private
theatres [. . .] is almost certain to prove, in its effect, injurious to the fe-

male performers." Jane Austen read Gisborne's book in 1805, writing to Cassandra, "I am glad you recommended 'Gisborne,' for having begun, I am pleased with it." Austen also participated in elaborate private plays staged by her older brother. These two facts—that Austen could like a book arguing against amateur plays yet still enjoy them herself—are not inherently contradictory. Despite a vague sense of danger surrounding them (or perhaps because of this), amateur plays were very fashionable. In practice, it was a question of *which* play to perform and whether it was appropriate for the circumstances. (Austen's neighbor Anne Lefroy once turned down an invitation to play the role of a jealous lover because she thought it inappropriate in the context of her real-life role as a wife and mother.)

Inchbald addressed the question of morality in plays herself. One of the added benefits to reading *The British Theatre* edition of *Lovers' Vows*, even the digitized copy, is that it includes Inchbald's new introductory remarks to her own play. In this preface she tackles the play's reputation for depicting "vice." Inchbald defends herself with a comment that I think Austen would agree with, as a writer committed to realism. Inchbald argues that the dramatist can't "be untrue to his science; which [. . .] is to follow nature through all her rightful course." That is to say, a playwright fails if she cannot faithfully re-create how people act in real life. And in real life, some people are rakes and rascals and worse. Inchbald was a committed writer of realism.

It's worth remembering that Austen's own tremendous skill for realism is what critics cited approvingly in their reviews, both in her lifetime and after her death. In his influential review of *Emma*, Walter Scott said Austen's talent for creating portraits of ordinary people was so strong that a "friend of ours, whom [Austen] never saw or heard of, was at once recognized by his own family as the original of Mr. Bennet," the heroine's father in *Pride and Prejudice*. This ability stood out among the novels published in the 1810s, when Austen was publishing, in which the characters more often felt like walking morals than actual people. (I myself had experienced this when I had thrown over Hannah More's *Coelebs in Search of a Wife* in disgust.)

Of course, another novel famous for its characters' realism was *A Simple Story*, published twenty years before Austen's first novel.

The connections between Inchbald and Austen continued to unfold. In that same preface to *Lovers' Vows*, Inchbald describes what she sees as the moral of the play: "to set forth the miserable consequences which arise from the neglect, and to enforce the watchful care, of illegitimate offspring." Only remove the word "illegitimate," and this comment describes the plot of *Mansfield Park*, in which the young adults' questionable activities occur while the patriarch of the house, Sir Thomas Bertram, is on an extended visit to his estate in Antigua. That's when one young woman, the soon-to-be married Maria, devotes herself to the idea of acting in *Lovers' Vows*. She takes on the role of the mother who was seduced outside of marriage, with lines like "I was intoxicated by the fervent caresses of a young, inexperienced, capricious man." In the end (spoiler, sorry), Maria does marry her fiancé—but then runs off with one of the other men from the play, ruining both their reputations and those of their families.

Once again, Austen was using reading as a means of revelation. She incorporated a play known for depicting "the crime of seduction" into her novel—foreshadowing the very same event that the play warns against. The characters who use *Lovers' Vows* to flirt have missed the point; the characters who see *Lovers' Vows* as a warning, like the heroine Fanny Price, prove much more level-headed.

———

Before this, I confess, *Mansfield Park* was my least favorite Austen novel. I didn't much like Fanny Price, whom I found irritatingly timid. When she's asked to take a role in the play and everyone awaits her reply, she is "shocked to find herself at that moment the only speaker in the room, and to feel that almost every eye was upon her." While others sparkle, she shrinks. But I've loved plenty of books with "unlikeable" heroines. In some cases, like *A Simple Story*, I've enjoyed the books *because* the heroines are unlikeable. Miss Milner is a total brat! And I love her!

Despite that, I've probably read *Mansfield Park* half a dozen times, more than any other Austen novel. I could never understand why something as simple as putting on a private private play would make Fanny so anxious. But I remained curious about it.

After reading *Lovers' Vows*—not just the play, but Inchbald's own interpretation of it, and Gisborne's commentary too—I picked up *Mansfield Park* again. This time, I considered that Fanny Price isn't *prudish*; she's *prudent*. She was a woman without fortune relying on the generosity of a capricious extended family. As such, Fanny was forced into a high-stakes game to survive. So she molded herself into a person who offended no one and helped everyone; someone you may not like, but whom you also wouldn't want to throw out.

Fanny was always a divisive character. When Austen gathered the opinions of her family on *Mansfield Park*, the answers about its heroine were split: of her brothers, "Edward admired Fanny—George disliked her"; her niece Fanny Knight was "delighted with Fanny"; another niece, Anna, "could not bear Fanny"; her close friend Miss Lloyd was also "delighted with Fanny"; but Austen's mother "thought Fanny insipid"; and Cassandra was "fond of Fanny." In a world in which we place so much value on a woman's "likeability," Fanny becomes something of a bellwether of what we each bring to our reading.

For years I couldn't understand why someone like Austen, who created strong-willed characters like Elizabeth Bennet and Emma Woodhouse, could depict a mouse like Fanny as the heroine. But in Austen's world, steadiness is strength. Austen was also an unmarried woman who had to rely on male relatives for support. After her father died, it was entirely up to her brothers' discretion how much money each of them would contribute to the upkeep of their mother and two sisters. Austen knew personally about the kind of strength that she gave Fanny Price.

I mulled over *Mansfield Park*, reading it as an audiobook this time because I had been planning to tackle a few big chores. The words swept over me while I packed books at the shop, then walked home. One moment, while folding laundry, I stopped with my hands midway into the basket as I realized something else about my experiences reading Austen and Inchbald. There is a reason it's fairly easy for a modern reader to pick up an Austen novel, but trickier to do the same with an Inchbald one.

It's not because Inchbald is an inferior writer. As a technician, she applies an outstanding precision honed over thousands of hours of work. Thanks to a career of watching how people react to every line of her performances, she is an expert at eliciting the emotion from her audience that she seeks. Inchbald's books achieve an elegance of execution that few can match. But one of Inchbald's stated aims, as she makes clear in her theater criticism (like the preface to the 1808 edition of *Lovers' Vows*), was to communicate as clearly as possible the moral of the story. This is what can make her difficult to read today.

Inchbald's commitment to a clear moral may have developed as a reaction to the criticisms she had received on her writing. Right after one of her biggest theatrical successes, *I'll Tell You What*, a close friend and advisor sent her a letter to register his disapproval of the moral ambiguity of one of the characters, calling it "poison which is imperceptibly [. . .] taken in" by audiences. Inchbald had an eighteenth-century audience to please, and so she adapted. She revised the drafts. But the heavy-handed moral was where I became disappointed in *A Simple Story*, which sags in the second part under the weight of Lord Elmwood's stony anger and his forsaken daughter's pious submission.

This is also why I hadn't liked *Mansfield Park*. In the Victorian era, *Mansfield Park* was held in high esteem among Austen readers. The great American literary critic and champion of the realist school of novels, William Dean Howells, said of *Mansfield Park* in 1900 that it was on par with "the highest art of any time." But today, *Mansfield Park* is often cited as one of the least liked of Austen's novels. Taking Goodreads as a massive (if imperfect) data set, *Mansfield Park* is just about tied with *Northanger Abbey* in ratings: *Mansfield Park* averages at 3.86 stars, with *Northanger Abbey* at 3.85. (*Pride and Prejudice* tops the ratings at 4.29 stars.) *Northanger Abbey* has the excuse of being the least polished of Austen's published novels of the 1810s, since an earlier version was sold and out of Austen's hands for many years. But it is *Mansfield Park* that is most relentless among Austen's novels in conveying its moral.

Mansfield Park is what we call "didactic," a work that doesn't hide the fact that it's trying to teach you something. Didactic novels were extremely popular in the nineteenth century—remember *Coelebs*—but they tend to annoy a modern reader. As a 1996 instructional manual for teachers and librarians says, "Didacticism usually puts readers off; therefore, it is best to avoid it when selecting literature." To my mind, Austen is at her best when she lets the moral of her stories follow by inference. Where she does slip in the moralizing, she often does it quickly. For instance, in *Pride and Prejudice*, when Caroline Bingley speaks with jealousy of Elizabeth Bennet, Austen notes only that "angry people are not always wise," before moving on.

Inchbald, too, is brilliant at asides like this. The first part of *A Simple Story* gallops along on the snappy bickering of Milner and Sandford that kept me riveted. But the second part of Inchbald's novel shifts into a kind of moralizing that's simply not to my taste as a modern reader.

A Simple Story was republished frequently throughout the nineteenth century. By tracing editions on the rare book marketplace and surveying library holdings in WorldCat, I could pinpoint at least eighteen different printings issued in the 1800s, an average of nearly two per decade. But Inchbald's balance of realism and blunt-force morality did not survive the shifting taste of the twentieth century; the frequency of reprints in that century declined dramatically. Had Inchbald finished *A Simple Story* after the happy marriage of Milner and Dorriforth, I would wager the book could have enjoyed active reading circulation today, a classic just like Austen's novels. It's that good.

Indeed, in 1779 Inchbald *had* initially submitted her manuscript without that cursed second part. When the novel gave the snotty Miss Milner a happy ending, publishers rejected it. Milner was too rebellious a heroine for the late eighteenth century; at one point, against the advice of everyone in the household, she attends a masquerade wearing men's clothing. Inchbald was able to sell *A Simple Story* only after adding the more conventional plot of the next generation to the end. In other words, Inchbald had to revise it to meet the requirements of her publishers for us to read *A Simple Story* at all. Even then, contemporaries read its morality ambiguously. In her review of the novel, Mary Wollstonecraft said Inchbald "evidently had a very useful moral in view [. . .] but it is to be lamented that she did not, for the benefit of her young readers, enforce it." Its moral wasn't considered clear enough to even such a liberal writer as Mary Wollstonecraft!

I would have loved a version of *A Simple Story* that ended as the earliest version did, with Milner getting her happy ending. But in the 1780s and '90s, when Inchbald was writing her novels and two decades before any of Austen's books saw print, the genre was still treated with moral suspicion. In 1785, the prominent critic George Steevens had attacked one of Charlotte Smith's early French translations, *Manon Lescaut*, because he disapproved of the main characters' actions. "How are the hero and heroine punished?" he commanded. In order to justify their art, novelists had to prove that they were writing explicitly moral works. One of the most famous defenses appears in the preface to the 1785 second edition of Frances Brooke's popular novel *The Excursion*, where she says: "the novel, which in other times, and other countries, has been too often made the vehicle of depravity and licentiousness, has here displayed the standard of moral truth, and breathed the spirit of purest virtue." This was the context of Inchbald's own novel writing. She had to make sure she bellowed the moral if she wanted to challenge the readers in any other way.

And Inchbald did love to challenge people. Miss Milner is not the perfect heroine of the eighteenth-century novel. She is spiteful, selfish, and immature. In the scholarly introduction to my Oxford paperback edition of the novel, Jane Spencer perceptively noted that the second part "can be read as a kind of atonement on Inchbald's part for the boldness of the first."

A generation later, when Austen published her novels, two major cultural shifts gave novelists a bit more flexibility in their artistic choices. First was the success of the Romantics, who made great gains in celebrating individual genius over conventional wisdom. Second, the novel as a genre had become far more accepted into England's literary culture. The old days of calling novels "rank treason against [. . .] Virtue" were viewed with the condescension of retrospect. While didactic novels remained fashionable

in the Regency period, the hysteria against the form as a whole had softened somewhat. Austen's novels had a little more room to simply *be*, apart
from any ostentatious display of goodness. The more subtle moral tone that
helped sustain Austen's popularity into the twenty-first century was almost
impossible to get past publishers before the nineteenth century. Inchbald
wrote a part two so Austen would never have to.

———————

When I finally got my hands on a first edition of *A Simple Story*, I still secretly
wished its four volumes had been released only as the first two. But knowing
why Inchbald wrote that second part allowed me to accept it. Grudgingly.
After reading Hannah More's books, I knew that I didn't have to like every
part of a story to enjoy it. I let go of the zero-sum game of *like* or *dislike*. The
moments of moralizing in *Lovers' Vows* were not to my taste, but plenty of
other moments absolutely delighted me. When Anhalt attempts to repay a
couple for taking care of the Baron's lost love, the husband turns him down.
He then turns to the wife with the bag of money, asking her to take it. She
quips, "I always obey my pastor," and receives it. Works by Inchbald can be
irritatingly moral, yes, and also genuinely funny. There is so much room in
the concept of "both."

Weaving between the plays, novels, and biographies; the first editions,
Victorian editions, and modern paperback editions, I kept thinking about
Inchbald's pocketbook diaries. They were not detailed, and most don't survive today. But she used them to record the everyday events of her life
for over fifty years, including scattered notes about what she was reading.
Inchbald was not formally educated. As an adult, she came to the books
of a traditional (read: upper-class male) English education—Plato, Ovid,
Milton—on her own. She also read Radcliffe's *Romance of the Forest* in 1792,
the year after it came out. The branches of this literary family tree were
slowly filling out: how Maria Edgeworth wrote with such admiration to
Inchbald, who in turn reviewed one of Edgeworth's works; and how Austen
names books by them both within her own novels.

However, we don't know what Inchbald thought of Radcliffe's novel.

That entry was made in a pocketbook that has not survived; we only know the fact at all because it was recorded by her first biographer, Boaden, who had access to Inchbald's pocketbooks and other private papers. One modern scholar, Patricia Sigl, tracked down evidence suggesting that the pocketbooks were preserved until about 1890, when most of them were burned. If only more people had considered such papers valuable! The eleven pocketbooks still known to survive are housed at the Folger Shakespeare Library, acquired by curators between 1905 and 1991 at auction and from dealers.

Collectors, curators, dealers: we might have different roles, but we share the same goal. We preserve material histories. We keep the evidence. It's a critical step that allows for the next one, where we look back at the past to make meaning from it. Over time, some of our values will inevitably change—which can, in turn, change our interpretation of that evidence. This was exactly what I was doing in going back to these writers' own books to determine their quality, rather than taking the word of outdated literary authorities. I had different values than Ian Watt; therefore, I had different interpretations. Every generation must, in its turn, scrape off the barnacles of previous generations' criticism and look at the evidence for themselves. But the evidence must be there.

I recorded these thoughts about Inchbald's and Austen's novels in my book journal as I finished them. This was a habit I'd started after reading about Inchbald's pocketbooks. I note the date I finished a book, what format I'd read the book in, and my initial thoughts after completion. The entries in my first book journal place Sonali Dev next to a reread of Austen's *Persuasion,* and Scarlett Peckham like a cry for help in a wilderness of biographies of Hannah More. Victor LaValle in paperback (with his main character a rare book dealer!) precedes two different Austen rereads on audiobook. Lauren Blackwood jumps in before a round of Inchbald biographies; I often like to have at least one fiction book and one nonfiction book going at the same time.

I chose a paper journal over a word processor, enjoying the enforced rumination that comes from taking longer to write out a thought by hand.

Within a few pages, I decided I needed to slow the process down further, so I began writing the entries in my nondominant hand. The clumsiness of the result is embarrassingly hard to read, but this journal isn't for others to read anyway. It is only for me.

Inchbald didn't write in her pocketbooks for others either. While she did work on a memoir through much of her later years, it was never published. Now all we have are a few of the surviving pocketbooks. They are tiny volumes, with space only for a few lines, and bound for carrying around in one's pocket. The area for entries is only about one centimeter high—and Inchbald would often turn the book ninety degrees to write up the margins. The modern editor of her diaries described the many practical problems of reading her handwriting: "In some cases it overlaps, and in some cases, the ink itself is too faded or blotted to decipher. To stretch her funds, Inchbald seems to have diluted her ink on some occasions, so the text sometimes is especially light." I doubt she anticipated others would want to leaf through them over two hundred years in the future. But she did go back herself to reference previous entries: "Lookd at my Old P: Books," she notes in a 1780 entry.

Like Inchbald, I enjoy looking back through my entries. As I read new books and reread Austen's, maintaining this book journal has allowed me to track the changes in my interpretations. *Northanger Abbey* becomes a very different story after reading Radcliffe's *Udolpho*; *Pride and Prejudice* builds on the blueprints set forth in Burney's *Evelina*; *Mansfield Park*'s central conflict makes a lot more sense after learning the plot of *Lovers' Vows*.

I also unintentionally tracked a different set of changes, not in how I viewed these books, but how I viewed myself. The entries for the earliest academic books I read for this project reflected how unsure I felt. I would read an argument I didn't agree with and assumed I must be the one in the wrong; these authors were, after all, specialists. But as I continued to read, and to collect, my entries changed. They were evidence of my very own turning point: in my inelegant, nondominant handwriting, I started arguing back. My rebuttals spiked with allusions to the various books I had read, recorded in the very same journal. My entries had begun as observations.

Now they were dialogues, honed by a life among these books. I was learning how to trust my own instincts.

My collection continues to grow. James Boaden's 1833 *Memoirs of Mrs. Inchbald: Including Her Familiar Correspondence* sits next to William Roberts's 1834 *Memoirs of the Life and Correspondence of Mrs. Hannah More*, two similar early-Victorian biographical portraits of very dissimilar women, practically sparking with their proximity to each other. I still haven't found a copy of *The British Theatre* I'm happy with, but I did acquire an original engraving of the same portrait of Inchbald used in the set. In this image, Inchbald turns to gaze directly at the viewer, her hands resting on a book. And, of course, I still have my 1988 reading copy of *A Simple Story*. I did once triumphantly snag a 1791 first edition of *A Simple Story* in full speckled calf bindings, but that one lives in a different collection. It was too perfect not to include in my rare book catalog tracing the history of romance that was ultimately destined for the rare book collections at the Lilly Library.

Finally, I included a different kind of book in my ever-increasing collection: my book journal. It belonged on the same shelf as the books that had shown me how to trust my own voice. The journal, and the books it sits alongside, marked what I chose to read, when, and why; how I saw myself in these books, or didn't. Entry by entry, acquisition by acquisition, the collection became a powerful act of self-definition: my own unconventional memoir.

Chapter Eight

HESTER LYNCH THRALE PIOZZI
(1741-1821)

**But all this, as my dear Mrs. Piozzi says, is flight & fancy &
nonsense.**

**—Letter from Jane Austen to her sister Cassandra,
December 9, 1808**

Like Elizabeth Inchbald, Mrs. Piozzi was a dutiful keeper of journals. But hers were of a different kind. A few months after her eightieth birthday, she added a new entry. In it, she listed every one of her "enemies outlived."

Hester Lynch Thrale Piozzi was a polarizing figure in her time. Her personal and professional choices were attacked relentlessly, but especially when they deviated from the broader expectations for an eighteenth-century British woman. Which was often. Piozzi's characteristic response was to commit more boldly to her course. Often she would host a party to celebrate that very course. When friends suggested she return from her European travels quietly, Piozzi instead announced a large welcome-home bash. When the lively and erudite Bluestocking hostesses abandoned her, Piozzi hosted her own dinners with literati. When she turned eighty and was expected to bow out of the public eye, she invited near seven hundred people to a debt-inducing birthday celebration in Bath.

Piozzi has remained a polarizing figure for over two centuries. Over the years, her rebellions have been cited repeatedly as proof that Piozzi was graceless, vain, and self-centered. But even a short description of a few of them is enough to inspire admiration to a modern reader (or perhaps I'm just telling on myself). There is some justification for either interpretation, as this oft-quoted 1781 passage from her journal captures: "Miss Owen & Miss Burney asked me if I had never been in Love; with myself, said I, & most passionately. when any Man likes me I never am surprized, for I think how should he help it? when any Man does *not* like me, I think him a Blockhead, & there's an End of the matter." (And yes: "Miss Burney" is our Burney.) No matter your reaction to such a passage, one point is clear: Hester Piozzi was never boring.

If you've spent any time reading about the world of eighteenth-century British literature, you know Piozzi already. Of all the women writers in this project, she was the only one with whom I was already quite familiar. At the same time, I hadn't known that she had written any books at all. Paradoxically, I knew she was considered a part of the canon, but I could not name a single one of her publications. How did that work?

———

To start, I didn't know her by the name under which she published, Hester Lynch Piozzi. The name I first knew her by was Mrs. Thrale. Perhaps that name is more familiar to you, too: it was her surname from her first marriage, during the years of her celebrated friendship with Samuel Johnson, the author of the great *Dictionary* and friend of Frances Burney, Charlotte Lennox, and Hannah More. Piozzi's first two books, both bestsellers, were based upon her friendship with Johnson: *Anecdotes of the Late Samuel Johnson* (1786), which went into an extraordinary five editions in a single year; and *Letters to and from the Late Samuel Johnson* (1788), which was also immediately reprinted despite its higher print run.

But these two publications marked just the beginning of Piozzi's literary career. She went on to publish three more fascinating books: *Observations and Reflections Made in the Course of a Journey* (1789), a European travelogue that Ann Radcliffe used as inspiration for her gothic landscapes; *British Synonymy* (1794), a groundbreaking book on English synonyms based on interactions with non-native speakers; and finally, *Retrospection* (1801), "the first world history ever written by [a British] woman," according to the modern scholar William McCarthy.

In the twentieth century, books unearthing previously unpublished Piozzi writings appeared with astonishing frequency. To name some of the best known, there are: *The Intimate Letters of Hester Piozzi and Penelope Pennington* (edited by Oswald G. Knapp, 1914); *The French Journals of Mrs. Thrale and Doctor Johnson* (edited by Moses Tyson and Henry Guppy, 1932); *Thraliana* (edited by Katherine C. Balderston, 1942); *The Children's Book or Rather Family Book* (edited by Mary Hyde in the book *The Thrales of Streatham Park*, 1977); and *The Piozzi Letters: Correspondence of Hester Lynch Piozzi, 1784–1821 (formerly Mrs. Thrale)* (edited by Edward A. Bloom and Lillian D. Bloom, 1989–2002). The Piozzi industry has remained strong for centuries.

I wondered why Piozzi continued to capture our imagination, for good and for ill, over so many years. Throughout my investigation into the lives and legacies of Austen's favorite women writers, I had narrowed in on turning points. I focused particularly on when and how each had fallen out of fashion, leading to their removal from the canon. I scouted for rare books with evidence of these moments. It is harder to find fancy, leather-bound copies of Burney's novels in the later nineteenth century, but easy to find beautiful editions of her journals, thanks to the buzzy 1840s publication of her *Diary and Letters* that transformed her reputation into a diarist first, novelist second. Lennox's novels disappeared entirely from the reprint scene in the twentieth century—I know because I've looked for them—until the 1970 edition of *The Female Quixote* that got people reading her again. But Piozzi is different. She hasn't disappeared from the canon. In every decade, across literary circles, she has been read, and debated, and ridiculed, and praised. So this time I didn't ask why she fell from the canon. I asked why she stayed.

Sometimes the first question you ask in an investigation leads you to a second question—and the second question is even more interesting. As I reviewed all those books mentioned above, I noticed that some people were continually willing to fight for her, even while others actively campaigned to bury her. Here's the second question: What was it about Hester Lynch Thrale Piozzi?

She was born in 1741 as Hester Lynch Salusbury, in Caernarfonshire, Wales, the only child of aristocratic but impoverished Welsh parents. Hester was the promised heir of wealthy relatives and raised as such, though in a slightly unorthodox manner for a girl. Her parents appreciated her intelligence at a young age and encouraged her. At age six, she already had a library of French books with which she was learning to translate; a few years later, she was reciting lines from Milton's *Paradise Lost* for the entertainment of a duke and duchess; and as a teenager, her parents employed a private tutor to teach her Latin. From childhood she was trained to perform her talents for others' entertainment. As she wrote in an autobiographical sketch much later, "although Education was a Word then unknown, as applied to Females; They had taught me [. . .] till I was half a Prodigy."

Hester did become half a prodigy, but ultimately not an heiress. When she was around seven years old, her mother's brother, Sir Robert Cotton, "openly declared he would generously provide for his little niece in his will," then died suddenly soon after—without having revised the will. The entire estate was therefore inherited by an estranged brother, and Hester's family suffered as a result; after the new heir took over, the family was forced to leave the London house where the late Robert Cotton had once granted them residence. The little aristocrat with the library of French books was now without a permanent home, and the family spent the next few years bouncing around between those of relatives. Not long after, in 1749 and again in 1752, Hester's father decided to sail to Nova Scotia in search of an income that would support the family. Despite two separate voyages across the Atlantic, he still came back destitute.

Her parents were once again forced to rely on family, and this time her father's brother Sir Thomas Salusbury stepped in. Sir Thomas and his wife were childless and, like the rest of the family, enchanted with Hester. She now became the heir apparent to the large fortune Sir Thomas had acquired upon his marriage to Lady Salusbury. This wealthy aunt had a facility with languages herself that she used to help teach Hester more French, alongside Italian and Spanish. As a teenager, Hester translated English essays into Italian and Spanish sermons into English. For fun, she would translate her favorite passages from *Don Quixote* into English, too. Taking joy in literature at an early age, Hester would long cherish dreams of becoming an author.

By eighteen, Hester was attracting attention from men who were drawn to her quick mind, her vivacity, and—let's be real—her expected inheritance. But her father was in no hurry to see her married. A letter from one occasion survives in which he outright threatened one young man who had sent her a love letter: "be then most certainly Assured that I will be avenged on you—much to the detriment of your Person and—So Help me God."

Then, several life-changing events occurred in quick succession. Lady Salusbury died. And Sir Thomas began to think of remarrying a widow named Mrs. King. Mrs. King disliked Hester, and the feeling was reciprocated. These developments were ominous because, as his new wife, Mrs. King might either produce an heir or convince her husband to cut off Hester. Hester's inheritance was in jeopardy once again, as she herself recognized: "my Uncle is on the point of being married himself to a fine young widow whose nearer Claim to his property & Affections must necessarily destroy mine." (This dilemma might sound familiar: the same fears plague Anne Elliot's family in *Persuasion*, when the widow Mrs. Clay endears herself to Anne's father with an eye toward his title and property.)

At the moment when Hester and her parents were worried about losing a second inheritance, they met a rich young brewer named Henry Thrale. Hester's mother adored him, as did her uncle Sir Thomas. Later in life Hester recalled that Sir Thomas thought Henry "an incomparable young Man [. . .] who was in short a Model of Perfection: ending his Panegyric by saying that he was a *real Sportsman*. Seeing me disposed to laugh, he looked very grave, said he expected us to like him—& that seriously." To

Sir Thomas, a marriage between Hester and Henry appeared an ideal solution. If she were to be married to a rich man, he wouldn't need to provide so extravagantly for her and could marry Mrs. King with (a little less) guilt about forsaking his niece. But her father judged him unfit for Hester. A brewer! Matched to his prodigy, descended from illustrious ancestors like Katheryn of Berain, who was known as "Mam Cymru," Mother of Wales! Hester's father furiously opposed the plans of his brother, declaring that he refused to see his daughter "exchanged for a Barrel of Porter." Then he died, unexpectedly, in December 1762.

Hester, who had not especially liked Henry, felt more vulnerable than ever. Friends of the family, particularly Hester's devoted Latin instructor, pressured Sir Thomas to formalize his promise of settling a fortune on her. Instead, Sir Thomas offered £10,000 as a dowry to Henry Thrale. Hester lost her strongest advocate when her mother refused to allow her to correspond with her Latin instructor any further because he had counseled against the marriage. In 1763 she married Henry Thrale. She convinced herself that they had a "mutual Preference for each other [. . .] not founded on Passion but on Reason." So Hester became the wife of a man she did not love, and thus began a marriage of nearly eighteen years that were to include some of the most miserable moments of her life.

Mr. Thrale was not much interested in his wife. When as a newlywed she attempted to write him some love poems, he ignored them as "Impertinent, or rejected [them] as superfluous." In addition, her new husband forbade her from one of her favorite hobbies, riding, because he thought it too "masculine." Mrs. Thrale had very few women friends in the early years of her marriage from whom she could seek counsel. The couple had moved into Streatham, a country manor turned grand by Henry's money, and also took a townhouse in Southwark near his brewery—but far from any casual company they might have. She later learned that Henry's interest in her began because she hadn't objected to living in such an unfashionable part of town, as other women had. Henry, ambitious in business, spent long days at the brewery. Hester did at least have the company of her widowed mother, who first stayed with them during the summers and soon became a fixture in the house. Until her death in 1773, her mother's presence was an immense comfort.

Hester Thrale soon had plenty to keep her busy, if not exactly happy. Henry loved hosting lavish dinners for his own friends and Hester was expected to entertain them. Soon Henry would run for and successfully gain a seat in Parliament, his wife canvasing by his side. She also became pregnant within the first year of her marriage, giving birth to a baby girl in 1764. For the next fifteen years, alongside all these plans, ambitions, and successes, Thrale would be either pregnant or recovering from pregnancy.

Thrale bore twelve children over the course of the marriage. Eight died young. Some passed quickly, like her second child Frances, who lived only nine days. A number of her children seemed to have issues with brain development, leading to headaches that caused the little ones great pain before they died. When her ninth child Ralph became ill with similar problems, she wrote to a friend: "The illness of this boy frights me for all the rest; if any of them have a headache it puts me in an agony, a broken leg would less affect my peace." Meanwhile, her husband had little patience with these worries and said so. As she recorded when one of her daughters was sick, she was "often told how little it signified whether she catch'd cold or no."

Many of Thrale's writings, whether in letters or in her own journals, describe the wretchedness of watching her children suffer. She records the daily details of motherhood—monitoring toothaches and hiring tutors—but underneath her mask of chattiness, grief swelled in her heart. When a friend once suggested that it would be worthwhile to keep correspondence to reminisce about twenty years later, she replied: "the sight of it would *not* revive the memory of cheerful times at all. God forbid that I should be less happy then than now, when I am perpetually bringing or losing babies, both very dreadful operations to me, and which tear mind and body both in pieces very cruelly."

The earliest biographies of Hester Thrale, all written by men, give very little consideration to the effect of so much childbearing and child-burying. But as a parent myself, I had a different interpretation. I distinctly remember the first time this feeling hit me. I was reading the 1987 second edition of James L. Clifford's foundational biography, *Hester Lynch Piozzi (Mrs. Thrale)*, on a flight across the country. I had reached the period when her little son Ralph grew sicker. His doctor advised sending him with a nurse to Brighton for the health benefits of bathing in the sea. Henry was comfortable leaving Ralph in the hands of medical professionals, and so the child went. He then insisted, against Hester's inclination, that he and Hester return to Streatham. But then word came that Ralph was near death, and Hester rushed back to him at Brighton, only to arrive after he had died.

The moment I read this, I was on a plane flying in the opposite direction of my own son, who was home being watched by his grandmother. Even though my child was in perfect health at the time, it was hard not to worry about him. Have you ever looked at the small hands of a child and ached at how fine, how fragile they appear? Felt the heat burning through the skin of a sick little boy and wished desperately that you could take the fever into yourself instead? I could not bear to imagine the depth of the pain she experienced, reaching Brighton and knowing he was gone. When Ralph died, she was still caring for a newborn, another daughter named Frances Anna who was then only two months old. Five months later, Frances Anna died too.

After her own mother had died a few years earlier, Hester didn't have many other people with whom she could talk about these harrowing experiences. In 1776, four months after the death of Frances Anna, nine-year-old Henry—the Thrales' final surviving son and heir—died suddenly of what was perhaps meningitis. This experience broke Henry Thrale as much as it did Hester; he plunged into a depression that rarely left him for the remainder of his life.

But despite losing three children in under a year, the couple did not talk about their anguish. Instead, they continued to host dinner parties that were by now famous, both for the lavish meals that Henry insisted upon and for the people who attended: the dramatist Arthur Murphy (who had brought the courtesan Ann Elliot to the stage), the painter Joshua Reynolds, the politician (and theorist of the sublime) Edmund Burke, the author Oliver Goldsmith, the lexicographer Samuel Johnson, the Bluestocking leader Elizabeth Montagu, and more.

These dinners were often viewed as rivals to Bluestocking events, though their character was different. Frances Burney, who became a regular guest at the Thrale home after her authorship of *Evelina* (1778) was revealed, recalled that Henry Thrale took "a singular amusement in hearing, instigating, and provoking a war of words [. . .] between clever and ambitious colloquial combatants." Hester herself gained a reputation as a consummate hostess at these events, all while dealing with multiple pregnancies and losses. As she wrote in a letter to Johnson, early on she had to "learn to be as gaily miserable [. . .] as I can." Skilled at social performance since childhood, she had crafted an elaborate mask to conceal her pain and disarm her visitors.

There are many stories of Hester's gaiety and talent for putting people at ease, including the dazzled Burney, who called her first visit to Streatham "the most consequential day I have spent since my birth." Later, Burney admitted of Thrale in her diary that "I am so much in love with her, that I shall be obliged to run away from the subject, or shall write of nothing else." Thrale equally impressed her male guests, though her erudition took some getting used to: one male visitor wrote that she "is a very learned lady, and joins to the charms of her own sex, the manly understanding of ours." Like Austen (and perhaps better than Lennox), Thrale balanced on the knife edge as a woman with wit. But it is also astonishing to think of how Thrale kept herself together despite poor health from so many pregnancies, and in constant anxiety and grief over her children, while putting on a show that impressed even the most illustrious of visitors. In a later self-portrait, Thrale recorded her own perception of these talents: her "Grace [was] more acquired than natural; for Strength & not Delicacy was the original Characterstick of the Figure."

Thrale needed that strength. While she took on the role of gracious hostess, she also became involved in work at the brewery. Initially Henry did not want her participation in his business—but after some of his foolhardy speculations to expand nearly bankrupted them, Hester stepped in to help stabilize it. Henry turned surly for her intervention, even as he let the task of saving the business fall to her. On one of these occasions in 1772, she spent the third trimester of one of her pregnancies scrounging up nearly £20,000 to keep the brewery afloat against over £130,000 in debt while Henry moped at home. The daughter born immediately after, Penelope, lived only ten hours. Hester was pregnant again within a matter of months.

By now the Thrales were famous enough that their doings made the papers—and not always positively. Henry was widely known to have mistresses, but in March of 1773, while Hester was pregnant again, one newspaper printed a malicious account of the gossip, stating that he was "more famed for his amours than celebrated for his beer." This was to be only the beginning of the press's mudslinging.

Privately, the situation was even worse. In 1776, Henry developed what was apparently a venereal disease; he refused to acknowledge it as such to Hester, but for treatment he saw a doctor who specialized in the field. Henry dealt with a painful swollen testicle that Hester tended to "every Night & Morning for an Hour together on my Knees"—while she was pregnant again, for the eleventh time. "Father's Prophecy was verified," she recorded in her diary, "who said If you marry that Scoundrel he will catch the Pox, /&/ for your Amusement set you to make his Pultices. This is now literally made out." The next year, her husband met a woman with whom he would become truly infatuated.

Hester Thrale became friends with Sophia Streatfeild in 1777, first meeting by chance on holiday at Brighton. They promptly established a mutual esteem based in part on their similar upbringings: Streatfeild had studied with the same tutor who had taught Hester Latin. (Streatfeild's specialty, however, was Greek.) Over the next few years, she became a popular addition to the Thrale social circle and, as a brilliant, beautiful, *single* woman, won the hearts of a number of men among their acquaintances. A postscript to the final entry in Thrale's early journal now known as *The Children's Book* revealed her growing awareness of the problem: "I will not fret about this Rival this S.S. no I won't." That sentence ended a journal begun twelve years earlier to record the growth of her children. Earlier in the entry, she speculated that she was pregnant again and prayed no more of her children would die before her. In January, Thrale confessed in her main journal (called *Thraliana*) that "Mr. Thrale is fallen in Love *really & seriously* [. . .] but there is no wonder in that; She is very pretty, very gentle, soft and insinuating."

Hester was never under any illusion that her marriage with Henry was based upon love. She tried not to allow this development to distress her. In the entries immediately after describing the affair, she puts on an air of amusement, calling herself "a disinterested Spectator." When Streatfeild insisted that her attentions to Henry were only signs of her affection for Hester, the diarist recorded that "I can hardly sometimes help laughing in her Face." But Hester Thrale was never a truly indifferent person, no matter how she affected it. Her gaiety was her defense against grief.

In comparison to her public persona, her journal entries are refreshing in their vulnerability. There, she takes off her mask. Direct and colloquial, her talents and flaws are both on display. Recording one conversation in which Hester had quoted Alexander Pope's translation of Homer, Henry remarked that Streatfeild "could have quoted the Lines *in the Greek*: his saying so, piqued me; & piqued me because it was true. I wish I understood Greek! Mr Thrale's preference of her to me never vexed me so much as my Consciousness—or Fear at least—that he had *Reason* for his Preference."

Sometimes, however, the mask slipped. At one dinner, when Hester was advanced in yet another pregnancy, Henry "very unceremoniously begged of me to change place [at the table] with Sophy ———— [*sic*], who was threatened with a sore-throat, and might be injured by sitting near the door." Her husband suggesting in company that she give up her pride of place at her own table—while pregnant—was too much. When no one objected, she left the dinner in tears.

Afterward, two of the dinner guests attempted to comfort her, admitting privately that her upset was justified. But Thrale understood the game. She responded, "I cannot help remarking with what blandness and composure you *witnessed* the outrage. Had this transaction been told of others, your anger would have known no bounds; but, towards a man who gives good dinners, &c., you were meekness itself!" Thrale then recorded that "I had not a word of answer from either." The dinner guests she had silenced were Edmund Burke and Samuel Johnson.

There was still more, and graver, to endure: Henry Thrale's health had been rapidly deteriorating. In 1779, he had a stroke, leading Hester to take up some responsibilities at the brewery again. Hester recorded one visit with Henry to the brewery a few months later, when he had partially recovered and she was far advanced in yet another difficult pregnancy:

> **Mr Thrale wished me to go, nay insisted on it, but seemed somewhat concern'd too, as he was well apprized of the Risque I should run. I went however, & after doing the Business I went to do, beg'd him to make haste home, as I was apprehensive bad Consequences might very quickly arise from the Joulting &c.—he would not be hurried—the probable Consequences *did* begin to rise, I pressed him to order the Coach— he could not be hurried—I told his Valet my Danger, & begged him to hasten his Master; no Pain, no Entreaties of mine could make him set out one *Moment* before the appointed hour—so I lay along in the Coach all the way from London to Streatham in a State not to be described, nor endured;—*but by me:*—& being carried to my Chamber the Instant I got home, miscarried in the utmost Agony before they could get me into Bed, after fainting five Times.—**

That was her final pregnancy as Mrs. Thrale.

Henry died in the spring of 1781. He left behind a widow with five daughters. In the following years, Hester Thrale and the other executors performed all the duties required to deal with the large estate, including setting up trusts for the daughters and selling the brewery. But the widow Thrale did not have sole authority over her children. According to the stipulations of her husband's will, all five of the named executors were appointed guardians of the children. Thrale was the only woman among them. She could make no significant decisions about her children's lives unless her husband's four male friends agreed with her.

Thrale was also almost immediately courted by men in her social circle. The sport became aggressive; Thrale recorded that at least one acquaintance "lays Wagers about me I find." Her response was to turn the gossip on its head: "they think they are doing me *honour* with these imaginary Matches, when, perhaps, the Man does not exist, who would do me honour by marrying me!"

Harried by suitors and gossip, Thrale began dreaming of a trip to Europe with her daughters to "see what the world could show me." But soon the dream became a practical idea as well: Thrale was running into money troubles. Keeping up Streatham was expensive without the brewery's regular income. And while she did receive a portion of the proceeds from the sale of the brewery, the vast majority went into her daughters' trusts, as stipulated by the will.

Just then a new problem developed in her long-standing feud with the woman Mrs. King, who had indeed become the new Lady Salusbury. After Thrale's uncle Sir Thomas had died in 1773, the relationship between that side of the family and the Thrales completely broke down. In 1782, less than a year after Thrale became a widow, Lady Salusbury opened and won a court case stipulating that Thrale must pay back a large amount of money that Sir Thomas had once loaned her parents. They settled at Thrale paying £7,500. Thrale was not ruined by this, but she did have to take out a large loan and she absolutely needed to economize.

Spending a few years in Europe would cut down her cost of living significantly compared to Streatham, and she could receive income by renting it out while away. As an added bonus, she could avoid all her suitors: "The persecution I endure from men too who want to marry me [. . .] is another reason for my desiring to be gone," she confided to her journal. "I wish to marry none of them." But one of the other guardians of her children "violently opposed the move," and Thrale was unable to pursue it.

Then a strange event occurred. Hester Thrale fell in love. And not with one of her genteel British suitors. A few years before Henry's death, she had made the acquaintance of Gabriel Mario Piozzi, an Italian musician. In 1780, she had engaged him to provide voice lessons for her eldest daughter, known in the family by the nickname Queeney. While Henry flirted with Streatfeild, Hester confessed in her journal that Piozzi's skill on the piano "fills the Mind with Emotions one would not be without, though inconvenient enough sometimes—I made him sing yesterday, & tho' he says his Voice is gone, I cannot some how or other get it out of my Ears,—odd enough!" Nevertheless, her journals mention him mainly in passing during the early years of their acquaintance. Then, in the fall of 1782, a year and a half after Henry Thrale's death: "that dear little discerning Creature Fanny Burney says I'm in love with Piozzi—very likely!" And Piozzi returned her affection.

After all Hester Thrale endured, falling in love should have been a triumph. Instead, it created a crisis. Piozzi was the wrong choice by every standard except love. He was a musician, not of her class, nor her financial equal. He was Italian, a serious problem in xenophobic eighteenth-century England, where marriage to foreigners was rarely approved of. He was Catholic, making a match with an English Protestant nearly as shocking to her contemporaries as proposing to an atheist. The four other guardians of the Thrale estate, who believed the marriage would disgrace the entire family, explicitly encouraged Thrale's children to hate him. And they did. Burney, too, immediately tried to talk Thrale out of her feelings, arguing that "while She possessed her Reason, nothing should seduce her to approve what Reason itself would condemn: that Children, Religion, Situation, Country & Character [. . .] were too much to Sacrifice to any One Man."

It is during this period that Thrale's journal entries are the most affecting. Even before Burney's intervention, Thrale wrote at length about the pros and cons of her new relationship in language as riveting as any passage about Radcliffe's Gothic halls or Burney's poignant misunderstandings between lovers. "I am not to think about myself, I married the first Time to please my Mother, I must marry the second Time to please my

Daughter—I have always sacrificed my own Choice to that of others, so I must sacrifice it again," she records. Then she continues:

> —but why? Oh, because I am a Woman of superior Understanding, & must not for the World degrade my self from my Situation in Life. but if I *have* superior Understanding, let me at least make use of it for once; & rise to the Rank of a human Being conscious of its own power to discern Good from Ill— the person who has uniformly acted by the Will of others, has hardly that Dignity to boast.

Hester Thrale was torn between society's expectations and her own happiness, between the mask and the heart underneath. Despite her feelings, she wasn't sure which choice to make, and she resented the fact that her friends and family were going to make her choose. "To what then am I Guardian?" she asked her journal in 1782: "to their Pride and Prejudice?"

There was that phrase again. Portions of Thrale's voluminous journals were gradually published after her death beginning in Abraham Hayward's important 1861 biography, *Autobiography, Letters, and Literary Remains of Mrs. Piozzi (Thrale)*. This entry was published for the first time there. In other words, it appeared long after Jane Austen's book *Pride and Prejudice* was published in 1813. But this was the third time I had run across it. Stumbling upon the tidbit that "pride and prejudice" appeared in Burney's *Cecilia* had been one of the singular catalysts to this quest. At the time, I thought it was definitive evidence. Austen had read *Cecilia*; she took that phrase from Burney's novel and turned it into a title for one of her own! It was a clear answer after a swift analysis, all the more appealing because it was simple.

But then I ran into the phrase, again, while reading a Charlotte Smith novel that Austen almost certainly read. Was there a chain of borrowings, a thread I could tug that connected all these women? And here, again, the phrase in Hester Thrale's private journal, not published until nearly eighty years later. *Cecilia* had come out in 1782, the year of Thrale's entry: perhaps she was alluding to her dear friend's new book. Or perhaps Burney had heard Thrale use it before. Or it was, perhaps, just a phrase. An eighteenth-century colloquialism. That would be logical: none of these women were writing separate from the influences of the world around them. They were of it, and from it.

It probably would have been a letdown if I had searched the history of the phrase "pride and prejudice" on the internet and found all these instances repeated as simple fact. Instead, I had sought out these books and experienced the phrase in the context of each of these authors' words. I remember the moment when I first ran across the phrase in Charlotte Smith's *Old Manor House*. I was reading the 1987 Pandora Mothers of the Novel paperback edition, its leaves toning just at the edges, its spine gradually creasing as I read under my lamp's yellow light. I dog-eared the page, then pulled up the note-taking app on my phone to type, "Did Austen get it from Burney or Smith . . . or both?" A few months later, I stumbled upon Thrale's journal entry as excerpted in the 1861 biography. This time, I had been reading on my laptop via Project Gutenberg, a vast digital library of public domain books. My daughter had wanted to go to the mall with her friends, so I sat scrolling at a table near a coffee shop while she larked about, texting me about spending her allowance on manga and lip gloss.

Reading is not separate from life. It is a thread of life. In the lives of these women and their books, I saw not a direct reflection, but a refraction of my experiences. When Hester Thrale asked, "To what then am I Guardian?," I felt the same scrunching in my heart that I remembered from the first time I had read Austen's *Pride and Prejudice* when I was a teenager. When Elizabeth reads Darcy's letter after refusing his proposal, it hits her that she has completely misjudged him. She reads it over and over again: "Mr. Darcy's letter, she was in a fair way of soon knowing by heart. She studied every sentence: and her feelings towards its writer were at times widely different." That part gets me every time. And now, reading Hester Thrale's journal entries, I realized that her real life was as moving to me as one of the greatest English novels ever published.

But I chose the wrong time to get invested in Thrale's fate, because then I read what happened next. She had finally decided that she would not marry Piozzi if her eldest daughter, Queeney, did not consent to it. Queeney did not. She had always had a difficult relationship with her mother because of their opposing temperaments: Thrale was fiery and capricious, while Queeney was cool and stoic. When she was a teenager, this natural disconnect was aggravated by Queeney's live-in Italian instructor, who loathed her mother and made malicious observations to Queeney like she "had more Sense, and would have a better Fortune than her Mother."

Queeney was not predisposed to consent to her mother's marriage, and her guardians and family friends encouraged this instinct. Frances Burney wrote to Queeney that her mother was "duped by ungovernable passions." (Thrale viewed Burney's actions at this time as a fundamental betrayal of their friendship; their relationship never recovered.) Burney's father Charles, a music instructor himself and the one who had first introduced Thrale and Piozzi, added that the marriage would "fling away [Thrale's] talents, situation in life, & character." As Austen later so aptly put it in *Persuasion*, "the public [. . .] is rather apt to be unreasonably discontented when a woman *does* marry again, than when she does *not*."

Queeney was then eighteen. She had always been capable and independent, matching her mother's intelligence. Yet she was also raised as an heiress who grew up in a famous household, and she was undeniably a snob. The idea of her mother marrying a foreigner of a lower class was horrifying. Thrale recorded Queeney telling her that "if I *would* abandon my Children, I *must*; that their Father had not deserved such Treatment from me." You know, the father who repeatedly and publicly cheated on her mother, and who refused to take her mother home when she was in the middle of a miscarriage. That father.

Thrale brought Queeney and Piozzi together to attempt to resolve the détente, recording that "I had but one heart for both him & Her—but that I would break it between them." Nevertheless, Queeney remained opposed to the match, and the couple capitulated. Piozzi gave all of Thrale's letters to Queeney and said, "Take your Mama—and make it of her a Countess— It shall kill *me* never mind—but it shall *kill her too*!" That was the end. Even though Piozzi had made a life and career in London, he arranged to return to Italy to make the break complete.

The following year was one of the most difficult of Thrale's life. Having given up her dreams of traveling in Europe, instead she moved to Bath, where she could live more economically. Almost immediately after, her youngest daughter Harriett, only four and a half years old, died. Now eight of the twelve children she had given birth to had died before her. She and her remaining four daughters suffered through a number of health scares, culminating in a catastrophe described by modern biographer James L. Clifford: "in November Sophia [her third eldest daughter] fell desperately ill. Despite her own nervous debility, Mrs. Thrale nursed her child through a long, dangerous siege and then collapsed. This last ordeal had broken what little resistance there was left."

Thrale's health had deteriorated rapidly over the course of the year, frightening her friends and family. Some of the physicians attending Thrale advised that the heartbreak over Piozzi had contributed to this decline. With this news, Queeney reversed her decision. She consented to the marriage, and Piozzi was called back to England.

Hester Lynch Thrale would become Hester Lynch Piozzi. But she was still a woman, and this was still eighteenth-century England. This triumph would exact stunning payment, and payment of a kind rarely required by male contemporaries. When word got out, many of her friends were horrified. Elizabeth Montagu—who had become godmother to one of Thrale's children only a few years before—immediately cut off her friendship with Thrale, writing to a fellow Bluestocking that "I am sorry and feel the worst kind of sorrow, that which is blended with shame [. . .] I am myself convinced that the poor Woman is mad." Thrale wrote to Queeney that another acquaintance, upon hearing the news, "prayed with true Presbyterian Tenderness and Devotion that Piozzi might be put in his Coffin before we met [to marry]—and this with a serious earnestness." When some physicians had recommended Piozzi's recall to help with Thrale's recovery, one doctor friend argued, in that case, Piozzi *"would not answer Mrs Thrale's Purpose* whose Health required a *Man."* Even among friends, Piozzi was a foreigner, a Catholic, and a musician; he wasn't on par with the rich Protestant Englishmen who had been courting Thrale. He wasn't even a man.

And that's before the press took up the news. In choosing Piozzi over an Englishman of her own class, Hester Lynch Piozzi had stepped out-of-bounds, therefore authorizing every kind of previously latent attack for sport. One print circulated at the time, captioned "Signor Piozzi Ravishing Mrs. Thrale," depicts Thrale sitting next to Piozzi while he plays a cello. One of his hands grasps the neck of the instrument in obviously phallic imagery. Thrale's speech bubble says, "Your Music has ravished me, and your Instrument is large & delightful." Piozzi's speech bubble responds, "And me like de Museek of your Guineas," efficiently combining xenophobia (imitating an accent and grammar errors of a non-native speaker) with classism (claiming he's after her for her money, though in reality Piozzi was by no means poor). One of the other figures in the tableau holds a horsewhip—think about that for a moment!—with a word bubble that says, "She had better have stuck to Home-brewed," a play on her late husband's trade alongside the physical threat and, of course, more xenophobia.

Their marriage became fodder for every joke and jeer, in part because it *was* a love match. That the widow Thrale would pursue a man she had fallen in love with, rather than demurely waiting for someone "worthy" of her to chase her, was inherently distasteful to the crowd aligned against her. Even over 150 years later, in the commentary to a printed collection of Queeney's letters he inherited, the Marquis of Lansdowne observed that "the pursuit of a second husband by a widow of maturer years must always be a somewhat undignified spectacle." (To be clear: the summer she married Piozzi, the widow in question was forty-three.)

I had searched for a first edition of this book, *The Queeney Letters* (1934), the design of which seemed to match Queeney's taste. It was printed on handmade paper that subtly spoke—to those who knew the signs—of its quality: soft but strong. The binding was in a simple but well-selected cream cloth. The spine was stamped in an elaborate gilt pattern, not with the most common ornament for books by women, flowers (you know how I feel about those), but with diamonds. I acquired a copy, then I read it.

To date, it's the only purchase for my collection that I regret.

As I investigated the lives and work of writers like Frances Burney and Charlotte Smith, I had come to understand that a love match held a precarious place in the wider cultural context of upper-class Great Britain. Love in marriage was fine, even desirable—if the lovers were of the same class. But marriage for love was often a secondary concern when wealth was involved. Recall that Burney's family thought she should accept the proposal of a man she had met once simply so that she would be financially provided for if her father died. Charlotte Smith was forced into a marriage that her father and stepmother viewed as a beneficial financial transaction, sold "like a Southdown sheep" without a care for her feelings. In Piozzi's sphere of wealth and aristocratic ancestry, marriage was fundamentally an economic arrangement meant to consolidate assets and secure them for future generations. And while a man might marry below his class for love without severe pushback, the same was not the case for women. These opinions still held in some circles well into the twentieth century, as when the Marquis of Lansdowne argued that marrying Piozzi must have meant Thrale "was suffering from what we should now call a 'sex complex.'" In print!

Nevertheless, Thrale planned her wedding. She also had to work with the four other guardians to make arrangements for her children. This sounds surprising, as one would assume the youngest would continue attending boarding school and the eldest daughters would continue living at home with their mother. But the four other guardians and the elder children refused, concerned that the infamy of this marriage would ruin the girls' own prospects of marriage. Thrale strongly disagreed: "As for me, the People who do not respect my Husband and my Daughters according to their Merit, or at least according to their Character, shall never be treated as Friends or even Companions by me." But she was outmatched. It was finally agreed that she and Piozzi would take a honeymoon in Italy, giving the girls distance (literally) from what they feared would be an event that could ruin their reputation. The girls no longer at school would remain in their own household in Brighton under a hired chaperone. Queeney was about to turn twenty.

Just before the ceremony in July 1784, Thrale wrote to her eldest daughter that "I do sincerely believe there is not so happy a Woman as I am, out of Heaven. Dear, precious, charming Queeney, accept my truest, my tenderest Thanks." Afterward, the couple left on their honeymoon, during which Piozzi wrote spirited letters to her daughters about their travels. They dined with nobility from across Europe. They became friends with an expat English community in Florence, with whom Piozzi published a miscellany of verses and other "scraps" written by the group. They climbed Mount Vesuvius. Always fascinated by languages, Piozzi loved noting the differences in Italian dialects. Catholic friends kept teasing her, a devout Protestant, for being a "Heretick" and priests tried to convert her to Catholicism, which she cheerfully resisted.

Nevertheless, even while abroad the British press gossiped about her. She recorded hearing "Reports of my Husband's having sold my Joynture [i.e., her settlement from the Thrale estate], & shut me up in a Convent." According to her journal, Piozzi published her first book in a gesture of defiance against the doubters: "to keep the English from fancying that I was *lost* to the World." But doing so fulfilled another of her long-standing dreams, to become an established author. Piozzi would ultimately publish five book-length works between 1786 and 1801.

Anecdotes of the Late Samuel Johnson was published in 1786, the year after Johnson's death, while Piozzi was still abroad. The modern scholar Michael John Franklin notes that the style of this biography—"informal, indeed intimate and conversational," and specifically feminine—re-created the atmosphere of her famed dinner parties in print. It sold out within hours, so quickly, according to Hayward, that when "the king sent for a copy of the 'Anecdotes' on the evening of the publication, there was none to be had." (The publisher ended up sending his own copy to the king instead.) Published in March, by mid-April it was already into a third edition; Hannah More remarked of it in an April letter to her sister that "Mrs. Piozzi's book is much in fashion." Piozzi followed it upon her return to England with *Letters to and from the Late Samuel Johnson* (1788), which was printed in twice the size of the print run of the *Anecdotes*. Even one of Piozzi's known enemies, the Shakespearean critic Edmond Malone, recorded that "I sat up till four o'clock reading away as hard as I could, and then my candle went out and I could read no more."

Piozzi followed these books related to Johnson with a bestselling work all her own, the travelogue of her European honeymoon, *Observations and Reflections Made in the Course of a Journey* (1789). It was a book-length defiance that celebrated her happy second marriage. *Observations* saw another edition the same year and a German translation the next. Frances Burney, who was then in royal service as "Keeper of the Robes," read it together with Queen Charlotte. She recorded in her *Diary*, "How like herself, how characteristic is every line!—Wild, entertaining, flighty, inconsistent, and clever!" Meanwhile, one modern scholar has argued that Ann Radcliffe turned to Piozzi's *Observations* for realistic descriptions of Europe for *Udolpho*, having not yet visited the Continent herself.

Each one of Piozzi's first three books was both praised and attacked in the press—and they all enjoyed healthy sales. A copy of each could be found in the library of Godmersham Park, the estate of Jane Austen's brother Edward Austen Knight, where Austen occasionally stayed and made use of those very shelves. But this success did not make the public forget about her controversial second marriage. Nor did Piozzi want them to: each book proudly bore "By Hester Lynch Piozzi" on the title page.

When the couple returned to England, a friend advised her to go by her maiden name of Salusbury rather than her new married name, arguing "that an Italian Name makes an awkward Jumble with the Smiths, Thomsons, Jacksons & all the Usual Names." Mrs. Piozzi did not do so. The same friend suggested she spend a few months in Bath first before making an appearance in London so that she might reenter British society quietly. Instead, Mr. and Mrs. Piozzi headed straight to London to attend a play at Drury Lane—exactly the kind of event one attended to see and been seen. (During this period, her love of the theater also led to a warm friendship with Elizabeth Inchbald.) A couple months later, Hester Piozzi threw a welcome-home party with nearly one hundred guests. Her gaiety had once been her mask to conceal her grief. But she didn't want to hide anymore. So she used it as a weapon to defy her critics.

Her oldest girls did not attend that party. Following Queeney's lead, they maintained a social distance from their mother. Queeney remained concerned that her mother's reputation would hurt their own marriage prospects. As a twenty-first-century woman, I can't help but admire Piozzi's audacity. From Queeney's perspective, I can also see how it made her daughters' lives more difficult. However, Piozzi herself was often convinced that this distance originated not with her daughters, but with the other guardians and family friends. She had reason: while she was away, one of the guardians had actually told her youngest daughter Cecilia that Gabriel Piozzi had locked her mother up in Milan, giving her only bread and water.

Piozzi would continue to have a strained relationship with her daughters for the rest of her life. The remaining four all blessedly outlived her, but she went through long periods of serious breaks with each for various reasons. Soon after her return to London, Piozzi and Queeney became estranged for six years over the question of living arrangements for Cecilia, then only ten years old. Queeney, fearing that Cecilia would be "corrupted" by their mother, had attempted to remove Cecilia from her boarding school before Piozzi could reunite with her. Piozzi's defiance was viewed by her daughters at the best of times as an irritation; at the worst of times, it was viewed as harmful. For her part, Piozzi's stubbornness increased whenever she felt wronged.

Piozzi's relationship with her daughters remained a fertile source of dispute for later commentators. Those against Piozzi argue that she was a terrible mother. Those for Piozzi emphasize Queeney's desire for respectability, which made her (and by extension, the younger daughters) vulnerable to believing the worst about their mother. But in between these two poles, small details hint at a more complicated truth. Queeney sent the Piozzis a lovely tea chest as a wedding gift, yet sent only infrequent letters to her mother during the honeymoon. Queeney herself waited until the age of forty-four to marry—making her one year older than her mother had been when marrying Piozzi. When she did, it was to one of the most decorated men in the United Kingdom, Admiral George Elphinstone, 1st Viscount Keith. She did not invite her mother to the wedding, nor to the birth of her own daughter (whose godparents were HRH the Prince of Wales and HRH the Duke of Clarence, two future kings of England). But she was nevertheless happy to introduce her mother to Walter Scott and the playwright Joanna Baillie upon request that same year. Queeney seems truly to have loved her mother, though ideally at a distance.

Through all the years of conflicts and reconciliations with her children, Piozzi recorded countless entries in her journal with both spiteful outbursts and extravagant love for her daughters. Piozzi's passionate nature, carefully filtered through her mask in company, had made her impressive at social events—one visitor referred to her "easy irresponsible charm." But at home, it made her difficult for her daughters to bear.

Piozzi's greatest strength was also her weakness: she allowed herself to feel everything fully. In the parlance of the time, she was too affected by sensibility, like Marianne in *Sense and Sensibility*. In fact, her daughter Cecilia compared her to another heroine famous for her sensibility: Emily, from Radcliffe's *The Mysteries of Udolpho*. Even after Frances Burney had broken with Piozzi over her second marriage, she still admired this quality in her former friend. Upon seeing a letter that Piozzi had written to a mutual friend, Burney observed that Piozzi was "full of spirit & fire, & all herself. I rejoiced to see such flash still in her."

Spirit, fire, and flash: to this new Piozzi, defiance was energizing. During her first marriage, she had kept her grief safely behind her mask. She had focused on being the kind of wife and mother that Henry Thrale expected: a sprightly host at the table, pregnant with a potential future heir. After Henry's death, Hester began to define her life on her own terms. That included setting her own boundaries. After Elizabeth Montagu and other Bluestockings had forsaken her, she called them "my unprovoked Enemies." When Montagu later attempted to reconcile, Piozzi recorded in her journal that "I dare say She does; but I will not be taken & left"—a sentiment I so admired that I want to applaud her from two hundred years off.

Meanwhile, she and her husband had begun constructing their ideal home in her native Wales. They named it Brynbella, formed from a combination of Welsh and Italian words. Gabriel had become a naturalized British citizen and Anglican, "slowly changing into a typical English squire." Unlike Henry Thrale, Gabriel Piozzi encouraged and supported his wife in every area, including her literary pursuits. Throughout their marriage, he proved the gossip about them unfounded: responsible with finances, "faithful & tender" to his wife, and "doating" on Cecilia as she grew up.

As a parent, Hester Piozzi remained the woman Burney once knew: "Wild, entertaining, flighty, inconsistent, and clever." Frankly, I would have struggled with that kind of mother as well. But to undermine Piozzi, detractors frequently chose to attack her as a mother, instead of judging her books on their own merits. We call that fallacy *ad hominem*. Many canonical writers were terrible fathers—Charles Dickens, William Faulkner—yet that subject rarely dominates critical conversations around them. What does Piozzi's literary legacy have to do with her parenting? These same critics tend to be silent on the subject of Henry Thrale as a father. While I don't think we should be silent on this subject, I do believe Piozzi should be judged by the same standards as her male peers. If a critic dislikes her, let it be for her books.

Hester Piozzi would go on to publish two more books, both of which were groundbreaking. In 1794, she released *British Synonymy*, a book on the English language that was something of a thesaurus mixed with a dictionary. Conceived in part from her experiences with her husband and other non-native English-speaking friends, it listed entries with an emphasis on the distinct connotations of words that are otherwise considered synonyms, such as "to abandon, forsake, relinquish, give up, desert, quit, leave." It was an innovative project, an experiment to make a place for herself within the authoritative landscape of books on language, then considered the province of men. As the modern literary scholar William McCarthy has argued, "Her position as a woman writer drove her to be resourceful."

In 1801, Piozzi published her final book, *Retrospection*, which McCarthy calls "the first world history ever written by [a British] woman." It was viciously panned at the time, with one reviewer calling it "History cooked up in a novel form reduced to light reading for boarding school misses, and loungers at a watering place." This method of attack—to denigrate a book for being enjoyed by teen girls, or as a beach read—remains in common use today. Yet McCarthy argued in 1985 that *Retrospection* is "a far more impressive work than it has ever been supposed [. . .] a work of great daring in every way." Queeney read the thousand-plus-page book *twice*. (This is one reason why I'm certain that she loved her mother.)

What particularly made Piozzi daring as an author was her style. Beginning with *Anecdotes* and through *Retrospection*, Piozzi mixed established genres—e.g., biography, travelogue, history—with personal writing. This gave her writing style an unusual "hybrid quality." Critics of her own time struggled with Piozzi's refusal to keep to form. An infamous 1801 review of her *Retrospection* argued its "style is often rendered abrupt and quaint, by the pursuit of what the French call *esprit*." But modern scholars have explored why she chose to break from that form. Piozzi was, according to Margaret D'Ezio, searching for a way to be an author true to herself in "a literary world still dominated by men." By taking this hybrid approach, Piozzi brought her social, feminine touch to these traditionally staid, masculine spheres. D'Ezio argues that Piozzi might be better appreciated by modern readers for this very reason—and as the recent rise of a similar hybrid form of personal essay with cultural criticism suggests. Piozzi's writing feels well suited to twenty-first-century audiences.

After the disheartening reception of *Retrospection*, Piozzi kept writing, though she did not publish further books. She remained a famous figure of literary England. As with Hannah More, many saw her as a legend: one woman remarked upon meeting Piozzi that she was "very like what I supposed Mrs. Piozzi to be." She still spent time in London to see her friends, like the novelist sisters Harriet Lee and Sophia Lee (the latter of whom published the landmark 1783 gothic novel *The Recess*), and the celebrated actress Sarah Siddons. But she now spent most of her time between Brynbella and Bath, where Gabriel sought treatment as a sufferer of gout. In Bath, the Piozzis moved next door to Hannah More—"Glorious creature! How she writes!" Piozzi once said of her. Despite Piozzi's unconventional marriage, she and More had much in common, as they were both deeply religious. (At the age of sixty-four, Piozzi decided to learn Hebrew to benefit her Bible study.) More also appreciated Piozzi's "gaiety, animation, and cheerfulness"; they enjoyed nearly daily visits before More retired to the country.

The very same year that Piozzi and More became neighbors, 1801, Jane Austen also moved to Bath after her father's retirement. Austen admired the famous writers living in her new hometown. We know this because of her extant letters to Cassandra. In one 1808 letter, after first teasing her correspondent, Austen joked that "all this, as my dear Mrs. Piozzi says, is flight & fancy & nonsense." She was slightly misquoting one of the celebrated letters from Piozzi's 1788 collection. (The line actually reads "Well! now all this is nonsense, and fancy, and flight.") Piozzi was such a well-known author in the family that Austen could quote that letter from memory and expect Cassandra to recognize the context.

Alongside the record of Piozzi's books belonging to the library at Godmersham Park, that single line of "flight & fancy & nonsense" had spurred me to add Piozzi to my list of Austen's favorite women writers. It was a slim bit of evidence, but it became a powerful catalyst. Looking back, I realized how quickly I had gotten attached to Piozzi from just that little nudge. While reading Piozzi, I found myself—to my surprise—barely thinking of Austen at all. When I began this project, Austen was my North Star. But as I progressed in my investigation, I gained more confidence in my own taste, and I didn't always need her anymore. Rather, I noticed that with each of my investigations, the world of women writers around her was becoming richer and more resonant.

––––––––––

In the end, Mr. and Mrs. Piozzi spent twenty-five happy years together. In 1809, Piozzi's beloved second husband died. The person who brought her so much happiness—and for whom she sacrificed so much—was gone. The final entry in *Thraliana* records his death: "Every thing most dreaded *has* ensued,—all is over." But Hester Thrale Piozzi kept going with verve, as she always had. She spent her final years in Bath, where she developed a number of significant new friendships and renewed old ones. As she joked when a friend brought his son to meet her, "I am now grown one of the Curiosities of Bath it seems & *one of the Antiquities.*"

In 1821, she threw an enormous party for her eightieth birthday, demonstrating that her defiant gaiety remained with her to the end of her life. Around seven hundred people attended the ball, which was followed by a lavish supper, all held at the famous Lower Assembly Rooms (and the same place Catherine Morland meets Henry Tilney in *Northanger Abbey*). Everyone who was anyone in Bath was there, and Piozzi herself "danced with astonishing elasticity," noted a friend who attended, the Irish writer Edward Mangin: "if anything could exceed the magnificent show of the assemblage, glittering in the gayest attire [. . .] it was the gracious and queen-like deportment of Mrs. Piozzi herself."

Piozzi died only a few months after the celebration. But she continued to be remembered, beginning with Mangin's 1833 collection, *Piozziana; or, Recollections of the Late Mrs. Piozzi.* And she continued to be the subject of gossip. In 1843, an anonymous pamphlet suddenly appeared suggesting that the widow Piozzi had fallen in love with one of her closest friends at the end of her life, the much younger actor William Augustus Conway (thirty at the time of their meeting). The pamphlet, *Love Letters of Mrs. Piozzi, Written When She Was Eighty, to William Augustus Conway*, printed seven of her letters to him and provoked a firestorm; the owner of the letters, Mrs. E. F. Ellet, published an indignant response stating that the "letters are so garbled and distorted as to change their character, for the apparent purpose of injuring the fair fame of [Piozzi]." Yet many still used it to make Piozzi appear ridiculous: once again, that woman with the "sex complex" had fallen in love and made a fool of herself.

Still, Piozzi had her champions. In 1927, a book-length defense of Piozzi titled *The True Story of the So-Called Love Letters* was published by Percival Merritt, a "painstaking historian and a scholarly collector of books." Today, the combination of modern criticism from scholars like Devoney Looser— who compellingly recast this friendship as one with Piozzi as "mentor" and

Conway as "would-be protégé"—and the availability of Piozzi's letters in the publication of the six-volume set edited by Edward A. Bloom, Lillian Bloom, and O. M. Brack Jr. make it clear that this was simply more sexist gossip aimed at one of the best-known literary women of the era. As I looked back at the *Love Letters* pamphlet, I thought it could have become a turning point, a moment that knocked her from her place in the canon. Yet: it didn't.

Through reading all these novels, biographies, books of letters, diaries, critical appraisals, and introductions, I had gotten a sense of the mechanics of how an author's legacy could rise and fall over the course of centuries. The right attack, at the right time, and by the right person, can be fatal. Recall how Wordsworth set the terms for Radcliffe's demise by turning her into a representative of a "lower" genre, rather than the best of a popular genre. Piozzi should have been displaced with the rest, but she wasn't. Yes, her value was constantly debated—but at least it *was* debated, rather than removed. It helped that she provided so much material to work with: as I mentioned, Piozzi's unpublished writings continued to be unearthed and published in the twentieth century. As late as 1942, the publication of her *Thraliana* journals kept her legacy alive, her name remaining in the story of eighteenth-century British letters. Well, sort of. Her first married name, Mrs. Thrale, remained part of it.

As I collected books related to Piozzi's life and works, tracing her legacy across centuries, the evidence as to why became unmistakable. Piozzi's image achieved longevity because it never fully revolved around her own life and creations. She remained in the conversation thanks to her close friendship with Samuel Johnson, perhaps the single most influential writer upon eighteenth-century British literature.

Unlike many of his contemporaries, Johnson welcomed some women as fellow intellectuals and writers. In his December 11, 1753, essay in *The Adventurer*, Johnson observed that "the revolution of years has now produced a generation of Amazons of the pen, who with the spirit of their predecessors have set masculine tyranny at defiance." This was the same Johnson who considered Frances Burney's comic characters superior to Fielding's;

who threw a book-launch party for Charlotte Lennox's first novel, then used his connections to ensure that *The Female Quixote* was published; who quoted Hannah More's own poetry back to her. At the time he had been encouraging Lennox's debut as a novelist, he was also working on the book that would shape his own legacy, the 1755 *Dictionary*. According to his friend and biographer James Boswell, he was commonly known after that point simply as "Dictionary Johnson."

Samuel Johnson and Hester Thrale met in 1765, a few months after the birth of her first child. They were introduced by a mutual friend, the playwright Arthur Murphy, who knew that Johnson would appreciate the generous dinners organized by Henry Thrale. Johnson soon became a weekly visitor at Streatham, and he and Hester Thrale developed a close friendship. When Johnson (who suffered from a number of physical and mental illnesses) experienced a particularly rough period of depression in 1766, the Thrales invited him for a long stay at their home. From that point until the death of Henry Thrale in 1781, Johnson was a constant presence there, treated more like a member of the family than a guest.

While Johnson respected Hester Thrale and other women writers of the period, it would be a mistake to say that he was a feminist. He was politically and socially conservative, as Piozzi makes clear in an anecdote about their argument over a lord who had left his wife of fourteen years to take up with "the Nursery Maid": "why says the Doctor I doubt not but it was the Lady's Fault." Nor did Johnson bestow his approbation upon every smart woman. He disliked the manner of Greek-reading Streatfeild, for instance. Most important, he prioritized traditionally feminine virtues of the time as far more important than intellectual accomplishments. He adored brilliant women who kept to social convention, and he disdained brilliant women who didn't. Thus he loved Mrs. Thrale, and he denounced Mrs. Piozzi.

When Johnson learned that the widow Thrale planned to marry Piozzi, he sent a stark letter warning against it: "If you have abandoned your children and your religion, God forgive your wickedness; if you have forfeited your fame and your country, may your folly do no further mischief." Thrale responded with head high: "I have this morning received from you so rough a letter [. . .] that I am forced to desire the conclusion of a correspondence which I can bear to continue no longer." This was the occasion of their final break. For my part, I once again wished to offer this woman a standing ovation. It could not have been easy to stand up to the most famous man of letters alive.

Piozzi's legacy has both benefited from and been impaired by her association with Johnson. The success of her first two books, published after his death in 1784, *Anecdotes of the Late Samuel Johnson* and *Letters to and from the Late Samuel Johnson*, obviously and unquestionably owed a debt to Johnson's reputation and the fame of their friendship. Yet when Piozzi published *British Synonymy*, "a rumor arose that the best parts of [it] had been pilfered from a manuscript" that Johnson had "allegedly left her." It was Lennox and *The Female Quixote* all over again. In fact, Piozzi was so worried that her friendship with Johnson would undermine her own achievements that she determined "I would not accept help from Doctor Johnson" and specifically "waited for his Death before I commenced Author."

Johnson and Thrale enjoyed a deep and meaningful friendship. Despite many attempts to suggest it was also romantic, there is no compelling evidence to support this. As early as 1773 newspapers were anonymously suggesting that the eldest Thrale son and heir was actually Johnson's child, for no other reason than that a friendship existed between a man and woman. After her first husband's death, it was widely reported that Thrale and Johnson would marry. Neither showed any interest in the idea—except in Thrale enjoying the dubious vindication of having predicted that exactly such rumors would circulate if her husband died before her. In fact, the day after Henry Thrale's funeral, James Boswell—frenemy of the Thrales and then-aspiring biographer of Johnson—composed a fake "Ode by Samuel Johnson to Mrs. Thrale upon Their Supposed Approaching Nuptials" that he jocularly circulated among friends.

One of the great modern biographers of Hester Lynch Piozzi, James L. Clifford, commented that this poem showed a "strange lack of taste," but there was nothing strange about it to me. It was utterly predictable. Because where a woman's name is commonly associated with a man's, sex jokes will inevitably follow. Even after her second marriage, one paper discussed her upcoming *Anecdotes of the Late Samuel Johnson* with printing-themed innuendo: "Report frequently whispered that a connubial knot would be tied between Mrs. Thrale and Dr. Johnson;—that event never took place, and yet Mrs. Piozzi and the Doctor, it seems, are shortly to be *pressed* in the same *sheets*."

In 1988, the scholar William McCarthy told an anecdote that demonstrates how common this leap remained, two hundred years later:

> **A Colleague (to me): Who are you writing about?**
> **I: Hester Lynch Piozzi.**
> **(Blank look.)**
> **I (trying to be polite): You know, "Dr. Johnson's Mrs. Thrale"?**
> **Colleague: Oh, Mrs. Thrale . . . didn't they have an affair or something?**

The mystery of why she has remained canonical is resolved by the name by which she is most remembered: Mrs. Thrale. This is the name that associated her with Johnson. The modern edition of Boswell's *Life of Johnson* (1791) that I read, for instance, indexes her name by "Thrale, Mrs. (afterwards Mrs. Piozzi)"—which I learned when I first tried to look her up under the *P*s. The Marquis of Lansdowne assured his readers in 1934 that "Mrs. Piozzi of Bath and Brynbella has not the same interest as Mrs. Thrale of Streatham, and her later letters to her daughters are of no special merit. Scattered among their pages, however, there are some further anecdotes of Dr. Johnson, never, I believe, published elsewhere, and deserving to be rescued from oblivion." He felt she was worthy of being remembered because of her friendship with Johnson, and only that.

But that is not why she should be remembered today. I was sick of reading about Johnson every time I picked up a book about Piozzi. I wanted to read about her opinions, her struggles, her literary creations, her victories. This chapter isn't about Johnson. It's about Hester Lynch Salusbury Thrale Piozzi. It was her own words that made me want to shout in triumph. Not

Johnson's quips, but her retorts. Not his pronouncements, but her teasing. Not his taste, but her heart. Because she revealed her heart, again and again, in her writing. When she sent a collection of her own letters to a friend for help arranging them, she warned "you will never again have the heart of any one so completely in your hand." That's why she deserves to be remembered today: for what she has to say about snatching happiness from a world aligned against you.

———

While married to Henry Thrale, Hester's existence was focused on meeting the expectations of others. Now she focused on making herself happy, rather than making others comfortable. And that wasn't the Mrs. Thrale whom Johnson and all his friends knew. To them, it was a betrayal. Her second marriage was, in many ways, a complete rejection of these friends and all they stood for. She married a foreigner who was both a musician and a Catholic, while she was simultaneously courted by Englishmen of her own class and religion. In her judgment, these men fell short—so they figured out a way to say that her judgment meant nothing. And they largely succeeded.

They turned on her, proudly and publicly. There was the critic, George Steevens, who called her second marriage a "disgrace" in a newspaper article; and John Wolcot, who wrote a satirical verse under his pen name Peter Pindar about the world "turn[ing] up the nose of scorn" at her marriage. Each of these men would end up on Piozzi's list of "enemies outlived." Nevertheless, the 1860 edition of the *Encyclopaedia Britannica* codified their campaign, in an aside about the Thrales in the entry for Johnson:

> **The kind and generous Thrale was no more; and it would have been well if his wife had been laid beside him. But she survived to be the laughing-stock of those who had envied her [. . .] While she was restrained by her husband, a man of sense and firmness, indulgent to her taste in trifles, but always the undisputed master of his house, her worst offences had been im-**

pertinent jokes, white lies, and short fits of pettishness ending
in sunny good humour. But he was gone [. . .] She soon fell
in love with a music-master from Brescia, in whom nobody
but herself could discover anything to admire. Her pride, and
perhaps some better feelings, struggled hard against this degrading passion.

That was printed in the encyclopedia! The entry was not even about
her! The animosity Piozzi inspired ran deep.

Yet every time a new detractor appeared to claim she was unworthy of
her more famous friend, it was Piozzi's own talents that won her new champions. One important twentieth-century admirer of Johnson who subsequently fell under Piozzi's charm was Mary Hyde, later Viscountess Eccles.
Hyde was a celebrated collector in the twentieth century whose Johnsonian
library (built with her first husband, Donald Hyde) ended up at the Houghton Library, the main repository for rare books and manuscripts at Harvard. Hyde was inspired to write about Piozzi after winning the manuscript
of *The Children's Book* at a London auction in 1969.

The Children's Book was Piozzi's family journal from 1766 to 1778,
when she was still Mrs. Thrale. This acquisition was a tense experience
for Hyde; her husband had died only a few years earlier, and he used to
handle arrangements like bidding at auction. Hyde asked a London representative, Winnie Myers, to do the bidding. The drama of the auction
room shines through in her account: "[I s]tayed in my hotel bedroom, by
the telephone [. . .] At last . . . she telephoned. Surprise! Joy! Success! *The
Children's Book* was ours!!"

Once it was in her hands, Hyde began to read it and "became increasingly curious" about the Thrale family. In 1977, she published *The Children's
Book* within a larger scholarly work, *The Thrales of Streatham Park*, that traced
the story of the family and their descendants into the twentieth century. *The
Children's Book* is now considered a critical primary source on Piozzi's life, as
well as offering "a rare insight into the life of an eighteenth-century family."
It is a fabulous example of the book collector's role in fueling discovery, cre-

ating scholarship, and shaping literary history. Naturally, I bought a signed first edition of *The Thrales of Streatham Park* for my own shelf.

––––––––––––

Even as the scholarship around Piozzi has shifted focus from her relationship with Johnson to an appreciation for the author in her own right, in the rare book world, Piozzi's value has largely remained tied to Johnson's. In dealer descriptions of first editions of *Anecdotes of the Late Samuel Johnson* and *Letters to and from the Late Samuel Johnson*, my colleagues naturally laid a great deal of emphasis on her more famous friend. But these descriptions rarely considered Piozzi's unique contributions in these books. The *Letters*, for example, contained more than two dozen examples of her own epistolary compositions, including one letter of advice to a young man getting married that earned special contemporary acclaim and became a favorite for anthologies of literary letters. Yet not one of my colleagues mentioned that celebrated composition in their catalog descriptions, even though it was first published here.

Even when Johnson had nothing to do with a book, many of the descriptions tended to make Piozzi's published works about him anyway. One description for a first edition copy of her first published book specifically *not* relating to Samuel Johnson, *Observations and Reflections Made in the Course of a Journey*, described Piozzi as a "Welsh-born diarist, author and patron of the arts, and is an important source of information on Samuel Johnson and 18th-century English life." There was no escaping Johnson, even in the book that chronicles her *honeymoon*.

Piozzi's *British Synonymy* was summarized by another rare book dealer without any description of the content at all except: "Contains some anecdotes regarding Samuel Johnson." A different dealer description for the same book noted, "She mentions Samuel Johnson some fifty times and uses his Dictionary as a source." Yet William McCarthy had already noted decades earlier in 1985 that "when she cites the *Dictionary* [. . .] she does so only to disagree with it."

They looked different to me now, all these beautiful volumes with

Piozzi's name printed on the title page. Octavos in full calf bindings, or quarter calf and marbled boards, or the ever-elusive original paper boards, or sometimes in lavish later rebinds. No matter the material, they carried Piozzi's heart. These dealer descriptions touted Johnson's eminence instead.

The formal work to correct this scholarship began decades ago. Many of the best mic-drop moments, like McCarthy's anecdote about fellow academics assuming Mrs. Thrale was Johnson's mistress, come from just such scholars' works in the 1970s and '80s. Yet professionals in adjacent fields—like people handling rare books—haven't caught up. Move away from specialist circles and into the most accessible places to find information, such as in Wikipedia pages, and the old narratives easily reassert their strength. As of this writing, the Wikipedia page for William Augustus Conway, the actor who became friends with Piozzi in Bath, notes that "Conway won the affections of Hester Piozzi, whose letters to him were published in 1843" (without any citation). That would be the seven letters, out of more than one hundred, that their owner said had been so "distorted as to change their character." We have the knowledge and the resources to know better. Yet we are still making these mistakes.

I say "we" here because I had done this myself. I still feel a knot in my stomach when I remember moments earlier in my career selling first editions of Boswell's *Life of Johnson, LL.D.*

Boswell's *Life of Samuel Johnson* is a classic of British literature. The first edition has been a highly sought trophy of rare book collectors for two centuries; I know it so well that I don't have to look up its date of publication (1791) and I can also recite from memory the typographical error—"gve" on page 135 of volume I—that indicates a first issue of the first edition. Boswell always nursed a great ambition for his biography, taking notes about his interactions with Johnson from their very first meeting in 1763. This seems to have caused some subtle tension between Boswell and (then) Hester Thrale, who was Johnson's biggest confidante; in 1769, he sent her a letter politely joking that "you and I [are] rivals for that great man." Only: he wasn't joking.

When Johnson died in 1784, a flood of reminiscences, reprints of his works, and biographies hit the marketplace. Piozzi's *Anecdotes* (1786) was by far the most popular of these works from the 1780s—outselling Boswell's own Johnsonian travelogue, *The Journal of a Tour to the Hebrides with Samuel Johnson, LL.D.* (1785). Boswell saw Piozzi's works as a threat to his planned biography's eminence, and he and his friends sought every opportunity to discredit her books about Johnson. His later followers followed, arguing that his biography was the only one worth reading; the others were trifling pretenders.

I, too, sold Boswell's book on the strength of his dominance. I can sell first editions of his *Life* for $10,000 to $15,000 (if it is an exceptionally well-preserved copy); first editions of Piozzi's *Anecdotes* currently fetch between $1,000 to $1,500. I never spent much time wondering why. Always, there was that easy answer: It's because he's the better writer, right? Meanwhile, Piozzi's great modern biographer James L. Clifford trusted Boswell so little that he only quoted from Boswell's prepublication notes of the *Life* wherever Piozzi was concerned. Clifford knew Boswell's narrative was not trustworthy. For his part, the scholar William McCarthy argued that "Boswell's treatment of her [. . .] did more to sink Piozzi's general reputation, probably than any other circumstance."

It sunk Piozzi's reputation, and cemented it in place. In the world of rare book collecting, she was always "Mrs. Thrale," her name during the years of her acquaintance with Johnson, not Hester Lynch Piozzi, her name as a published author. Or more to the point: when *I* mentioned Mrs. Thrale, I talked about her only in relation to Samuel Johnson. I remember how, in my early years as a dealer, I loved that a woman became a celebrated literary figure because she was able to banter with Johnson on a level few others could manage. I didn't even realize she had published any books until I read a biography of her years later.

I had helped bury Hester Lynch Piozzi.

The mechanics of the profession had led my colleagues and me here. Johnson was more famous: more sellable. Therefore he is mentioned more prominently and more often. At the first rare book firm where I worked, we jokingly referred to the "Shakespeare Principle": any rare book becomes more sellable if it can be tied in some way to Shakespeare. An otherwise unremarkable book on botany suddenly becomes much more desirable when it includes examples of flowers from Shakespeare's hometown of Stratford-upon-Avon. A book of engravings can double in price if it includes a portrait of Shakespeare.

The Shakespeare Principle can be applied to anyone who is more famous than the creator of the book in question, as long as a connection can be made to the better-known person. I had already seen it happen to Charlotte Lennox when associated with Samuel Johnson. And I had even indulged in this fallacy myself as I formulated this project. I had decided to explore Piozzi's life and works simply because Austen had called her "my dear Mrs. Piozzi." Like so many before me, I had found Piozzi on someone else's merits. But once I read her books, journals, letters, and poetry, I came to appreciate her for her own. I wanted as many of her publications as possible in my collection.

Like Mary Hyde, I will also occasionally bid at auction. I don't prefer to because it's incredibly labor-intensive; most auctions are caveat emptor, buyer beware. Bidders are expected to do their own due diligence to check if the book is right because auction terms typically dictate no returns, even for mis- or under-described material. I also determine in advance exactly how much I will bid because the drama of the auction room is, as Hyde knew, very real. If I don't have a number already in mind, I'm putting myself in danger of getting carried away by the excitement and spending more than I intended. So if I'm bidding at an auction, I will do hours of research in advance, then spend the day watching it, and often only acquire 10 percent of the books I wanted. However, it occurred to me that in this context I could use Piozzi's underestimated reputation to my advantage. To achieve big numbers at auction requires at least two people bidding against each other; less interest means fewer people bidding, and possibly a lower price.

A presentation copy, marked in ink "From the Author / 1797," of Piozzi's *Letters* was coming up in New York. It had an estimate of $1,000 to

$2,000, meaning that Christie's expected the bidding to end within that range. At this level, I would be buying it for my company—but I could only do so if I could nab it under that estimate. Otherwise I wouldn't be able to keep the margin I needed for the business. I thought I just might achieve it.

Like Hyde, I wasn't in the auction room. But I did bid for myself—I'm the kind of person big collectors like Hyde call when they want someone to bid for them. In this instance, the auction was conducted entirely online. Due to the COVID pandemic, auction houses ramped up their internet capabilities, so the process has become much smoother than it had been in previous years. My children quickly acclimated to the sounds of auction patter in the background when I bid from home. That said, online bidding is not entirely devoid of its own risks. Once, in trying to switch between open windows on my screen, I accidentally clicked the big red "BID" button on a lot of Winston Churchill letters that I absolutely did not want. I experienced a harrowing five seconds until someone unknowingly committed an act of mercy and outbid me.

The bidding started at half the auction's low estimate, $500. Sometimes I wait to join in, but this time I had to be in early—otherwise, I would not be in at all. I bid. Someone followed me at $600. It was my turn at $700. This was my last chance. Auction houses also charge a "buyer's premium," an additional percentage of the "hammer" price achieved at the winning bid. This auction's premium was 26 percent. If I missed this book at $700, another person would bid at $800, then I would be at $900; with the premium, that would mean (sorry, math) a final price of $1,134. Too much. I needed the $700 to stick. I bid.

It stuck.

Piozzi's *Letters* was mine. Temporarily, at least. It was still meant for my rare book company. As I said, it was too expensive for what I was acquiring in my own humble collection. The next step would be to catalog it, writing a description that both captured the book's importance and recorded the physical traits of this particular copy. I can't offer it for sale until I do so. That auction occurred in 2022. I still have not cataloged it.

When I do, you can bet that I will emphasize Piozzi's style, how intrepid she was as a writer. She brought to her books the daring she had learned from her personal life. I saw in her a writer whom I admired for her courage to experiment, to combine genres as the surest way to stay true to herself. A model, perhaps, for my own writing. A model for this book.

Chapter Nine

MARIA EDGEWORTH
(1768-1849)

I have made up my mind to like no Novels really, but Miss Edgeworth's, Yours & my own.

—Letter from Jane Austen to Anna Austen, September 28, 1814

In the early years of my rare book apprenticeship a first edition appeared at auction that, even now, makes my breath catch just to think of it. It was bound in paper wrappers: cheap, unremarkable, drab. The text block of printed pages was detaching, and there were ink splots, some staining, and other spotting to the leaves. But none of that mattered to me because it was a copy of *Emma* that had been owned by Maria Edgeworth.

As the scattered references to her throughout this book indicate, Edgeworth was one of the most popular and respected novelists of the early nineteenth century, and one of Jane Austen's favorite authors. This copy was not only owned by Edgeworth; it was the copy sent to Edgeworth at the request of Austen herself. This was a bold act on the part of the younger, less established author. It was also a gesture of literary kinship, a way to show the esteem Austen held for Edgeworth as one of her most beloved models. Even when Austen joked about disliking her "competitors" in novel writing, as she did when writing to a niece about their shared literary ambitions, she always made an exception for Edgeworth: "I have made up my mind to like no Novels really, but Miss Edgeworth's, Yours & my own."

Austen's high opinion of Edgeworth was shared by her contemporaries. Edgeworth's major modern biographer Marilyn Butler sums up her reputation as "easily the most celebrated and successful of practising English novelists" from 1800 to 1814. Radcliffe had dominated the category in the previous generation of the 1790s; Walter Scott would in the following generation. Edgeworth fit between them: in 1792, the year after Radcliffe published her breakout *The Romance of the Forest*, Edgeworth wrote to her cousin about the book, "It has been the fashionable novel here, everybody read and talked of it." In 1814, Scott would publish *Waverley*, the first of his Scottish historical novels that would secure that position. In that book's postscript, Scott praised Edgeworth's novels as the model he himself sought to "emulate."

Scott and Edgeworth later became friends on the strength of their mutual esteem. Edgeworth even once visited Scott at his home in Scotland. Afterward, Scott's son-in-law described the famed fifty-five-year-old novelist thus: "a little, dark, bearded, sharp, withered, active, laughing, talking, impudent, fearless, outspoken, honest, Whiggish, unchristian, good-tempered, kindly ultra-Irish body. I like her one day, and damn her to perdition the next." If ever there was a description of a woman calculated to make me love her, it would be this one. (Aside from the Irish part I cannot claim, someone please put this on my tombstone.) Scott himself referred to her as "the great lioness of Edinburgh" during her visit, and he "was always quoting Miss Edgeworth, or alluding to some of her characters."

Today Austen has eclipsed them both. But Scott hasn't exactly been forgotten. To start, he was featured side by side with Austen as the headliner in a chapter from that 2005 introduction to the English novel I read at the beginning of this investigation, the one that had skipped all those generations between Sterne and Austen. And while I didn't grow up reading Scott's books, such as his epic poem *The Lady of the Lake* (1810) or his Scottish historical novel *Waverley*, I've worked with collectors who did (and to whom I've sold Scott's books). Both Austen and Scott looked up to Maria Edgeworth; both sought to "emulate" her. I had categorically missed her. Why?

Edgeworth found success from her very first novel, *Castle Rackrent* (1800), a historical epic about multiple generations of Anglo-Irish landowners in Ireland. In 1801, she published *Belinda*, a novel about a young woman entering society who learns to rely upon herself while buffeted about by other characters in the book, especially her mentor, Lady Delacour—who is, admittedly, hard to resist. *Belinda* is one of the three novels that Austen approvingly mentioned in *Northanger Abbey* (along with Burney's *Cecilia* and *Camilla*).

But the publication that firmly cemented Edgeworth as the best of her generation was *Tales of Fashionable Life*, which was published as two collections almost a decade later, and included her acclaimed novels *Ennui* (1809) and *The Absentee* (1812). In other words, during the primary years when Austen was working to get published—from first selling her novel *Susan* in 1803 to first seeing her novel *Sense and Sensibility* in print in 1811—Maria Edgeworth was the most renowned novelist in England.

Imagine how Austen's heart must have pounded, daring to send that copy of *Emma* to the one and only Maria Edgeworth. Books like these are called association copies, meaning that they were once owned or used by someone who has some association with the author or work. They feel weighted with extra significance. As anyone with a family Bible knows, books passed from one person to another become memory holders. In the case of a book like Edgeworth's copy of *Emma*, these come to represent branches in a tree of literary ancestry—a symbol of the generative relationship that can blossom between two artists.

Books of all kinds can carry this extra significance, even those without such distinguished provenance. This is why I will never give up my childhood copy of Beverly Cleary's *Ramona Quimby, Age 8*, which I read at age seven, while I impatiently awaited my eighth birthday. I keep that worn paperback, featuring Ramona on the cover, her hair sticking out like she's just emerged from a blanket fort, on a shelf next to the sturdy mid-century calculus textbook of my late grandfather, who died before I was born. My bookshelves are like family photo albums, each volume capturing a particular time and place in my life.

Not too far from *Ramona Quimby, Age 8*, and my late grandfather's calculus textbook, is a copy of *Emma*. I first read *Emma* in college. I can remember exactly where I was and who I was with: I was lying on a grass slope near my dorm with a guy I was dating. He always kept paperbacks of whatever he was reading in his back pocket. That day, I think, he had Kerouac's *On the Road*. I brought *Emma* in my bag. He looked at the painting of a woman in Regency dress on the cover of my Austen book and said, "I wish I could get away with reading that in public." I paused to hold my place with a finger and asked him, "Why don't you think you can?" Looking back on that scene now, everything about it evokes my life as a college student. I loved having the freedom of choosing how to spend my time—reading in the park all day, if I so chose. That memory is forever tied up with my experience of reading *Emma*. I wondered where Edgeworth was when she read its first sentence: "Emma Woodhouse, handsome, clever, and rich, with a comfortable home and happy disposition, seemed to unite some of the best blessings of existence."

Edgeworth's copy of *Emma* sold for £79,250, even though it was missing one of the three volumes, a factor that normally tanks a price on the collectible market, and had a number of serious condition issues. It fetched a higher price than any other item at that auction, including a presentation copy, warmly inscribed by Charles Dickens, of his first novel *The Pickwick Papers*; and far surpassing an original document signed by King Henry VIII. Edgeworth's copy of *Emma* did well because it was an association copy of an Austen novel, but there was more to it than that: there was another association copy of *Emma* in the same auction that fetched significantly less. It was itself an important association, owned by Martha Lloyd, Austen's dear friend who lived with her, her mother, and her sister Cassandra at Chawton cottage during the period when Austen published her novels. Its sale price was £37,250.

The Edgeworth copy of *Emma* also had Edgeworth's ownership signature in volume one—a light scribble of "Maria Edgeworth" just above

"EMMA" on the title page—but again, there was more to it than that. There were other books inscribed by Edgeworth in this auction fetching much less. If books are memory holders, this one stored a core memory: a famed woman writer had sent it to another famed woman writer, a role model, someone who had shown her what it meant to be a woman of letters. It was evidence that Austen had ambition. She had seen Edgeworth's work as the standard of what she wanted to achieve.

This copy of *Emma* also revealed the lie I had once believed so easily, that there were no great women writers in English before Austen. Austen knew the truth. There were quite a few. She read these writers, enjoyed their work, and hoped to be as great as they were. Edgeworth's success offered both a model and a goal to an aspiring writer.

Edgeworth's career as a novelist could have been cut short before it even began. I learned this when I read her first published work, *Letters for Literary Ladies*, which was published in 1795, when Edgeworth was twenty-seven years old. As if I could skip a book with a title like that! Austen had advised readers in the pages of *Northanger Abbey* to seek out Edgeworth's books, and here was a book by Edgeworth offering advice for "literary ladies." I . . . I was a literary lady. I wanted to know what Edgeworth had to say to someone like me.

Letters for Literary Ladies was not what I expected. It is a collection of fictional letters on the subject of women's education, beginning with a correspondence between two men. The first letter, by one gentleman to his dear friend who is the new father of a baby girl, denounces formally educating girls: "you will say that we have been amply repaid for our care,—that ladies have lately exhibited such brilliant proofs of genius, as must dazzle and confound their critics. I do not ask for proofs of genius, I ask for solid proofs of utility." I may have cursed out loud when I read that sentence.

As I read this first letter, I silently cataloged the logical fallacies employed according to category, a pastime I had adopted years ago when reading the comments of trolls on social media who still make remarkably similar errors in judgment. When the first correspondent says, in the eighteenth century: "In which of the useful arts, in which of the exact sciences, have we been assisted by female sagacity or penetration?" and I think: *argumentum ad ignorantiam*, arguing that women's education cannot help society because he cannot think of examples of it doing so. And I think of the faceless, nameless online avatars today that like to claim there have been no important women scientists—*argumentum ad lapidem*, dismissing the very idea as ridiculous and ignoring all evidence to the contrary. This is what happens when you study both Latin and philosophy in college.

Letters for Literary Ladies was inspired by real events in Edgeworth's life. The first letter was, in fact, a re-creation of an actual one sent by a close family friend to her father, Richard Lovell Edgeworth. In 1782, when Maria was still a teenager, her father had set her the task of translating a popular French work on education told through a series of letters. Richard Lovell was so pleased with Maria's work that he made plans for its publication in London—but while it was at the printer, another person's translation of the same work came out, making the work redundant.

The news must have been devastating for young Maria. But one of Richard Lovell's friends, Thomas Day, used it as an opportunity to send a "congratulatory letter," which included that denunciation "against female authorship." Day argued, in the most rational and supposedly disinterested terms, that Richard Lovell should not allow Maria to publish works under her own name. Richard Lovell responded in defense of women authors. But as Maria recounted many years later, the "impression however, which the eloquence of Mr. Day's letter made, though I heard it read only once [. . .] remained for years in my mind." While her *Letters for Literary Ladies* three years later was presented as a "fictional" dialogue, it was based on real conversations Edgeworth heard growing up.

That Edgeworth had something of a champion in her father played an enormous role in creating the environment she needed for a successful literary career. He was an unusual father of an unusual family. Married four times, Richard Lovell had twenty-two children, of whom Maria Edgeworth (born in 1768) was the second eldest to survive into adulthood. Richard

Lovell took a proactive role in the education of his children alongside their mothers, blending the ideas of writers like John Locke and Jean-Jacques Rousseau into a comprehensive philosophy that, among other things, encouraged learning by play. As early as fourteen, Maria became indispensable in assisting with the care of children in the household.

Informed by her practical experience, Edgeworth's second publication was a children's book that would become one of the most influential of its generation, *The Parent's Assistant* (1796). It was a collection of stories meant specifically for children, including "some minor masterpieces in the genre," according to her modern biographer Marilyn Butler. Their quality was what made them innovative: "Before Maria Edgeworth, masterpieces like *Gulliver's Travels* and *Robinson Crusoe* were read by children, but there were no masters of writing for children." Next, Richard Lovell and Maria wrote several books together on pedagogy, the earliest and most famous of which was *Practical Education* (1798). Before she became famous as a novelist, Maria Edgeworth was already well respected as an author.

Edgeworth was encouraged by her father at home—but step beyond the threshold of their house, and she didn't always receive the same support from others. This was clear in the first letter of *Letters for Literary Ladies*. Yet the second letter, by the character based upon her father, responded that "women of literature are much more numerous of late than they were a few years ago." Women like Frances Burney and Elizabeth Montagu offered models for other literary ladies, both in print and in the drawing room. The fact that they existed could be both a comfort and inspiration to someone like Edgeworth. She would need it. As an aspiring author who was also a woman, she lived in a contradictory state. Yes, of course, live the life of a literary lady. Also, expect people to judge you for it.

That tension is visible in how Austen's brother Henry worked to shape her reputation in his "Biographical Notice" published after her death. In that piece he undersold her eagerness to publish: "For though in composition she was equally rapid and correct, yet an invincible distrust of her own judgement induced her to withhold her works from the public, till time and many perusals had satisfied her." He couldn't have known that modern scholars would be able to compare this statement to other sources, proving that was far from the truth. But they did. First, there was the 1797 letter by Austen's father, attempting to sell Austen's novel *First Impressions* (later revised into *Pride and Prejudice*) as a book "About the length of Miss Burney's *Evelina*." Or the 1809 letter Jane Austen herself wrote to the publisher who had bought and never published her novel *Susan* (later *Northanger Abbey*), in which she essentially writes *publish it or give it back*. The fact was, Austen desperately wanted to see her novels in print. But her brother felt that bold truth should be hidden.

Much of Henry Austen's account about his sister's literary life has been thrown into question from the evidence of her own letters. According to Henry, "Neither the hope of fame nor profit mixed with her early motives," but he conveniently left out her growing pleasure at making money from her novels, as she wrote regarding her desire for a second edition of *Mansfield Park*: "I am very greedy & want to make the most of it." Later, she remarked that "People are more ready to borrow & praise, than to buy," concluding "tho' I like praise as well as anybody, I like what Edward calls *Pewter* too." Her "anonymous" authorship was also an open secret that Henry explained as her need to "shrink from notoriety," but after the success of *Pride and Prejudice*, she approached her anonymity laughingly: "I shall rather try to make all the Money than all the Mystery I can of it." It was in opposition to Henry's published portrait of his sister that the modern scholar Jan Fergus stated, "for Austen, being a professional writer was, apart from her family, more important to her than anything else in her life." Nevertheless, even Austen herself would not have admitted it in print; we only know how she felt at all because of these private letters.

This tension felt personal to me, all these years (and many waves of feminism) later. The rare book trade is dominated by men in positions of power and influence. But I had models whose example sustained me while I learned the trade. The company where I was first hired is among the few of substantial size in the US with a decades-long track record of training, paying well, and promoting women: the cofounder was a woman, as was the general manager, and the other male cofounder was as feminist in practice as either of them. I was guided through my apprenticeship in an environment where I was allowed to prove myself, not despite the fact that I was a woman, but simply as a bookseller. That may sound normal. As soon as I attended a book fair or visited another antiquarian book shop, I learned how abnormal it was: the membership in the nation's leading trade organization for antiquarian booksellers is made up of less than 20 percent women. Even today, as the cofounder of a company with a track record of selling millions of dollars of rare books, some still assume it is my male cofounder who is the driving force behind the business we built together.

But I have also had the opportunity to recognize and appreciate the example of other women booksellers who must navigate this tension. At one book fair, a woman dealer asked a male dealer for his best price on a book, a typical conversation between colleagues in the trade. He replied with a number, then added, "But I might be willing to go lower if you let me buy you a cup of coffee." She bantered back, "Ah, but the coffee is free in the conference center." I remember that wit as a deft way to reject a man without having to worry about scuttling the deal. Should women have to do this? No. But it is a necessary skill for a woman in the rare book trade.

Without others around you facing similar struggles, you can start to wonder if the people who doubt you are right. But if you have models, you know there are others who made it through—and therefore, you can too. In my experience, it's not the actual work that makes building a career so difficult. It's all the outside pressures and assumptions that drain one's determination. Models are a comfort, an affirmation, an antidote as you try.

Jane Austen had named both Frances Burney and Maria Edgeworth as models; I wondered if she had read *Letters for Literary Ladies* and felt a similar vindication, knowing that there were other women like her who were building careers as writers. Perhaps she felt comfort simply seeing other women in her field succeed, just as she hoped she would.

If Edgeworth was Austen's model, writing a book as good as *Belinda* was her goal. *Belinda* was Edgeworth's first courtship novel. The titular character has come into society for the first time, without many resources herself, through the assistance of wealthy family friends. The setup is similar to Burney's first novel, *Evelina*—and also not unlike that of Austen's *Northanger Abbey*. But there is one aspect that sets *Belinda* apart: the character who takes Belinda under her wing, Lady Delacour. She is the celebrated society wit whose cynicism is reformed over the course of the novel, but who never loses her flair.

The conditions that led to Maria Edgeworth creating a character like Lady Delacour make the novel stand out even more. Because novels of the late eighteenth century had a Heroine Problem. A heroine must experience something remarkable to hold the reader's interest; yet in this era, saying that a woman had "adventures" was a euphemism for illicit liaisons that would likely lead to being cast out of high society. She must be both faultless and yet, somehow, not boring. That's the Heroine Problem: How could authors compose an exciting story when moral authorities demanded that their main character never be a "bad example" to other young women readers?

In twenty-first-century parlance, we have transformed this into "likability." A quick scan of any Goodreads page with reviews for a novel featuring a woman protagonist is going to turn up complaints about her not being "likable" for a variety of reasons. Since I myself had not much liked *Mansfield Park*'s Fanny Price for many years, I checked in to see what Goodreads reviewers thought of her. "Fanny had a rubbish personality, she was judgemental [*sic*], self-righteous, insipid, obedient, and always bloody tired. The girl couldn't walk or talk for five seconds without wanting to collapse."

But Fanny Price is an easy target. What of Austen's most beloved heroine, Elizabeth Bennet? "I know I'm supposed to like Elizabeth, but she just talks smack the entire novel. We'll call it 'wit' if you want, but when we do, realize I mean 'snarky gossip about people she dislikes at the moment.'" I'm quoting these examples because, in fact, I appreciate them. But in such reactions one can also detect a whiff of moral judgment, carried across centuries from the debates of 1700s London, about how made-up heroines ought to act. Not too perfect; then they're insipid, like Fanny. Not too flawed; then they're snarky, like Elizabeth. We may tire of the heavy-handed moral in novels like Inchbald's, but we have our own version of it in concepts like "likability."

Frances Burney solved this problem by making the mistakes of her heroines, like Evelina, ones of naivete. This gave her heroine plausible deniability whenever she did something that led to trouble. Ann Radcliffe solved the problem by making the atmosphere surrounding her heroine so menacing that she had no choice but to act (or, alternatively, faint). Maria Edgeworth attempted a different strategy: she created her perfect heroine Belinda—but gave her a constant companion in the dazzlingly imperfect Lady Delacour, who cannot make it a page without offering a highly quotable pronouncement, whether brazen, charming, or both. In one of the earliest scenes, one woman worries about whether they will all have time to change their dresses before a party. Lady Delacour is quick to advise. "Not at all too late, my dear," she said; "never too late for women to change their minds, their dress, or their lovers."

Lady Delacour is introduced as "the most fascinating person she [Belinda] had ever beheld." Her parties are famous, her bons mots are quoted in the newspapers, and her tastes inspire fashions. Lady Delacour reigns in the London social scene, and she doesn't do it because she's young or beautiful or good, but because she is wise, witty, and bold. (She sounds, in fact, a lot like Hester Thrale Piozzi—whose personality may have partially inspired a similar, minor character in her former friend Burney's third novel, *Camilla*.)

Edgeworth begins the novel with Belinda coming to live with Lady Delacour for the season, thus creating a structure that neatly circumvents the Heroine Problem. Belinda can be as boring as virtue requires; we have Lady Delacour there to entertain us. "Follow my example, Belinda; elbow your way through the crowd: if you stop to be civil and beg pardon, and 'hope I didn't hurt ye,' you will be trod under foot," she advises. Or rather, she commands: Lady Delacour dominates every room. Others give way before her because she has earned their awe. It reminded me of Hester Thrale Piozzi. But it also reminded me of someone else: Emma Woodhouse.

The further I read into *Belinda*, the more I began to see glimmers of

Emma. Emma Woodhouse is around Belinda's age, but has Lady Delacour's personality traits. She is a character who is both young and beautiful, and witty and bold. Early in the book we are told that the hero "Mr. Knightley, in fact, was one of the few people who could see faults in Emma Woodhouse." Austen knew she was taking a risk. In a letter to her family, she called Emma "a heroine whom no one but myself will much like," indicating that she knew well the Heroine Problem. Perhaps, with the example before her of what a novelist could accomplish with a character like Lady Delacour, Austen felt she could experiment in her own courtship novels. And what a success. In placing a spellbinding egoist at center stage, Austen wrote "the most perfect example in English fiction in which character shapes events quietly but irresistibly," at least according to no less an artist than Edith Wharton.

These characters not only share personality traits, but plotlines. Belinda works with the hero, a favorite of Lady Delacour's, to "reform" the lady, which—thank heavens—does not mean robbing her of her wit, but rather helping her reconcile with her estranged husband. The happy ending is only possible when Lady Delacour admits she's made an error of judgment. Meanwhile, *Emma*'s conflict is similarly spurred by mistakes the heroine makes in her friendship with the innocent Harriet, all the while observed, criticized, and advised—in short, "reformed"—by the hero Mr. Knightley.

But *Emma* is by no means a simple imitation of *Belinda*. Instead, it is as if Austen is in dialogue with Edgeworth. Where Edgeworth gives us Lady Delacour admitting she didn't always lead Belinda well, Austen gives us Emma realizing that she led Harriet astray. It's the same theme, but inverted in perspective. Reading the two together feels something like a jazz session: one author tries out melody; the other listens and plays back, building in their own unique deviations and flourishes.

We do know how Edgeworth reacted to *Emma*, even though Austen didn't. In her private letters, published in 1867, Edgeworth wrote that she had enjoyed *Mansfield Park*, a bit of intel that Austen would have been extremely gratified to learn. But Edgeworth described being underwhelmed by the plot of *Emma*, and especially disliking the frivolous complaints of Emma's father. In fact, her negative reaction to the book explained the mystery of why the copy at auction had only two volumes instead of all three: according to Marilyn Butler, "after reaching the end of the first volume Maria passed the remaining two volumes on to a friend, observing: . . . 'there was no story in it.'" This, you may recall, was a common contemporary criticism of Austen's work. What was then viewed as too ordinary to be considered high art is what we now praise as compelling realism.

Edgeworth read a number of Austen's books, and occasionally recorded reactions to them in her letters. But the modern reader can share Austen's torture of not knowing Edgeworth's opinion when it comes to *Pride and Prejudice*. In a letter to her brother after the book came out in 1813, Edgeworth tantalizingly wrote, "I am desired not to give you my opinion of 'Pride and Prejudice,' but desire you to get it directly, and tell us yours." The closest glimpse we get of Edgeworth's judgment would come twenty-five years later, when she reread *Emma* and *Pride and Prejudice* and wrote that she "liked them better than ever." Edgeworth also read *Northanger Abbey*, which she thought a bit too unrealistic. She also didn't record any comments about seeing her own novel *Belinda* praised in it. Since *Northanger Abbey* was published after Austen's death, Austen never knew that Edgeworth would see her praise in print.

The concept of "genius" tends to convey isolation: that a person is above—and therefore separate—from the rest of us mere mortals. But geniuses do not live apart from the world. They respond to others' work, as Austen did with the writers on my shelf. This does not always mean imitation or even necessarily admiration. Models can be someone not only to aspire to, but also to react against. I have long accepted that I am easily motivated by spite. It would not be *entirely* wrong to say that I built that mammoth collection of romance novels to sell to an institution specifically to spite colleagues in the rare book trade who had ignored or actively derided these novels. It is possible to build something new, something productive and even something important, that was first inspired by such low feelings as spite, anger, frustration, or loneliness. We all experience these feelings;

we can nurse them and allow them to poison us, or we can transform them into fuel to address the roots of those pains. That's what Maria Edgeworth did when she disagreed with one of her models: her beloved father who had educated her.

———————

Richard Lovell Edgeworth supported his daughter becoming a literary lady, but of a certain kind. He did not appreciate novels in the "Burney tradition," and wanted Maria to focus solely on educational or, as he put it, "useful" publications. Together they had published a number of successful books on practical education, and this was the model Richard Lovell wanted Maria to continue. But Maria did appreciate novels like Burney's: in one letter she talks about rereading Burney's novel *Cecilia*, "which entertains me as much at the third reading as it did at the first." She would try to find a middle way. Beginning with her second novel, *Belinda*, Maria would write in the "Burney tradition," but try to spin her work so as to please her father as well. The opening "Advertisement" (that is, a notice from the author at the beginning of the book) of the first edition states that *Belinda*

> **is offered to the public as a Moral Tale—the author not wishing to acknowledge a Novel. Were all novels like those of Madame de Crousaz, Mrs. Inchbald, Miss Burney, or Dr. Moore, she would adopt the name of Novel with delight: But so much folly, errour and vice are disseminated in books classed under this denomination, that it is hoped the wish to assume another title will be attributed to feelings that are laudable, and not fastidious.**

Now Austen's rebuke in *Northanger Abbey* took on a new layer of meaning where she had said, "I will not adopt that ungenerous and impolitic custom so common with novel-writers, of degrading by their contemptuous censure the very performances, to the number of which they are themselves adding." Austen was scolding her own model! But in the same passage

Austen also praises her, citing *Belinda* itself against Edgeworth's argument. Edgeworth wanted her books to be called "moral tales" instead of "novels." Austen wanted Edgeworth to own her title as "novelist," and she said so. Perhaps that famous passage in *Northanger Abbey* wasn't directed at Austen's readers at all—they were, after all, reading a novel at that very moment. Perhaps it was directed at Maria Edgeworth.

Of course, Austen could proudly take a stand in support of the genre: she had a father supportive of her novel writing. Edgeworth did not. Writing to a friend a few years after the publication of *Belinda*, Edgeworth explained of her father, "he has pointed out to me that to be a mere writer of pretty stories & novellettes [*sic*] would be unworthy of his partner, pupil & daughter & I have been so touched by his reason or his eloquence or his kindness or all together, that I have thrown aside all thoughts of pretty stories." But she didn't throw them aside. Instead, she transformed them.

The novels to come, especially *Ennui* and *The Absentee*, blended the practical philosophies Edgeworth explored alongside her father with fictional narratives of "fashionable life." They were a delight to read, yet they also had a purpose, impressing on readers the values of personal responsibility, duty to community, and financial constraint. This kind of social-reform novel would become the heart of the genre in the Victorian era, with Edgeworth's "epoch-making" work among its biggest catalysts. And it still has a place in the canon—for instance, in the works of Charles Dickens, for whom Edgeworth was also unquestionably a model. In the case of Edgeworth, however, critics like to use the career-killing word "didactic." But I've read both *Ennui* and *The Absentee*, and that is not how I experienced them.

I finished *Ennui* in a rush over the course of a single afternoon, reading a gorgeous copy of the second edition bound in what is known as "Spanish calf," striped with veins of subtle green across the caramel hue of the leather. Edgeworth brings her characters to life in small, incidental details. You cannot help but love a count in *The Absentee* whose pet goat is always in the way: "the Angora goat [. . .] with long, curling, silky hair, was walking about the room with the air of a beauty and a favourite." The public loved these books, too: they quickly went into multiple editions, with one reviewer calling her tales "actually as perfect as it was possible to make them." Edgeworth pushed back against her most important model, her father, and demonstrated that she could make "pretty stories" with real cultural impact.

While Edgeworth's father had initially critiqued her desire to write novels, he eventually became her biggest champion. For her part, Edgeworth never forgot the importance of her father's support in that career. In her later book *Memoirs of Richard Lovell Edgeworth, Esq. Begun by Himself and Concluded by His Daughter* (1820), she faithfully chronicled her first efforts at writing books through the encouragement of Richard Lovell, and spoke warmly of the years of their "literary partnership, which, for so many years, was the pride and joy of my life." For Edgeworth, too, writing was a dialogue with one's models.

With the publication of the two series of *Tales of Fashionable Life* (1809 and 1812), the period's critics named Edgeworth's novels a landmark in the development of the form. Her skill was in composing specific details that make characters resonate with the reader, which heralded a new era of realism (not just a goat, but an *Angora* goat!). As John Wilson Croker remarked in the *Quarterly Review* upon the publication of the *Tales* that included *The Absentee*, "Other writers have caught nothing but the general feature, and in their description, everything that is Irish is pretty much alike, lords, peasants, ladies and nurses; to Miss Edgeworth's keen observation and vivid pencil it was reserved to separate the genus into its species and individuals." With Edgeworth, the art of the novel had reached a new level of maturity.

Edgeworth's own life ended in 1849 with her place in the canon seemingly assured. But here in the twenty-first century, I knew it wasn't. I wanted to know why, and this time, it was not merely curiosity that drove me. It was surprise. After reading her novels myself, I was genuinely astonished that they aren't still read.

For much of the nineteenth century, critics would rarely discuss Austen's name without first bringing up Edgeworth. A well-known Victorian textbook, George Lillie Craik's *A Compendious History of English Literature and of the English Language* (1861), names Austen and Edgeworth as "generally admitted to have been the first female novelists of the last age." Then, Austen-Leigh's *A Memoir of Jane Austen* (1870) was published, spurring the first wave of Austen fandom and buoying Austen's reputation. A turning point. In the meantime, Edgeworth's own reputation began to shift. She became known not as a novelist, but as an Irish novelist.

I traced evidence for this turning point in Edgeworth's career in the popular 1889 publication *Some Eminent Women of Our Times*, by Millicent Garrett Fawcett. The essays in this book were first published to wide readership in the magazine the *Mother's Companion*, then printed (and quickly reprinted) here in book form. According to Fawcett, "Maria Edgeworth may be said to have invented the modern novel"—a statement many modern scholars agree with. But she then goes on to describe Edgeworth's influence on other writers specifically in terms of what "Edgeworth had done for Ireland and the Irish peasantry." The epic scale for which Edgeworth was once celebrated was narrowed down to a single point: the regional novel.

Maria Edgeworth wrote a lot of terrific novels, but the primary ones that remained on canonical lists in the generations after her death were those she set in Ireland, especially *Castle Rackrent* and *The Absentee*. They were so celebrated for their depictions of the country that they became "national sketches," as the novelist and critic Margaret Oliphant described them in her 1882 *Literary History of England*. But this was the very problem: novels about Ireland were viewed as regional novels of "extreme remoteness" from the center of British letters, London. Edgeworth became a great novelist for depicting Ireland, rather than, simply, a great novelist. This shift is evident even in the design of Edgeworth's popular reprints; one well-known set of her novels from 1893 is bound in lime green and covered in four-leaf clover ornaments.

Compare this with the evolution of Austen's legacy. To readers of her era and immediately after, Austen's focus on limited settings and ordinary life in quiet English towns made her seem "provincial." After Ralph Waldo Emerson read her novels, he recorded in his journal that "I am at a loss to understand why people hold Miss Austen's novels at so high a rate [. . .] Never was life so pinched and narrow." But after Austen rose to the level of canon, she became relatable, "everybody's Jane," even to readers who had never been to England. In the twenty-first century, the word you see a lot is "universal."

"Universal": a key word used in canonizing an author. It is also used to keep authors out of the canon. In one recent Austen book, the author quickly dismisses some writers of Austen's time who "would never become household words [. . .] they lacked her own gift of universality." This is one way Edgeworth's slide into becoming an "Irish novelist" first hurt her broader legacy. Austen went from the narrow to the universal; Edgeworth went from the universal to the narrow.

By 1894, the year after that lime-green, clover-leafed set of Edgeworth's novels was published, William Minto admitted that "Edgeworth must certainly be pronounced to have gone out of fashion [. . .] yet novel-readers who have exhausted the novels of their own generation might do worse than give 'Belinda' or 'Castle Rackrent' a trial." Edgeworth was no longer popular, but readers "might do worse." Not long after came another turning point: Edmund Gosse argued in 1898 that Edgeworth's greatest value was that she "prepare[d] the way for the one prose writer of this period whose genius has proved absolutely perdurable": Jane Austen.

Like Burney's, Edgeworth's books were now being used to emphasize Austen's superiority. By the mid-twentieth century, one biographer of Edgeworth stated that Austen was "much the better novelist," while arguing that Edgeworth "may be the more important" because of her influence—on Austen, Scott, and others. Scott, too, was a "regional writer" about Scotland—but, like Austen, his towering fame eventually eclipsed the work of his predecessors and peers. Scott became *the* regional writer, as Austen was *the* realist writer. Edgeworth was no longer the model, as Austen and Scott themselves viewed her. She was the precursor, just a step on the ladder of their ascent. This provided the critical framework to pass over Edgeworth, the literary force of her generation, in favor of Austen and Scott in the subsequent one.

I learned all this gradually, book by book, acquisition by acquisition. (Yes, of course I bought one of those clover-covered sets of Edgeworth's novels.) When I first began investigating these women writers, I had felt ignorant. Why hadn't my training in rare books, which required knowledge of the history of the novel in English, included these women? Was I the only one who struggled with this omission? But it wasn't just me. As soon as I made up my mind to look, I found others who felt as I did. Scholars had remarked upon the loss of these authors from the literary landscape, had researched and recovered the lives and works of these women. For some, this might deflate the novelty of my project; it wasn't an objective "rediscovery" of these "forgotten" women. But instead of being disappointed that I wasn't the first, I was comforted by the company.

In the early 1980s, when I was just a toddler, an Australian professor named Dale Spender began her own investigation into the great lie that Austen was the first major woman writer: "far from standing at the beginning of women's entry to fiction writing, Jane Austen was the inheritor of a long and well-established tradition of 'women's novels.'" When I started this project, one of the first books I turned to was her *Mothers of the Novel: 100 Good Women Writers Before Jane Austen* (1986). Just like me, Spender reacted to this discovery with deep feeling: "on the one hand there has been the delight of discovering this treasure chest; on the other hand, there has been sadness, frustration, and anger, that such treasures ever should have been buried."

Mothers of the Novel was one of the most influential works of its era to reverse the "Great Forgetting," that name given to the disappearance of women writers in English before Austen. In it, Spender celebrated the "continuity of women's literary traditions," tracing the line of authorial heritage from seventeenth-century authors up to Frances Burney, from there to Maria Edgeworth and, of course, Jane Austen, alongside other successful novelists of their time like Mary Brunton, author of *Self Control* (1811), and Amelia Opie, author of *Adeline Mowbray* (1804).

Many other scholars have built upon, argued against, and otherwise engaged with Spender's fundamental premise that these writers were worthy of reclamation. Along with these academic studies came reprints of the books in question, often for student use. It was while collecting reprints of Charlotte Lennox's *Female Quixote* that I found an edition of that novel with a series name similar to Spender's academic work: it was a "Mothers of the Novel" book. The cover design looked so familiar. Then I had a realization—followed quickly by sheepishness. I glanced at my shelf and spotted the same design on Spender's book, *Mothers of the Novel*: an all-white paperback with a central square vignette in a muted color palette. I hadn't even known a reprint series had followed Spender's landmark book. New editions of Lennox, Smith, Inchbald, Edgeworth, and more, labeled "100 good women writers before Jane Austen." Well. Clearly, I had to collect the entire series in twenty volumes.

In the process of following leads from the various acquisitions in my collection, I had pushed the project's parameters further, extending my exploration of Austen's literary ancestry to including other critics' work in their recovery. This is what I love about book collecting. It had led me to discover the scholarship by another woman, nearly forty years before me, who had pursued a similar project of reading and writing about women writers before Jane Austen. First in reading Austen's letters, then finding Lennox's books, then discovering Spender's reprint series, I watched an entire literary ancestry grow tall behind me, the branches of the tree reaching out. I wasn't alone at all.

Spender was not a book collector, but a scholar. And one part of Spender's book that struck me was her struggle to find copies of these early books in order to read them. In the section about Edgeworth, Spender lamented that she had been unable to read some of Edgeworth's novels because they hadn't been published recently and she hadn't been able to track down rare editions. At one point, she joked about one of the most influential studies of the novel in the twentieth century that "I can only presume that Ian Watt does not rank [Edgeworth] among the originators of the novel because he has not read her work." There was truth underlying it. In the 1980s, one could not read about *Belinda* in *Northanger Abbey*, then simply walk into the local bookshop to purchase a copy. I confirmed this using a few tricks of the rare book trade, like WorldCat. While an edition of *Castle Rackrent* was published by Oxford University Press during this period, there was no edition of Austen's favorite. That meant a bookshop specializing in new releases would not have stocked *Belinda* when Spender was looking for it. A reader in the 1980s could try their luck in a secondhand bookshop, but they would indeed have to be lucky: aside from a couple mid-century sets of Edgeworth's *Tales and Novels,* I found no record of any individual editions of *Belinda* published after 1925. A desire to read *Belinda* did not mean that an Austen fan could actually read *Belinda*.

This reality made reclamation projects especially difficult. "I would dearly love to have a course on Maria Edgeworth's novels," Spender says, "but predictably most of her work is not in print." It was not a coincidence that those who worked on the slow reclamation project of women writers before Jane Austen enjoyed special access of some kind: they worked at a university with a stellar special collections department; they inherited old libraries, or had the funds to purchase expensive early editions of these works from rare book dealers; they lived in a city with a vibrant antiquarian book scene. But a popular revival does not occur only in rare book shops, a truth to which I can ruefully attest. The role of the reprint in the shaping of what we continue to read is difficult to overstate. This was why the Mothers of the Novel series of humble paperbacks was so important.

Forty years later and walking the same path as Spender, I have new tools. I can retrieve in seconds just about any book in the public domain for free; every one of Edgeworth's novels is now available and accessible online. Or I can find print copies at a variety of price points with a simple online search. The stock of antiquarian book dealers from across the world is posted to internet marketplaces, where I can purchase a $3,000 first edition, or a $20 edition from 1910, or a $5 edition from 1986. Shockingly, I have spent more money on some twenty-first-century academic titles than I did for the first appearance ever in print of Austen's works from when she was a teenager. Thirty dollars—for a first edition of a Jane Austen book! Readers today have the privilege of access that generations before us didn't have. For the book curious, the internet age is a new golden age.

Many of my colleagues in the rare book trade don't like the changes wrought by the internet. Antiquarian booksellers called the moment of transition into digital the Great Glut because suddenly thousands of books became available online—and this rush upended our previous perceptions about rarity. Books that once seemed rare, like a first edition of J. D. Salinger's *The Catcher in the Rye* (1951), are now easily found by an online search. This has largely benefited collectors, but it does make the work of a rare book dealer more difficult. We can no longer say, "This book is rare, and this is your only way to purchase it, so you must give me money if you want it." Now collectors can compare our copy right next to copies of all our competitors. Hence the grumbling of some dealers, and the excitement of collectors.

One dampening effect of this new accessibility where I do agree with my more pessimistic colleagues is that it can easily kill the romance of the hunt in collecting. Finding that one book you were seeking at a serendipitous moment, standing snugly between others on a folding shelf at a book fair, can feel miraculous. I remember one day visiting a fair for ephemera, the category of materials that weren't meant to be saved: playbills, valentines, postcards, and more. A stack of brightly printed sheets caught my eye in the corner of one dealer's booth. I could tell immediately that they were labels for the boxes of late nineteenth-century French board games. (I realize that's an oddly specific thing to clock at ten feet, but I am, after all, a professional.) I started leafing through them when I came across something so astounding that I actually gasped aloud. It was a set of the *En L'An 2000* cards. These cards are legendary. They were produced for the 1900 Paris Exposition on the theme of imagining what the world would be like a century into the future. They feature scenes with atomic energy, electric trains, and a device very like Zoom, all in an exuberant steampunk style that calls to mind Jules Verne. And they are incredibly rare, with only a few seventy-eight-card sets known. I bought it. To date, it remains one of my favorite finds.

It can take a serious commitment of time, energy, and focus to find a specific book in these environments. For that reason, it tends to feel more satisfying when you finally do. Collecting in the wild brings with it that thrill of bibliomancy, magic momentarily sparking in your life. But on internet marketplaces, you have only to type in the title and publisher information to find twelve copies from twelve different sellers, with differences in prices varying sometimes by thousands of dollars. It no longer feels miraculous. It feels . . . confusing. No one wants to make a mistake if they are committing to rare book–level prices—and how do you know which listing of the twelve is the right one for you? Faced with too much information, the hunt loses its romance and is replaced by anxiety.

Over the last few years, I have found balance in a combined approach. The internet gave me access, but chaos. I needed to use my experience as an antiquarian book dealer to bring curation to that chaos. I found this new approach both satisfying and effective. But it took me time to get it right because it took time to develop the skills and confidence. Today I can navigate the confusion of online listings because I know, for instance, that it's a red flag to see a dealer call a book a "first edition" when it's clearly a later printing: "first edition" in the world of book collecting means "first edition, first printing," i.e., the very first batch printed. Collectors pick up these bits of knowledge naturally in the process of the hunt. You learn as you go.

When I started to build my collection, I already had this knowledge of the marketplace. Still, it took me time to develop the confidence about *what* I should add to my shelf, and why. I had always admired Jane Austen's confidence. In that, she has been my model. Austen is one of the most confident writers I can remember reading. Yes, she created appealing and varied heroines; yes, she's witty. But also: in every line of her novels, it seems to me that Jane Austen knows who she is as a writer. There is an ease to her style that speaks to an underlying mastery, a complete control over her art. I chose to investigate Austen's favorite women writers so that I could trace the contours of her confidence. Bit by bit, I could understand how it took shape. In Austen, I saw what it looked like when someone made art from a deep sense of self. And, just as I looked back to Austen for reassurance to go forward, Austen did, too. That's what that passage in *Northanger Abbey* naming her predecessors is all about.

Austen could both be an original and a part of a literary ancestry. Yet this ancestry was quickly minimized by her earliest biographers. Even though Austen stated—both privately and publicly—that Edgeworth's novels were some of her favorites, her earliest biographers ignored this preference. In the first sketch of Jane Austen's life, the 1817 "Biographical Notice," her brother Henry mentions only Samuel Richardson among novelists she liked. Yes, she did love Richardson. And: in *Northanger Abbey*, the very book this "Biographical Notice" precedes, Austen states that she considers Edgeworth's *Belinda* and Burney's *Cecilia* and *Camilla* as some of the best novels ever written ("in which the greatest powers of the mind are displayed").

Perhaps this was a hedge from Henry. We already saw this problem with the gothics of the 1790s to 1800s; the field of the novel was still very much contested on gendered terms in the 1810s. Burney's final novel, *The Wanderer* (1814), had just received a scathing review in the *Edinburgh Review* by William Hazlitt that attacked it for what he argued were uniquely feminine traits. Burney "is a quick, lively, and accurate observer of persons and things; but she always looks at them with a consciousness of her sex." He went on to deliver what would become known as a phrase of execution. He states that she is "a mere common observer of manners, and also a very woman." The modern scholar Laura Runge summarizes the effect of this review: "Hazlitt's essay signals a change in the status of the female novelist, one in which 'female' takes on a greater importance than 'novelist.'" By bringing up Richardson, rather than any of her favorite women novelists, it's possible that Henry was attempting to spare Austen the treatment Burney had experienced.

Then came her nephew James Edward Austen-Leigh's landmark biography, *A Memoir of Jane Austen* (1870), that major turning point in Austen's popular and critical reputation. Austen-Leigh repeated her love of Richardson, and also left out Burney and Edgeworth among her favorite writers, listing "Johnson in prose, Crabbe in verse, and Cowper in both." Well, he doesn't leave out Burney entirely. Instead of describing Austen's love for the novelist, he repeats a common criticism of Burney—that she copied Samuel Johnson's style—in order to compliment Austen: "It is well that the native good taste of [Austen] saved her from the snare into which a sister novelist had fallen, of imitating the grandiloquent style of Johnson." That old canard: Burney isn't worth reading because she's not as good as Austen. Meanwhile, *Northanger Abbey* was being printed and reprinted, praising Burney explicitly. Readers took her relatives as authorities on Austen's taste—rather than look to her own words.

Today we have even more evidence of what Austen really thought because there are now over 150 of her letters in print. We can see for ourselves that Austen refers warmly to characters from Burney's novels throughout her life. This is the case from some of her earliest letters extant, such as the September 1796 letter to Cassandra in which she compares herself to a Burney heroine, "To-morrow I shall be just like Camilla." In 1815, less than two years before her death, she refers to two characters from *Evelina*, when she writes, "Sweet amiable Frank! why does <u>he</u> have a cold too? Like Capt. Mirvan to Mde Duval, 'I wish it well over within him.'" And this is just the beginning. We have seen her write a hero who isn't ashamed to admit that he loves Radcliffe's gothics, praise Lennox's *Female Quixote* as a reread, admit she will probably like Hannah More's *Coelebs in Search of a Wife*, record her youthful preference for Charlotte Smith's non-hero Delamere, build an entire plot around Inchbald's *Lovers' Vows*, quote a line in a letter by Piozzi from memory, and joke that the only novelist she likes outside her family is Maria Edgeworth.

Some early scholars did pick up on these threads. In 1929, Clara Thomson published *Jane Austen: A Survey*, the first book-length investigation of Austen's craft and influences, including Edgeworth. But these scholars more typically followed the lead of Austen's early biographers. Take, for instance, this conclusion published in an academic journal in the 1970s after listing a number of parallels between Austen's works and Edgeworth's: "None of these parallels have been, or should be, considered as evidence that Jane Austen was drawing on the works of Maria Edgeworth for inspiration [. . .] in all cases the themes and issues are common to so many novels of the period as to make the question of influence largely an irrelevant one." It's true that we have no extant document from Austen stating, *I took inspiration from Lady Delacour in creating the character of Emma Woodhouse.* We have only clues: novels and letters in which Austen describes Edgeworth as one of her favorite novelists; *Belinda* as a beloved novel; a transgressive main character showing many traits in common with a major character in the novel she admired; a copy sent, audaciously, to her model.

These scholars kept setting Austen apart. Instead of positioning Austen as a branch on the tree, they put Austen "above" her literary ancestry, where she became a kind of lone genius. One 2013 book on Austen asks, "why, if Austen's writing is so firmly grounded in the literature of her contemporaries, is her own work so strikingly and consistently different?" I confess, I found this question baffling after reading Burney, Lennox, and Edgeworth. Austen is a tremendous writer, yes, but "so strikingly and consistently different"? No, I couldn't agree with that.

The need for Austen to be a lone genius, ex nihilo, kept reminding me of patterns in modern book collecting. The value we give to being "first" is reflected in the value of "first edition." For over one hundred years, the biggest trend in rare book collecting in the US has centered upon this idea of the "first edition." The first edition of the book is a powerful concept because it romanticizes the moment when those words were first widely available to the public. Imagine being among the first people to read Charles Darwin's *On the Origin of Species* (1859), which sold out its entire edition on the first day. There are some books that feel like meteor strikes, creating a "before" and "after." Collectors who chase after the first edition want to capture the moment of impact. I myself have gotten goose bumps holding a first edition of *Origin of Species*.

But Darwin wasn't the first scientist to suggest a theory of evolution; he was the first to propose a theory of evolution *by means of natural selection* in book form. Jean-Baptiste Lamarck, a French biologist, had sketched out an earlier theory of evolution, and many others had theorized along similar lines—including Darwin's own grandfather, Erasmus Darwin (who was also a close friend of Maria Edgeworth and her father). The germ of Charles Darwin's idea began more than twenty years before the publication of his book, after discussing his findings on the voyage of the *Beagle* with fellow scientists like Charles Lyell and John Gould. He was finally spurred to publication when another scientist, Alfred Wallace, sent Darwin his own ideas on the same mechanism of natural selection. He and Wallace even published a paper together on the subject a year before *Origin of Species*.

None of these facts takes away from the power of that moment when *Origin of Species* sold out. Instead, each additional layer of context—of dialogue between specialists—makes the story of Darwin's famous book even more fascinating. I know all this because, as a rare book dealer, I've worked with a lot of Darwin collectors. A collection of Charles Darwin's first editions is wonderful; a collection that includes not only Darwin, but also Lamarck and Lyell and Gould and Wallace? That gets my pulse moving.

Despite our cultural admiration for the "lone genius," no thinker works in a vacuum. The same applies to authors as it does scientists. The concept of the first edition takes part of its power from the assumption that there really was a clear "before" and "after." But there never was. According to a collector who values only first editions, the fifth edition of *Origin of Species* is undesirable. But this is the edition in which the phrase "survival of the fittest" (itself borrowed from philosopher Herbert Spencer) is first included. Even after the book's publication, Darwin continued to be influenced by others, considering their contributions and revising his own work and thinking as it, er, evolved. The word "evolution" doesn't even appear in *Origin of Species* until the sixth edition, published thirteen years after the first edition.

The concept of the first edition so dominates the rare book marketplace that most people don't even realize book collecting doesn't have to be about first editions at all. Once you realize this—that you don't have to chase after what everyone else is seeking, that you can go your own way—all sorts of new paths open up.

Some of my own collections explore these new paths. It's a more difficult pursuit because untrodden can often mean uncertain. But I have models here, too. Lisa Unger Baskin built a monumental collection on the subject of "women at work" for decades, able to form it on a modest budget because she had very few competitors on the marketplace. In 2015, she sold the collection to Duke University's Rubenstein Library. I thought about Baskin often as I built my collection of romance novels. I bought them over many years, when few collectors were paying attention to Harlequin paperbacks, then sold the collection to an institution, Indiana University's Lilly Library, only after interest in romance at rare book libraries had increased sufficiently to make it practical. But it was a gamble. I was only able to pull that off by a conviction that romance deserved more attention in the rare book world. So I took the risk and I didn't look back, even as I sunk thousands of dollars into books most people would simply throw away. Not only did the idea of collecting romance raise eyebrows among a few of my colleagues, it went against the old-school belief that the first edition was the most important. Harlequin began in 1949 as a publisher of reprints, not first editions.

———

In 1979, one of the most important works from the modern feminist recovery movement was published: *The Madwoman in the Attic* by Sandra M. Gilbert and Susan Gubar. In it, they argued persuasively that women authors find strength in their precursors, not weakness: they are "actively seeking a *female* precursor who, far from representing a threatening force to be denied or killed, proves by example that a revolt against patriarchal literary authority is possible." The woman novelist in English did not begin with Jane Austen. *Isn't that exciting?*

The same year as Gilbert and Gubar's book was published, Audre Lorde argued at a conference on feminism that it was more than literary ancestry that women needed: it was also community. This lecture, called "The Master's Tools Will Never Dismantle the Master's House," is one of Lorde's most famous and influential. "[I]nterdependency between women is the only way to [. . .] freedom," Lorde asserted; "the need and desire to nurture each other is not pathological but redemptive." But we don't have to fit into the same mold to do so. Lorde argues that "community must not mean a shedding of our differences, nor the pathetic pretense that these differences do not exist."

Over the years that I'd been reading Austen and Austen's favorite women writers, my conviction about moving away from the idea of lone genius toward a tree of literary ancestry grew stronger. In the meantime, I had been reading other books, too—and that tree cast its branches over all my reading. I noticed it as I reread Lorde's lecture in the landmark anthology *This Bridge Called My Back*, an anthology compiled by "radical women of color," as the subtitle says. This book was meant to carve out a space where women of color could share their stories, where they could agree, where they could disagree, where they could explore who they were. It was a gorgeous, generative dialogue between authors. It was a work of community building.

The originality I was coming to value in these books was not about being first, but rather about the particular ways in which a writer might make something her own within a larger conversation. Now I read these books as dialogues within a community of women. In 1809, Maria Edgeworth read Elizabeth Inchbald's *A Simple Story* for the fourth time, remarking that the two lovers of the first part "appeared to me real persons whom I saw and heard." Immediately after reading the book, Edgeworth had to revisit her own *Belinda*, published eight years before; Anna Laetitia Barbauld needed a revised and edited version of it for her upcoming anthology, *The British Novelists*, that created the "first novelistic-canon" in English.

Initially, the contrast Edgeworth noticed between *A Simple Story* and *Belinda* was painful to her, having just experienced the liveliness of Inchbald's characters: "I really was so provoked with the cold tameness of that stick or stone Belinda, that I could have torn the pages to pieces; and, really, I have not the heart or the patience to *correct* her." The Heroine Problem! But Edgeworth was also an artist, and her frustration evolved quickly into inspiration: "As the hackney coachman said, 'Mend *you*! better make a new one.'" The skill of another writer encouraged Edgeworth, already by then quite famous, to continue to hone her craft. Her next novel, *The Absentee* (1812), was judged by her contemporaries as one of the "landmarks in the history of the novel" and became one of her most enduring.

As I had with the other women on my shelf, I traced Edgeworth's rise and fall from the canon through the slow acquisition of books for my collection. When did we stop caring about Edgeworth, and why? My collection held the evidence. The solid green cloth of the Oliphant set, in which her novels become "national sketches," sat next to the attractive mid-century dust jacket design of the Newby biography that argued her most important contribution was setting the stage for Austen. I followed that with a 1973 biography of Edgeworth issued via Bucknell University Press as part of their Irish Writers Series—the series name yet another tell in Edgeworth's transformation, focusing on her importance as an "Irish writer."

In reading Dale Spender, Margaret Anne Doody, Marilyn Butler, and so many others, I kept seeing ghosts. Here I was, attempting to navigate the hazy labyrinth of history, only to turn a corner and see the flickering image of a woman who had been there before me. Annibel Jenkins sees me on the path of Elizabeth Inchbald, and I imagine her smiling at me conspiratorially, spurring me forward through the maze. I can see Loraine Fletcher, writing about Charlotte Smith, saying "follow me." And I do. Sometimes, as when I read Marilyn Butler's 1987 preface to her new edition of *Jane Austen and the War of Ideas*, I am floored by the brilliance of an observation that builds on a thought I believed was mine alone: any deflation I feel about not being the "first" is well compensated by the opportunity to explore the shared idea in the work of such a perceptive scholar. Later, when I returned to the description of that auction lot for the copy of *Emma* sent to Maria Edgeworth, I noticed the traces here too. Care to guess who owned it before it came up for sale? It was Marilyn Butler.

Other times, I think of Constance Hill and Ellen Hill—much earlier explorers of Austen's world who published *Jane Austen: Her Homes and Her Friends* in 1902—giving me a shrug when I take a left where they went right. More than one hundred years after that, Glory Edim started the book club Well Read Black Girl, which she said "led me to discover my life's purpose: Uplifting the narratives of Black women." I inhaled her collection of the same name with essays by Black women writers on books they loved by other Black women writers. And right after I finished the first draft of this book, I was thrilled to get my hands on a copy of Devoney Looser's *Sister Novelists*, about Jane Porter and Anna Maria Porter, two more women writers whom Scott's reputation effaced and "who paved the way for Austen and the Brontës."

Every time I read a new book or article saying something smart about these women, I momentarily felt sheepish for having missed their work for so long. But all of us who dare to navigate the labyrinth of the past will feel this way at some point. The most important realization was that I was not alone in that labyrinth.

Not all of my predecessors were women; they were people who simply shared this drive to understand literary women whom they also esteemed. Rictor Norton brought light to the corridors of Ann Radcliffe's life, and William McCarthy and James L. Clifford championed Hester Lynch Piozzi. Sara Ahmed captured my growing sentiment when she described citation as feminist work in *Living a Feminist Life*: "Citation is how we acknowledge our debt to those who came before; those who helped us find our way when the way was obscured because we deviated from the paths we were told to follow." Like collecting, citation is a form of preservation. I cite these writers not only to acknowledge them, but also to form a connection with them.

———

There was one more book I knew I wanted to add to this part of my collection. After more than three years into the project, I decided I would return to a book that I knew fit in the tradition of feminist recovery, but that I hadn't read since college. I bought a new copy of Joanna Russ's *How to Suppress Women's Writing* (1983), an ironic "guide" to the mechanics of ignoring, discrediting, and erasing the contributions of women to our literary heritage.

I had originally come across *How to Suppress Women's Writing* in college, in those heady days when my earliest blushes of feminist rage found support in works like this. Back then, I was struck by the book's tone—clipped and unyielding, bold and no-nonsense—and by the stories Russ told of these literary women. This time around, it felt like reading an entirely different book. After years in the rare book trade, I knew those stories well. I've sold multiple copies of the first edition of Woolf's *Room of One's Own*, of the first editions of Emily Dickinson's *Poems* put together by her friends and family after her death, and of Plath's *Bell Jar*. Because this time those stories lacked the novelty of a first read, my attention shifted instead to Russ's focus on the mechanisms of sexism in the lives and afterlives of these women. That's what I had been doing, for a different group of women in an earlier period. Russ's specialty as a scholar was primarily Victorian literature, while I had been reading mostly eighteenth-century material. As she laid bare the fallacies used in each section, it hit me: Russ's book was the direct literary ancestor of my own. I had even followed her method of categorizing arguments by fallacy! Flickering ghosts, here again.

I love the cover of the first edition of *How to Suppress Women's Writing* because it prints each fallacy that Russ dissects in the book. "*She didn't write it.*" I had seen this happen to Charlotte Lennox, when critics claimed that Johnson wrote the penultimate chapter of *Female Quixote*. "*She wrote it, but she shouldn't have.* (It's political, sexual, masculine, feminist.)" I had seen this in Charlotte Smith's works, where Smith defends her political writing in the preface to her novel set during the French Revolution, *Desmond*. "*She wrote it, but look what she wrote about.* (The bedroom, the kitchen, her family. Other women!)" I thought of Hazlitt's damning phrase about Burney: "a mere common observer of manners, and also a very woman." "*She wrote it, but she wrote only one of it.*" Who cares if Hannah More wrote a novel so popular that it laid the foundation for the national bestsellers of the Victorian era? It's not like she was a career novelist. "*She wrote it, but she isn't really an artist, and it isn't really art.* (It's a thriller, a romance, a children's book. It's sci fi!)" Here was the fate of Radcliffe's gothic romances, shunted into a separate category from the "higher" genre, literary realism. "*She wrote it, but she had help.*" The success of Piozzi's *Anecdotes* was attributed to the genius of Johnson, yet that doesn't account for it outstripping every other Johnsonian work of the 1780s in popularity. "*She wrote it, but she's an anomaly.*" And there's Jane Austen.

When I reached the end of Russ's book for the second time, I heard her speak to me like I never had before. Her book ends like this:

"I've been trying to finish this monster for thirteen ms. pages and it won't," she complained. "Clearly it's not finished."

Then she gave a command that felt like a stare, right into my own eyes, across forty years: "*You* finish it."

It was as if she knew that I would take up this project of investigating Austen's bookshelf. And she did know. Because she knew someone would. She had seen the flickering ghosts herself. But I won't finish it either. Some of you will take it from here. Hello: welcome. I'm delighted that you're here.

CONCLUSION

Five years after I started collecting Jane Austen's Bookshelf, I decided to return to one of the works that I had read when I first had the idea to build this collection, Frank W. Bradbrook's *Jane Austen and Her Predecessors* (1966). Back then I had found myself shipwrecked on his chapter surveying "the feminist tradition in the English novel." It was the one that had made me wonder whether my entire idea was ill-conceived, that I was setting off to explore a sea of terrible books—thanks to sentences like this one: "Jane Austen turns inferior work by her predecessors and contemporaries to positive and constructive uses." But this time around, I had actually read those books. And I'd enjoyed them. I thought I might read Bradbrook's monograph differently now. Boy did I.

This time as I reread his work, it lit me up with fire and fury. Over and over again, the author argued that Austen's positive debts were to the men who influenced her—Johnson, Shakespeare, Wordsworth—while those debts clearly owed to her favorite women writers were only improved by Austen's use of them. Austen "showed her usual critical shrewdness in using the conventions of the novel as written by Fanny Burney, who admired Dr Johnson, as a framework for her own fiction." Someone please explain why

Johnson is in that sentence. Of course, even when Johnson was removed from the conversation, Bradbrook still spoke with confidence of the "skill of Jane Austen in transforming the material that Fanny Burney supplied."

In another passage, Bradbrook turned Radcliffe's influence on Austen into a conduit for a more respectable influence, Shakespeare: "The influence of Shakespeare on Ann Radcliffe has been frequently noted [. . .] Jane Austen occasionally appears to have absorbed Shakespeare through the medium of Ann Radcliffe." On the very next page, he expressed hope that a passage from Austen was influenced by Wordsworth instead of Radcliffe, even while admitting it wasn't: "Did Jane Austen recall Wordsworth's sonnet, or is the passage in *Mansfield Park* a direct reminiscence of *The Mysteries of Udolpho*? There can be little doubt that Jane Austen had the passage from Ann Radcliffe's novel in mind." He wrote an entire book about the literary tree of Austen's ancestors, then did acrobatics to jump over certain branches.

I found myself disagreeing with Bradbrook's commentary on almost every page. Had we read the same books?

And then I realized that Bradbrook hadn't, in fact, read many of the books he was talking so authoritatively about.

The real smoking gun appeared on page 104, about halfway through the chapter. There, Bradbrook described Charlotte Smith's novel *The Old Manor House*, after making it clear that, "Occasionally, Jane Austen may be indebted to Charlotte Smith for an odd phrase, or she may mock a certain cliche or vulgarism used by the less critical novelist." Because of its acclaimed reputation—less critical novelist indeed—*The Old Manor House* had been the first Charlotte Smith novel I read. Bradbrook devoted nearly two pages to a discussion of "the heroine Isabella." But Isabella is not the heroine of *The Old Manor House*. Isabella is the hero's sister, and her story weaves in and out of the narrative as a contrasting tale of warning. She's a subplot at best: calling her the heroine of the novel would be like calling Lydia Bennet the heroine of *Pride and Prejudice*. Anyone who read even the first ten pages of *The Old Manor House* would know that it is the orphan with "the dramatic and uncommon name of Monimia," raised

Cinderella-like as a servant to her aunt, who is the heroine. The only logical conclusion is that Bradbrook had read *about* the book, but hadn't read the book itself.

I experienced a wave of secondhand embarrassment for Bradbrook. I was sympathetic, for a few reasons. I knew in reading the scholarship of feminist recovery that many academics struggled to gain access to these texts to read them. I also know we quite literally don't have the time to read every book. Hence the practicality of the canon. But the longer I thought about it, the less merciful I was inclined to be. Surely a critic must read the books if he is going to analyze them in such an extended comparison with others. So when Bradbrook argued that "Charlotte Smith's fiction was only of negative use to Jane Austen," I no longer believed him. Because I knew better. I had actually read her books.

It was as if I had been given the key to decipher the code for Bradbrook's work. When he stated that Edgeworth's "prose is without wit and epigrammatic grace," I knew that didn't mean he was right. It meant that Bradbrook probably hadn't read *Belinda*, which features Lady Delacour, the single wittiest character in any novel I had read from the period—including Austen's. When Bradbrook argued that "Fanny Burney is not able to show a character developing or changing or being transformed in the consciousness of another person," I knew he probably hadn't read *Camilla*, since that's pretty much the entire arc of the novel.

Jane Austen and Her Predecessors was published in the 1960s, before the momentum for the recovery of these authors had truly taken hold. Over the decades, multiple scholars in this new wave chipped away at the assumption that Austen's favorite reads must have been, somehow, bad. And they had made great strides. But the lure of the canon is powerful. And, according to the modern scholar Jan Gorak, it has two problematic side effects: "to freeze responses to the texts inside it and to exclude other [ones]."

The authority we ascribe to the canon can make us complacent. We know what's good—see, there's a list—so whatever doesn't make that list must not be. Why investigate further? We fall into Bradbrook's error, allowing the mammoth place Austen holds in the canon to overshadow the contributions of the women writers who came before her. In a popular book about Jane Austen published in 2004, the author stated that Austen was "the first woman to earn repeated comparisons to Shakespeare." I read that with a pang for Ann Radcliffe. In an otherwise clever 2016 book that generated tremendous talk about Austen outside of academic circles, the author stated that "Jane was the only novelist of this period to write novels that were set more or less in the present day and more or less in the real world—or, at any rate, a world recognizable to her readers as the one in which they actually lived." I gasped when I read that line, thinking about when Edgeworth's *Patronage*—published in 1814, between Austen's *Pride and Prejudice* (1813) and *Mansfield Park* (1814)—caused an uproar in London because readers of the time placed "the action in or near the present day, which encouraged critics to try to identify characters and incidents."

As of this writing, Austen's Wikipedia page states, "Part of Austen's fame rests on the historical and literary significance that she was the first woman to write great comic novels. Samuel Johnson's influence is evident, in that she follows his advice to write 'a representation of life as may excite mirth.'" Reading those sentences, my temples grew hot: they are far better suited to describe Burney, who was both influential and acclaimed for this very trait—comic realism—a generation before. (Remember: Burney's friends joked about being "afraid" she would satirize them as characters in her books.) Austen followed Burney as her model in this trait as least as much as she was following Johnson.

It would be folly to claim every difference in opinion between critics is because one of them hasn't actually read the book. I also read attacks on books that I loved from plenty of critics who actually read them, like the 1966 *Time* magazine review of *Udolpho* calling it "a travesty of the romantic ethos." Further, not every book I read in my investigation was great. I couldn't even finish the first chapter of *Coelebs*. And I've already been clear that I'd like to see the second half of *A Simple Story* locked up with some arcane magic that eliminates it from this universe's timeline. But hear me out: I do rather feel that publishing as a professional about a book's literary merit (or lack thereof) should require one to open it. You know, as a rule.

Why do we make definitive statements about books we haven't read? And I do mean "we": we have all claimed at some point to have read a book that we haven't. You haven't? You must be a perfect heroine from an eighteenth-century novel. Because I sure have.

Most of the times I have told that kind of little white lie, I have done so in service of keeping the conversation moving. If I say I haven't read the book, then the flow of the discussion collapses because the other person feels they must stop to explain the context. But in the past, I know I've also done it to buttress my literary credentials. Forget Bradbrook: I'm embarrassed for myself, admitting that.

The job of a bookseller requires learning how to talk with authority about books you haven't read, either because you've read a lot *about* those books, or because you can place that book in a wider historical context that you do know well. This is what I saw these Austen scholars doing when they made statements that overstepped. This is how I myself had overstepped when I confidently sold Boswell's *Life of Johnson* as the only biography of the man worth noticing, having never read any of Piozzi's works (nor Boswell's!).

But the deeper my literary knowledge became, the weaker too became my urge to claim I'd read any given book. I was comfortable with the boundaries of my knowledge. I had stopped caring whether someone thought less of me because I hadn't read, say, all of Shakespeare's historical plays. (I haven't.) Scholars today can praise Austen without making statements about other writers they can't back up with evidence. Austen doesn't need hyperbole. She's great. End of story.

Over the course of my investigation it became clear that many of the scholars who had actually read Austen's favorites also loved them. Far from the "lack of fastidiousness" asserted by Bradbrook, Loraine Fletcher argued that Charlotte Smith's novels had "forcefulness and originality." And unlike the argument that Austen was the first to be compared to Shakespeare, Rictor Norton spells out the actual context:

What Ann Radcliffe achieved was to place her novels within the Great Tradition of High Art—many of her contemporaries joined in one breath the names of Shakespeare, Milton, Ariosto, Radcliffe. She seems to have accomplished this quite self-consciously, deliberately and in a manner that we now call feminist. She asserted the right of women's work to be deemed a masterpiece: *The Mysteries of Udolpho* occupied a place on the top shelf in the canon of literature for three generations.

Nevertheless, we have decided that Austen is the best. And maybe she is, in some ways. But if we're using comparison as a tool for rating authors, it's not difficult to flip that narrative. Austen paints with a smaller palette than Burney. She is not as moving as Radcliffe. She is less daring than Lennox. She has less conviction than Hannah More. She is less philosophical than Smith. She is not as witty as Inchbald. She doesn't have as much heart as Piozzi. She lacks the depth of wisdom of Edgeworth. But does that change my love for Austen? Of course not. When we use comparison as a way to rank rather than to reveal, all we do is dim our curiosity. Such an approach limits the potential of our reading, making the canon function as "yes, but"—as when we assume a book is no longer canonical because it isn't any good. The canon is most useful when we say "yes, and"—using it as a starting point for a richer and more expansive approach to our reading.

We have decided that Austen is the best. And because we venerate the concept of "first" so much, we easily elide the two: *best* must also be *first*. But that's where the trouble lies. To call Austen not only the best but the "first great woman writer in English" requires simplifying the narrative, erasing her literary ancestry. To hold a first edition copy of *Emma* is to feel the thrill of traveling through time, to witness the first moment when people would have met these families in Highbury. But I also loved my copy of Edgeworth's *Patronage* published in 1986, from the Pandora Mothers of the Novel series that was issued as a companion to Dale Spender's book. Even with its bent corners, its three-dollar pencil price at the top corner of the first leaf, and its growing creases to the spine as I worked through its six-hundred-plus pages. It was not a "first," but that didn't mean it was insignificant.

I want to separate "best" and "first." Austen's reputation today is so high that it feels counterintuitive to suggest any other writer of her era compared with her. But there is no need to degrade or even erase the women writers who came before in order to elevate her. Nevertheless, Austen criticism remains full of arguments that follow this pattern, like: "Jane Austen shows in *Northanger Abbey* that she *could* have written a Radcliffian best-seller every bit as bloodcurdling as *Mysteries of Udolpho*." Absolutely no, she could not. As Elizabeth Inchbald observed in a humorous 1807 article on "the art of writing Novels": "Beware how you imitate Mrs. Radcliffe or Maria Edgeworth; you cannot equal them."

Commentators have often used Austen to keep other women out of the canon. In this investigation, Austen helped me create a more expansive view of the canon. Austen didn't see herself as the "first" or the "only" anything. After reading all her surviving letters, I believe that Austen herself would have rolled her eyes at this treatment today. That's what she's doing in that passage in *Northanger Abbey* when she criticizes readers who proudly discuss Milton but are too embarrassed to admit they're reading novels. While it's wonderful to imagine her happiness at achieving such a high reputation, I think she would have been equally shocked that *Northanger Abbey* is still read, but that the magnificent novels she mentions in it (*Belinda*, *Camilla*, *Cecilia*, and of course *Udolpho*) have fallen far below her in popular circulation. In fact, her brother Henry's biography incidentally revealed that we have this all backward: Austen "sent into the world those novels, which by many have been placed on the same shelf as the works of a D'Arblay [i.e., Burney] and an Edgeworth." Henry was proud to say that Jane Austen had earned a place next to *them* on the shelf. Now we make these authors earn a place next to her.

The canon has always changed, responding to the needs, values, and tastes of each generation. Bradbrook clearly did not feel that the novels of these women writers should be included in the canon, but I went on to read many other scholars who believed the question was worthy of debate.

This disconnect between generations, in which a younger generation overlooks the contributions of a previous one, isn't an unusual pattern. I had already learned through collecting that reprints were one of the primary mechanisms used to preserve that book's status as a classic. Reprints say: this book should keep being read beyond its initial publication, so we've made it conveniently available for another generation. But this is where women's contributions often got swept away by later critics. The scholar Olivia Murphy has pointed out that Barbauld's 1810 canonizing anthology, *The British Novelists*, reprinted many works by women—including Burney, Radcliffe, Lennox, Smith, Inchbald, and Edgeworth—but of these women, Walter Scott's 1821–24 reprint series, Ballantyne's Novelist's Library, kept only Radcliffe and Smith. Just one-third survived. Classic books can only remain part of the canon from generation to generation if readers can access the texts. To be reread, books have to be reprinted. Every few years, a new crop of reprints must reaffirm a book's classic status, or not, as each generation with a new tastemaker deletes or adds based on their own critical authority—often disguised as objective universality.

Until our generation, when hubs for public domain books have sprouted and matured across the internet, making it easy to read the text of just about any book out of copyright. Now we don't have to rely on the canonizers and the reprints. If I want to read a nineteenth-century French novel about Ann Radcliffe as the head of a troupe of vampire hunters, it's only my level of French that's stopping me, not my access to the book.

When that Pandora Press series of reprints called Mothers of the Novel was founded, the publishers announced that they intended to reprint one hundred "novels written in England by women before 1820." The scholar Anne K. Mellor celebrated this development in 1988: "The availability of such works in affordable paperback editions may radically change the way we teach the eighteenth-century novel. It will certainly make possible for the first time undergraduate courses in eighteenth-century women writers." But the Pandora series ended with only twenty of those one hundred titles published, for reasons that are unclear (funding? lack of demand?).

Eighty of those one hundred titles weren't given their chance at canonical resuscitation for that generation. Today, you can read them all for free online.

––––––––––

I don't think we should abandon the canon. Nor am I advocating indiscriminate reading. But I do think we need to take advantage of the fact that we are living in an unprecedented moment thanks to the access that the internet has given us. The internet is sometimes viewed as inimical to the world of reading—but I think it's the breaker of the cycle: we no longer have to lose wonderful authors with each subsequent generation. More people have access to more books today than at any time in history. It is easier now than ever to explore great works of the past on our own terms, outside the classroom and beyond the recommendations of literary authorities. Most are in the public domain and can be pulled up within seconds to read on a laptop, as I had done countless times over the course of this investigation. Other times, when I needed a break from screens, I used internet marketplaces to find and acquire some old reprint of a novel that I would not likely have found in my local secondhand bookstore. All this access gives us significant power to determine what we read not because we "should," but because we want to. Because we are curious, and the internet gives us the power to act on that curiosity.

Tracing my fingers across the spines on my Jane Austen Bookshelf, I could literally feel the difference that time made on our "timeless" opinions: the leather spines with raised bands mixed with the gilt-stamped cloth ones, all alongside the books in dust jackets I had protected with archival plastic sleeves, and the paperbacks creased along the spines. Austen's critical reputation was in the same spot around 1930 as that of these writers today; she was the subject of a number of biographies and the darling of select critics, but not so mainstream that her place in the canon was accepted without quibble. In that case, why couldn't these authors follow Austen's model and rejoin the canon? Once again, it was Austen's own example that suggested the fate of the women in this book could be turned around—if people actually decided to read their books and find meaning in them again.

Next to my Jane Austen Bookshelf, one stack of books balanced precariously along the edge of the nightstand. A tiny copy of Ann Radcliffe's *Romance of the Forest*, printed in Exeter in 1834, lay there, its type too small to read without a bright light shining directly onto its leaves. Other stacks sprouted across the floor in the corner, awaiting yet another bookshelf I promised myself I'd buy. On my desk downstairs, three further stacks of books with varying heights and states of stability towered above my laptop, set in front of yet another row of books kept upright by antique bookends. In a different corner of that room, I kept the books checked out from the library in a separate row, ready to be gathered in my arms, their buckram-bound corners projecting out at all angles, for hauling back to the return bin. I always checked out far too many to be able to read within the lending timeline, but the challenge of it thrilled me: maybe this time I'd finish them all before I had to return them. (I didn't.)

Among the books I had purchased in my investigation, many of the modern ones were now scribbled with my marginalia. I underlined. I dog-eared. I argued with the authors at the bottom of the page. I penciled in exclamation points, smiley faces, and broken hearts. I didn't write in the older books, but I kept notes in an app on my phone as I read them, then printed out the notes and organized them into color-coded folders that I then slid into place on the same bookshelves, next to the reading journal I started after reading about Inchbald's pocketbooks. Like the library books, I had also segregated some of the older books that needed special attention. The original scaleboard binding of an 1810 Boston edition of Hannah More's poetry was hanging on by a thread, in need of a conservator's hand to strengthen it so it could be read again. A lone volume two of that first US edition of *Pride and Prejudice*, the one retitled *Elizabeth Bennet: or, Pride and Prejudice* (1832), waited for the day when I discovered a similarly bereft copy of volume one to complete the set.

In the process of building this collection, I had tracked down the evidence and traced the turning points. I found lies: Radcliffe "died of the horrors," and Piozzi wrote love letters to a man one-third her age; I found insults: Burney was "a mere common observer of manners, and also a very woman," and Hannah More was "like a huge conger-eel in an ocean of dingy morality" (a line that still baffles me). I found cover-ups: Johnson receiving credit for Lennox's most famous chapter in *The Female Quixote*, while Edgeworth's novels were named "didactic" instead of "philosophical." And I found one other thing: literary ancestors.

My collection became a space where I could be surrounded by these ancestors. When the frenetic pace of the world set my mind buzzing, I could turn to *Thraliana* to meet Piozzi, in Italy, after she finally got to take that trip she had always dreamed of with her beloved second husband. Or I could compare Radcliffe's *Udolpho* with the 1802 pirated abridgment of it, *The Veiled Picture*, that I had acquired after hours of determined internet searching for copies of Radcliffe imitations. On a quiet afternoon, I could track how an Austen letter was edited across editions from 1869, 1884, 1913, 1925—all the way up to the definitive version compiled by Deirdre Le Faye, tracing what parts were considered by her male relatives too bold to see in print. In the mornings before work, I would sit among them and simply enjoy how they spoke to me. One bringing heat to my skin in fury all over again. Another standing in silent reproof because I hadn't read it yet. Another, a bibliography, needling me into the urge to hunt for more books to add to my collection.

Even the experience of belatedly finding this community of literary ancestors was a path that others had trod before me. When I had first started this investigation, I had run across a line from Alice Walker that had encouraged me to continue in spite of my initial disappointments: "My discovery of them [. . .] came about, as many things of value do, almost by accident." In that same book, *In Search of Our Mothers' Gardens*, Walker also describes "that wonderful feeling [. . .] of being *with* a great many people, ancient spirits, all very happy to see me consulting and acknowledging them, and eager to let me know, through the joy of their presence, that, indeed, I am not alone."

To get here, I had researched and built upon the work of all those feminist scholars whose recovery of these women writers began many years ago. If I had tried to attempt this book collection back then, it too would have been the work of decades. A number of earlier collectors did just that, like Mary Hyde Eccles's pursuit of Hester Thrale Piozzi. But now I had two benefits they didn't. I had the foundation they built, and I had internet access to secondhand copies and e-books.

This new access to texts online didn't depress my desire to own physical copies of these books. On the contrary, it vastly increased the number of books that I wanted to add to my collection. I started to take notes on books mentioned within other books. I seesawed between twenty-first-century studies of Austen and searching for the nineteenth-century books about her that they described. I read a collection of her compositions as a teenager, *Love and Freindship* [*sic*], in a copy from their first appearance in print in 1922. It contained so many scenes that reminded me of Charlotte Lennox's *Female Quixote* that I decided to swing back to Lennox again, pulling up an e-book copy of her 1762 novel *Sophia*.

Looking over the notes I took on my phone while reading *Love and Freindship*, I can pinpoint the exact moment when I made the connection to Lennox. In the novella, two young ladies make judgments about everyone they meet according to standards they've taken from novels. At one point, the young women don't believe a relative cares about them because "though he told us that he was much concerned at our Misfortunes, yet by his own account it appeared that the perusal of them, had neither drawn from him a single sigh, nor induced him to bestow one curse on our vindictive stars—." By page 28 I had noted, "Officially convinced that the entirety of Love and Freindship is a spoof on the Female Quixote model." The more I read, the less alone "the first great woman writer in English" appeared. Austen's work was one branch in that larger tree of literary ancestry. My bookshelf was a partial re-creation of all those roots and branches.

In 1986, the writer and critic Italo Calvino published one of the most influential and frequently cited essays on the definition of a "classic" called

"Why Read the Classics?" Both a meditation on the pleasures of reading and a philosophical interrogation, this essay supplies increasingly refined definitions of a "classic." Having observed the joy of the reread, Calvino's definition #6 is: "A classic is a book that has never finished saying what it has to say." Check. In fact, a number of Calvino's definitions fit my readings of these women on Austen's shelf. #9: "Classics are books which, upon reading, we find even fresher, more unexpected, and more marvelous than we had thought from hearing about them." I experienced this kind of delightful surprise again and again: Burney's comedic set pieces, Radcliffe's cavernous hallways, Lennox's bold witticisms, More's commonalities with Wollstonecraft, Inchbald's honed elegance, Piozzi's unrepentant heart, and Edgeworth's irresistible characters. And #11: "*Your* classic author is the one you cannot remain indifferent to, who helps you to define yourself in relation to him, even in dispute with him" [emphasis original]. By that definition, these authors were my classics now.

Building this collection led me to question the canon. I did not throw it out, but I've learned the confidence to distinguish between the taste of "authorities" and my own. Look into the past and read whatever resonates with you, not what we're told are the "best" authors. You don't have to read any of the books I read in my investigation. Calvino argues that, outside of school, "we don't read classics out of duty or respect, only read out of love."

The process itself is the point. Like so many women before me, I had felt alone as a solitary reader. As a collector investigating Austen's favorite women writers, I found the warmth and affirmation of models. I didn't "discover" these writers; I reconnected with them, like my predecessors had done before me. I gave a chance to writers like Radcliffe, Inchbald, and Edgeworth, and I loved their books so much that they're now part of my personal canon. I hope you find yours, too.

ACKNOWLEDGMENTS

Michelle Brower, my agent: in any record of acknowledgments for this book, your name must be the first two words. Thank you. I owe further thanks to Brian Cassidy, for his unflagging confidence in me; to Lynne M. Thomas, for her enthusiasm and perceptiveness; to Emily Simonson and Brittany Adames, whose valuable work helped shape this book; and to my children, Ellie and Kit, simply for being themselves.

My deepest thanks to the many rare book institutions, dealers, scholars, and collectors whose work has made this book possible. The records created by cataloguers, whether in libraries or rare book stores, have been critical finding aids. The digitization of texts undertaken by rare book repositories involves a tremendous amount of specialized work of which I have taken every advantage. The scholars who have tread this ground in their own ways, not just over decades, but over centuries: I am so grateful for the opportunity to learn from you. And the collectors: I love your drive, your obsession, your delight in material history. It starts with you. Thank you.

APPENDIX

Selected Books from the Jane Austen Bookshelf

JANE AUSTEN

Austen, Jane. *Mansfield Park*. **London: Richard Bentley, 1833.**
First English illustrated edition and first single-volume edition. Half contemporary calf and marbled boards, sympathetically rebacked with original spine laid down. Marbled endpapers and marbled edges. Engraved frontispiece and engraved vignette title page by Pickering, followed by printed Bentley's Standard Novels title page and Mansfield Park title page. [4], 424 pages. Some rubbing to boards, with light edgewear, spine label slightly chipped. Engraved frontis and title page foxed, with a couple small marginal stains not affecting images. Gilson D3.

Austen-Leigh, J. E. *A Memoir of Jane Austen*. **London: Richard Bentley, 1870 [but 1869].**
First edition. Original green cloth with blind border ornament to boards, central gilt ornament on front board, gilt-lettered spine. Dark blue coated endpapers, edges uncut. Illustrated with the Andrews portrait of Jane Austen, based on Cassandra Austen's watercolor; and four full-page engraved plates. Title page printed in red and black, red border around text throughout. viii, 236 pages. Bookplate to front pastedown; ink gift inscription, dated year of publication, to verso of front flyleaf. Light rubbing to extremities, spine a touch toned. Gilson M125.

Adams, George Fay. *The Story of Jane Austen's Life*. **Chicago: A. C. McClurg, 1891.**

First edition. Original full blue cloth, spine and front board stamped in gilt with floral ornaments. Frontispiece illustration of Austen based on the Andrews portrait. Publisher's ads at rear. [4], viii, 9–277, [1], [6] pages. Ink owner name on front pastedown aggressively rubbed out, with some loss of paper. Light toning to spine, faint ripple to rear board. A couple spots to early leaves, else clean with only gentle toning to margins. Gilson M182.

Austen, Jane. *Pride and Prejudice*. **London: George Allen, 1894. Illustrated by Hugh Thomson; preface by George Saintsbury. The "Peacock" edition.**

Original dark green pictorial cloth elaborately stamped in gilt with peacock design. Endpapers with Art Nouveau peacock design, all edges gilt. Illustrated by Thomson with tissue-guarded frontispiece and black-and-white images throughout. xviii, 476, [2] pages. Touch of soil to fore-edge of frontispiece and title page. Book with one tiny closed tear to head of spine, slight lean. Gilt bright, hinges firm. Gilson E78.

Hill, Constance. *Jane Austen: Her Homes & Her Friends*. **London: John Lane, 1902. Illustrated by Ellen G. Hill.**

First edition. Original pictorial navy cloth, gilt-lettered spine, front board and spine stamped in white after an "embroidery upon a muslin scarf worked in satin-stitch by Jane Austen." Top edge gilt, other edges uncut. Illustrated with frontispiece image of Austen (Andrews portrait, after Cassandra Austen's watercolor); black-and-white reproductions throughout, many full-page; some photogravure, some based upon Ellen G. Hill's drawings. xiv, 279, [1] pages. Ink gift inscription, dated November 1901, to second flyleaf. Offsetting to endpapers. Faint rubbing to spine ends, slight lean. Interior clean; hinges tight. Gilson M251.

Austen-Leigh, William, and Richard Arthur Austen-Leigh. *Jane
Austen: Her Life and Letters. A Family Record.* **London: Smith,
Elder, 1913.**
First edition. Original red cloth, front board and spine lettered in gilt. Photogravure frontispiece of the Zoffany portrait; two folding leaves of family
trees before index. Publisher's ads at rear. xvi, 437, [1], [2] pages. Top edge
soiled; spine toned, with some wear to spine ends. Offsetting to endpapers;
moderate foxing to first and last few leaves. Hinges strong. Gilson M313.

Austen, Jane. *Love & Freindship* **[sic]** *And Other Early Works
Now First Printed from the Original Ms. by Jane Austen.* **London:
Chatto & Windus, 1922. Preface by G. K. Chesterton. Containing
the juvenilia "Love and Freindship," "Lesley Castle," "The
History of England," "Collection of Letters," and "Scraps."**
First edition, "Special Edition de Luxe." Original pink and yellow silk cloth,
leather spine label lettered in gilt. One of 260 numbered copies printed
on handmade paper; this copy number 208. Top edge gilt, other edges
uncut. Color pictorial endpapers reproducing Cassandra Austen's drawings
for "The History of England." Spine a touch sunned, with label toned to
brown. A couple small stains to cloth. Some foxing and offsetting to endpapers. Interior crisp. Gilson F3.

Austen, Jane. *Fragment of a Novel* **[*Sanditon*]. Oxford, UK:
Clarendon Press, 1925. Edited and with notes by R. W. Chapman.**
First edition thus, a full transcription of the manuscript. Original quarter
white cloth, blue paper boards, printed paper spine label reading "Sanditon." Uncut. [12], 170, [38] pages. Floral bookplate of Nancy Douglass to
front pastedown. Light soil to boards, faint toning to spine, tiny crease to
label. Some offsetting to endpapers. Gilson F6.

Austen, Jane. *Volume the Third.* **Oxford, UK: Clarendon Press,
1951. Edited by R. W. Chapman.**

First edition, containing the juvenilia "Evelyn" and "Kitty, or the Bower" (now known as "Catharine, or the Bower"). Original quarter white cloth, blue paper boards, printed paper spine label. Uncut and partially unopened. viii, 133, [1] pages. Touch of soil to spine, else clean and fresh. Gilson F14.

Austen, Jane. *Northanger Abbey*. **New York: Paperback Library, 1965.**

First edition thus, a Paperback Library Gothic. Original color pictorial wrappers (art uncredited, but likely Lou Marchetti), cover price 60c, 53– 873. Front cover copy reads: "The terror of Northanger Abbey had no name, no shape—yet it menaced Catherine Morland in the dead of night!" All edges stained orange. Publisher's ads at rear. 206, [2] pages. Faint spine crease, trace shelf wear. Leaves gently toned.

FRANCES BURNEY

[Burney, Frances] "by the author of *Evelina." Cecilia, or Memoirs of an Heiress*. **London: Printed for T. Payne and Son [. . .] and T. Cadell, 1782.**

First edition. Five 12mo volumes. Contemporary full sprinkled calf sympathetically rebacked, red goatskin spine labels. [2], 293, [1]; [2], 263, [1]; [2], 365, [1]; [2], 328; [2] 398 pages. Ink ownership inscription of Bethia Coman, dated 1784, to front free endpapers, her name again on the title page and another name on the following leaf of each volume; ink notation by Coman in vol. V, "By accident a strawbury [*sic*] fell into the Book which has stained the leaves": reddish residue to rear board of vol. IV and edges of vol. V. Moderate edgewear.

[Burney, Frances]. *Evelina; or, the History of a Young Lady's Entrance into the World*. **London: W. Lowndes, 1794.**

Early edition. Two 12mo volumes. Contemporary half calf, drab brown paper boards, gilt-stamped spines with weblike ornaments. xii, 237; 281,

[1] pages. Early ink owner name, "Christine Anderson / St. Germain" to title pages. Spines rubbed and dry; joints cracking but still holding. Text block lightly foxed and toned.

[Burney, Frances] "by the author of *Evelina* and *Cecilia*."
***Camilla: Or, a Picture of Youth*. London: Andrew Strahan for**
T. Payne, T. Cadell, Jun., & W. Davies, 1796.
First edition. Five octavo volumes. Early-twentieth-century full dark brown morocco by Birdsall, raised bands, spines elaborately stamped in gilt, triple-gilt rules. Gilt dentelles, all edges gilt. With subscriber's list in vol. I including "Miss J. Austen, Steventon." xlviii, 390; [4], 432; [4], 468; [4], 432; [4], 556 pages. Lengthy ink inscription to flyleaf of vol. I; early ink owner inscriptions to title pages. A fine copy.

Barrett, Charlotte, ed. *Diary and Letters of Madame D'Arblay,*
***Author of Evelina, Cecilia, &x. Edited by Her Niece*. London:**
Henry Colburn, 1842–1846.
First edition. Seven volumes. Contemporary half tan goatskin, marbled paper boards, raised bands, black spine labels. Red speckled edges. Engraved frontispiece in each volume; two folding facsimile plates of Burney's diary and a letter in vol. I. Half titles in vols. II, III, IV, and VI. xxviii, 436; xii, 434; 477, [1]; [4], 427, [1]; [2], 446; [4], 377, [1]; [2], 401, [1] pages. Bookplates of John Capel Philips to front pastedowns. Some rubbing to spines and corners; foxing to plates and a bit to first and last few leaves. Tight.

Macaulay, Thomas. *Critical and Historical Essays Contributed to*
***the Edinburgh Review*. London: Longmans, Green, 1874.**
Later edition. Full tree calf, spine elaborately stamped in gilt, raised bands, red goatskin spine label. Marbled endpapers, all edges marbled. x, 850 pages. Ink gift inscription in Latin, dated 1875, to second flyleaf; a few notes in pencil to rear endpaper. Binding remarkably clean, with one spot of wear to rear board, else bright and firm.

Ellis, Annie Raine, ed. *The Early Diary of Frances Burney, 1768–1778. With a Selection from Her Correspondence, and from the Journals of Her Sisters Susan and Charlotte Burney.* **London: George Bell and Sons, 1889.**

First edition. Two volumes. Original maroon cloth, gilt-lettered spines. Yellow coated endpapers. xcii, 327, [1]; [4], 385, [1] pages. Some edgewear and rubbing to boards. Moderate foxing to first and last few leaves.

Seeley, L. S., ed. *Fanny Burney and Her Friends: Select Passages from Her Diary and Other Writings.* **London: Seeley, 1890.**

First edition thus, an abridgement of Burney's *Diary*. Original blue cloth, gilt-lettered spine, front board stamped in gilt in neoclassical frame. Illustrated with nine photogravures, including frontispiece portrait of Burney. Publisher's catalog at rear. xii, 331, [1], 16 pages. Moderate wear to extremities, touch of toning to spine.

Burney, Fanny [Frances]. *Evelina.* **London: Macmillan, 1903. Introduction by Austin Dobson, illustrated by Hugh Thomson.**

First edition thus, with Thomson's illustrations. Original emerald-green cloth elaborately stamped in gilt to spine and front board. All edges gilt. Illustrated by Thomson with full-page images and vignettes in black and white. Publisher's ads at rear. xxxvi, 477, [1], [2] pages. Bookplate of Alice and Graham Spence to front pastedown. Spine toned, with shallow wear to extremities. Slight lean. Some foxing, primarily to endpapers.

Dobson, Austin. *Fanny Burney.* **English Men of Letters Series. London: Macmillan, 1903.**

First edition, presentation copy. Original red cloth, gilt-lettered spine. Top edge gilt. Publisher's ads at rear, including catalog for the English Men of Letters series (with Austen and Edgeworth listed). viii, 216, [4] pages. Blind circular emboss "presentation copy" to title page; "Laurel Book Service" (Hazelton, PA) bookseller ticket to rear pastedown. Light toning to spine, offsetting to endpapers. Crisp.

Tinker, Chauncey Brewster, ed. *Dr. Johnson and Fanny Burney, Being the Johnsonian Passages from the Works of Mme. D'Arblay.* New York: Moffat, Yard, 1911.

First edition. Original brick-red cloth, gilt-lettered spine and front board. Frontispiece portrait of Samuel Johnson. xl, 252 pages. Some wear to extremities, gilt on spine slightly effaced. Leaves gently toned.

ANN RADCLIFFE

Boaden, James. *Fountainville Forest, a Play in Five Acts (Founded on the Romance of the Forest), as Performed at the Theatre-Royal Covent-Garden.* London: Printed for Hookham and Carpenter, 1794.

First edition of a dramatic adaption of *The Romance of the Forest*. Early-twentieth-century brad-bound plain paper wrappers, paper printed title label. [6], 70 pages. Ink name "James Boaden" and date "1794" to title label. Moderate wear to spine. Some soil to edges of text.

Radcliffe, Ann. *The Mysteries of Udolpho.* London: Printed for G. G. and J. Robinson, 1794.

First edition. Four 12mo volumes, 6.75 x 4 inches. Full contemporary speckled calf, gilt-ornamented spines, green and black goatskin spine labels. With all half titles. [4], 428; [4], 478; [4], 463, [1]; [4], 428 pages. Ink owner name of Sarah Price Clarke (heiress of Sutton Scarsdale Hall, Derbyshire) on front pastedown of each volume, dated 23 June 1794 in vol. 1 (and partially effaced in vol. 3). A few gatherings partially sprung and/or standing proud, with edges correspondingly softened. Light rubbing to bindings. Faint scattered foxing. Firm.

Sammelband of Periodical-Format Gothics issued by *Marvellous Magazine,* including two unauthorized abridgements of Radcliffe novels. *The Cavern of Horrors; or, The Mysteries of Miranda: A Neopolitan Tale / The Secret Oath of the Blood-Stained Dagger / The Southern Tower; or, Conjugal Sacrifice, and Retribution / The Veiled Picture; or, The Mysteries of Gorgorno &c.* London: Printed for T. Hurst, [1802–1804].

Four chapbooks bound together, *The Southern Tower* a pirated abridgement of *Sicilian Romance* and *Veiled Picture* a pirated abridgement of *Mysteries of Udolpho*. Full contemporary mottled calf, gilt-stamped spine. Illustrated with engraved frontispieces at front of each volume. 72 pages each. Light foxing to title pages and frontispieces, with a bit of cracking to joints (still sound).

Wheelwright, C. A. *Poems, Original and Translated; Including Versions of the Medea and Octavia of Seneca.* London: Printed by A. J. Valpy [. . .] sold by Longman, Hurst, Rees, Orme, and Brown, 1810.

First edition, containing a footnote erroneously stating Radcliffe died of "*the horrors.*" Contemporary half calf, gilt-stamped raised bands, blind-stamped compartments and boards. Red speckled edges. xxxii, 303, [1] pages. Lacking spine label. Moderate wear to joints and boards. Light scattered foxing.

Dunlop, John. *The History of Fiction: Being a Critical Account of the Most Celebrated Prose Works of Fiction, from the Earliest Greek Romances to the Novels of the Present Age.* London: Printed for Longman, Hurst, Rees, Orme, and Brown, 1814.

First edition. Three 8mo volumes. Contemporary brown-wave patterned boards, black morocco spine labels. Errata leaf at rear of each volume. xx, 416, [2]; [4], 410, [2]; [4], 436, [2] pages. Armorial bookplate of John Adolphus, Esquire, to front pastedown of each volume. Some pencil notes to endpapers, primarily vol. I, including "many original phrases in this volume." Expert repairs to spine labels and some joints. Some dampstain to each volume, heavier to vol. III. A bit of rippling to boards.

Radcliffe, Anne [*sic*]; and [Thomas Talfourd]. *Gaston de Blondeville, or the Court of Henry III. Keeping Festival in Ardenne, a Romance.* [With] *Memoir of the Life and Writings of Mrs. Radcliffe.* **London: Henry Colburn, 1826.**

First edition, with *Memoir* printed in first part of vol. I. Four 12mo volumes. Contemporary half calf, marbled paper boards, black morocco spine labels. Red speckled edges. [4], 132, 1–186; [4], 399, [1]; [4], 375, [1]; [6], 331, [1] pages. Contemporary ink owner name, "Mrs Edward Flowers," to second flyleaf of all volumes; additional early ink owner name to title page of vols. III and IV. Pencil owner notes to rear endpapers of vols. I and III. Touch of cracking to rear joint of vol. I (still firm); moderate wear to boards. Some soil to edges and endpapers. Interiors largely clean.

[Radcliffe, Ann] "Mrs. Ratcliffe." *The Romance of the Forest. Interspersed with Some Pieces of Poetry.* **Exeter, UK: J. & B. Williams, 1834.**

Early-Victorian reprint. Two 32mo volumes. Full contemporary sheep, gilt-stamped spines. 186; 184 pages. Pencil gift inscription, dated 1899, to early leaves. Some edgewear to boards. Toning and light scattered foxing to leaves.

Gillies, R. P. *Memoirs of a Literary Veteran; Including Sketches and Anecdotes of the Most Distinguished Literary Characters from 1794 to 1849.* **London: Richard Bentley, 1851.**

First edition, printing for the first time letters from Wordsworth, et al. Three volumes. Publisher's blue blind-stamped cloth, spines lettered in gilt. Yellow endpapers. xii, 344; vi, 339, [1]; vi, 340 pages. Bookplate of John Sparrow to front pastedowns. Vol. I recased, endpapers renewed. Cracking to joints (still holding). Spines toned; moderate edgewear to boards. Interiors fresh.

Radcliffe, Ann. *The Mysteries of Udolpho.* **London: J. M. Dent & Sons, 1931. Introduction by R. Austin Freeman.**

Everyman's Library edition. Two volumes. Original red cloth, gilt-lettered spines, blind-stamped front boards. In original red pictorial dust jackets. Red swirl-patterned endpapers. Publisher's catalog at rear of each volume. xiv, 336, 16; [6], 344, 16 pages. Some pencil marginalia throughout. Jackets with a touch of toning to spines. Top edges dusty. Bright.

Tompkins, J. M. S. *The Popular Novel in England: 1770–1800*. London: Constable and Co., 1932.

First edition. Original green cloth, gilt-stamped spine. In original unclipped (12/6 net) typographic dust jacket. xii, 388 pages. From the library of Barry Bloomfield, bibliographer of Auden and Larkin, and former director of collection development at the British Library. Jacket with several archival paper repairs to verso, moderate foxing to edges and flaps. Book with lightly toned spine, a bit of spotting to fore-edges.

CHARLOTTE LENNOX

[Lennox, Charlotte]. *The Female Quixote; or, The Adventures of Arabella*. London: Printed for A. Millar, 1752.

Second edition. Two 12mo volumes. Modern fine bindings by Sol Rébora with intricately textured and hand-painted cloth in multiple layers, incorporating Japanese papers in various hues. xvi, 271, [1]; [2], 322 pages. Archival repairs to edges of a number of leaves. Housed in custom gray cloth clamshell box, with accompanying paper chemise containing remnants of eighteenth-century calf boards.

[Lennox, Charlotte] "by the author of *The Female Quixote.*" *Shakespear Illustrated: Or the Novels and Histories, on Which the Plays of Shakespear Are Founded, Collected and Translated from the Original Authors. With Critical Remarks*. London: Printed for A. Millar, 1753, 1754.

First edition. Three 12mo volumes. Contemporary full speckled calf, gilt-stamped spine, raised bands, red goatskin spine labels. Speckled edges, some leaves unopened. Publisher's ads at rear of volume II. xii, [2], 292; [4], 274, [2]; [4], 308 pages. From the library of Frances Mary Richardson Currer, with her engraved bookplate on front pastedown of each volume; vol. I with small contemporary ink notation on front free endpaper. Some flaking and sympathetic repairs to spines, small areas of wear and tiny bit of cracking to joints (still firm). Some marginal toning and soil to leaves. Light spot of dampstaining to lower margin of vol. II. Well preserved and lovely.

Johnson, Samuel. *A Dictionary of the English Language: In Which the Words Are Deduced from Their Originals, and Illustrated in Their Different Significations by Examples from the Best Writers. To Which Are Prefixed, a History of the Language, and an English Grammar.* **London: Printed by W. Strahan, for J. and P. Knapton; T. and T. Longman; C. Hitch and L. Hawes; A. Millar; and R. and J. Dodsley, 1755.**

First edition. Two folio volumes. Contemporary full speckled calf sympathetically rebacked with elaborately gilt-stamped spine in period style, raised bands, red and black goatskin spine labels. Red speckled edges, new marbled endpapers and flyleaves. Engraved armorial bookplates of the House of Abercairny in Scotland on front pastedowns. Contemporary calf boards with moderate rubbing, light expert restoration to corners and edges. A few short marginal paper repairs. A bit of browning and faint foxing to some gatherings, minor wormholing to vol. I, overall very clean.

[Lennox, Charlotte, trans.]. *Memoirs of Maximilian de Bethune, Duke of Sully, Prime Minister to Henry the Great* **[. . .]. London: Printed for A. Millar, in the Strand; R. and J. Dodsley, in Pall-Mall; and W. Shropshire, in New-Bond-Street, 1756.**

First edition in English, extra illustrated with 193 additional plates bound in. Three quarto volumes. Nineteenth-century full maroon straight-grain morocco by Bayntun, raised bands, elaborately gilt-stamped spines, large gilt cornerpieces and triple-gilt rules to boards. Gilt dentelles, marbled endpapers, all edges gilt. Extra illustrated with portraits, landscapes, dramatic scenes, inter alia. Half titles in first two volumes. [4], 540; [4], viii, 555, [1]; viii, 408 pages plus index. Only light rubbing to joints.

[Lennox, Charlotte, trans.] "Translated from the French, by the author of *The Female Quixote*." *Memoirs for the History of Madame de Maintenon and of the Last Age*. London: Printed for A. Millar, and J. Nourse, in the Strand; R. and J. Dodsley, in Pallmall; L. Davis, and C. Reymer, in Holbourn, 1757.

First edition thus, Lennox's translation. Five 12mo volumes. Twentieth-century full black straight-grain morocco, raised bands, tan and red morocco spine labels, large gilt ornaments to compartments. All edges gilt, reddish brown endpapers. Dedication and preface erroneously bound in vol. V. [8], 316; [8], 304; [8], 314; [6], 318; [8], xxiv, 348 pages. Bookplates of C. Sewell Thomas and Marie Wade Thomas to front pastedowns. Small repair to gutter of early leaves in vol. IV. Touch of wear to a couple spine heads, a tiny bit of foxing, else clean and bright.

Lennox, Charlotte, trans. *Meditations and Penitential Prayers, Written by the Celebrated Duchess de La Valliere, Mistress of Lewis [sic] the Fourteenth of France*. [London]: Printed for J. Dodsley, in Pall Mall, 1774.

First edition, with Lennox noted as translator on title page, of the memoirs of Louis XIV's famous mistress. 16mo. Modern three-quarter calf, marbled boards, gilt-ruled raised bands, red morocco spine label. With half title. [4], 192 pages. Ink owner name, "Eliza Bastable / The Gift of Her Grandmother / Mary Bastable," to front flyleaf. Soil to first and final leaves, lighter soil to margins throughout.

Burgoyne, John. *The Heiress. A Comedy in Five Acts*. London: Printed for J. Debrett, 1786.

First edition, largely based upon Lennox's *The Sister*, went into seven editions in its first year. Modern paper wrappers. [2], 112 pages. Only a bit of foxing.

Wilson, Mona. *These Were Muses*. London: Sidgwick and Jackson, 1924.

First edition, with a chapter on Charlotte Lennox, beginning with the story of Johnson (sourced from Boswell) at dinner with Elizabeth Carter, Hannah More, and Frances Burney, during which he named Charlotte Lennox "superior to them all." Original quarter blue cloth, blue marbled boards, printed paper spine label. Errata and additional paper label at rear. Illustrated with nine full-page plates, including a portrait of Lennox by Joshua Reynolds. x, 235, [1] pages. Light peeling and toning to paper label; slight lean. Some foxing to prelims.

Lennox, Charlotte. *The Female Quixote: Or the Adventures of Arabella*. London: Oxford University Press, 1970. Edited and with introduction by Margaret Dalziel.

First edition thus, in the Oxford English Novels series. Original orange cloth boards, spine stamped in gilt and teal. In original price-clipped orange and teal typographic dust jacket. 427, [1] pages. Ink owner name, "M. M. J. Rubel / Oxford, 1978" to front free endpaper. Slight sunning to spine, else clean and bright.

Lennox, Charlotte. *The Female Quixote: or the Adventures of Arabella*. London: Pandora, 1986.

"Mothers of the Novel" series. Original white pictorial wrappers with design and illustration by Marion Dalley. Publisher's ads for Brunton's *Self-Control* and Edgeworth's *Belinda* at rear. xvi, 423, [3] pages. Distributor sticker (Unwin Hyman / Winchester, MA) to rear wrapper. Some foxing to wrappers, spine creases, spot of rubbing to rear joint. Marginal toning to leaves.

HANNAH MORE

More, Hannah. *Sir Eldred of the Bower, and the Bleeding Rock: Two Legendary Tales.* **London: Printed for T. Cadell, 1776.**
First edition. Modern half calf, marbled paper boards, brown spine label. With half title. Publisher's catalog at rear. [6], 49, [1] pages.

[More, Hannah]. *Percy, a Tragedy. As It Is Acted at the Theatre-Royal in Covent-Garden.* **London: Printed for T. Cadell, in the Strand, 1778.**
First edition. Modern quarter bright blue cloth, gilt-lettered spine, gray-blue paper boards. Publisher list ("Lately Published by the same Author") at rear. [6], 87, [1] pages. Later ink notations to first leaf, including "the prologue and epilogue are both written by David Garrick, who is said to have assisted in the writing of the play." Some foxing and soil to text block edges, lightly toned.

Yearsley, Ann. *Poems, on Several Occasions.* **London: Printed for T. Cadell, in the Strand, 1785. Bound with two roughly contemporary, but shorter, imprints.**
First edition. Contemporary half calf, speckled paper boards, black morocco spine label. Yellow stained edges. With prefatory letter to Elizabeth Montagu and subscriber's list. xxx, 168; [4], 12; [4], 16 pages. Spine somewhat dry and rubbed, corners lightly bumped.

[More, Hannah]. *Thoughts on the Importance of Manners of the Great to General Society.* **London: Printed for T. Cadell, in the Strand, 1788.**
First edition. Contemporary red morocco, marbled paper boards, gilt-lettered spine. Marbled endpapers. [4], 102 pages. Some wear and toning to spine. Light scattered foxing.

[More, Hannah]. *Cheap Repository Number 22. The Harvest Home*. Philadelphia: B. & J. Johnson, 1800.
First US edition. Original pictorial self-wrappers. 36 pages. Likely once bound into a sammelband, now disbound: remnants of glue to spine. Leaves uniformly toned, some edgewear, with scattered light foxing. Sound.

More, Hannah. *Strictures on the Modern System of Female Education*. Boston: Printed for Joseph Bumstead, 1802.
Third US edition "with considerable additions." Two 12mo volumes in one. Contemporary full sheep, gilt-stamped goatskin spine label. viii, 312 pages. Ink owner inscriptions, "Property of Misses / Sophia, Judith Greenleaf [. . .] / and Susanna Northend / 1803" and "Hallowell Jane 1830" to second flyleaf. Short verse in ink to rear pastedown. Significant wear and patches of scratching to boards. Leaves browned. Firm.

More, Hannah. *Coelebs in Search of a Wife. Comprehending Observations on Domestic Habits and Manners, Religion, and Morals*. London: Printed for T. Cadell and W. Davies, 1808.
First edition. Two octavo volumes. Contemporary full speckled calf, sympathetically rebacked. Speckled edges. xii, 351, [1]; [4], 469, [1] pages. Engraved bookplate of John Smith, Esq., to front pastedowns; his ink owner name to title page of vol. II. Some dryness to boards, repaired. A few shallow ink stains to edges of vol. II title, else quite clean.

[More, Hannah]. *The Shepherd of Salisbury Plain [. . .] to Which Is Added, The Sorrows of Yamba; or the Negro Woman's Lamentation*. Boston: Printed by Samuel Avery, 1810.
Early US edition. 24mo. Original pink paper spine, gray-blue paper over scaleboard. 107, [1] pages. Spine partly perished, with boards hanging by threads. Old spine tape repair peeling. Wear to boards, exposing some scaleboard underneath. Text toned and foxed.

Roberts, William. *Memoirs of the Life and Correspondence of Mrs. Hannah More.* **London: R. B. Seeley and W. Burnside, 1834.**

First edition. Four octavo volumes. Contemporary half olive calf, marbled paper boards, tan morocco spine labels, gilt-rules, blind-stamped spine compartments. Red speckled edges. Engraved frontispiece portrait of More in vol. I. xii, 407, [1]; [2], 478; [2], 502; [2], 399 pages. Vol. II lacking spine label; two leaves tipped in at gutter in vol. IV. Faint soil, some rubbing to boards.

CHARLOTTE SMITH

Smith, Charlotte. *Emmeline, the Orphan of the Castle.* **London: Printed for T. Cadell, 1788.**

First edition, the copy of Mary Hill, Marchioness of Downshire. Four 12mo volumes. Contemporary tree calf, spine labels with Mary Hill's gilt-stamped monogram. [2], 292; [2], 268; [2], 319, [1]; [2], 393, [1] pages. Ink owner name, "Mary Hillsborough," to title pages. Spines lacking a number of labels, with some cracking to joints (all still firm). A couple gatherings sprung.

Smith, Charlotte. *Elegiac Sonnets. The Fifth Edition, with Additional Sonnets and Other Poems.* **London: Printed for T. Cadell, 1789.**

First illustrated edition. Two 16mo volumes. Contemporary tree calf, spines elaborately stamped in gilt, red morocco spine labels, gilt rules. Marbled endpapers. Illustrated with ten full-page engraved plates, including frontispiece portrait of Smith in vol. II. Subscriber's list in both volumes; publisher's catalog at rear. [4], 139; [16], 117, [1], [2] pages. Some rubbing to joints, else bright and clean.

Smith, Charlotte. *Desmond. A Novel.* **London: Printed for G. G. J. and J. Robinson, 1792.**

.

First edition, provincial circulating library copy. Three 12mo volumes. Contemporary half calf, marbled paper boards, red goatskin spine labels, gilt-ruled spines. With half titles. Publisher's catalog at rear of vol. III. [4], xii, 280; [4], 296; [4], 348, [4] pages. Terms leaf for D. Towler's Public Circulating Library, Bungay, and later bookseller ticket below, to front pastedowns. Rubbing and wear to marbled paper, with some exposure of boards and calf corners underneath; vol. III with front joint and part of spine sympathetically repaired, joints of vol. II just cracking but firm. Dampstaining to first few leaves of vol. II, primarily at margins, else largely clean.

Smith, Charlotte. *The Old Manor House. A Novel, in Four Volumes.* **London: Printed for J. Bell, 1793.**

First edition. Four 12mo volumes. Contemporary full speckled calf, black goatskin spine labels, double rules in gilt. Marbled endpapers, yellow stained edges. Publisher's catalog at rear of vol. IV. [2], 280; [2], 320; [2], 353, [1]; [2] 363, [1] pages. Significant loss to front endpaper and subsequent flyleaves of vol. I, with slightly damaged lower corner of several gatherings thereafter and front board. Spines somewhat dry and rubbed, light general wear. Sound.

[Woolston, Thomas, ed.]. *The Young Gentleman and Lady's Poetical Preceptor.* **Coventry, UK: Printed and sold by M. Luckman, 1794.**

First edition, presentation copy from the editor, of this textbook of canonical poets for students. Includes Milton, Pope, Burns, et al., alongside Charlotte Smith, whose poems are called "some of the most exquisite Sonnets, perhaps, ever written." 36mo. Contemporary tree calf, rebacked, maroon spine label, gilt rules to boards. Publisher's catalog at rear. xii, 310, [2] pages. Ink inscription, "The Gift of the / author April 24th / 1795" to front flyleaf. Subtle paper repairs to gutters of first few leaves. Boards rather rubbed at corners, with some dry crackling to contemporary leather, else neat and clean.

Smith, Charlotte. *Elegiac Sonnets, and Other Poems.* **London: Jones & Company, 1829.**
Beautifully bound late Georgian sammelband of poetic imprints from Jones & Company, including works by John Dryden, Virgil, Lord Lyttelton, and Charlotte Smith. 12mo. Contemporary full paneled calf, raised bands, green spine label, spine elaborately stamped in gilt, boards with multiple gilt rules and ornamental cornerpieces. Marbled endpapers and edges. xii, 139, [3], [2: ads]; viii, 108; 23, [1]; 12; vi, 34; viii, 13–26; iv, 22, [2: ads]; xii, 48; ii, 12 pages. Some foxing to early and last leaves, small spot of soil to first Dryden leaf (A2r). Binding lovely with only trace shelf wear.

Sharp, Mrs. William. *Women's Voices: An Anthology of the Most Characteristic Poems by English, Scotch, and Irish Women.* **London: Walter Scott, 1887.**
First edition, including poems by Charlotte Smith, Hannah More, and Hester Piozzi ("Three Warnings"). Full pebbled goatskin, gilt-lettered spine and front board. Errata slip. xx, 419, [1] pages. Touches of rubbing to extremities. Bright.

Smith, Charlotte. *Emmeline.* **London: Pandora, 1987. Introduction by Zoë Fairbairns.**
"Mothers of the Novel" series. Original white pictorial wrappers with design and illustration by Marion Dalley. Publisher's ads at rear. xiv, 553, [1], [8] pages. Small HarperCollins price sticker to rear wrapper. A few knicks and spots of rubbing to wrappers. Marginal toning to leaves.

Smith, Charlotte. *The Old Manor House.* **London: Pandora, 1987. Introduction by Janet Todd.**
"Mothers of the Novel" series. Original white pictorial wrappers with design and illustration by Marion Dalley. xii, 516 pages. Creasing and some rubbing to spine, light foxing to wrappers. Marginal toning to leaves.

Curran, Stuart, ed. *The Poems of Charlotte Smith*. Oxford, UK: Oxford University Press, 1993.

First edition thus, collected and with introduction by Curran. Original maroon cloth, gilt-lettered spine and boards. xxx, 335, [1] pages. Only trace edgewear.

ELIZABETH INCHBALD

[Inchbald, Elizabeth]. *Appearance Is Against Them. A Farce, in Two Acts, as It Is Acted at the Theatre Royal, Covent Garden.* London: Printed for G. G. J. & J. Robinson, 1785.

First edition. Modern paper wrappers. [4], 48 pages. A bit of soil to last leaf.

[Inchbald, Elizabeth] "Mrs. Inchbald." *I'll Tell You What. A Comedy, in Five Acts, as It Is Performed at the Theatre Royal, Haymarket.* London: Printed for G. G. J. and J. Robinson, 1786.

First edition. Modern paper wrappers. [6], 88 pages. Faint early ink owner name to title page. Light spotting. Soil to last leaf.

[Inchbald, Elizabeth] "Mrs. Inchbald." *Next Door Neighbours; a Comedy, in Three Acts.* London: Printed for G. G. J. & J. Robinson, 1791.

First edition. Modern paper wrappers. With half title. Contemporary ink ownership inscription, "J. Rees Stokes." [8], 82 pages. Light soil to first and last few leaves.

The Ladies' Own Memorandum-Book [. . .] *for the Year 1798.* London: Printed for G. G. J. & J. Robinson, [1797].

Pocketbook of the same kind used by Elizabeth Inchbald, with many portions filled in by a contemporary owner. 32mo. Modern quarter straight-grained tan morocco, marbled paper boards, black morocco spine label.

Illustrated with two engraved fashion plates: "Ladies in the Dresses of the Year 1797" and folding plate "Head Dresses of the Year 1797." Unpaginated. Contemporary ink marginalia throughout, covering a large number of entries and keeping accounts. Some dampstain and foxing to engravings. First and last few leaves heavily soiled. Top edge closely trimmed. Firm.

Boaden, James. *Memoirs of Mrs. Inchbald: Including Her Familiar Correspondence with the Most Distinguished Persons of Her Time* [. . .]. **London: Richard Bentley, 1833.**
First edition. Two octavo volumes. Contemporary half navy calf, marbled paper boards. Marbled edges and endpapers. Frontispiece portrait of Inchbald in vol. I. xii, 380; viii, 375, [1] pages. Front joints expertly repaired. Some wear and light rubbing to boards.

[Inchbald, Elizabeth]. Engraved portrait used in The British Theatre series and in Boaden's *Memoirs*. **[N.p.]: n.p., circa 1830s.**
Single engraved sheet, measuring 10 x 8 inches, matted. Caption reads: "Mrs. Inchbald / Engraved by Dean from an Original Painting." Fine.

Inchbald, Elizabeth. *A Simple Story* [with] *Nature and Art*. **London: Richard Bentley, 1833.**
Bentley Standard Novels edition (no. XXVI), the same series that reprinted Austen's novels in the 1830s. Octavo. Contemporary half calf, marbled paper boards, shallow gilt-stamped raised bands, black goatskin spine label. Marbled endpapers. Engraved frontispiece and title page; printed titles for both *Simple Story* and *Nature and Art*. xii, 434 pages. Armorial bookplate of Baron Henley to front pastedown; blurred ink owner stamp to second flyleaf, offset to frontispiece. Contemporary binding somewhat rubbed and worn, with tiny bit of cracking to head of joints (still strong). Engraved plates and last few leaves foxed. Firm.

[Inchbald, Elizabeth] "Mrs. Inchbald." *Nature and Art*. **London: Cassell and Company, 1886.**

Cassell's National Library edition, in which Inchbald is the first woman published among canonical authors such as Byron, Scott, Johnson, Shakespeare, Swift, et al. Original full pictorial brown cloth, elaborately stamped in black, gilt-lettered front board. Contemporary ads ("Barber & Company's French Coffee"; "Coventry Machinists' Co. Bicycles & Tricycles") to endpapers; further ads and publisher's catalogs at rear. 192, [4] pages. Trace wear to spine ends. Fresh and bright.

Inchbald, Elizabeth. *A Simple Story*. London: Pandora, 1987. Introduced by Jeanette Winterson.
"Mothers of the Novel" series. Original white pictorial wrappers with design and illustration by Marion Dalley. xii, 294 pages. Distributor sticker (Unwin Hyman / Winchester, MA) to rear wrapper. Some foxing and soil to wrappers, spine creases. Leaves toned.

Inchbald, Elizabeth. *A Simple Story*. Oxford, UK: Oxford University Press, 1988. Edited by J. M. S. Tompkins, new introduction by Jane Spencer.
Oxford World's Classics edition. Original color pictorial wrappers. Publisher's catalog at rear. xxxiv, 345, [5] pages. Contemporary price sticker to rear wrapper. Light pencil annotations to margins; a number of leaves with folded corners. Faint shelf wear. Leaves gently toned.

HESTER LYNCH PIOZZI

Piozzi, Hester Lynch. *Letters to and from the Late Samuel Johnson, LL.D.* London: Printed for A. Strahan, and T. Cadell, 1788.
First edition, presentation copy. Two octavo volumes. Contemporary full speckled calf, sympathetically rebacked and recornered, tan morocco spine labels, gilt rules. [2], 397, [1]; xii, 424 pages. Ink inscription, "Mrs. Lambart

/ given her by her friend / the Authoress in two Vols." Additional owner name of Hamilton Lambart, in pencil and ink, in each volume respectively. Boards a touch dry, rather rubbed at fore-edges; a few light stains to edges. Interior fairly clean.

[Wolcot, John] "Peter Pindar." *Bozzy and Piozzi, or, the British Biographers. A Town Eclogue.* **London: Printed for G. Kearsley, 1788.**

Ninth edition of this satirical poem on the literary rivalry between James Boswell and Hester Lynch Piozzi. A sample verse: "For that Piozzi's wife, Sir John, exhort her, / To draw her immortality from porter; / Give up her anecdotical inditing, / And study housewifery instead of writing." Quarto. Modern wrappers. Frontispiece engraving depicting Piozzi accosting Boswell. Publisher's catalog at rear. 57, [1] pages. Crisp and clean.

[Croker, J. W., ed.]. *Johnsoniana; or, Supplement to Boswell.* **London: John Murray, 1836.**

First edition thus, a collection of biographical works on Samuel Johnson, beginning with an edited version of Piozzi's *Anecdotes*. Octavo. Contemporary three-quarter green morocco, raised bands, gilt-stamped spine, gilt rules to boards. All edges gilt, marbled endpapers. Illustrated with 45 full page steel-engraved plates, including title page and vignette adaptation of Reynolds's portrait of "Mrs. Thrale, afterwards Mrs. Piozzi." xxiv, 530 pages. Spine somewhat toned, minor rubbing to boards. Interior clean.

[Anonymous]. *Love Letters of Mrs. Piozzi, Written When She Was Eighty, to William Augustus Conway.* **London: John Russell Smith, 1843.**

First edition. Original printed wrappers. 39, [1] pages. Spine carefully repaired; wrappers somewhat soiled, minor wear.

Hayward, A., ed. *Autobiography Letters and Literary Remains of Mrs. Piozzi (Thrale), Edited with Notes and an Introductory*

Account of Her Life and Writings. London: Longman, Green, Longman, and Roberts, 1861.

First edition. Two octavo volumes. Original blind-stamped plum cloth, gilt-lettered spines. Brown coated endpapers, uncut edges. Engraved frontispieces in each volume. Publisher's catalog at rear of vol. I. [8], 358, 24; [8], 407, [1] pages. Minor, subtle repairs to spine ends of vol. I. Spines lightly toned, slight lean. Gentle bumping and shelf wear, else bright and firm.

[Piozzi, Hester Lynch] "Mrs. Piozzi." *Glimpses of Italian Society in the Eighteenth Century from the "Journey" of Mrs. Piozzi*. London: Seeley, 1892. Introduction by Countess Evelyn Martinengo Cesaresco.

First edition thus, an abridgement of *Observations and Reflections Made in the Course of a Journey through France, Italy, and Germany* (1789). An interesting companion volume to Seeley and Co.'s *Fanny Burney and Her Friends* (1890). Original full green cloth, spine and front board stamped in gilt. Illustrated with 16 full-page plates. [4], 327, [1] pages. Small early bookplate of Frances Waring Robinson to front pastedown. Shallow scuffing to boards. Small nick to front free endpaper. Bright.

Merritt, Percival. *The True Story of the So-Called Love Letters of Mrs. Piozzi: "In Defence of an Elderly Lady."* Cambridge, MA: Harvard University Press, 1927.

First edition, limited to 350 copies, with presentation card from the author. Original quarter blue cloth, blue and red flower-patterned paper boards. Top edge gilt, other edges uncut. [10], 85, [1] pages. Author's card, ink "With the compliments of" in Merritt's hand above printed name, tipped into gutter of title page with early tape. Some edgewear to boards. Light offsetting to endpapers. Clean.

Lansdowne, The Marquis of, ed. *The Queeney Letters: Being Letters Addressed to Hester Maria Thrale by Doctor Johnson[,] Fanny Burney[,] and Mrs. Thrale-Piozzi*. London: Cassell, 1934.

First edition. Original full cream cloth, elaborately gilt-stamped spine. xxxii, 275, [1] pages. Early bookseller ticket and bookplate of John A. Parker to front pastedown. Faint pencil erasure to front free endpaper. Some wear to spine ends, with minute repair to chipping at spine head. Faint toning.

Balderston, Katherine C., ed. *Thraliana: The Diary of Hester Lynch Thrale (Later Mrs. Piozzi), 1776–1809*. Oxford, UK: Clarendon Press, 1942.
First edition. Two volumes. Original full gray cloth, gilt-stamped spines. In original printed dust jackets. xxxii, 610, [2]; [4], 611–1191, [1] pages. Contemporary clipped review laid in. Jackets with shallow chipping to spine ends, some toning. Firm.

Hyde, Mary [later Mary Hyde Eccles]. *The Thrales of Streatham Park*. Cambridge, MA: Harvard University Press, 1977.
Inscribed first edition, including the first appearance of Hester Thrale's *The Children's Book*. Original full black cloth, gilt-lettered spine. In original color pictorial dust jacket with illustrations by Felix Kelly. Numerous full-page illustrations in black and white. xviii, 373, [1] pages. Inscribed by Hyde in ink to front free endpaper: "For Canon George De Mille— / a present from Darwin / Kirby, with added good wishes from / Mary Hyde / Christmas / 1977." Jacket with three-inch closed tear to rear panel, repaired with tape to verso; light toning to spine. Clean.

MARIA EDGEWORTH

Edgeworth, Maria. *Tales of Fashionable Life*. London: Printed for J. Johnson, 1809; 1812.
First editions of both series of *Tales* in uniform contemporary bindings, including her acclaimed *Ennui* and *The Absentee*. Six 12mo volumes. Con-

temporary half calf, marbled paper boards, raised bands, black morocco spine labels. x, 400; [4], 338; [2], 369, [1]; [2], viii, 460; [2], 392; [2], 466 pages. Only light rubbing to bindings.

Edgeworth, Maria. *Tales of Fashionable Life*. London: Printed for J. Johnson, 1809.

Second edition, published the same year as the first, of the first series of *Tales*. Tales included are *Ennui, Almeria, Madame de Fleury, The Dun*, and *Manoeuvring*. Three 12mo volumes. Contemporary full Spanish calf with green striations, gilt-stamped spines, floriated gilt rules to boards. Red speckled edges, thin green silk ribbon markers. With half titles. viii, 417, [1]; [4], 390; [4], 388 pages. Contemporary ink owner name and clipped engraved bookplate to endpapers of first two volumes. Spine label of vol. I lacking; spine label of vol. II partially effaced. Light wear to joints, some toning to spines. A few spots to text, else clean.

Edgeworth, Maria. *Patronage*. London: Printed for J. Johnson, 1814. Preliminary "To the Reader" note by Richard Lovell Edgeworth.

First edition, in original boards. Four 12mo volumes. Publisher's blue paper boards with tan paper spines, printed paper spine labels. Errata leaf to rear of vol. IV. [4], 418; [4], 431, [1]; [4], 402; [4], 390 pages. Housed in custom clamshell boxes with facsimiles of printed paper spine labels. Contemporary ink manuscript arithmetic to front board of vol. III. Joints overall fairly weak, with areas of loss to spine ends. Light toning, scattered foxing to leaves.

Edgeworth, Maria. *Harrington, a Tale; and Ormond, a Tale*. London: Printed for R. Hunter [. . .] and Baldwin, Cradock, and Joy, 1817.

First edition. Three 12mo volumes. Contemporary half calf, marbled paper boards. Red speckled edges. Publisher's catalog at rear of vol. III.

[2], 521, [1]; [2]; 422; [2], 352, [2] pages. Contemporary ink owner name to title page of vol. I; small, faint ink initials to all title pages. Light rubbing and wear to binding. Tight.

Edgeworth, Maria. *Helen, a Tale*. **London: Richard Bentley, 1834.**
First edition. Three 12mo volumes. Contemporary full muslin, black goatskin spine labels, vol. III rebacked with original spine laid down. With half titles. [4], 336; [4], 336; [4], 322 pages. Moderate foxing. Spines toned, with expert repairs to a couple joints. Firm and sound.

Edgeworth, Maria. *Stories from Ireland: Castle Rackrent and the Absentee*. **London: George Routledge and Sons, 1886. Introduction by Henry Morley.**
Morley's Universal Library edition of Edgeworth's best-known novels set in Ireland. Original full gray-green cloth, paper printed spine label reading "Stories of Ireland. Edgeworth." Edges uncut. Endpapers with publisher's ads for titles in Morley's Universal Library series to front and other Routledge series to rear. 287, [1] pages. Small orange paper ad for upcoming title in Morley's Universal Library series, Aristophanes, tipped to front endpaper. Contemporary ink owner name to verso of half title. Spine somewhat toned, with rubbing to label. Leaves toned, more so at edges.

Edgeworth, Maria. *The Novels of Maria Edgeworth*. **London: J. M. Dent, 1893.**
Extravagantly Irish-packaged late Victorian set. Twelve volumes. Original lime-green cloth stamped in repeating pattern of dark green clovers; spines stamped in gilt with Celtic knots, front boards with gilt-stamped titles within ornamental lyres. Top edges stained light green, other edges uncut. Printed lyre and clover decorative bookplate design to front pastedowns. Engraved title pages and frontispieces in each volume (except *Patronage*, vol. I, lacking its individual title). Contemporary ink gift inscription, "M.R.A. / from / G.A. / April 28 1895" to front free endpaper of each volume; vol. I only,

ink owner name dated 1963 to front pastedown. Light toning to spines, with a bit of dustiness overall. Some thin spots of red to boards of *Belinda* and *Leonora* volumes, else largely clean.

Edgeworth, Maria. *Castle Rackrent and the Absentee*. London: Macmillan, 1895. Illustrated by Chris Hammond; introduction by Anne Thackeray Ritchie.
The "Peacock" edition, featuring Albert Angus Turbayne's yellow peacock endpapers and elaborately gilt-stamped binding in Art Nouveau style. Original gilt-stamped emerald-green cloth, all edges gilt. l, 382 pages. Ink gift inscription, "To Ella H. Dobson / from W. R. Hamddon / Xmas 1918," to half title. Moderate foxing to frontispiece and title page, a few scattered spots of soil, else bright and tight.

[Fawcett, Millicent Garrett] "Mrs. Henry Fawcett." *Some Eminent Women of Our Times: Short Biographical Sketches*. London: Macmillan, 1889.
First edition. Octavo. Original full blue cloth stamped in light green. viii, 231, [1] pages. Rather shaken, with cracking to hinges and gutters (still holding). Offsetting and some foxing to endpapers, light edgewear.

Hare, Augustus J. C., ed. *The Life and Letters of Maria Edgeworth*. Boston: Houghton Mifflin, 1895.
First US edition. Two volumes. Original full dark green cloth, spine lettered in gilt, double rules in gilt to spine and front board. Top edges gilt, other edges uncut. Illustrated with frontispieces in each volume. viii, 339, [1]; vi, 341–704 pages. Vol. I with some cracking to gutter at title page, rear hinge starting. Else only light edgewear.

BIBLIOGRAPHY

Abbott, John L. "Defining the Johnsonian Canon: Authority, Intuition, and the Uses of Evidence." *Modern Language Studies* 18, no. 1 (Winter 1988): 89–98.

Achebe, Chinua. "Colonialist Criticism." Excerpted in *Debating the Canon*, ed. Lee Morrissey. New York: Palgrave Macmillan, 2005.

Ahmed, Sara. *Living a Feminist Life*. Durham, NC: Duke University Press, 2017.

Amory, Hugh. "Lennox [née Ramsay], (Barbara) Charlotte." *Oxford Dictionary of National Biography*. Oxford, University Press, 2004, https://doi.org/10.1093/ref:odnb/16454.

Anonymous. "Books: Extricating Emily." Review of *The Mysteries of Udolpho*, by Ann Radcliffe. *Time*, April 22, 1966, https://content.time.com/time/subscriber/article/0,33009,899190-1,00.html.

Anonymous. "Correspondence. Mysteries of Udolpho." *Critical Review* 12, 2nd series (November 1794).

Anonymous. "Mrs. Lenox." *British Magazine and Review* (September 1783).

Anonymous. "On Novels and Romances." *Scots Magazine; or General Repository of Literature, History, and Politics, for the year MDCCCII* 64 (1802): 470–74.

Auerbach, Emily. *Searching for Jane Austen*. Madison: University of Wisconsin Press, 2004.

[Austen, Henry]. "Biographical Notice." In *Northanger Abbey: and Persuasion. With a Biographical Notice of the Author*. London: John Murray, 1818.

Austen, Jane. "Catharine, or the Bower." In *Volume the Third*. Oxford, UK: Clarendon Press, 1951.

[Austen, Jane]. "By the author of 'Pride and Prejudice,' &c. &c." *Emma: A Novel*. London: John Murray, 1816.

Austen, Jane. *Love & Freindship [sic] and Other Early Works Now First Printed from the Original Ms.* London: Chatto & Windus, 1922.

[Austen, Jane]. "By the author of 'Sense and Sensibility,' and 'Pride and Prejudice.'" *Mansfield Park: A Novel*. London: Printed for T. Egerton, 1814.

———. "By the author of 'Pride and Prejudice,' 'Mansfield-Park,' &c." *Northanger Abbey: and Persuasion. With a Biographical Notice of the Author*. London: John Murray, 1818.

———. "By the author of 'Sense and Sensibility.'" *Pride and Prejudice: A Novel*. London: Printed for T. Egerton, 1813.

———. "By a lady." *Sense and Sensibility: A Novel*. London: Printed for the author [. . .] and published by T. Egerton, 1811.

Austen-Leigh, J. E. *A Memoir of Jane Austen*. 2nd ed. London: Richard Bentley and Son, 1871.

Backscheider, Paula R. *Eighteenth-Century Women Poets and Their Poetry: Inventing Agency, Inventing Genre*. Baltimore: Johns Hopkins University Press, 2005.

Baker, William. *Critical Companion to Jane Austen: A Literary Reference to Her Life and Work*. New York: Facts on File, 2008.

Baldwin, Olive, and Thelma Wilson. "Elliot, Ann." *Oxford Dictionary of National Biography*, https://doi.org/10.1093/ref:odnb/64332.

Barbauld, Anna Laetitia. "Miss Burney." In *The British Novelists*, vol. XXXVIII. London: F. C. & J. Rivington, 1810.

———. "Mrs. Radcliffe." In *The British Novelists*, vol. XLIII. London: Printed for F. C. & J. Rivington, 1820.

Bell, Mackenzie. *Christina Rossetti: A Biographical and Critical Study*. London: Thomas Burleigh, 1898.

Bent, William. *The London Catalogue of Books, Selected from the General Catalogue Published in MDCCLXXXVI, and Including the Additions and Alterations to September MDCCXCI. Classed under the Several Branches of Literature, and Alphabetically Disposed under Each Head, with Their Sizes and Prices*. London: Printed for W. Bent, 1791.

Berenger, Richard. "On the Mischiefs of Romances," July 4, 1754, essay in *The World*, no. 79. In *The British Essayists: Containing the Spectator, Tatler, Guardian . . .* vol. IV. London: Jones and Company, 1828.

Betham, Matilda. "Lines to Mrs. Radcliffe, on First Reading *The Mysteries of Udolpho*." In *Poems*. London: J. Hatchard, 1808.

Birkhead, Edith. *The Tale of Terror: A Study of the Gothic Romance*. London: Constable & Co., 1921.

Blackstone, William. *Commentaries on the Laws of England. Book the First*. Oxford, UK: Clarendon Press, 1765.

Blagdon, Francis William. *Flowers of Literature, for 1806: Or, Characteristic Sketches of Human Nature, and Modern Manners. to Which Are Added, a General View of Literature during That Period; Portraits and Biographical Notices of Eminent Literary, and Political Characters; with Notes, Historical, Critical, and Explanatory.* London: J. G. Barnard, 1807.

Blakey, Dorothy. *The Minerva Press, 1790–1820.* London: Bibliographical Society, 1939.

Bloom, Edward A., Lillian D. Bloom, and Joan E. Klingel. "Portrait of a Georgian Lady: The Letters of Hester Lynch (Thrale) Piozzi, 1784–1821." *Bulletin of the John Rylands University Library* 60, no. 2 (Spring 1978): 304–30.

Boaden, James. *Memoirs of Mrs. Inchbald.* London: Richard Bentley, 1833.

Boswell, James. *Letters of James Boswell.* Edited by Chauncey Brewster Tinker. Oxford, UK: Clarendon Press, 1924.

———. *The Life of Samuel Johnson, LL.D. A New Edition, with Numerous Annotations and Notes, by John Wilson Croker, LL.D. F.R.S.* London: John Murray, 1831.

———. *The Life of Samuel Johnson.* New York: Alfred A. Knopf, 1992.

Brack, O. M., Jr., and Susan Carlile. "Samuel Johnson's Contributions to Charlotte Lennox's 'The Female Quixote.'" *Yale University Library Gazette* 77, no. 3/4 (April 2003): 166–73.

Bradbrook, Frank W. *Jane Austen and Her Predecessors.* Cambridge, UK: Cambridge University Press, 1966.

Bromley, Anne E. "Faulkner as Father: Student's Prize-Winning Research Reveals Conflicted Portrait." *UVA Today,* November 9, 2016. Accessed April 30, 2024, https://news.virginia.edu/content/faulkner-father-students-prize-winning -research-reveals-conflicted-portrait.

[Brooke, Frances] "Mrs. Brooke." *The Excursion: A Novel.* 2nd ed. London: Printed for T. Cadell, 1785.

Brown, Stephen P. "Steven [*sic*] King Shining Through." *Washington Post,* April 9, 1985, https://www.washingtonpost.com/archive/lifestyle/1985/04/09/ste ven-king-shining-through/eaf662da-e9eb-4aba-9eb9-217826684ab6/.

Bucke, Charles. *On the Beauties, Harmonies, and Sublimities of Nature.* New edition, greatly enlarged. London: Printed for Thomas Tegg and Son, 1837.

Burke, Edmund. *A Philosophical Enquiry into the Origin of Our Ideas of the Sublime and Beautiful.* London: Printed for R. and J. Dodsley, 1757.

[Burney, Frances] "By the author of *Evelina.*" *Cecilia, or Memoirs of an Heiress.* London: Printed for T. Payne and Son, 1782.

————. "Madame d'Arblay." *Diary and Letters of Madame d'Arblay, Edited by Her Niece*. London: Henry Colburn, 1842.

Burney, Frances. *The Early Journals and Letters, Volume II: 1774–1777*. Edited by Lars E. Troide. Montreal: McGill-Queen's University Press, 1991.

————. *The Early Journals and Letters, Volume III: The Streatham Years: Part 1, 1778–1779*. Edited by Lars E. Troide and Stewart J. Cooke. Montreal: McGill-Queen's University Press, 1994.

[Burney, Frances.] "Fanny Burney." *Evelina, or the History of a Young Lady's Entrance into the World*. Introduction by Austin Dobson. London: Macmillan, 1903.

————. "Madame D'Arblay." *Memoirs of Doctor Burney, Arranged from His Own Manuscripts, from Family Papers, and from Personal Recollections*. London: Edward Moxon, 1832.

————. "By the author of *Evelina*; *Cecilia*; and *Camilla*." *The Wanderer; or, Female Difficulties*. 2nd ed. London: Printed for Longman, Hurst, Rees, Orme, and Brown, 1814.

Burnim, Kalman A. *David Garrick, Director*. Pittsburgh: University of Pittsburgh Press, 1961.

Butler, Marilyn. *Jane Austen and the War of Ideas*. Oxford, UK: Oxford University Press, 1990. Reissue, with new introduction, from the 1975 first publication.

————. *Maria Edgeworth: A Literary Biography*. Oxford, UK: Clarendon Press, 1972.

Calvino, Italo. "Why Read the Classics?" In *The Uses of Literature*. New York: Harcourt Brace Jovanovich, 1986.

Carlile, Susan. *Charlotte Lennox: An Independent Mind*. Toronto: University of Toronto Press, 2018.

[Carter, Elizabeth]. *A Series of Letters between Mrs. Elizabeth Carter and Miss Catherine Talbot, from 1741 to 1770*. Edited by Montagu Pennington. London: Printed for F. C. and J. Rivington, 1809.

————. *A Series of Letters from Mrs. Elizabeth Carter to Mrs. Montagu, between the Years 1755 to 1800*. Edited by Montagu Pennington. London: Printed for F. C. and J. Rivington, 1817.

Castle, Terry. *Masquerade and Civilization: The Carnivalesque in Eighteenth-Century English Culture*. Stanford: Stanford University Press, 1986.

Chancellor, Gordon. "Darwin's *Origin of Species*, Sixth Edition (1872): An Introduction." *Darwin Online*, accessed May 12, 2024, https://darwin-online.org.uk/EditorialIntroductions/Chancellor_Origin6th.html.

Chapman, R. W. *Jane Austen: Facts and Problems.* Oxford, UK: Clarendon Press, 1948.

Chisholm, Kate. "The Burney Family," 7–22. In *The Cambridge Companion to Frances Burney.* Edited by Peter Sabor. Cambridge, UK: Cambridge University Press, 2007.

Christmas, Danielle. "Lord Mansfield and the Slave Ship *Zong.*" *Persuasions* 41, no. 2 (Summer 2021).

[Churchill, Charles]. *The Ghost.* London: Printed for the author, and sold by William Flexney, 1762.

Civale, Susan. "The Literary Afterlife of Frances Burney and the Victorian Periodical Press." *Victorian Periodicals Review* 44, no. 3 (Fall 2011): 236–66.

Clarke, Norma. *Dr. Johnson's Women.* London: Hambledon and London, 2000.

———. *The Rise and Fall of the Woman of Letters.* London: Pimlico, 2004.

Clifford, James L. *Hester Lynch Piozzi (Mrs. Thrale).* Second edition with a new introduction by Margaret Anne Doody. New York: Columbia University Press, 1987.

Collins, Paul. *Edgar Allan Poe: The Fever Called Living.* New York: Amazon, 2014.

Coolidge, Archibald C., Jr. "Charles Dickens and Mrs. Radcliffe: A Farewell to Wilkie Collins." *Dickensian* 58, no. 337 (May 1962): 112–16.

Corman, Brian. *Women Novelists before Jane Austen: The Critics and Their Canons.* Toronto: University of Toronto Press, 2008.

Cox, Octavia. "'& Not the Least Wit': Jane Austen's Use of 'Wit,'" *Humanities* 11, no. 6 (2022): 132.

The Critical Review, or Annals of Literature. Volume xxxii. London: Printed by and for S. Hamilton, 1801.

Csengei, Ildiko. "'She Fell Senseless on His Corpse': The Woman of Feeling and the Sentimental Swoon in Eighteenth-Century Fiction." In *Romantic Psyche and Psychoanalysis.* Edited by Joel Faflak. Romantic Circles Praxis Series (December 2008).

Curran, Stuart, ed. *The Poems of Charlotte Smith.* Oxford, UK: Oxford University Press, 1993.

Curties, T. J. Horsley. *Ancient Records; or, The Abbey of Saint Oswythe. A Romance.* London: Minerva Press, 1801.

Davison, Carol Margaret. *History of the Gothic: Gothic Literature, 1764–1824.* Cardiff: University of Wales Press, 2009.

D'Ezio, Marianne. "'As Like as Peppermint Water Is to Good French Brandy': Ann

Radcliffe and Hester Lynch Salusbury (Thrale) Piozzi." In *Locating Ann Radcliffe*. Edited by Andrew Smith and Mark Bennett. London: Routledge, 2020.

———. *Hester Lynch Piozzi: A Taste for Eccentricity*. Newcastle upon Tyne: Cambridge Scholars, 2010.

Demers, Patricia. *The World of Hannah More*. Lexington: University Press of Kentucky, 1996.

Destrée, Pierre. "Aristotle on Why We Laugh at Jokes." In *Laughter, Humor, and Comedy in Ancient Philosophy*. Edited by Pierre Destrée and Franco V. Trivigno. Oxford, UK: Oxford University Press, 2019.

Dobson, Austin. *Fanny Burney (Madame d'Arblay)*. London: Macmillan, 1903.

Dodsley, Robert. *A Collection of Poems in Six Volumes, By Several Hands*. London: Printed by J. Hughs, for R. and J. Dodsley, 1758.

Donkin, Ellen. *Getting into the Act: Women Playwrights in London, 1776–1829*. London: Routledge, 1995.

Doody, Margaret Anne. *Frances Burney: The Life in the Works*. New Brunswick, NJ: Rutgers University Press, 1988.

———. *Jane Austen's Names: Riddles, Persons, Places*. Chicago: University of Chicago Press, 2015.

Dorset, Catherine. "Charlotte Smith." In Walter Scott, *Miscellaneous Prose Works, vol. IV: Biographical Memoirs, vol. II*. Edinburgh: Robert Cadell, 1834.

Doyle, Arthur Conan. *The New Annotated Sherlock Holmes*. Edited by Leslie S. Klinger. New York: W. W. Norton, 2005.

Drake, Nathan. *Literary Hours, or Sketches Critical and Narrative*. London: Printed by J. Burkitt and sold by T. Cadell, Junior, and W. Davies, 1798.

Dunlop, John. *The History of Fiction*. London: Printed for Longman, Hurst, Rees, Orme, and Brown, 1814.

Eagleton, Terry. *The English Novel: An Introduction*. Malden, MA: Blackwell, 2005.

[Edgeworth, Frances Anne Beaufort] "Mrs. Edgeworth." *A Memoir of Maria Edgeworth*. London: Joseph Masters and Son, 1867.

Edgeworth, Maria. *Belinda*. London: Pandora Press, 1986.

[Edgeworth, Maria]. *Letters for Literary Ladies. To Which Is Added, an Essay on the Noble Science of Self-Justification*. London: Printed for J. Johnson, 1795.

Edgeworth, Maria. *Memoirs of Richard Lovell Edgeworth, Esq. Begun by Himself and Concluded by His Daughter*. London: R. Hunter and Baldwin, Cardock, and Joy, 1820.

———. *Patronage*. London: Pandora Press, 1986.

————. *Stories of Ireland: Castle Rackrent and the Absentee*. London: George Routledge and Sons, 1886.

Eger, Elizabeth, and Lucy Peltz. *Brilliant Women: 18th-Century Bluestockings*. New Haven, CT: Yale University Press, 2008.

The Encyclopaedia Britannica, or Dictionary of Arts, Sciences, and General Literature. 8th ed. Edinburgh: Adam & Charles Black, 1856.

Erickson, Lee. "The Economy of Novel Reading: Jane Austen and the Circulating Library." *Studies in English Literature, 1500–1900*, 30, no. 4, Nineteenth Century (Autumn 1990): 573–90.

Errington, Philip W. *J. K. Rowling: A Bibliography 1997–2013*. London: Bloomsbury, 2015.

Evans, M. J. Crossley. *Hannah More*. Bristol, UK: Bristol Branch of the Historical Association, 1999.

[Fawcett, Millicent] "Mrs. Henry Fawcett." *Some Eminent Women of Our Times*. London: Macmillan, 1889.

Feldman, Paula R., and Daniel Robinson. *A Century of Sonnets: The Romantic-Era Revival, 1750–1850*. Oxford, UK: Oxford University Press, 1999.

Fergus, Jan. "The Professional Woman Writer." In *The Cambridge Companion to Jane Austen*. Edited by Edward Copeland and Juliet McMaster. Cambridge, UK: Cambridge University Press, 1997.

Ferguson, Moira. "Mansfield Park: Slavery, Colonialism, and Gender." *Oxford Literary Review* 13, no. 1/2, Neocolonialism (1991): 118–39.

Fielding, Henry. "Proceedings at the Court of Censorial Enquiry." *Covent Garden Journal*, no. 14 (April 20, 1752).

Fletcher, Loraine. *Charlotte Smith: A Critical Biography*. New York: Palgrave, 2001.

Ford, Charles Howard. *Hannah More: A Critical Biography*. New York: Peter Lang, 1996.

Fordyce, James. *Sermons to Young Women*. London: Printed for A. Millar and T. Cadell . . . , 1766.

Forsyth, William. *The Novels and Novelists of the 18th Century*. New York: D. Appleton, 1871.

Foster, James R. "Charlotte Smith, Pre-Romantic Novelist." *PMLA* 43, no. 2 (June 1928): 463–75.

Fowler, Catherine. "Revisiting Mansfield Park: The Critical and Literary Legacies of Edward W. Said's Essay 'Jane Austen and Empire' in *Culture and Imperialism* (1993)." *Cambridge Journal of Postcolonial Literary Inquiry* 4, no. 3 (2017): 362–81.

Fowler, Karen Joy. *The Jane Austen Book Club*. New York: G. P. Putnam's Sons, 2004.

Francus, Marilyn. "Why Austen, not Burney? Tracing the Mechanisms of Reputation and Legacy." *ABO: Interactive Journal for Women in the Arts, 1640–1830*, 13, no. 1, article 6 (Summer 2023).

Franklin, Michael John. *Hester Lynch Thrale Piozzi*. Cardiff: University of Wales Press, 2020.

Garnai, Amy. *Revolutionary Imaginings in the 1790s: Charlotte Smith, Mary Robinson, Elizabeth Inchbald*. New York: Palgrave Macmillan, 2009.

Garside, Peter. "The English Novel in the Romantic Era: Consolidation and Dispersal." In *The English Novel 1770–1829: A Bibliographical Survey of Prose Fiction Published in the British Isles, Volume II: 1800–1829*. Edited by Peter Garside and Rainer Schöwerling, 15–103. Oxford, UK: Oxford University Press, 2000.

The Gentleman's Magazine: And Historical Chronicle. For the Year MDCCXCVIII. Volume LXVIII [sic]. Part the Second. London: Printed by John Nichols, 1798.

Gilbert, Sandra M., and Susan Gubar. *The Madwoman in the Attic: The Woman Writer and the Nineteenth-Century Literary Imagination*. 2nd ed. New Haven, CT: Yale University Press, 2000.

Gillespie, Iseult. "The Wicked Wit of Jane Austen." TED-Ed, accessed April 28, 2024, https://ed.ted.com/lessons/the-wicked-wit-of-jane-austen-iseult-gillespie.

Gillies, R. P. *Memoirs of a Literary Veteran; Including Sketches and Anecdotes of the Most Distinguished Literary Characters from 1794 to 1849*. London: Richard Bentley, 1851.

Gilson, David. *A Bibliography of Jane Austen*. Oxford, UK: Clarendon Press, 1985.

Gisborne, Thomas. *An Enquiry into the Duties of the Female Sex*. London: Printed for T. Cadell, Junior, and W. Davies, 1797.

Gorak, Jan. *The Making of the Modern Canon*. London: Athlone, 1991.

Gordon, Mary Wilson. *"Christopher North": A Memoir of John Wilson*. Edinburgh: Edmonston and Douglas, 1862.

Gosse, Edmund. *A Short History of Modern English Literature*. New York: D. Appleton, 1898.

Gottlieb, Robert. *Great Expectations: The Sons and Daughters of Charles Dickens*. New York: Farrar, Straus and Giroux, 2012.

Grau, Joseph A. *Fanny Burney: An Annotated Bibliography*. New York: Garland, 1981.

Gregory, John. *A Father's Legacy to His Daughters*. London: Printed to W. Strahan et al., 1774.

Grosart, Alexander B., ed. *The Prose Works of William Wordsworth*. London: Edward Moxon, 1876.

Halperin, John. *The Life of Jane Austen*. Baltimore: Johns Hopkins University Press, 1984.

Halsey, Katie. *Jane Austen and Her Readers, 1786–1945*. London: Anthem Press, 2012.

Hamilton, Catherine J. *Women Writers: Their Works and Ways*. London: Ward, Lock, Bowden, 1892.

Hare, Augustus J. G. *Maria Edgeworth: Life and Letters*. Boston: Houghton Mifflin, 1894.

Harman, Claire. *Fanny Burney: A Biography*. New York: HarperCollins, 2000.

———. *Jane's Fame: How Jane Austen Conquered the World*. New York: Henry Holt, 2009.

Harris, Jocelyn. *Jane Austen's Art of Memory*. Cambridge, UK: Cambridge University Press, 1989.

Hawkins, John. *The Life of Samuel Johnson, LL.D.* London: Printed for J. Buckland et al., 1787.

[Hays, Mary]. "Mrs. Charlotte Smith." In *British Public Characters, 1800–1801*, vol. 3. London: Printed for R. Phillips, 1801.

Hayward, A. *Autobiography, Letters and Literary Remains of Mrs. Piozzi (Thrale) Edited with Notes and an Introductory Account of Her Life and Writings*. London: Longman, Green, Longman, and Roberts, 1861.

Hazlitt, William. *Lectures on English Comic Writers*. London: Printed for Taylor and Hessy, 1819.

Hemlow, Joyce. *The History of Fanny Burney*. Oxford, UK: Clarendon Press, 1958.

Hill, Constance. *Jane Austen: Her Home & Her Friends*. London: John Lane, 1902.

Honan, Park. *Jane Austen: Her Life*. New York: St. Martin's Press, 1987.

Hopkins, Mary Alden. *Hannah More and Her Circle*. New York: Longmans, Green, 1947.

Howells, W. D. *Heroines of Fiction*. New York: Harper & Brothers, 1901.

Hughes, Charles. *Mrs. Piozzi's Thraliana, with Numerous Extracts Hitherto Unpublished*. London: Simpkin, 1913.

Hume, David. *Essays, Moral and Political*. Edinburgh: Printed by R. Fleming and A. Alison, for A. Kincaid, 1741.

Hume, Robert D. "The Value of Money in Eighteenth-Century England: Incomes, Prices, Buying Power—and Some Problems in Cultural Economics." *Huntington Library Quarterly* 77, no. 4 (Winter 2014): 373–416.

Hyde, Mary [later Mary Hyde Eccles]. *The Thrales of Streatham Park*. Cambridge, MA: Harvard University Press, 1977.

Hyde Eccles, Mary. "Unending Pursuit." *Grolier Club Gazette*, no. 42. New York: Grolier Club, 1990, 89–100.

Inchbald, Elizabeth. *Lovers' Vows.* In *The British Theatre.* London: Printed for Longman, Hurst, Rees, and Orme, 1808.

———. *A Simple Story.* Edited by J. M.S. Tompkins, introduction by Jane Spencer. Oxford, UK: Oxford University Press, 1988.

———. *A Simple Story.* Introduction by Anna Lott. Ontario: Broadview Press, 2007.

Jackel, David. "Leonora and Lady Susan: A Note on Maria Edgeworth and Jane Austen." *ESC: English Studies in Canada* 3, no. 3 (Fall 1977): 278–88.

Jenkins, Annibel. *I'll Tell You What: The Life of Elizabeth Inchbald.* Lexington: University Press of Kentucky, 2003.

Johnson, Claudia. "'Let Me Make the Novels of a Country': Barbauld's 'The British Novelists' (1810/1820)." *NOVEL: A Forum on Fiction* 34, no. 2, Romantic-Era Novel (Spring 2001): 163–79.

Johnson, Samuel. *A Dictionary of the English Language* [. . .]. London: Printed by W. Strahan [. . .], 1755.

———. *The Works of Samuel Johnson, LL.D.* London: J. Buckland et al., 1787.

Kaplan, Deborah. *Jane Austen among Women.* Baltimore: Johns Hopkins University Press, 1992.

Kauvar, Elaine M. "Jane Austen and *The Female Quixote,*" *Studies in the Novel* 2, no. 2, British Neo-Classical Novel (Summer 1970): 211–21.

Kelly, Helena. *Jane Austen: The Secret Radical.* New York: Alfred A. Knopf, 2017.

Kim, Boram. "Faint or Feint?: Literary Portrayals of Female Swooning in the Eighteenth Century." *English Studies* 29 (2009): 148–66.

Knapp, Oswald G., ed. *The Intimate Letters of Hester Piozzi & Penelope Pennington, 1788–1821.* London: John Lane, 1914.

Knox, Vicesimus. *Essays, Moral and Literary.* London: Printed for Edward and Charles Dilly, 1779.

Korshin, Paul J. "Types of Eighteenth-Century Literary Patronage." *Eighteenth-Century Studies* 7, no. 4 (Summer 1974): 453–73.

Labbe, Jacqueline M. *Charlotte Smith: Romanticism, Poetry and the Culture of Gender.* Manchester, UK: Manchester University Press, 2003.

———. "Introduction." In *The Works of Charlotte Smith,* pt. III, vol. 14. London: Pickering & Chatto, 2007.

———. *Reading Jane Austen after Reading Charlotte Smith.* London: Palgrave Macmillan, 2020.

———. *Writing Romanticism: Charlotte Smith and William Wordsworth, 1784–1807.* New York: Palgrave Macmillan, 2011.

Lansdowne, Henry William Edmund Petty-FitzMaurice, Marquis of. *The Queeney Letters: Being Letters Addressed to Hester Maria Thrale by Doctor Johnson, Fanny Burney and Mrs. Thrale-Piozzi*. London: Cassell & Company, 1934.

Le Faye, Deirdre, comp. and ed. *Jane Austen's Letters*. 4th ed. Oxford, UK: Oxford University Press, 2011.

[Lennox, Charlotte]. *The Female Quixote; or, the Adventures of Arabella*. 2nd ed., rev. and corrected. London: Printed for A. Millar, 1752.

Lennox, Charlotte. *The Life of Harriot Stuart, Written by Herself*. Madison, NJ: Fairleigh Dickinson University Press, 1995.

[Lennox, Charlotte]. "By the Author of *The Female Quixote*." *Shakespear Illustrated: Or the Novels and Histories, on Which the Plays of Shakespear Are Founded, Collected and Translated from the Original Authors. With Critical Remarks*. London: Printed for A. Millar, 1753, 1754.

Littlewood, S. R. *Elizabeth Inchbald and Her Circle*. London: Daniel O'Connor, 1921.

[Lockhart, John Gibson]. *Memoirs of the Life of Sir Walter Scott, Bart*. Edinburgh: Robert Cadell and John Murray and Wittaker, 1837–38.

Lodge, Henry Cabot, ed. *The Best of the World's Classics*. New York: Funk & Wagnalls, 1909.

Loe, Thomas. "Gothic Plot in 'Great Expectations.'" *Dickens Quarterly* 6, no. 3 (September 1989): 102–10.

Looser, Devoney. *The Making of Jane Austen*. Baltimore: Johns Hopkins University Press, 2017.

———. *Sister Novelists*. New York: Bloomsbury, 2022.

———. *Women Writers and Old Age in Great Britain*. Baltimore: Johns Hopkins University Press, 2008.

Lorde, Audre. "The Master's Tools Will Never Dismantle the Master's House." *This Bridge Called My Back: Writings by Radical Women of Color*. 4th ed. Edited by Cherríe Moraga and Gloria Anzaldúa. Albany, NY: SUNY Press, 2015.

Lustig, Irma S. "Boswell at Work: The 'Animadversions' on Mrs Piozzi." *Modern Language Review* 67, no. 1 (January 1972): 11–30.

Macaulay, Thomas. "Madame D'Arblay." *Critical and Historical Essays Contributed to the Edinburgh Review*. London: Longmans, Green, 1874.

Mandal, Anthony. *Jane Austen and the Popular Novel: The Determined Author*. Basingstoke, UK: Palgrave Macmillan, 2007.

[Mangin, Edward]. *Piozziana; or, Recollections of the Late Mrs. Piozzi, with Remarks. By a Friend*. London: Edward Moxon, 1833.

Manvell, Roger. *Elizabeth Inchbald: England's Principal Woman Dramatist and Independent Woman of Letters in 18th Century London, a Biographical Study*. Lanham, MD: University Press of America, 1987.

[Mathias, Thomas James]. *The Pursuits of Literature: A Satirical Poem in Dialogue*. 4th ed., rev. London: Printed for T. Becket, 1797.

Maynadier, Gustavus Howard. *The First American Novelist*. Cambridge, MA: Harvard University Press, 1940.

Mayo, Robert D. "Gothic Romance in the Magazines." *PMLA* 65, no. 5 (September 1950): 762–89.

Mazzeno, Laurence W. *Jane Austen: Two Centuries of Criticism*. Rochester, NY: Camden House, 2011.

McCarthy, William. *Hester Thrale Piozzi: Portrait of a Literary Woman*. Chapel Hill: University of North Carolina Press, 1985.

———. "The Repression of Hester Lynch Piozzi; or, How We Forgot a Revolution in Authorship." *Modern Language Studies* 18, no. 1, Making and Rethinking the Canon: The Eighteenth Century (Winter 1988): 99–111.

McDonagh, Josephine. "Place, Region, and Migration." *The Nineteenth Century Novel 1820–1880*. Edited by John Kucich and Jenny Bourne Taylor. Oxford, UK: Oxford University Press, 2012.

Medwin, Thomas. *The Life of Percy Bysshe Shelley. A New Edition [. . .] with an Introduction and Commentary by H. Buxton Forman, C.B.* London: Humphrey Milford, 1913.

Merriam-Webster. "Old Fashioned Names for Diseases and Ailments." Accessed April 22, 2024. https://www.merriam-webster.com/wordplay/illnesses-ailments-diseases-history-names.

Miles, Robert. "What Is a Romantic Novel?" *NOVEL: A Forum on Fiction* 34, no. 2, Romantic-Era Novel (Spring 2001): 180–201.

Minto, William. *The Literature of the Georgian Era*. Edinburgh: William Blackwood and Sons, 1894.

[Moir, George]. *Treatises on Poetry, Modern Romance, and Rhetoric*. Edinburgh: Adam & Charles Black, 1839.

Montagu, Lady Mary Wortley. *The Letters and Works*. 2nd ed., rev. Edited by Lord Wharncliffe. London: Richard Bentley, 1837.

[More, Hannah]. *Coelebs in Search of a Wife. Comprehending Observations on Domestic Habit and Manners, Religion and Morals*. London: Printed for T. Cadell and W. Davies, 1808.

More, Hannah. *An Estimate of the Religion of the Fashionable World: By One of the Laity.* London: Printed for T. Cadell, 1791.

———. *Slavery: A Poem.* London: Printed for T. Cadell, 1788.

———. *The Sunday School.* Dublin: Sold by William Watson, Printer to the Cheap repository for religious and moral tracts: and by the booksellers, chapmen and hawkers in town and country, [ca. 1800].

———. *Strictures on the Modern System of Female Education. With a View of the Principles and Conduct Prevalent among Women of Rank and Fortune.* 3rd American ed. Boston: Printed for Joseph Bumstead, 1802.

———. *The Works of Hannah More.* Philadelphia: Edward Earle, 1813.

More, Martha. *Mendip Annals: Or, a Narrative of the Charitable Labours of Hannah and Martha More in Their Neighbourhood; being the Journal of Martha More.* Edited by Arthur Roberts. London: James Nisbet, 1859.

Mudrick, Marvin. *Jane Austen: Irony as Defense and Discovery.* Princeton, NJ: Princeton University Press, 1952.

Murphy, Olivia. *Jane Austen the Reader: The Artist as Critic.* Basingstoke, UK: Palgrave Macmillan, 2013.

Nardin, Jane. "Jane Austen, Hannah More, and the Novel of Education." *Persuasions: Journal of the Jane Austen Society of North America* 20 (1998): 15–20.

Nelson, Bonnie. "Emily Herbert: Forerunner of Jane Austen's *Lady Susan.*" *Women's Writing* 1, no. 3 (1994): 317–23.

Newby, P. H. *Maria Edgeworth.* London: Arthur Baker, 1950.

Newcomer, James. *Maria Edgeworth.* Lewisburg, PA: Bucknell University Press, 1973.

Newton, A. Edward. *The Amenities of Book-Collecting and Kindred Affections.* Boston: Atlantic Monthly Press, 1918.

Norton, Rictor, ed. *Gothic Readings: The First Wave, 1764–1840.* London: Leicester University Press, 2000.

———. *Mistress of Udolpho: The Life of Ann Radcliffe.* London: Leicester University Press, 1999.

Oliphant, Mrs. *The Literary History of England: In the End of the Eighteenth and Beginning of the Nineteenth Century.* London: Macmillan, 1882.

Omasreiter, Ria. "Maria Edgeworth's Tales: A Contribution to the Science of Happiness." *Functions of Literature: Essays Presented to Erwin Wolff on His Sixtieth Birthday.* Edited by Ulrich Broich, Theo Stemmler, and Gerd Stratmann. Tübingen, Germany: M. Niemeyer, 1984.

Pakenham, Valerie, ed. *Maria Edgeworth's Letters from Ireland*. Dublin: Lilliput Press, 2018.

Patten, Robert L. *Charles Dickens and "Boz": The Birth of the Industrial-Age Author.* Cambridge, UK: Cambridge University Press, 2012.

Pedicord, Harry William, and Frederick Louis Bergmann. *The Plays of David Garrick, Vol. 3: Garrick's Adaptations of Shakespeare, 1744–1756*. Carbondale: Southern Illinois University Press, 1980.

Pennington, Sarah. *An Unfortunate Mother's Advice to Her Absent Daughters; in a Letter to Miss Pennington*. London: Printed by S. Chandler, 1761.

Phemister, Mary Anne. *Hannah More: The Artist as Reformer*. Sisters, OR: Deep River Books, 2014.

Phillips, Nicola Jane. *Women in Business, 1700–1850*. Woodbridge, UK: Boydell Press, 2006.

Pickering, Samuel, Jr. "Hannah More's *Coelebs in Search of a Wife* and the Respectability of the Novel in the Nineteenth Century." *Neuphilologische Mitteilungen* 78, no. 1 (1977): 78–85.

Piozzi, Hester Lynch. "Autobiographical Remains." In *Autobiography, Letters and Literary Remains of Mrs. Piozzi (Thrale)*. Edited by A. Hayward. London: Longman, Green, Longman, and Roberts, 1861.

———. *British Synonymy; or, an Attempt at Regulating the Choice of Words in Familiar Conversation. Inscribed with Sentiments of Gratitude and Respect, to Such of Her Foreign Friends as Have Made English Literature Their Peculiar Study*. London: G.G. and J. Robinson, 1794.

———. *Letters to and from the Late Samuel Johnson, LL.D. To Which Are Added Some Poems Never Before Printed*. London: Printed for A. Strahan and T. Cadell, 1788.

———. *Thraliana. The Diary of Mrs. Hester Lynch Thrale (Later Mrs. Piozzi), 1776–1809*. Edited by Katharine C. Balderston. Oxford, UK: Clarendon Press, 1942.

Pollitt, Katha. "Hers; The Smurfette Principle." *New York Times*, April 7, 1991.

Potter, Franz. *The History of Gothic Publishing, 1800–1835: Exhuming the Trade*. London: Palgrave Macmillan, 2005.

Quayle, Eric. *Early Children's Books: A Collector's Guide*. Newton Abbot, Devon: David & Charles, 1983.

Quinby, Jane. *Beatrix Potter: A Bibliographical Check List*. New York: Jane Quinby, 1954.

Raleigh, Walter. *Six Essays on Johnson*. Oxford, UK: Clarendon Press, 1910.

Raven, James, and Antonia Forster, ed. *The English Novel, 1770–1829: A Bibliograph-

ical Survey of Prose Fiction Published in the British Isles. Oxford, UK: Oxford University Press, 2000.

Rees, Thomas. *Reminiscences of Literary London from 1779–1853. With Interesting Anecdotes of Publishers, Authors, and Book Auctioneers of that Period, &c., &c*. New York: Francis P. Harper, 1896.

Reeve, Clara. *The Old English Baron*. Kansas City, MO: Valancourt Press, 2009.

———. *The Progress of Romance and the History of Charoba, Queen of Aegypt, Reproduced from the Colchester Edition of 1785, with a Bibliographical Note by Esther M. McGill*. New York: Facsimile Text Society, 1930.

Regis, Pamela. *A Natural History of the Romance Novel*. Philadelphia: University of Pennsylvania Press, 2003.

Reilly, Robin. *Wedgewood*. London: Stockton Press, 1989.

Roberts, Bethan. *Charlotte Smith and the Sonnet: Form, Place, and Tradition in the Late Eighteenth Century*. Liverpool: Liverpool University Press, 2019.

Roberts, William. *Memoirs of the Life and Correspondence of Mrs. Hannah More*. 3rd ed. London: R. B. Seeley and W. Burnside, 1835.

Robertson, Ben P., ed. *The Diaries of Elizabeth Inchbald*. London: Pickering and Chatto, 2007.

Robinson, Daniel. "'Work without Hope': Anxiety and Embarrassment in Coleridge's Sonnets." *Studies in Romanticism* 39, no. 1 (Spring 2000): 81–110.

Rogers, Deborah D. *Ann Radcliffe: A Bio-Bibliography*. Westport, CT: Greenwood Press, 1996.

Romney, Rebecca. "On Feminist Practice in the Rare Books and Manuscripts Trade: Buying, Cataloguing, and Selling." *Criticism* 64, no. 3 (2022): 413–31.

———. *The Romance Novel in English: A Survey in Rare Books, 1769–1999*. Silver Spring, MD: Type Punch Matrix, 2021.

Ross, Deborah. *The Excellence of Falsehood: Romance, Realism, and Women's Contribution to the Novel*. Lexington: University Press of Kentucky, 1991.

Rothschild, Nathaniel Mayer Victor Rothschild, Baron. *The Rothschild Library: A Catalogue of the Collection of Eighteenth-Century Printed Books and Manuscripts Formed by Lord Rothschild*. Cambridge, UK: Cambridge University Press, 1954.

Rothstein, Edward. "At the Morgan, the Jane Austen Her Family Knew." *New York Times*, November 6, 2009. https://www.nytimes.com/2009/11/07/arts/design/07austen.html.

Runge, Laura. "Momentary Fame: Female Novelists in Eighteenth-Century Book Reviews." In *A Companion to the Eighteenth-Century English Novel and Culture*. Edited by Paula R. Backscheider and Catherine Ingrassia. Malden, MA: Blackwell, 2005.

Sabor, Peter. "Annie Raine Ellis, Austin Dobson, and the Rise of Burney Studies." *Burney Journal* 1 (1998): 25–45.

Said, Edward. *Culture and Imperialism*. London: Chatto & Windus, 1993.

Santiáñez-Tió, Nil. "Nuevos mapas del Universo: Modernidad y ciencia ficción en la literatura española del siglo XIX (1804–1905)." *Revista Hispánica Moderna* 47, no. 2 (December 1994): 269–88.

Schellenberg, Betty L. *The Professionalization of Women Writers in Eighteenth-Century Britain*. Cambridge, UK: Cambridge University Press, 2005.

Schürer, Norbert. *Charlotte Lennox: Correspondence and Miscellaneous Documents*. Lewisburg, PA: Bucknell University Press, 2012.

Scott, Walter. "Prefatory Memoir to Mrs Ann Radcliffe." In *The Novels of Mrs. Ann Radcliffe*, Ballantyne's Novelist's Library. London: Hurst, Robinson, 1824.

[Scott, Walter]. *Waverley: Or 'tis Sixty Years Since*. Edinburgh: Archibald Constable and Co., 1814.

Séjourné, Philippe. *The Mystery of Charlotte Lennox: First Novelist of Colonial America (1727?–1804)*. Aix-en-Provenance: Publications des annales de la faculté des lettres, 1967.

Sher, Richard B. *The Enlightenment and the Book*. Chicago: University of Chicago Press, 2008.

Siskin, Clifford. *The Work of Writing: Literature and Social Change in Britain, 1700–1830*. Baltimore: Johns Hopkins University Press, 1999.

Small, Miriam Rossiter. *Charlotte Ramsay Lennox: An Eighteenth Century Lady of Letters*. Albany, NY: Archon Books, 1969. First published in 1935.

Smith, Charlotte. *Desmond: A Novel*. London: Printed for G. G. J. and J. Robinson, 1792.

———. *Emmeline, the Orphan of the Castle*. London: Printed for T. Cadell, 1788.

———. *The Old Manor House*. London: Pandora Press, 1987.

Smith, Goldwin. *Life of Jane Austen*. London: Walter Scott, 1890.

Southam, B. C., ed. *Jane Austen: The Critical Heritage, Volume 1: 1811–1870*. London: Routledge, 1968.

———. *Jane Austen: The Critical Heritage, Volume 2: 1870–1940*. London: Routledge, 1987.

Spencer, Jane. "*Evelina* and *Cecilia*." In *The Cambridge Companion to Frances Burney*. Edited by Peter Sabor, 23–38. Cambridge, UK: Cambridge University Press, 2007.

———. *The Rise of the Woman Novelist: From Aphra Behn to Jane Austen*. Oxford, UK: Basil Blackwell, 1986 (reprinted 1989).

Spender, Dale. *Mothers of the Novel: 100 Good Women Writers before Jane Austen*. London: Pandora Press, 1986.

Stanton, Judith Phillips. *The Collected Letters of Charlotte Smith*. Bloomington: Indiana University Press, 2003.

———. "Statistical Profile of Women Writing in English from 1660–1800." In *Eighteenth-Century Women and the Arts*. Edited by Frederick M. Keener and Susan E. Lorsch. Westport, CT: Greenwood Press, 1998.

Steele, Valerie. *The Corset: A Cultural History*. New Haven, CT: Yale University Press, 2001.

Stoker, Bram. *Dracula*. 6th ed. Westminster, UK: Archibald Constable and Co., 1899.

Stoodt, Barbara D., Linda B. Amspaugh, and Jane Hunt. *Children's Literature: Discovery for a Lifetime*. Melbourne: Macmillan, 1996.

Stott, Anne. *Hannah More: The First Victorian*. Oxford, UK: Oxford University Press, 2003.

Talfourd, Thomas Noon. "Memoir of the Life and Writings of Mrs. Radcliffe." In *Gaston de Blondeville*, I.1–132. London: Henry Colburn, 1826.

Thaddeus, Janice Farrar. *Frances Burney: A Literary Life*. London: Macmillan, 2000.

Tompkins, J. M. S. *The Popular Novel in England: 1770–1800*. London: Constable and Co., 1932.

Townshend, Dale. *Gothic Antiquity: History, Romance, and the Architectural Imagination, 1760–1840*. Oxford, UK: Oxford University Press, 2019.

Townshend, Dale, and Angela Wright, ed. *Ann Radcliffe, Romanticism, and the Gothic*. Cambridge, UK: Cambridge University Press, 2014.

Troide, Lars E. "Joyce Hemlow and the McGill Burney Project." In *A Celebration of Frances Burney*. Edited by Lorna J. Clark, 10–17. Newcastle upon Tyne: Cambridge Scholars Publishing, 2007.

Walker, Alice. *In Search of Our Mothers' Gardens: Womanist Prose*. San Diego: Harcourt Brace Jovanovich, 1983.

Watt, Ian. *The Rise of the Novel: Studies in Defoe, Richardson and Fielding*. Berkeley: University of California Press, 1957.

Watt, James. *Contesting the Gothic: Fiction, Genre and Cultural Conflict, 1764–1832*. Cambridge, UK: Cambridge University Press, 1999.

Weekes, Ann Owens. *Irish Women Writers: An Uncharted Tradition*. Lexington: Kentucky University Press, 1990.

Wells, Juliette. *Everybody's Jane: Austen in the Popular Imagination*. London: Continuum, 2011.

———. *A New Jane Austen: How Americans Brought Us the World's Greatest Novelist*. London: Bloomsbury, 2023.

———. "A Note on Henry Austen's Authorship of the 'Biographical Notice.'" *Persuasions* 38, no. 1 (Winter 2017). Accessed April 23, 2024. https://jasna.org/publications-2/persuasions-online/vol38no1/wells.

Wells, Mary. *Memoirs of Mrs. Sumbel Late Wells*. London: C. Chapple, 1811.

Wharton, Edith. *The Writing of Fiction*. New York: Scribner, 1925.

Wheelwright, C. A. *Poems, Original and Translated*. London: Longman, Hurst, Rees, Orme, and Browne, 1810.

Whitehead, W. "On the Ignorance and Indecency of Modern Romance Writers." In *The British Essayists: Containing the Spectator, Tatler, Guardian* [. . .] vol. IV. London: Published by Jones and Company, 1828.

Wickham, Hill, ed. *Journals and Correspondence of Thomas Sedgewick Whalley, D.D. of Mendip Lodge, Somerset*. London: Richard Bentley, 1863.

Wingrove, Ann. *Letters, Moral and Entertaining*. Bath: R. Cruttwell, 1795.

[Wolcot, John]. "Peter Pindar." *Bozzy and Piozzi: Or the British Biographers. A Town Eclogue*. 9th ed. London: Printed for G. Kearsley, 1788.

Wollstonecraft, Mary. *A Vindication of the Rights of Woman*. London: J. Johnson, 1792.

Wordsworth, William. *Lyrical Ballads, with Other Poems*. 2nd ed. London: Printed for T. N. Longman and O. Rees, 1800.

Worsley, Lucy. *Jane Austen at Home: A Biography*. New York: St. Martin's Griffin, 2021.

Yearsley, Ann. *Poems, on Several Occasions*. London: Printed for T. Cadell, 1785.

Zall, Paul M. *Coleridge's "Sonnets from Various Authors."* Glendale, CA: La Siesta Press, 1968.

NOTES

INTRODUCTION

1 *"'You see, but you do not observe'"*: Arthur Conan Doyle, *The New Annotated Sherlock Holmes*, ed. Leslie S. Klinger (New York: W. W. Norton, 2005), I.10.

5 *"the first great woman writer"*: John Halperin, *The Life of Jane Austen* (Baltimore: Johns Hopkins University Press, 1984), 69.

5 *"was one of the most fertile"*: Terry Eagleton, *The English Novel: An Introduction* (Malden, MA: Blackwell, 2005), 94.

5 *from that Leading Literary Theorist's bookshelf*: In fairness, of these eight women, Eagleton does briefly name-check Maria Edgeworth as an "Irish" novelist in his discussion of Scott (96). None of the remaining seven appear even in passing.

5 *"It is my business to know"*: Doyle, *The New Annotated Sherlock Holmes*, I.217.

5 *Grimms' fairy tales contains a typo*: See Eric Quayle, *Early Children's Books: A Collector's Guide* (Newton Abbot, Devon, UK: David & Charles, 1983), 71.

5 *El Anacronópete (1887) describes a time machine*: Nil Santiáñez-Tió, "Nuevos mapas del Universo: Modernidad y ciencia ficción en la literatura española del siglo XIX (1804–1905)," *Revista Hispánica Moderna* 47, no. 2 (December 1994): 285.

5 *copies that Beatrix Potter printed privately*: Jane Quinby, *Beatrix Potter: A Bibliographical Check List* (New York: Jane Quinby, 1954).

6 *more women published novels than men*: Robert Miles, "What Is a Romantic Novel?" *NOVEL: A Forum on Fiction* 34, no. 2, Romantic-Era Novel (Spring 2001): 181n1.

6 *It's called the Great Forgetting*: Clifford Siskin, *The Work of Writing: Literature and Social Change in Britain, 1700–1830* (Baltimore: Johns Hopkins University Press, 1999), 216; see also Betty L. Schellenberg, *The Professionalization of*

Women Writers in Eighteenth-Century Britain (Cambridge, UK: Cambridge University Press, 2005), 162.

6   *"while the abilities of the nine-hundredth abridger"*: Jane Austen, *Northanger Abbey: and Persuasion* (London: John Murray, 1818), I.62–64.

9   *"not particularly distinguished"*: Frank W. Bradbrook, *Jane Austen and Her Predecessors* (Cambridge, UK: Cambridge University Press, 1966), 90.

9   *"Jane Austen turns inferior work"*: Bradbrook, *Jane Austen and Her Predecessors*, 104.

13   *"My discovery of them"*: Alice Walker, *In Search of Our Mothers' Gardens: Womanist Prose* (San Diego: Harcourt Brace Jovanovich, 1983), 9.

CHAPTER ONE:
JANE AUSTEN (1775–1817)

17   *"Mrs Martin tells us that her Collection"*: Quoted in Deirdre Le Faye, ed., *Jane Austen's Letters*, 4th ed. (Oxford, UK: Oxford University Press, 2011), 27.

17   *Austen's path to canonicity*: Claire Harman, *Jane's Fame: How Jane Austen Conquered the World* (New York: Henry Holt, 2009).

17   *book about her American champions*: Juliette Wells, *A New Jane Austen: How Americans Brought Us the World's Greatest Novelist* (London: Bloomsbury, 2023).

17   *"the best romance novel ever written"*: Pamela Regis, *A Natural History of the Romance Novel* (Philadelphia: University of Pennsylvania Press, 2003), 75.

18   *"let Emma help you"*: Jane Austen, *Emma* (London: John Murray, 1816), I.45.

18   *"she had not got beyond the words 'delightful'"*: Jane Austen, *Pride and Prejudice: A Novel* (London: Printed for T. Egerton, 1813), III.23.

19   *"To generations of Austen worshippers"*: Lucy Worsley, *Jane Austen at Home: A Biography* (New York: St. Martin's Griffin, 2021), 7.

19   *"a little under £600"*: Halperin, *Life of Jane Austen*, 24.

19   *Jane was one of eight*: When referring to Austen's childhood, I often use her first name; otherwise, I default to using her surname—unless distinguishing between two people with the same surname in the same paragraph, in which case I typically refer to both by their first names (e.g., "Jane and Cassandra"). I have followed this convention for the other writers throughout.

19   *Jane's "favorite" brother*: Halperin, *Life of Jane Austen*, 22.

19   *sister to whom Jane was devoted*: Austen's nephew quotes Jane and Cassandra's mother as saying, "If Cassandra were going to have her head cut off, Jane

would insist on sharing her fate." J. E. Austen-Leigh, *A Memoir of Jane Austen*, 2nd ed. (London: Richard Bentley and Son, 1871), 15.

19 *"great Novel-readers"*: Letter from Jane Austen to Cassandra Austen, December 18–19, 1798, in Le Faye, *Letters*, 27.

20 *"once I knew her to take up a volume of* Evelina*"*: Quoted in Katie Halsey, *Jane Austen and Her Readers, 1786–1945* (London: Anthem Press, 2012), 19.

20 *Austen did not purchase many books for herself*: David Gilson surveys the books she owned in their own section, *K*, of his bibliography: David Gilson, *A Bibliography of Jane Austen* (Oxford, UK: Clarendon Press, 1985). See also Murphy for an argument that one particular case in the Godmersham Park library kept her books: Olivia Murphy, *Jane Austen the Reader: The Artist as Critic* (Basingstoke, UK: Palgrave Macmillan, 2013), 177–81. For Austen's use of circulating libraries, see Mary Margaret Benson, "Parasols & Gloves & Broches & Circulating Libraries," *Persuasions* 19 (1997): 205–10; and Lee Erickson, "The Economy of Novel Reading: Jane Austen and the Circulating Library," *Studies in English Literature, 1500–1900* 30, no. 4, Nineteenth Century (Autumn 1990): 573–90.

20 *The barn was the perfect place*: Halperin, *Life of Jane Austen*, 29.

20 *James was considered the literary darling*: Harman, *Jane's Fame*, 8; see also Park Honan, *Jane Austen: Her Life* (New York: St. Martin's Press, 1987), 56–65.

20 *Austen enjoyed a supportive environment*: Halsey, *Jane Austen and Her Readers*, 20.

20 *"No! Never shall it be said that I obliged my Father"*: Jane Austen, *Love and Freindship [sic] and Other Early Works Now First Printed from the Original Ms.* (London: Chatto & Windus, 1922), 10.

20 *"pay Jane Austen Spinster"*: Austen, *Love and Freindship*, 45.

21 *One of these was her neighbor Madame Anne Lefroy*: Honan, *Jane Austen*, 40–41.

21 *"I write only for Fame"*: Letter from Jane Austen to Cassandra Austen, January 14–15, 1796, quoted in Le Faye, *Letters*, 3.

21 *In 1796, Austen began the book*: I use the dating of drafts according to Cassandra's notes many years after the fact. In this I'm following Gilson et al., though with acknowledgment of Helena Kelly's warning that critics "have tended to treat this document as if it were completely reliable; they really shouldn't." Helena Kelly, *Jane Austen: The Secret Radical* (New York: Alfred A. Knopf, 2017), 18.

21 *revised and retitled*: See Gilson, *Bibliography*, 7.

21 *"apart from her family"*: Jan Fergus, "The Professional Woman Writer," in *The*

Cambridge Companion to Jane Austen, ed. Edward Copeland and Juliet McMaster (Cambridge, UK: Cambridge University Press, 1997), 13.

22   *"smaller than I expected"*: Letter from Jane Austen to Cassandra Austen, May 21–22, 1801, quoted in Le Faye, *Letters*, 92. Honan notes gossip from Anna Lefroy that Austen "fainted" at the news of the move. Honan, *Jane Austen*, 155.

22   *"rather a dull affair"*: Letter from Jane Austen to Cassandra Austen, May 12–13, 1801, quoted in Le Faye, *Letters*, 88.

23   *total of £450 per year*: Honan, *Jane Austen*, 214.

23   *for his mother and sisters*: Their dear family friend, Martha Lloyd, also moved in with them. Lloyd's sister was married to Jane's oldest brother, James.

23   *Her brother Henry negotiated*: Anthony Mandal, *Jane Austen and the Popular Novel: The Determined Author* (Basingstoke, UK: Palgrave Macmillan, 2007), 78.

24   *"that its sale would not repay"*: Henry Austen, "Biographical Notice," in *Northanger Abbey: and Persuasion* (London: John Murray, 1818), I.xiii.

24   *sold well enough to bring her £140*: Gilson, *Bibliography*, 8.

24   *Multiple volumes provided the ability to charge more*: James Raven, "Historical Introduction," in *The English Novel 1770–1829: A Bibliographical Survey of Prose Fiction Published in the British Isles*, ed. James Raven and Antonia Forster (Oxford, UK: Oxford University Press, 2000), I.96.

24   *When Austen's characters mention "the Library"*: See Benson, "Parasols & Gloves & Broches & Circulating Libraries," 205–10.

24   *"A present [. . .] now and then"*: Jane Austen, *Sense and Sensibility: A Novel* (London: printed for the author [. . .] and published by T. Egerton, 1811), I.22.

25   *"worthy of particular commendation"*: Quoted in B. C. Southam, ed., *Jane Austen: The Critical Heritage, Volume 1: 1811–1870* (London: Routledge, 1968), 35.

25   *"I am never too busy"*: Letter from Jane Austen to Cassandra Austen, April 25, 1811, in Le Faye, *Letters*, 190.

25   *"Letter from At. Cass."*: Gilson, *Bibliography*, 8; also quoted in Mandal, *Jane Austen and the Popular Novel*, 81.

25   *The first edition had an estimated 1,500 copies*: Gilson, *Bibliography*, 24.

26   *"as delightful a creature"*: Letter from Jane Austen to Cassandra Austen, January 29, 1813, in Le Faye, *Letters*, 210.

26   *"It is far superior to almost all"*: Quoted in Southam, *Jane Austen: The Critical Heritage, Volume I*, 41.

26   *"which only makes me long for more"*: Letter from Jane Austen to Francis Austen,

July 3, 1813, in Le Faye, *Letters*, 226. She continues, "I have something in hand—which I hope on the credit of P.&P. will sell well."

26 *Printed in an estimated edition of 1,250 copies*: Gilson, *Bibliography*, 48–49, 59–60.

26 *the specter of the slave trade*: See Catherine Fowler, "Revisiting Mansfield Park: The Critical and Literary Legacies of Edward W. Said's Essay 'Jane Austen and Empire' in *Culture and Imperialism* (1993)," in *Cambridge Journal of Postcolonial Literary Inquiry* 4, no. 3 (2017): 362–81.

26 *Of* Mansfield Park, *her mother did not like it*: Quoted in Southam, *Jane Austen: The Critical Heritage, Volume I*, 49.

27 *"has read and admired all your publications"*: Austen-Leigh, *Memoir*, 113.

27 *"no one but myself will much like"*: Austen-Leigh, *Memoir*, 148.

27 *published in an edition of two thousand copies*: Gilson, *Bibliography*, 67–69.

27 *Its title page, however, is dated 1816*: Except in cases of speaking to the precise month and date of publication, I typically default to the convention of stating the year of publication as that listed on the title page.

28 *but in fact by Walter Scott*: According to Juliette Wells, it was not until 1930 that Charles Beecher Hogan published an article definitively attributing the piece to Scott. Wells, *New Jane Austen*, 142.

28 *"subjects are not often elegant"*: Quoted in Southam, *Jane Austen: The Critical Heritage, Volume I*, 67.

28 *rarely evoke the same transcendent response*: The modern version of this is the tendency to consider fiction set during wartime as more "important" or "literary" than fiction about more ordinary events that most people experience, such as falling in love.

28 *"It has not however that elevation of virtue"*: Quoted in Southam, *Jane Austen: The Critical Heritage, Volume I*, 12.

28 *"Big Bow-wow strain"*: Quoted in Southam, *Jane Austen: The Critical Heritage, Volume I*, 106.

28 *"No, I must keep to my own style"*: Austen-Leigh, *Memoir*, 117.

29 *signs of serious illness*: Austen, "Biographical Notice," I.vii–viii.

29 *Based on her symptoms, scholars have suggested*: See Honan, *Jane Austen*, 392, for a discussion of possible diagnoses.

29 *The edition numbered 1,750 copies*: Gilson, *Bibliography*, 83–84.

29 *"had the satisfaction of informing"*: Austen-Leigh, *Memoir*, 130.

29 *"closely resembles, except for a few details"*: Marvin Mudrick, *Jane Austen: Irony as Defense and Discovery* (Princeton, NJ: Princeton University Press, 1952), 48.

30　*"one of the very best of Miss Austen's productions"*: Quoted in Southam, *Jane Austen: The Critical Heritage, Volume I*, 83; Whately in 1821 (below) references the characterization of the Thorpes with praise, but moves quickly onto *Persuasion*.

30　*"superior to all"*: Quoted in Southam, *Jane Austen: The Critical Heritage, Volume I*, 102. This review, later identified as by Richard Whately, archbishop of Dublin, was a smart, comprehensive assessment of Austen's work and became the second landmark in Austen criticism alongside Scott's.

30　*Henry revealed Jane Austen's name*: Juliette Wells has pointed out that we don't know definitively that Henry composed this notice; according to her research, that attribution began with Reginald Brimley Johnson in 1892 and was supported by "family tradition." Wells suggests that Cassandra may have had a hand in it as well. See Juliette Wells, "A Note on Henry Austen's Authorship of the 'Biographical Notice,'" *Persuasions* 38, no. 1 (Winter 2017).

30　*"Her merit consists altogether in her remarkable talent"*: Quoted in Southam, *Jane Austen: The Critical Heritage, Volume I*, 80, 81.

30　*At the time of her death, it was by no means clear*: See Devoney Looser, *The Making of Jane Austen* (Baltimore: Johns Hopkins University Press, 2017), 4. This observation has been important to a number of Austen monographs, including Harman, *Jane's Fame*; Southam, *Jane Austen: The Critical Heritage*; Laurence W. Mazzeno, *Jane Austen: Two Centuries of Criticism* (Rochester, NY: Camden House, 2011); and Emily Auerbach, *Searching for Jane Austen* (Madison: University of Wisconsin Press, 2004).

31　*"favored adjectives such as sweet"*: Auerbach, *Searching for Jane Austen*, 6.

31　*"a little bit of ivory"*: Austen, "Biographical Notice," I.xvii.

32　*"triumphing over the married women"*: R. W. Chapman, *Jane Austen: Facts and Problems* (Oxford, UK: Clarendon Press, 1948), 67; also partially quoted in Harman, *Jane's Fame*, 90.

32　*Henry sold to publisher Richard Bentley*: Harman, *Jane's Fame*, 80–81. Publisher Murray actually approached the family first for *Pride and Prejudice*, but that deal did not go through. The Bentley series also featured a slightly expanded version of the "Biographical Notice."

32　*first illustrated editions of Austen's novels in English*: Looser, *Making of Jane Austen*, 19. The first illustrated Austen novel was actually a French edition of *Persuasion*, *La Famille Eliot*, in 1821 (Looser, *Making of Jane Austen*, 18).

32　*"For nearly half a century England has possessed an artist"*: Quoted in Southam, *Jane Austen: The Critical Heritage, Volume I*, 148.

32 *"a carefully fenced, highly cultivated garden"*: Quoted in Southam, *Jane Austen: The Critical Heritage, Volume I*, 126, 127.

33 *The engaging* A Memoir of Jane Austen . . . *received significant attention*: See B. C. Southam, ed., *Jane Austen: The Critical Heritage, Volume 2: 1870–1940* (London: Routledge, 1987), 1–45.

34 *"my dear aunt Jane"*: Austen-Leigh, *Memoir*, 1.

34 *decision to call her "dear aunt Jane" himself*: Unsigned (but by Richard Simpson) review of *Memoir* in the *North British Review*, April 1870, quoted in Southam, *Jane Austen: The Critical Heritage, Volume I*, 265.

34 *The image was eagerly embraced*: Looser, *Making of Jane Austen*, 7–10.

34 *"On the contrary, it failed frequently"*: Quoted in Auerbach, *Searching for Jane Austen*, 7.

34 *bequeathed to various family members*: Charles got "Volume the First"; Frank "Volume the Second"; James Edward Austen-Leigh "Volume the Third"; Caroline Austen "The Watsons"; Anna Lefroy "Sanditon" and unused chapters of *Persuasion*; Fanny Knight "Lady Susan" and most of the letters. See Harman, *Jane's Fame*, 90.

34 *the Bentley "Steventon Edition" of her works*: Harman, *Jane's Fame*, 119.

35 *Austen-Leigh's* Memoir *was the catalyst*: Southam, *Jane Austen: The Critical Heritage, Volume 2*, 1–3.

35 *containing the ninety-four letters he had inherited*: Southam, *Jane Austen: The Critical Heritage, Volume 2*, 39–41.

35 *ushered in a new generation of scholarship*: See Southam, *Jane Austen: The Critical Heritage, Volume 2*, 40.

35 *"writing simply, honestly, [and] artistically"*: Wells, *New Jane Austen*, 88–89.

35 *Adams published the earliest critical edition*: Wells, *New Jane Austen*, 1–2.

35 *Austen became a favorite for teaching*: See "Textbook Austens" in Looser, *Making of Jane Austen*.

36 *"are spoken of respectfully as classics"*: Goldwin Smith, *Life of Jane Austen* (London: Walter Scott, 1890), 65. See also Southam, *Jane Austen: The Critical Heritage, Volume 2*, 19.

36 *"every person of education has read"*: Quoted in Looser, *Making of Jane Austen*, 202.

36 *Allen's 1894 "Peacock"* Pride and Prejudice: Gilson, *Bibliography*, 267.

37 *Saintsbury, coins the term "Janite"*: See Harman, *Jane's Fame*, 128–29.

37 *Constance Hill and Ellen Hill's 1902 bestseller*: Looser, *Making of Jane Austen*, 8–9.

This was also the book that first made public the revelation of Bigg-Wither's ill-fated proposal to Austen; see Wells, *New Jane Austen*, 36.

37   *"from a muslin scarf that was satin-stitched by Austen"*: Constance Hill, *Jane Austen: Her Home & Her Friends* (London: John Lane, 1902), xiv.

37   *"a national memorial to the novelist"*: Quoted in Harman, *Jane's Fame*, 178.

37   *Austen's triumphant narrative continued*: Mazzeno, *Jane Austen: Two Centuries of Criticism*, 2; Harman, *Jane's Fame*, 206. See also Auerbach, *Searching for Jane Austen*. For information on the contributions of Austen collectors and fans, see Juliette Wells, *Everybody's Jane: Austen in the Popular Imagination* (London: Continuum, 2011), and Wells, *New Jane Austen*.

CHAPTER TWO:
FRANCES BURNEY (1752–1840)

39   *"if to PRIDE and PREJUDICE"*: Frances Burney, *Cecilia, or Memoirs of an Heiress* (London: Printed for T. Payne and Son, 1782), V.380.

39   *The flames consumed all of Burney's manuscripts*: Frances Burney, *The Wanderer* (London: Printed for Longman, Hurst, Rees, Orme, and Brown, 1814), xxi. This event is also described in Frances Burney ("Madame D'Arblay"), *Memoirs of Doctor Burney* (London: Edward Moxon, 1832), II.125.

40   *a now-classic of the field*: A. Edward Newton, *The Amenities of Book-Collecting and Kindred Affections* (Boston: Atlantic Monthly Press, 1918), 199–200. This is where I first read of it as a young bookseller.

40   *She vividly re-created her heroine's interior world*: See Claire Harman, *Fanny Burney: A Biography* (New York: HarperCollins, 2000), 91, 97.

41   *"he is a very Young Man"*: Letter from Jane Austen to Cassandra Austen, June 2, 1799, quoted in Le Faye, *Letters*, 44.

41   *"There are two Traits in her Character"*: Letter from Jane Austen to Cassandra Austen, September 15–16, 1796, quoted in Le Faye, *Letters*, 9.

43   *once considered the dunce of the lot*: Burney ("Madame D'Arblay"), *Memoirs of Doctor Burney*, II.124.

43   *only Burney child who did not receive a formal education*: Burney ("Madame D'Arblay"), *Memoirs of Doctor Burney*, I.197. See also Harman's *Fanny Burney*, which does an excellent job of contrasting Frances Burney's upbringing with her siblings' precocity.

44   *he owned only one novel*: Burney, *The Wanderer*, xxii.

44   *"closet up two pair of stairs"*: Burney ("Madame D'Arblay"), *Memoirs of Doctor Burney*, II.169.

44   *"dangerous"*: Vicesimus Knox, "On Novel Reading," in *Essays Moral and Literary* (London: Printed for Edward and Charles Dilly, 1779), II.189.

44   *"extreme indecency"*: W. Whitehead, "On the Ignorance and Indecency of Modern Romance Writers," *The World*, no. 19 (May 10, 1753), in *The British Essayists* (London: Jones and Company, 1828), IV.34.

45   *"the corruption occasioned by these books"*: Hannah More, "On Female Study," in *Strictures on the Modern System of Female Education*, in its updated form in *The Works of Hannah More* (Philadelphia: Edward Earle, 1813), V.123. Earlier versions of *Strictures* have a slightly different wording.

45   *"fatal poison"*: James Fordyce, *Sermons to Young Women* (London: Printed for A. Millar and T. Cadell, 1766), I.144.

45   *"aloud to the ladies"*: Austen, *Pride and Prejudice*, I.154.

45   *"must in her soul be a prostitute"*; *"a horrible violation of all decorum"*: Fordyce, *Sermons*, I.148–9.

45   *"but a useless employment"*: Richard Berenger, "On the Mischiefs of Romances," *The World*, no. 79 (July 4, 1754), in *The British Essayists*, IV.138.

46   *"nourish a vain and visionary indolence"*: Hannah More, *Strictures of the Modern System of Female Education* (Boston: Printed for Joseph Bumstead, 1802), 103.

46   *"hence the mind is secretly corrupted"*: Thomas Gisborne, *An Enquiry into the Duties of the Female Sex* (London: Printed for T. Cadell Junior and W. Davies, 1797), 216–17.

46   *learn from their own informal reading*: Halsey, *Jane Austen and Her Readers*, 30.

46   *"are apt to give a romantic Turn"*: Sarah Pennington, *An Unfortunate Mother's Advice to Her Absent Daughters; in a Letter to Miss Pennington* (London: Printed by S. Chandler, 1761), 40.

46   *"such a lover as her romantic imagination had represented"*: Ann Wingrove, *Letters, Moral and Entertaining* (Bath: R. Cruttwell, 1795), 6.

46   *"I know several unmarried ladies"*: Berenger, "On the Mischiefs of Romances," 138.

47   *"around 50 percent every decade starting in the 1760s"*: Judith Phillips Stanton, "Statistical Profile of Women Writing in English from 1660–1800," in *Eighteenth-Century Women and the Arts*, ed. Frederick M. Keener and Susan E. Lorsch (Westport, CT: Greenwood Press, 1998), 248.

47   *women wrote more than 50 percent*: Miles, "What Is a Romantic Novel?," 181n1, speaking of the period between 1785 and 1820.

47   *"forbid your readers"*: Whitehead, "On the Ignorance and Indecency of Modern Romance Writers," IV.34.

47   *This set the tone for critical commentary*: See Claudia Johnson, "'Let Me Make the Novels of a Country': Barbauld's 'The British Novelists' (1810/1820)," *NOVEL: A Forum on Fiction* 34, no. 2, The Romantic-Era Novel (Spring 2001): 163–79.

48   *"So early was I impressed myself"*: Burney, *The Wanderer*, xx.

48   *"she considered it her duty"*: Burney ("Madame D'Arblay"), *Memoirs of Doctor Burney*, II.125.

48   *"thought it prudent to consume it in the garden"*: Burney, *The Wanderer*, xxi.

48   *"I have resolved, neck or nothing"*: Frances Burney, *The Early Journals and Letters, Volume II: 1774–1777*, ed. Lars E. Troide (Montreal: McGill-Queen's University Press, 1991), 70 (June 15, 1769, entry), 73 (June 25, 1769, entry).

49   *"From Nobody I have nothing to fear"*: Frances Burney, *Diary and Letters of Madame d'Arblay, Edited by Her Niece* (London: Henry Colburn, 1842), I.34.

49   *"the old lady"*: Burney, *Diary and Letters*, I.xvi.

49   *"I looked like a most egregious fool"*: Burney, *Early Journals and Letters*, II.239.

49   *"gaily, without reading a word of the work"*: Burney ("Madame D'Arblay"), *Memoirs of Doctor Burney*, II.127.

49   *The rights were sold to publisher Thomas Lowndes*: Margaret Anne Doody, *Frances Burney: The Life in the Works* (New Brunswick, NJ: Rutgers University Press, 1988), 70.

50   *surprise bestseller of the same decade*: Richard B. Sher, *The Enlightenment and the Book* (Chicago: University of Chicago Press, 2008), 254.

50   *Austen received only ten pounds*: See letter from Jane Austen to B. Crosby & Co., April 5, 1809, quoted in Le Faye, *Letters*, 182. See also Gilson, *Bibliography*, 82.

50   *anonymous authorship was a respected convention*: One publisher did turn it down because of Burney's request for anonymity; Lowndes, the second publisher approached, had no such qualms. See Joyce Hemlow, *The History of Fanny Burney* (Oxford, UK: Clarenden Press, 1958), 64.

50   *"This is what Stephen King would write"*: Stephen P. Brown, "Steven [*sic*] King Shining Through," *Washington Post*, April 9, 1985, https://www.washington post.com/archive/lifestyle/1985/04/09/steven-king-shining-through/eaf 662da-e9eb-4aba-9eb9-217826684ab6/.

50   *"exceeding odd sensation"*: This paragraph was silently elided in the 1842 edition of Burney's *Diary and Letters*, but can be found in later editions, e.g., the 1892 London edition from Frederick Warne, I.62.

51   *didn't even pretend to hide their smiles*: Burney ("Madame D'Arblay"), *Memoirs of Doctor Burney*, II.132.

51   *Burney fell sick soon after the book's publication*: Harman, *Fanny Burney*, 101; Burney ("Madame D'Arblay"), *Memoirs of Doctor Burney*, II.133.

52   *"they had concluded it to be the work of a man!"*: Burney, *Diary and Letters*, I.38.

52   *"I must own I suffered great difficulty"*: Burney, *Diary and Letters*, I.39.

52   *four further editions published*: According to the English Short Title Catalogue (ESTC), after the 1778 first edition, three more London editions were published in 1779, as well as one Dublin edition.

52   *"one of the most sprightly, entertaining & agreeable productions"*: *Monthly Review*, April 1778, quoted in Frances Burney, *Early Journals and Letters, Volume III: The Streatham Years: Part 1, 1778–1779*, ed. Lars E. Troide and Stewart J. Cooke (Montreal: McGill-Queen's University Press, 1994), 15; and Harman, *Fanny Burney*, 100.

52   *"he must be a man of great abilities!"*: Burney, *Diary and Letters*, I.43.

52   *"conscious intellectual disgrace"*: Burney ("Madame D'Arblay"), *Memoirs of Doctor Burney*, II.124.

53   *"If she had conceived an illegitimate child"*: Harman, *Fanny Burney*, 104.

53   *"with fear and trembling"*: Quoted in Burney ("Madame D'Arblay"), *Memoirs of Doctor Burney*, II.169.

53   *"wrought up in a most extraordinary manner"*: Quoted in Burney, *Diary and Letters*, I.44.

53   *"How little did I dream"*: Burney, *Diary and Letters*, I.44.

53   *"Henry Fielding never did anything equal"*: Hester Lynch Thrale Piozzi, *Thraliana*, ed. Katharine C. Balderston (Oxford, UK: Clarendon Press, 1942), I.329; also quoted in Harman, *Fanny Burney*, 118.

53   *"seemed more like a romance"*: Burney ("Madame D'Arblay"), *Memoirs of Doctor Burney*, II.143.

54   *"I have already, I fear"*: Burney, *Diary and Letters*, I.50.

54   *Thackeray used in writing* Vanity Fair: See Kate Chisholm, "The Burney Family," in *The Cambridge Companion to Frances Burney*, ed. Peter Sabor (Cambridge, UK: Cambridge University Press, 2007), 8.

55   *"He's terribly afraid"*: Quoted in Hemlow, *History of Fanny Burney*, 127.

55 *"Scarcely any name, if any, stands higher"*: Anna Laetitia Barbauld, "Miss Burney," in *The British Novelists* (London: F. C. & J. Rivington, 1810), XXXVIII.i.

55 *"monuments of genius"*: Unsigned review of *Life and Adventures of Peter Wilkins*, 1823, in *Retrospective Review*; quoted in Southam, *Jane Austen: The Critical Heritage*, Volume 1, 108.

55 *"Born in the same rank of life"*: Unsigned review of *Life and Adventures of Peter Wilkins*, 1823, in *Retrospective Review*; quoted in Southam, *Jane Austen: The Critical Heritage*, Volume 1, 109.

55 *"extraordinary"*; *"among the classical novels of England"*; *"surpassed"*: Thomas Macaulay, "Madame D'Arblay," in *Critical and Historical Essays Contributed to the Edinburgh Review* (London: Longmans, Green, 1874), 712; 710; 731.

56 *Burney was a watered-down version of Austen*: See also Marilyn Francus, "Why Austen, not Burney? Tracing the Mechanisms of Reputation and Legacy," *ABO: Interactive Journal for Women in the Arts, 1640–1830*, 13, no. 1, article 6 (Summer 2023).

56 *"it was Jane Austen who completed the work"*: Ian Watt, *The Rise of the Novel: Studies in Defoe, Richardson and Fielding* (Berkeley: University of California Press, 1957), 298.

56 *"is more responsible than anyone else"*: Lars E. Troide, "Joyce Hemlow and the McGill Burney Project," in *A Celebration of Frances Burney*, ed. Lorna J. Clark (Newcastle upon Tyne, UK: Cambridge Scholars Publishing, 2007), 10. Troide succeeded Hemlow as director of the Burney Centre (which she founded in 1960).

56 *"Essentially then, Jane Austen admired"*: William Baker, *Critical Companion to Jane Austen: A Literary Reference to Her Life and Work* (New York: Facts on File, 2008), 510.

56 *"It is as if there were a quota"*: Doody, *Frances Burney*, 2.

57 *"accented by a lone female"*: Katha Pollitt, "Hers; The Smurfette Principle," *New York Times*, April 7, 1991.

57 *"an iconic figure"*: Susan Civale, "The Literary Afterlife of Frances Burney and the Victorian Periodical Press," *Victorian Periodicals Review* 44, no. 3 (Fall 2011): 236.

58 *When Burney's reputation as a diarist soared*: For example, a contemporary review in the *Eclectic Review* refers to Burney as "little Fanny Burney"—using quotation marks, indicating the phrase came from the book—instead of the title page's "Madame d'Arblay." See Civale, "The Literary Afterlife of Frances Burney," 245.

59   *Burney was one of the first women included*: See Civale, "The Literary Afterlife of Frances Burney," 252. Burney was the third woman of five included in the series: after Victorians Elizabeth Gaskell and George Eliot, and before Maria Edgeworth and Jane Austen. This series had two parts; the first part was launched with a biography of Samuel Johnson by Leslie Stephen—the father of Virginia Woolf.

59   *Dobson's was the first book-length biography*: See Peter Sabor, "Annie Raine Ellis, Austin Dobson, and the Rise of Burney Studies," *Burney Journal*, vol. 1 (1998): 25.

59   *"high above [her] efforts as a novelist"*: Austin Dobson, *Fanny Burney (Madame D'Arblay)* (London: Macmillan, 1903), 205.

59   *"'Fanny' is a patronizing diminutive"*: Doody, *Frances Burney*, 6. See also Janice Farrar Thaddeus, *Francis Burney: A Literary Life* (London: Macmillan, 2000), 225–26.

61   *"we begin to experience gender as a restriction of possibility"*: Sara Ahmed, *Living a Feminist Life* (Durham, NC: Duke University Press, 2017), 7.

61   *romance is the only major genre with a thoroughly feminine reputation*: It's important to note that people of all genders always have participated in the romance genre as authors, editors, publishers, critics, and readers; yet also inescapably, the wider reputation of the genre as dominated by women has always played a role in the genre's larger reception.

62   *Poe conceived of such stories as miniature puzzles*: Paul Collins, *Edgar Allan Poe: The Fever Called Living* (New York: Amazon, 2014), 59.

67   *"to be sure, they said, I should not want for friends"*: Frances Burney, *Evelina, or the History of a Young Lady's Entrance into the World.* (London: Macmillan, 1903), 281.

67   *"Evelina's breathless letters to her guardian"*: Harman, *Fanny Burney*, 22.

68   *"Then coming up close to me, he said"*: Burney, *Diary and Letters*, II.375.

68   *"We were merry, & laughed"*: Quoted in Harman, *Fanny Burney*, 5.

68   *"Miss Burney looks so meek and so quiet"*: Burney, *Diary and Letters*, I.77.

69   *"'Harry Fielding never drew so good a character!'"*: Burney, *Diary and Letters*, I.78.

69   *Burney was a gloriously complex person*: Janice Farrar Thaddeus's biography emphasizes Burney's "many-sidedness," describing "three Burneys: the one who fears to do wrong, the one who represses her rage, and the one who unleashes her rage." Thaddeus, *Frances Burney*, 5, 6.

69   *"I suppose my consciousness betrayed my artifice"*: Burney, *Evelina*, 37.

70   *They "all seemed shocked and amazed"*: Burney, *Evelina*, 37–46.

71 *"Suppose You to lose yr Father"*: Quoted in Burney, *Early Journals and Letters*, II.123.

72 *he printed only five hundred copies*: Hemlow, *History of Fanny Burney*, 148.

72 *about three hundred copies of the* Philosopher's Stone: Philip W. Errington, *J. K. Rowling: A Bibliography 1997–2013* (London: Bloomsbury, 2015), A1(a).

74 *"woman in the room whom it would not be a punishment"*: Austen, *Pride and Prejudice*, I.20. Technically, Darcy is referring to all the women in the room except Bingley's sisters.

74 *"a poor weak girl"*: Burney, *Evelina*, 32.

74 *The first-ever appearance of Jane Austen's name in print*: According to Sabor, Ellis was the first person to notice this in her introduction to an 1881 edition of *Evelina*. See Sabor, "Annie Raine Ellis, Austin Dobson, and the Rise of Burney Studies," 27.

75 *"a Manuscript Novel"*; *"form of elaborate homage"*: Harman, *Jane's Fame*, 20; 17. See also Gilson, *Bibliography*, 24; Honan, *Jane Austen*, 122.

76 *Dobson's wonder about the "irony"*: Dobson, *Fanny Burney*, 196.

78 *much more violent than Austen's*: On this topic see also Doody, *Frances Burney*, 2–3.

CHAPTER THREE:
ANN RADCLIFFE (1764–1823)

79 *"'while I have Udolpho to read'"*: Austen, *Northanger Abbey: and Persuasion*, I.73.

79 *"'But, my dearest Catherine'"*: Austen, *Northanger Abbey*, I.68–69.

80 *"when I had once begun it"*: Austen, *Northanger Abbey*, I.250.

80 *"all-Jane-Austen-all-the-time book club"*: Karen Joy Fowler, *The Jane Austen Book Club* (New York: G. P. Putnam's Sons, 2004), 5.

80 *"'You've read* The Mysteries of Udolpho?'"*: Fowler, *Jane Austen Book Club*, 139.

81 *"Wedgwood supplied the science"*: Rictor Norton, *Mistress of Udolpho: The Life of Ann Radcliffe* (London: Leicester University Press, 1999), 28. Much of this biographical section is indebted to a combination of Norton and Thomas Noon Talfourd, "Memoir of the Life and Writings of Mrs. Radcliffe," in *Gaston de Blondeville* (London: Henry Colburn, 1826), I.1–132.

81 *"Wedgwood & Bentley" mark*: See Robin Reilly, *Wedgwood* (London: Stockton Press, 1989).

82 *"During the sitting of Parliament"*: Thomas Rees, *Reminiscences of Literary London from 1779–1853* (New York: Francis P. Harper, 1896), 133; and quoted in Norton, *Mistress of Udolpho*, 60.

82 *"So far was she from being subjected"*: Talfourd, "Memoir," 8.

83 The Castles of Athlin and Dunbayne *received only a little notice*: Review of *Castles of Athlin and Dunbayne* in the *Critical Review*, in Raven and Forster, *The English Novel*, 483. See also Norton, *Mistress of Udolpho*, 57.

83 *"Adventures heaped on adventures"*: Walter Scott, "Prefatory Memoir to Mrs. Ann Radcliffe," in *The Novels of Mrs. Ann Radcliffe*, Ballantyne's Novelist's Library (London: Hurst, Robinson, 1824), iv.

83 *"It has been the fashionable novel here"*: Quoted in Augustus J. G. Hare, *Maria Edgeworth: Life and Letters* (Boston: Houghton Mifflin, 1894), I.27.

83 *publish under her own name*: Norton, *Mistress of Udolpho*, 82. See also Deborah D. Rogers, *Ann Radcliffe: A Bio-Bibliography* (Westport, CT: Greenwood Press, 1996), 8–9.

84 *It shares the same root as the word "new"*: Deborah Ross, *The Excellence of Falsehood: Romance, Realism, and Women's Contribution to the Novel* (Lexington: University Press of Kentucky, 1991), 2.

84 *"a heroic fable"*: Clara Reeve, *The Progress of Romance* (New York: Facsimile Text Society, 1930), 111.

84 *"the Shakespeare of Romance Writers"*: Nathan Drake, *Literary Hours, or Sketches Critical and Narrative* (London: Printed by J. Burkitt and sold by T. Cadell, Junior, and W. Davies, 1798), 249.

85 *expanded its Monthly Catalogue of "Novels"*: Norton, *Mistress of Udolpho*, 89.

85 *he wagered £10 against it*: Talfourd, "Memoir," 12.

85 *Burney had proved that women could write novels just as good*: For a discussion of this, see Jane Spencer, "*Evelina* and *Cecilia*," in *The Cambridge Companion to Frances Burney*, ed. Peter Sabor (Cambridge, UK: Cambridge University Press, 2007), 23.

85 *Readers reported staying up all night*: Talfourd, "Memoir," 11.

85 *Poets printed odes inspired by it*: Matilda Betham, "Lines to Mrs. Radcliffe, on First Reading *The Mysteries of Udolpho*," in *Poems* (London: J. Hatchard, 1808), 11–14.

85 *"the most interesting novel in the English language"*: Anonymous, "Correspondence. Mysteries of Udolpho," in *Critical Review*, 2nd series, vol. 12 (November 1794): 359–60. Dale Townshend and Angela Wright, ed., in *Ann Radcliffe, Ro-*

manticism, and the Gothic (Cambridge, UK: Cambridge University Press, 2014), attribute this anonymous review and response to Samuel Taylor Coleridge; Norton's biography *Mistress of Udolpho* argues against this attribution.

87 *"in the hands of Mrs Radcliffe"*: John Dunlop, *The History of Fiction* (London: Printed for Longman, Hurst, Rees, Orme, and Brown, 1814), III:393.

88 *Dickens read Radcliffe's books as manuals*: See Archibald C. Coolidge Jr., "Charles Dickens and Mrs. Radcliffe: A Farewell to Wilkie Collins," *Dickensian* 58, no. 337 (May 1962): 112–16; and Thomas Loe, "Gothic Plot in 'Great Expectations,'" *Dickens Quarterly* 6, no. 3 (September 1989): 106–8. See also Norton, *Mistress of Udolpho*, 255.

88 *"passages that lead to nothing"*: Dunlop, *History of Fiction*, III:387. Dale Townshend notes that Dunlop is himself referencing a Thomas Gray poem in this wording. Dale Townshend, *Gothic Antiquity: History, Romance, and the Architectural Imagination, 1760–1840* (Oxford, UK: Oxford University Press, 2019), 134.

89 *"some of the most finished pictures"*: November 1825 issue of the *Monthly Review*, quoted in Norton, *Mistress of Udolpho*, 107.

89 *she had never left the country before*: Talfourd, "Memoir," 14.

90 *"ghosts and goblins"*: Edmund Burke, *A Philosophical Enquiry into the Origin of Our Ideas of the Sublime and Beautiful* (London: Printed for R. and J. Dodsley, 1757), 273–75.

91 *"to shelter my own daring"*: Preface to the 1765 second edition of Walpole's *The Castle of Otranto*, quoted in *Gothic Readings: The First Wave, 1764–1840*, ed. Rictor Norton (London: Leicester University Press, 2000), 7.

92 *not some grand attempt to begin a new genre*: See James Watt, *Contesting the Gothic: Fiction, Genre and Cultural Conflict, 1764–1832* (Cambridge, UK: Cambridge University Press, 1999), 6–7.

92 *"unite the most attractive and interesting circumstances"*: Clara Reeve, *The Old English Baron* (Kansas City, MO: Valancourt Press, 2009), 3. Walpole did not like what Reeve did with it, calling *The Old English Baron* "a professed imitation of mine, only stripped of the marvelous; and so entirely stripped, except in one awkward attempt at a ghost or two, that it is the most insipid dull thing you ever saw." Quoted in Watt, *Contesting the Gothic*, 32.

92 Emmeline *brought gothic elements into the Burney-esque courtship novel*: See James R. Foster, "Charlotte Smith, Pre-Romantic Novelist," *PMLA* 43, no. 2 (June 1928): 463–75.

93 *one-third of the entire fiction market*: Robert D. Mayo, "Gothic Romance in the

Magazines," *PMLA* 65, no. 5 (September 1950): 766; Carol Margaret Davison, *History of the Gothic: Gothic Literature, 1764–1824* (Cardiff: University of Wales Press, 2009) also references different accountings with similar results, such as in Franz Potter's *The History of Gothic Publishing, 1800–1835: Exhuming the Trade* (London: Palgrave Macmillan, 2005) and Peter Garside's "The English Novel in the Romantic Era: Consolidation and Dispersal," in *The English Novel 1770–1829: A Bibliographical Survey of Prose Fiction Published in the British Isles, Volume II: 1800–1829*, ed. Peter Garside and Rainer Schöwerling (Oxford, UK: Oxford University Press, 2000).

93 *"a most singular revolution"*: *Gentleman's Magazine*, vol. 84 (1798): 786.

93 *One publisher, the Minerva Press*: Potter, *History of Gothic Publishing*, 15.

93 *"the Shakespeare of Romance Writers"*: Drake, *Literary Hours*, 249.

93 The Italian *went into another edition*: Raven and Forster, *The English Novel*, I.727.

94 *publishing a heap of fake "posthumous" works*: See Norton, *Mistress of Udolpho*, 204.

94 *an appendix of "Spurious Attributions"*: Rogers, *Ann Radcliffe*, 191–94.

94 *"In a high window of the tower a light"*: Quoted in Talfourd, "Memoir," 98.

94 *Radcliffe always sat in the orchestra*: Talfourd, "Memoir," 100.

95 *"altho' I know next to nothing about her"*: Mackenzie Bell, *Christina Rossetti: A Biographical and Critical Study* (London: Thomas Burleigh, 1898), 91.

95 *"I despair and withdraw"*: Bell, *Christina Rossetti*, 92; also described in Norton, *Mistress of Udolpho*, 4–5.

95 *"awakening public interest in an author virtually forgotten"*: Southam, *Jane Austen: The Critical Heritage*, Volume 2, 2.

96 *"Mrs. Ann Radcliffe, the ingenious authoress"*: C. A. Wheelwright, *Poems, Original and Translated* (London: Longman, Hurst, Rees, Orme, and Browne, 1810), 275.

96 *"a fit of depression or fright"*: *Merriam-Webster* summarizes the horrors as "a shuddering or shivering as symptomatic of a fever, or a fit of depression or fright as occurs with mental delirium" (see "Old Fashioned Names for Diseases and Ailments," *Merriam-Webster*, accessed April 22, 2024, https://www.merriam-webster.com/wordplay/illnesses-ailments-diseases-history-names). The context of the Radcliffe reference in Wheelwright's poem makes it clear he is referring to the latter definition.

96 *Radcliffe was taking walks in the park*: Extensively described by Talfourd in "Memoir."

96 *Even the thought of such an inelegant letter*: Talfourd, "Memoir," 95.

97   *"When we know the full extent of any danger"*: Burke, *Philosophical Enquiry*, 43.

98   *"is that which is raised by a delineation of guilt"*: Dunlop, *History of Fiction*, III:396.

99   *"That her genius was poetical"*: Quoted in Norton, *Mistress of Udolpho*, 232, from an unauthorized collection of her *Poems* (1815).

100   *"the most excellent, but at the same time the most difficult"*: Quoted in Raven and Forster, *The English Novel*, I.727.

100   *"it has been the fashion to make Terror the order of the day"*: Quoted in Potter, *History of Gothic Publishing*, 22.

100   *Minerva Press was notorious for flooding the market*: See also Edith Birkhead, *Tale of Terror: A Study of the Gothic Romance* (London: Constable & Co., 1921), 185, attributing this to authors writing gothics: "as a lucrative trade, not as an art."

100   *"So closely identified with cheap fiction"*: Dorothy Blakey, *The Minerva Press, 1790–1820* (London: Bibliographical Society, 1939), 1.

100   *"vapid and servile imitations"*: Quoted in Raven and Forster, *The English Novel*, I.761.

100   *more women published novels than men*: Miles, "What Is a Romantic Novel?," 181n1.

100   *Women drove that genre*: Influential exceptions like Matthew Lewis's *The Monk* (1796) specifically attempted to "masculinize" the genre.

100   *gothics were a symbol of emotion over reason*: J. M. S. Tompkins, *The Popular Novel in England: 1770–1800* (London: Constable & Co., 1932), 210.

101   *"the grossest and most immoral novelists"*: Francis William Blagdon, *Flowers of Literature, for 1806* (London: J. G. Barnard, 1807), lxxiv.

101   *"when female invention will employ itself"*: T. J. Horsley Curties, *Ancient Records; or, The Abbey of Saint Oswythe. A Romance* (London: Minerva Press, 1801), I.viii.

101   *"caught from an enthusiastic admiration of Udolpho's"*: Curties, *Ancient Records*, I.vi.

101   *"Many 'serious' male poets borrowed the poetic phrases"*: Norton, *Mistress of Udolpho*, 250–53.

101   *Shelley loved her novels unabashedly*: Thomas Medwin, *The Life of Percy Bysshe Shelley. A New Edition [. . .] with an Introduction and Commentary by H. Buxton Forman, C.B.* (London: Humphrey Milford, 1913), 25.

101   *Byron was so taken with Radcliffe's description*: Norton, *Mistress of Udolpho*, 252.

102   *"degrading thirst" for "frantic novels"*: William Wordsworth, *Lyrical Ballads, with Other Poems*, 2nd ed. (London: Printed for T. N. Longman and O. Rees, 1800), xix.

102   *"Radcliffe school"*: Letter from William Wordsworth to R. P. Gillies, April 25, 1815, quoted in R. P. Gillies, *Memoirs of a Literary Veteran; Including Sketches and*

Anecdotes of the Most Distinguished Literary Characters from 1794 to 1849 (London: Richard Bentley, 1851), II.158.

102 *"mighty magician of* Udolpho*"*: Thomas James Mathias, *The Pursuits of Literature: A Satirical Poem in Dialogue*, rev. 4th ed. (London: Printed for T. Becket, 1797), 14.

102 *seesawed between brusque criticisms and backhanded compliments*: See Norton, *Mistress of Udolpho*, 259, who argues that in this biography "Scott had cleverly planted the seeds of his rival's downfall."

102 *"the use of opiates"*: Scott, "Prefatory Memoir," vii.

102 *"she may have been disgusted"*: Scott, "Prefatory Memoir," xiv.

103 *"was probably carried to its perfection by Mrs. Radcliffe"*: George Moir, *Treatises on Poetry, Modern Romance, and Rhetoric* (Edinburgh: Adam & Charles Black, 1839), 197, 204.

103 *printing a number of Wordsworth's letters*: Gillies, *Memoirs*, II.158.

103 *"the gloomy horrors of the Radcliffe school"*: William Forsyth, *The Novels and Novelists of the 18th Century* (New York: D. Appleton, 1871), 307, 322.

103 *"name everybody knows"*: Mrs. Oliphant, *The Literary History of England: In the End of the Eighteenth and Beginning of the Nineteenth Century* (London: Macmillan, 1882), II.277.

103 *"the fashion of objecting to Radcliffe's explanations"*: William Minto, *The Literature of the Georgian Era* (Edinburgh: William Blackwood and Sons, 1894), 109.

104 *"crude romance-writers"*: Edmund Gosse, *A Short History of Modern English Literature* (New York: D. Appleton, 1898), 294.

104 *nothing by Radcliffe herself*: Henry Cabot Lodge, ed., *The Best of the World's Classics* (New York: Funk & Wagnalls, 1909).

105 *A separate tradition of gothic studies grew*: See Watt, *Contesting the Gothic*, 1–2.

105 *"tenth-rate fiction"*; *"Others had paddled toy-boats"*; *"two chief facts"*: Tompkins, *The Popular Novel in England*, vii; 248; 1.

105 *"literary degradation"*: "The quantitative increase [in novels] was not in any way matched by an increase in quality. [. . .] much of it reveals only too plainly the pressures towards literary degradation which were exerted by the booksellers and circulating library operators." Watt, *The Rise of the Novel*, 290.

106 *"when I had once begun it"*: Austen, *Northanger Abbey*, I.250.

106 *"imbecility of the mind"*: Anonymous, "On Novels and Romances," *Scots Magazine; or General Repository of Literature, History, and Politics, for the Year MDCCCII*, 64 (1802): 471.

107   *"Northanger Abbey may attack Gothic fiction"*: Halperin, *Life of Jane Austen*, 113.

108   *"I [. . .] think Signor Montoni right"*: Ann Radcliffe, *The Mysteries of Udolpho* (London: J. M. Dent and Sons, 1931), I.207.

108   *"Yes, I will leave the castle"*: Radcliffe, *Mysteries of Udolpho*, I.269.

109   *"Long suffering had made her spirits peculiarly sensible to terror"*: Radcliffe, *Mysteries of Udolpho*, I.336.

109   *"It was too pathetic for the feelings of Sophia"*: Austen, *Love and Freindship*, 16.

110   *"even a moderately laced corset"*: Valerie Steele, *The Corset: A Cultural History* (New Haven, CT: Yale University Press, 2001), 70.

110   *"delicate taste"*: David Hume, *Essays, Moral and Political* (Edinburgh: Printed by R. Fleming and A. Alison, for A. Kincaid, 1741), 4.

110   *Modern scholarship has demonstrated*: See Ildiko Csengei, "'She Fell Senseless on His Corpse': The Woman of Feeling and the Sentimental Swoon in Eighteenth-Century Fiction," in *Romantic Psyche and Psychoanalysis*, ed. Joel Faflak, Romantic Circles Praxis Series (December 2008); and Boram Kim, "Faint or Feint?: Literary Portrayals of Female Swooning in the Eighteenth Century," *English Studies* 29 (2009): 148–66.

111   *"Yet if in 1794 her virginal vaporings"*: Anonymous, "Books: Extricating Emily," review of *The Mysteries of Udolpho*, by Ann Radcliffe, *Time*, April 22, 1966, https://content.time.com/time/subscriber/article/0,33009,899190-1,00 .html. See also Rogers, *Ann Radcliffe*, 105.

112   *"weeps on every other page with unintendedly comic pathos"*: Honan, *Jane Austen*, 139.

113   *"Radcliffe has been ejected from her rightful position"*: Norton, *Mistress of Udolpho*, 253.

113   *"want of taste"*: Gillies, *Memoirs*, II.158.

114   *"no one would give me the slightest explanation"*: Bram Stoker, *Dracula*. 6th ed. (Westminster, UK: Archibald Constable and Co., 1899), 9.

115   *"genius," "unrivalled," and "the great enchantress"*: Betham, "Lines to Mrs. Radcliffe," 11; Charles Bucke, *On the Beauties, Harmonies, and Sublimities of Nature*, new edition, greatly enlarged (London: Printed for Thomas Tegg and Son, 1837), I.x; among others.

115   *Contemporaries associated her with Homer*: See Dunlop, *History of Fiction*, III.396; Anna Laetitia Barbauld, "Mrs. Radcliffe," in *The British Novelists*, vol. XLIII (London: Printed for F. C. and J. Rivington, 1820), viii; and Stendahl's 1804 letter to his sister Pauline, quoted in Norton, *Mistress of Udolpho*, 133.

CHAPTER FOUR:
CHARLOTTE LENNOX (C. 1729-1804)

117   *"Female Quixotte [. . .] now makes our evening amusement"*: Letter from Jane Austen to Cassandra Austen, January 7–8, 1807, quoted in Le Faye, *Letters*, 120.

117   *"I am not without some little ambition"*: Letter from Charlotte Lennox to John Boyle, Earl of Cork and Orrery, October 29, 1758; Letter 31 in Norbert Schürer, *Charlotte Lennox: Correspondence and Miscellaneous Documents* (Lewisburg, PA: Bucknell University Press, 2012), 88–89.

117   *"reputation for candor"*: Letter from Charlotte Lennox to David Garrick, August 4, 1774; Letter 52 in Schürer, *Charlotte Lennox*, 147.

119   *These verses came to the notice of Lady Isabella Finch*: Anonymous, "Mrs. Lenox," *British Magazine and Review* (September 1783): 9; see also Susan Carlile, *Charlotte Lennox: An Independent Mind* (Toronto: University of Toronto Press, 2018), 38.

119   *"own history"*: James Boswell, *The Life of Samuel Johnson, L.L.D. A New Edition, with Numerous Annotations and Notes, by John Wilson Croker, L.L.D. F.R.S.* (London: John Murray, 1831), I:208f2.

119   *"a lady of great distinction at court"*: Charlotte Lennox, *The Life of Harriot Stuart, Written by Herself* (Madison, NJ: Fairleigh Dickinson University Press, 1995), 169–70.

119   *"monstrous abuse of one of the very few women"*: Letter from Montagu to the Countess of Bute, March 1, 1752, quoted in Lady Mary Wortley Montagu, *The Letters and Works*, 2nd ed. rev., ed. Lord Wharncliffe (London: Richard Bentley, 1837), III.22; also quoted in Carlile, *Charlotte Lennox*, 66. In this letter, Montagu also criticizes the heroine Harriot, "who, being intended for an example of wit and virtue, is a jilt and a fool in every page."

120   *"Let a soft sigh steal out"*: Quoted in Miriam Rossiter Small, *Charlotte Ramsay Lennox: An Eighteenth Century Lady of Letters* (Albany, NY: Archon Books, 1969), 234.

120   *"intolerably provoking to see people"*: Letter from Carter to Miss Talbot, December 1, 1750, in Elizabeth Carter, *A Series of Letters between Mrs. Elizabeth Carter and Miss Catherine Talbot, from 1741 to 1770*, ed. Montagu Pennington (London: Printed for F. C. and J. Rivington, 1809), 367.

120   *"Not Sappho more the yielding soul could move"*: *Gentleman's Magazine*, vol. 19 (June 1749), 278.

120   *"consisted wholly in hopes and expectations"*: Anon., "Mrs. Lenox," *British Magazine and Review* (September 1783), 9.

121 *"I was miserably poor"*: James Boswell, *The Life of Samuel Johnson* (New York: Alfred A. Knopf, 1992), 39.

121 *"magnificent hot apple-pye"*: John Hawkins, *The Life of Samuel Johnson, LL.D.* (London: Printed for J. Buckland et al., 1787), 286.

121 *"the period's icon of empowered feminine genius"*: Elizabeth Eger and Lucy Peltz, *Brilliant Women: 18th-Century Bluestockings* (New Haven, CT: Yale University Press, 2008), 85.

122 *"These ladies that are distinguished for their wit"*: Lennox, *The Life of Harriot Stuart*, 170.

122 *"If Wit into the scale is thrown"*: Charles Churchill, *The Ghost* (London: Printed for the author, and sold by William Flexney, 1762), 23.

124 *"Nothing very remarkable happen'd during this Journey"*: Charlotte Lennox, *The Female Quixote; or, the Adventures of Arabella*, 2nd ed, rev. and corrected (London: Printed for A. Millar, 1752), II.242.

124 *parallels between these two books are obvious*: See also Elaine M. Kauvar, "Jane Austen and *The Female Quixote*," *Studies in the Novel* 2 no. 2, British Neo-Classical Novel (Summer 1970): 211–21.

125 *"we changed it for the 'Female Quixotte'"*: Letter from Jane Austen to Cassandra Austen, January 7–8, 1807, quoted in Le Faye, *Letters*, 120.

125 *"said he was Sensible"*: Austen, *Love and Freindship*, 24.

126 *"make it necessary to write a new Book"*: Letter from Charlotte Lennox to Samuel Richardson, November 22, 1751; quoted in Schürer, *Charlotte Lennox*, 15.

126 *"I am quite charm'd with the lovely Visionary's Absurdity"*: Quoted in Schürer, *Charlotte Lennox Documents*, 12.

127 *"struck me as wanting souls"*: Quoted in Southam, *Jane Austen: The Critical Heritage, Volume 2*, 11.

127 *"true Humour"*: Henry Fielding, "Proceedings at the Court of Censorial Enquiry," *Covent Garden Journal*, no. 14 (April 20, 1752): 55.

127 *"some historical Anecdotes"*: Lennox, *Female Quixote*, II.137.

128 *"you speak like an Orator"*: Lennox, *Female Quixote*, II.145.

128 *Lennox made heavy philosophical topics interesting*: Carlile, *Charlotte Lennox*, 82.

128 *"no Superior in Wit, Elegance, and Ease"*: Lennox, *Female Quixote*, II.229.

128 *the calendar for the current publishing season*: Letter from Charlotte Lennox to Samuel Johnson, February 3, 1752, in Schürer, *Charlotte Lennox*, 24 (see also endnote 2). In this letter, Lennox once again asks Johnson for a favor, that he can persuade Millar to "hurry the printing" to make the current season.

Schürer also cites Raven's "Historical Introduction" in *The English Novel*, I.83; Raven more explicitly says the traditional season was "November to May" in "Historical Introduction," I.26.

129 *"I do very earnestly recommend it"*: Fielding, "Proceedings at the Court of Censorial Enquiry," 54–55.

130 *"A Woman's Wit: Jane Austen's Life and Legacy"*: See Edward Rothstein, "At the Morgan, the Jane Austen Her Family Knew," *New York Times*, November 6, 2009, https://www.nytimes.com/2009/11/07/arts/design/07austen.html.

130 *"TED's youth and education initiative"*: Iseult Gillespie, "The Wicked Wit of Jane Austen," TED-Ed, accessed April 28, 2024, https://ed.ted.com/lessons/the-wicked-wit-of-jane-austen-iseult-gillespie. For the description of TED-Ed, see https://ed.ted.com/about.

130 *"naturally drawn"*: Unsigned review of *Sense and Sensibility* in the *Critical Review*, February 1812; quoted in Southam, *Critical Heritage, Volume I*, 35.

130 *"first major critical notice"*; *"finished up to nature"*: Southam, *Critical Heritage, Volume I*, 58; 67.

130 *"keenest relish for wit"*: Austen, "Biographical Notice," I.xi.

130 *"'Aunt Jane' was the delight of all her nephews and nieces"*: Austen-Leigh, *Memoir*, 2. Austen-Leigh also adds that she is "sympathising, and amusing," but here is in contrast to "clever" and comes from the perspective of a writer who knew her only as a boy: she was excellent at engaging young children's attention. See also Auerbach, *Searching for Jane Austen*, 15, for ways in which Austen-Leigh removed references to wit in Austen's writings.

130 *"subtle humor"*: Catherine J. Hamilton, *Women Writers: Their Works and Ways* (London: Ward, Lock, Bowden, 1892), 206; also quoted in Mazzeno, *Jane Austen*, 25. Austen herself had a complicated relationship with the word "wit," since it wasn't always used positively in her lifetime. In her own works, she often uses it ironically. See Octavia Cox, "'& Not the Least Wit': Jane Austen's Use of 'Wit,'" *Humanities* 11, no. 6 (2022): 132.

130 *"If it is unusual to find an eleven- or twelve-year-old"*: Halperin, *Life of Jane Austen*, 35.

131 *"with all the éclat of a proverb"*: Austen, *Pride and Prejudice*, I.210.

131 *"the tide of feminine sensibility in novels of the time"*: Mudrick, *Jane Austen*, 17; this turning point and Kennedy's work on Jane Austen are discussed in Mazzeno, *Jane Austen*, 69–70.

131 *"wit, irony, light laughter"*: Mudrick, *Jane Austen*, 181.

131   *"Women Aren't Funny"*: The name of the 2014 film on the subject directed by Bonnie McFarlane.

131   *The element of surprise*: See Pierre Destrée, "Aristotle on Why We Laugh at Jokes," *Laughter, Humor, and Comedy in Ancient Philosophy*, eds. Pierre Destrée and Franco V. Trivigno (Oxford, UK: Oxford University Press, 2019), 35–51. The element of the unexpected, for Aristotle, mostly concerns what we might call today witticisms or puns. Octavia Cox quotes Addison in the *Spectator* asserting that two elements "essential to Wit" are "Delight and Surprize" (see Cox, "'& Not the Least Wit': Jane Austen's Use of 'Wit'"). We know from Austen-Leigh that Austen was "well acquainted" with the *Spectator* (Austen-Leigh, *Memoir*, 84).

132   *"sort of coquetry"*: Letter from Elizabeth Carter to Catherine Talbot, August 27, 1757, quoted in Carter, *A Series of Letters*, II.260.

133   *"probably the first study by a feminist critic"*: Norma Clark, *Dr. Johnson's Women* (London: Hambledon and London, 2000), 111.

133   *"mangled and defaced"*: Charlotte Lennox, *Shakespear Illustrated: or the Novels and Histories, on Which the Plays of Shakespear Are Founded, Collected and Translated from the Original Authors. With Critical Remarks* (London: Printed for A. Millar, 1753, 1754), III.261. The third volume was published the next year in 1754, but I couldn't resist using this particular example first brought to my attention in Carlile, *Charlotte Lennox*, 116.

133   *"you are a bird of Prey"*: Quoted in Schürer, *Charlotte Lennox*, 45.

134   *"who seemed to think Shakespear was the Sanctum Sanctorum"*: Quoted in Schürer, *Charlotte Lennox*, 37–38.

134   *"were perhaps stronger Proofs of my Zeal"*: Letter from David Garrick to Charlotte Lennox, August 12, 1753; Letter 17 in Schürer, *Charlotte Lennox*, 47. Schürer discusses Garrick's more public criticism in 49f.8.

135   *"an anonymous critick"*: Carlile, *Charlotte Lennox*, 127.

136   *He quoted Lennox in the* Dictionary *more than a dozen times*: Carlile, *Charlotte Lennox*, 136. See also sjdictionarysources.com.

136   *"Persons who possess the true talent of raillery"*; *"Slight satire; satirical merriment"*: Samuel Johnson, *A Dictionary of the English Language* [. . .] (London: Printed by W. Strahan [. . .], 1755), 26C[1v]; and 21C[1v].

137   *By 1820 it had been printed nineteen times*: See Carlile's appendix, "Publications, Editions, and Reprints," in *Charlotte Lennox*, 438–39 (cross-checked against WorldCat, dealer catalogs, and online antiquarian bookseller marketplaces).

137   *"not the least Wit"*: Quoted in Auerbach, *Searching for Jane Austen*, 15.

137   *"Wit is the most dangerous talent you can possess"*: John Gregory, *A Father's Legacy to His Daughters* (London: Printed to W. Strahan et al., 1774), 30; partially quoted in Auerbach, *Searching for Jane Austen*, 44.

137   *"well-timed sprightliness"*: March 1813 review in the *Critical Review*, quoted in Southam, *Jane Austen: The Critical Heritage, Volume I*, 46.

138   *"wit, like wine, intoxicates the brain"*: George Lyttelton, "Advice to a Lady," excerpted in Robert Dodsley, *A Collection of Poems in Six Volumes, by Several Hands* (London: Printed by J. Hughs, for R. and J. Dodsley, 1758), II.42.

138   *"Because of their natural weakness"*: Quoted in Carlile, *Charlotte Lennox*, 174.

138   *condemned for their personal lives by their critics*: This arc is traced in detail by Jane Spencer, *Rise of the Woman Novelist: From Aphra Behn to Jane Austen* (Oxford, UK: Basil Blackwell, 1986, reprinted 1989).

138   "Punk *and* Poetess *agree so pat*": This verse is quoted in Spencer, *Rise of the Woman Novelist*, 28. Later, she shows how "disparaging references to Manley's life have often been substituted for criticism of her work" (Spencer, *Rise of the Woman Novelist*, 56).

139   *understood the labor and expertise involved*: In fact, Lennox said she found translation "a good deal easier then [*sic*] Composition," Letter from Charlotte Lennox to Samuel Johnson, February 3, 1752, quoted in Schürer, *Charlotte Lennox*, 23.

139   *"an instant classic"*: Carlile, *Charlotte Lennox*, 149.

139   *a form of royal patronage*: This kind of patronage from the Crown was significantly less common in the eighteenth century than it had been in previous centuries, and speaks to the merit that the Duke of Newcastle saw in Lennox's work. See Paul J. Korshin, "Types of Eighteenth-Century Literary Patronage," *Eighteenth-Century Studies* 7, no. 4 (Summer 1974): 453–73, for a clear overview. Lennox also later benefited from a different kind of patronage from this family when the Duchess of Newcastle arranged for Lennox and her children to live, with royal approval, at Somerset House for a number of years. Lennox not only dedicated works to both the Duke and Duchess of Newcastle, but gave her firstborn daughter the middle name "Holles," referencing their last name, Pelham-Holles. See Carlile, *Charlotte Lennox*, 233.

139   *a royal pension of £300*: Boswell, *Life of Johnson*, 235.

139   *"the duke's promise not immediately taking effect"*: Anonymous, "Mrs. Lenox," in the *British Magazine and Review*, 9–10.

140   *Lennox laid the blame for the disruption on another playwright*: See Small, *Charlotte*

Ramsay Lennox, 38; and Ellen Donkin, *Getting into the Act: Women Playwrights in London, 1776–1829* (London: Routledge, 1995), 106. Donkin argues that this incident with Lennox, as well as another with Burney in 1779, "suggest that Cumberland's sense of world order did not include tolerating women either as colleagues or as competitors" (10).

140 *He feared that Lennox would encourage more women writers*: See above, as well as Carlile, *Charlotte Lennox*, 235.

140 *"and hiss it, because she had attacked Shakespeare"*: Boswell, *Life of Samuel Johnson* (1992 edition), 944.

142 *weighing the possibility that Johnson wrote a chapter*: One of the most influential examples was Allen Hazen, *Samuel Johnson's Prefaces & Dedications* (New Haven, CT: Yale University Press, 1937), considered a foundational reference work for Johnsonians; see page 95 for his statement that the chapter was "almost certainly by Johnson." Bad attributions based upon "style" have long been a known problem in Johnson studies, since he was known to write so much anonymously. John L. Abbott includes a section in his article calling attention to the problem of Hazen's use of "intuition" in making Johnsonian attributions: John L. Abbott, "Defining the Johnsonian Canon: Authority, Intuition, and the Uses of Evidence," in *Modern Language Studies* 18, no. 1 (Winter 1988): 89–98.

143 *article by O. M. Brack Jr. and Susan Carlile*: Letter from Charlotte Lennox to Samuel Johnson, March 12, 1752; Letter 10 in Schürer, *Charlotte Lennox*, 29. Following in the foosteps of Duncan Isles, Robert Hay Carnie, and others (as mentioned in their article), see O. M. Brack Jr. and Susan Carlile, "Samuel Johnson's Contributions to Charlotte Lennox's 'The Female Quixote,'" *Yale University Library Gazette* 77, no. 3/4 (April 2003): 166–73.

145 *"as a person, she is perhaps most human"*: Hugh Amory, "Lennox [née Ramsay], (Barbara) Charlotte," *Oxford Dictionary of National Biography* (Oxford, UK: Oxford University Press, 2004), https://doi.org/10.1093/ref:odnb/16454. This entry ends: "Not that the kitchen was her proper sphere, but, a true Quixote, she was at her best humorously braving her shabby reputation for traditional womanly skills, instead of helplessly ranting against such spiteful slander."

145 *consult many standard books for rare book cataloging*: See Rebecca Romney, "On Feminist Practice in the Rare Books and Manuscripts Trade: Buying, Cataloguing, and Selling," *Criticism* 64, no. 3 (2022): 413–31.

145 *"The ESTC notes that the translator"; "Samuel Johnson wrote the dedication"*: Descrip-

tions found on AbeBooks and viaLibri, June 4, 2022, screenshots of each recorded.

146 Rasselas, *contains a similar sentiment*: Small, *Charlotte Ramsay Lennox*, 81.

146 *"the most important single fact in Mrs. Lennox's literary life"*: Small, *Charlotte Ramsay Lennox*, 1.

147 *analyzed in detail how she influenced Johnson*: Carlile, *Charlotte Lennox*, 82–85.

147 *But before 1970, there had been no new edition of* The Female Quixote: Carlile, *Charlotte Lennox*, 17.

CHAPTER FIVE:
HANNAH MORE (1745-1833)

149 *"Of course I shall be delighted when I read it"*: Letter from Jane Austen to Cassandra Austen, January 24, 1809, quoted in Le Faye, *Letters*, 177.

149 *"nourish a vain and visionary indolence"*: More, *Strictures*, 103.

149 *pronounced "see-libs"*: Mary Anne Phemister gives this pronunciation, noting Anne Stott's connection of the name to the word "celibate." Mary Anne Phemister, *Hannah More: The Artist as Reformer* (Sisters, OR: Deep River Books, 2014), 105; Anne Stott, *Hannah More: The First Victorian* (Oxford, UK: Oxford University Press, 2003), 274.

150 *the work was a phenomenon in More's (and Austen's) time*: Brian Corman, *Women Novelists before Jane Austen: The Critics and Their Canons* (Toronto: University of Toronto Press, 2008), 24; Mary Alden Hopkins, *Hannah More and Her Circle* (New York: Longmans, Green, 1947), 224.

150 *Some modern critics even argue that its massive popularity*: See Samuel Pickering Jr., "Hannah More's *Coelebs in Search of a Wife* and the Respectability of the Novel in the Nineteenth Century," in *Neuphilologische Mitteilungen* 78, no. 1 (1977): 78–85.

150 *"I had hoped to see you respectable and good"*: Jane Austen, "Catharine, or the Bower," *Volume the Third* (Oxford, UK: Clarendon Press, 1951), 111. Also quoted in Stott, *Hannah More*, 278.

151 *"woman's highest honour"*: Coelebs is actually quoting Milton here, defending Milton's praise of Eve as a support to Adam. Hannah More, *Coelebs in Search of a Wife. Comprehending Observations on Domestic Habit and Manners, Religion and Morals* (London: Printed for T. Cadell and W. Davies, 1808), 4.

153   *"Mr. More, who was remarked for his strong dislike of female pedantry"*: William Roberts, *Memoirs of the Life and Correspondence of Mrs. Hannah More*, 3rd ed. (London: R. B. Seeley and W. Burnside, 1835), I.11, 12.

153   *"she might one day be rich enough"*: Roberts, *Memoirs*, I.14.

154   *"the robbery he had committed upon her time"*: All quotes in this paragraph are from Roberts, *Memoirs*, I.31–33.

154   *"to devote herself to her literary pursuits"*: Roberts, *Memoirs*, I.33.

155   *Johnson quoted one of More's own poems to her*: Roberts, *Memoirs*, I.48; a commonly told story (e.g., Stott, *Hannah More*, 28), sourced from Roberts.

155   *"not only the finest genius, but the finest lady"*: Roberts, *Memoirs*, I.53.

155   *"don't mind dress! Come in your blue stockings!"*: Burney ("Madame D'Arblay"), *Memoirs of Doctor Burney*, II.263. See also Eger and Peltz, *Brilliant Women*, 16.

156   *"you are doing so much honour to your sex"*: Roberts, *Memoirs*, I.58.

157   *"the pride of your friends and the humiliation of your enemies"*: Roberts, *Memoirs*, I.124.

157   *"the only two monsters in the creation"*: All quotes in this paragraph are from Roberts, *Memoirs*, I.72; I.77; I.127.

157   *"Again I am annoyed by the foolish absurdity"*: Roberts, *Memoirs*, I.65.

158   *"has been reading your Essays"*: Roberts, *Memoirs*, I.190–91.

160   *"We never see a human face but each other's"*: Roberts, *Memoirs*, I.167.

160   *"a Milker of Cows"*: Stott, *Hannah More*, 72.

161   *"a roster of the Bas Bleu"*: Hopkins, *Hannah More*, 123.

161   *"had an Estate of near Six pounds a year"*: Letter from Hannah More to Elizabeth Montagu, August 27, 1784, quoted in Stott, *Hannah More*, 71–72.

161   *"to cloathe her family and furnish her House"*: Letter from Hannah More to Elizabeth Montagu, June 1785, quoted in Stott, *Hannah More*, 74.

161   *"I hear she [Yearsley] wears very fine Gauze Bonnets"*: Letter from Hannah More to Elizabeth Montagu, July 21, 1785, digitized at the Huntington Library, https://hdl.huntington.org/digital/collection/p16003coll18/id/44228/rec/1.

162   *"For mine's a stubborn and a savage will"*: Ann Yearsley, *Poems, on Several Occasions* (London: Printed for T. Cadell, 1785), 72.

162   *"I am utterly against taking her out of her station"*: Letter from Hannah More to Elizabeth Montagu, September 27, 1784, quoted in Stott, *Hannah More*, 72.

162   *establishing him in a profession*: Hopkins, *Hannah More*, 125.

163   *finally succeeding in 1807*: The outlawing of slavery itself across the British Empire occurred years later, just before Wilberforce's death in 1833.

163   *used her talents to sway public opinion*: Patricia Demers, *The World of Hannah More* (Lexington: University Press of Kentucky, 1996), 58.

163   *"raves of mercy, while she deals out death"*: Hannah More, *Slavery: A Poem* (London: Printed for T. Cadell, 1788), 3.

163   *"something must be done for Cheddar"*: Martha More, *Mendip Annals: Or, a Narrative of the Charitable Labours of Hannah and Martha More in Their Neighbourhood; being the Journal of Martha More*, ed. Arthur Roberts (London: James Nisbet, 1859), 13.

164   *"that my plan for instructing the poor is very limited"*: More, *Mendip Annals*, 6.

164   *Some mothers even argued*: Hopkins, *Hannah More*, 165.

164   *The Cheddar School was the first of many*: See M. J. Crossley Evans, *Hannah More* (Bristol, UK: Bristol Branch of the Historical Association, 1999), 11.

165   *"though the leaders designed the instruction"*: Hopkins, *Hannah More*, 161.

166   *"Good Hannah More is killing herself"*: Quoted in Stott, *Hannah More*, 134.

166   *More made a staggering £2,000*: Stott, *Hannah More*, 281.

167   *"I'm not Hannah More!"*: Hopkins, *Hannah More*, 116.

167   *"the Reverend Sir Archibald MacSarcasm"*: Demers, *World of Hannah More*, 18–19.

167   *"one of the most detestable writers that ever held a pen"*: Quoted in Demers, *World of Hannah More*, 21, from two separate Birrell essays: "Hannah More" in the 1894 *Men, Women, and Books* and "Hannah More Once More" in the 1905 *In the Name of the Bodleian and Other Essays*.

170   *"As the morals of my own sex are the great object"*: More, *Mendip Annals*, 7.

170   *"humble the sinner and exalt the Saviour"*: Hannah More, *An Estimate of the Religion of the Fashionable World: By One of the Laity* (London: Printed for T. Cadell, 1791), 228.

170   *"poison for the soul"*: Hannah More, *The Sunday School* (Dublin: Sold by William Watson, Printer to the Cheap repository for religious and moral tracts: and by the booksellers, chapmen and hawkers in town and country, [ca. 1800]), 19.

170   *"she used to send her children to the shop on Sundays"*: More, *The Sunday School*, 6.

173   *"nourish a vain and visionary indolence"*: More, *Strictures*, 103.

175   *"It is a singular injustice"*: More, *Strictures*, iii.

175   *"that the minds of women are enfeebled"*: Mary Wollstonecraft, *A Vindication of the Rights of Woman* (London: J. Johnson, 1792), 2.

175   *"time and industry"*: More, *Strictures*, 100.

176   *"are still reckoned a frivolous sex"*: Wollstonecraft, *Vindication*, 8.

176 *"the women who are amused by the reveries"*: Wollstonecraft, *Vindication*, 425.

176 *"there is something fantastic and absurd in the very title"*: Letter from Hannah More to Horace Walpole, August 18, 1792, quoted in Eger and Peltz, *Brilliant Women*, 117; see also Roberts, *Memoirs*, II.372.

176 *But the fact that they could agree on this subject*: Upon reading Spencer's *Rise of the Woman Novelist*, 168, I was vindicated to see that she had noted the resemblance between More and Wollstonecraft, too.

177 *"corruption"*: More, *Strictures*, 105.

177 *"embodies the lesson in Hannah More's* Strictures*"*: Honan, *Jane Austen*, 337–38.

177 *"subtle, dark, and difficult book"*: Jane Nardin, "Jane Austen, Hannah More, and the Novel of Education," *Persuasions: Journal of the Jane Austen Society of North America* 20 (1998): 20.

177 *"I do not like the Evangelicals"*: Letter from Jane Austen to Cassandra Austen, January 24, 1809, quoted in Le Faye, *Letters*, 177.

178 *"I am by no means convinced"*: Letter from Jane Austen to Fanny Knight, November 18–20, 1814, in Le Faye, *Letters*, 292.

CHAPTER SIX:
CHARLOTTE SMITH (1749-1806)

179 *"'You have read Mrs Smith's Novels'"*: Austen, "Catharine, or the Bower," *Volume the Third*, 44.

179 *"I imagine I shall die in a prison"*: Letter from Charlotte Smith to William Hayley, March 26, 1797, quoted in Judith Phillips Stanton, *The Collected Letters of Charlotte Smith* (Bloomington: Indiana University Press, 2003), 262.

180 *"so disagreeable & indeed dreadful"*: Letter from Charlotte Smith to Thomas Cadell Jr. and William Davies, March 9, 1797, quoted in Stanton, *Collected Letters*, 256. Stanton also provides excellent additional context for each of these letters in the endnotes.

180 *"She had read more than any one in the school"*: Catherine Dorset, "Charlotte Smith," in Walter Scott, *Miscellaneous Prose Works, Vol. IV: Biographical Memoirs, Vol. II* (Edinburgh: Robert Cadell, 1834), 22.

181 *"a considerable fortune"*: Mary Hays, "Mrs. Charlotte Smith," in *British Public Characters, 1800–1801*, vol. 3 (London: Printed for R. Phillips, 1801), 46.

181 *"thought it a prodigious stroke of domestic policy"*: Letter from Charlotte Smith to

the Earl of Egremont, February 4, 1803, quoted in Stanton, *Collected Letters*, 522.

181 *he beat her*: Letter from Charlotte Smith to the Earl of Egremont, January 25, 1804, quoted in Stanton, *Collected Letters*, 607: "I could have brought another person, a relation of mine, who would have taken the most solemn oath that she has seen him strike & kick me &, once at table, throw a quartern loaf at my head without provocation at all but the phrenzy, for so it seemed at the moment." Loraine Fletcher summarizes: Benjamin's "violence to herself [Charlotte] would intensify, and this was the reason she always gave for the separation." *Charlotte Smith: A Critical Biography* (New York: Palgrave, 2001), 77.

181 *"blowing up the walls of the house"*: Letter from Charlotte Smith to an unnamed recipient, circa July 1784, quoted in Stanton, *Collected Letters*, 5.

182 *"the chicanery of law"*: Hays, "Mrs. Charlotte Smith," 50.

182 *"for such things there was no sale"*: Hays, "Mrs. Charlotte Smith," 51.

182 *"their melody, feeling, and pathos touch the heart"*: Hays, "Mrs. Charlotte Smith," 52.

183 *including nine children*: Hays says she had seven children with her on the voyage, with the elder boys being sent ahead (59); Fletcher puts the count with her at nine (*Charlotte Smith*, 5). Dorset ("Charlotte Smith," 26) also says this was the winter of 1783, but I again defer to Fletcher's attribution of 1784. Fletcher's account of this period is fantastic and well worth reading; she considers it a central turning point in Smith's life.

183 *"so many little beings clinging about me"*: Letter from Charlotte Smith to an unnamed friend, spring 1785, quoted in Hays, "Mrs. Charlotte Smith," 56; and Stanton, *Collected Letters*, 6.

183 *"to recover a fortune through breeding them"*: Fletcher, *Charlotte Smith*, 7–8.

183 *"forebodings that she should not survive"*: Dorset, "Charlotte Smith," 41.

184 *"purchase her freedom from a vile husband"*: "I was glad to find that you were pleased with the 'Orphan of the Castle.' I heartily wish it was fashionable enough to be of any essential benefit to the author, who has been obliged to purchase her freedom from a vile husband." Letter from Elizabeth Carter to Elizabeth Montagu on reading *Emmeline*, June 30, 1788, quoted in Elizabeth Carter, *A Series of Letters from Mrs. Elizabeth Carter to Mrs. Montagu, between the Years 1755 to 1800*, ed. Montagu Pennington (London: Printed for F. C. and J. Rivington, 1817), III.295.

184 *"the very being or legal existence of the woman"*: William Blackstone, *Commentaries on the Laws of England* (Oxford, UK: Clarendon Press, 1765), I.430. See Nicola

Jane Phillips, *Women in Business, 1700–1850* (Woodbridge, UK: Boydell Press, 2006), 25, for a modern commentary on this passage as relates to a professional like Charlotte Smith.

185   *"my admirable talents"*: Letter to an unnamed recipient [underline *sic*], December 8, 1791, quoted in Stanton, *Collected Letters*, 40. See also Fletcher, *Charlotte Smith*, 87–88: payment on her own funds was "completely at [the Trustee's] discretion."

185   *"convince him I had no malice against him"*: Letter from Charlotte Smith to Thomas Cadell Sr., January 14, 1788, quoted in Stanton, *Collected Letters*, 13.

186   *"Alas! No—Mr Smith himself is come from Scotland to oppose it"*: Letter from Charlotte Smith to Joseph Cooper Walker, June 23, 1799, quoted in Stanton, *Collected Letters*, 327–28.

186   *"so capricious and often so cruel"*: Letter from Charlotte Smith to Joseph Cooper Walker, October 6, 1793, quoted in Stanton, *Collected Letters*, 79.

187   *"could only regret the measure had not been adopted years before"*: Dorset, "Charlotte Smith," 48.

187   *"to be compelled to live only to write"*: Letter from Charlotte Smith to Dr. Thomas Shirley, August 22, 1789, quoted in Stanton, *Collected Letters*, 23.

187   *"rendered [it] ineffectual"*: Hays, "Mrs. Charlotte Smith," 48.

187   *"the magic sum necessary"*: Fletcher, *Charlotte Smith*, 58.

187   *"decades of delay and litigation"*: Stanton, *Collected Letters*, xxix.

188   *"I shall probably never see him again"*: Letter from Charlotte Smith to Joseph Cooper Walker, April 30, 1794, quoted in Stanton, *Collected Letters*, 113.

188   *Dickens was often paid by the installment*: Robert L. Patten, *Charles Dickens and "Boz": The Birth of the Industrial-Age Author* (Cambridge, UK: Cambridge University Press, 2012), 244.

189   *imitates Smith's style*: Jacqueline M. Labbe, *Writing Romanticism: Charlotte Smith and William Wordsworth, 1784–1807* (New York: Palgrave Macmillan, 2011), 2.

189   *"turning over the leaves of Charlotte Smith's sonnets"*: See Jacqueline M. Labbe, "Introduction," in *The Works of Charlotte Smith*, pt. III, vol. 14 (London: Pickering & Chatto, 2007), 164, also referencing *Journals of Dorothy Wordsworth*, edited by Mary Moorman.

189   *"a lady to whom English verse is under greater obligations"*: Quoted in Alexander B. Grosart, ed., *The Prose Works of William Wordsworth* (London: Edward Moxon, 1876), III.151. In his 1993 edition of her poetry, editor Stuart Curran also notes the major Wordsworth references and argues that Smith "was the first poet in

England whom in retrospect we would call Romantic." Stuart Curran, ed., *The Poems of Charlotte Smith* (Oxford, UK: Oxford University Press, 1993), xix.

189 *"they who first made the Sonnet popular"*: Quoted in Paul M. Zall, *Coleridge's "Sonnets from Various Authors"* (Glendale, CA: La Siesta Press, 1968), 13. Bethan Roberts also quotes this and traces the rise of the sonnet in the eighteenth century in her book *Charlotte Smith and the Sonnet: Form, Place, and Tradition in the Late Eighteenth Century* (Liverpool, UK: Liverpool University Press, 2019).

189 *"followed directly Charlotte Smith's lead"*: Daniel Robinson, "Work without Hope': Anxiety and Embarrassment in Coleridge's Sonnets," *Studies in Romanticism* 39, no. 1 (Spring 2000): 82.

189 *"Elegiac Sonnet to a Mopstick"*: See Paula R. Feldman and Daniel Robinson, *A Century of Sonnets: The Romantic-Era Revival, 1750–1850* (Oxford, UK: Oxford University Press, 1999), 11–13. The "Elegiac Sonnet to a Mopstick" is composed by one of the heroines in William Beckford's satirical novel *Azemia*; see also Robinson, "Work without Hope," 83.

189 *"sonnet has been revived by Charlotte Smith"*: *Critical Review* 34 (January 1802): 393; also partially quoted in Paula R. Backscheider, *Eighteenth-Century Women Poets and Their Poetry: Inventing Agency, Inventing Genre* (Baltimore: Johns Hopkins University Press, 2005), 316. Thanks to the work of many modern critics like Stuart Curran, Jacqueline Labbe, and Paula Backscheider, Smith's poetry is now viewed as a critical link from Milton and Gray to Coleridge, Wordsworth, Byron, and Keats.

191 *focused largely on her poetry*: As Labbe notes, Smith's first reappraisal began with the wave of feminist recovery (*Writing Romanticism*, 3). Labbe describes the academic evolution from gender analysis to poetics in her own books and particularly notes the influence of Curran on refocusing critical attention on Smith as a major Romantic poet: "Anyone who works on Charlotte Smith owes much to Stuart Curran." Jacqueline M. Labbe, *Charlotte Smith: Romanticism, Poetry and the Culture of Gender* (Manchester, UK: Manchester University Press, 2003), ix.

191 *"the culture we call Romanticism"*: Labbe, *Writing Romanticism*, 2.

193 *bluebells meant kindness*: "The Language of Flowers," *Smithsonian Gardens*, accessed May 12, 2024, https://gardens.si.edu/wp-content/uploads/2020/05/SIGardens_HistBloom_Language_of_Flowers.pdf.

195 *The typical range for a book of sonnets*: See letter from Charlotte Smith to Thomas Cadell Sr., June 3, 1787, quoted in Stanton, *Collected Letters*, 11; that the price

proposed there was accepted can be seen in William Bent, *The London Catalogue of Books* [. . .] (London: Printed for W. Bent, 1791), 63. Compare to Brydges's Sonnets in the same catalog at 2s. 6d. and Knight's at 3s.

196 *proposals for subscription editions survive*: These proposals are collected in Schürer, *Charlotte Lennox*, as numbers 14, 54, and 78. Schürer, xli, also notes that she had at least two further subscription plans, one for *Female Quixote* in 1773 and one for "an opera, probably *Philander*" in the 1790s.

196 *cost more than a week's wages*: These numbers should be taken with the usual caveats of the difficulty of translating monetary means vs. costs across centuries and come from Robert D. Hume, "The Value of Money in Eighteenth-Century England: Incomes, Prices, Buying Power—and Some Problems in Cultural Economics," *Huntington Library Quarterly* 77, no. 4 (Winter 2014): 385, with further extrapolation from his note that "An item costing 1s. would represent a whole day's wages." In his discussion of these prices, Hume also notes the critical fact that "most of the culture we now study is inarguably elite: it was mostly consumed by the top 1 percent or 0.5 percent of the English population" (Hume, 373).

197 *"marked the high point of Smith's sonnet success"*: Roberts, *Charlotte Smith and the Sonnet*, 100.

197 *"price Miss Burney obtain'd"*: Letter from Charlotte Smith to George Robinson, June 18, 1789, quoted in Stanton, *Collected Letters*, 20.

197 *"it is my poverty and not my will"*: Letter from Charlotte Smith to Thomas Cadell, August 22, 1790, quoted in Stanton, *Collected Letters*, 27.

197 *"I am quite delighted with them"*: Austen, "Catharine, or the Bower," *Volume the Third*, 44.

197 *"pivotal in Austen's development as a writer"*: Jacqueline M. Labbe, *Reading Jane Austen after Reading Charlotte Smith* (London: Palgrave Macmillan, 2020), 1.

197 *Academics and casual readers alike have noticed the influence of* Emmeline: Labbe, *Reading Jane Austen after Reading Charlotte Smith*, 25.

198 *"Emmeline of Delamere"*: Austen, *Love and Freindship*, 93.

198 *"temper growing more irritable"*: Charlotte Smith, *Emmeline, the Orphan of the Castle* (London: Printed for T. Cadell, 1788), II.148.

198 *a scene from Smith's life*: Smith's contemporaries also knew the portrait of the couple was autobiographical, as Fletcher recounts, *Charlotte Smith*, 100–101.

199 *"Others have, in their husbands, protectors and friends"*: Smith, *Emmeline*, III.239; IV.242.

199 *"a virtuous heroine must marry the first person"*: Fletcher, *Charlotte Smith*, 98.

200 *"I was right in submitting to her"*: All Austen quotes in this paragraph are from Austen, *Persuasion*, III.59; IV.272; and IV.295.

200 *"reads* Emmeline *and revisits it"*: Labbe, *Reading Jane Austen*, 24.

200 *"first novelistic-canon"*: Johnson, "'Let Me Make the Novels of a Country,'" 166.

201 *"if to PRIDE and PREJUDICE you owe your miseries"*: Burney, *Cecilia*, V.380.

201 *"these fits of half repentance, originating in pride and prejudice"*: Charlotte Smith, *The Old Manor House* (London: Pandora Press, 1987), 258, 280.

202 *they also don't suffer for their evil deeds*: A similarly unethical family of ambition in Maria Edgeworth's novel *Patronage* (1814) eventually comes to ruin, which consequence fits with Edgeworth's own moral philosophy, quite different from Smith's realism.

202 *"most overtly feminist novel"*: Fletcher, *Charlotte Smith*, 150; the detail that Benjamin handled the contract also comes from Fletcher, 152. Charlotte Smith's sister is one of those who agreed with the condemnation of *Desmond*: "not only on account of its politics, but its immoral tendency." Dorset, "Charlotte Smith," 39.

203 *"The man may range from his unhappy wife"*: Quoted in Norma Clarke, *The Rise and Fall of the Woman of Letters* (London: Pimlico, 2004), 127.

203 *"to shew you that I cannot afford to lose the smallest profit"*: Letter from Charlotte Smith to Thomas Cadell Sr., April 1792, quoted in Stanton, *Collected Letters*, 45.

204 *"women it is said have no business in politics"*: All Smith quotes in this paragraph are from Charlotte Smith, *Desmond: A Novel* (London: Printed for G. G. J. and J. Robinson, 1792), I.iii–iv.

205 *"abused, poor, and often pregnant"*: Stanton, *Collected Letters*, xxv.

205 *"Of course I cannot see her want"*: Letter from Charlotte Smith to Sarah Rose, February 14, 1805, quoted in Stanton, *Collected Letters*, 680.

205 *"Even the most enthusiastic advocates of domesticity"*: Deborah Kaplan, *Jane Austen among Women* (Baltimore: Johns Hopkins University Press, 1992), 22.

205 *"'allow me to ask, what you mean by happily married?'"*: Maria Edgeworth, *Patronage* (London: Pandora Press, 1986), 149.

205 *"never to marry at all"*: Smith, *Emmeline*, IV.116–17.

208 *"as her resources grew so did her appetite"*: See Bernard Quaritch, Ltd., "The English & Anglo-French Novel 1740–1840: A catalogue, including books from

the library of Mary Hill, Marchioness of Downshire," Catalogue 1442 (London: Bernard Quaritch, 2020). With special thanks to Donovan Rees for his cataloging.

209 *"Instead therefore of giving way to tears and exclamations"*: Smith, *Emmeline*, I.13.

CHAPTER SEVEN:
ELIZABETH INCHBALD (1753-1821)

210 *"'Lovers Vows!'"*: Jane Austen, *Mansfield Park: A Novel* (London: Printed for T. Egerton, 1814), I.275.

210 *"By the time you receive this"*: James Boaden, *Memoirs of Mrs. Inchbald* (London: Richard Bentley, 1833), I.7; I.18. The majority of information we have today (including most of that recounted here) about Inchbald's early life comes from Boaden's book.

210 *"one of the most important [English] writers"*; *"the cleverest self-educated woman"*: See Annibel Jenkins, *I'll Tell You What: The Life of Elizabeth Inchbald* (Lexington: University Press of Kentucky, 2003), 3; and the introductory advertisement to Boaden, *Memoirs*, I.iii.

211 *"In spite of your eloquent pen"*: Boaden, *Memoirs*, I.15.

212 *"She wrote out all the words"*: Boaden, *Memoirs*, I.7.

213 *"frightening you to death"*: Boaden, *Memoirs*, I.27.

213 *"terrified and vexed beyond measure"*: Boaden, *Memoirs*, I.29.

214 *"her husband might consider that her rising talent"*: Boaden, *Memoirs*, I.31.

214 *"Mr. Inchbald came home we had High Words"*: Ben P. Robertson, ed., *The Diaries of Elizabeth Inchbald* (London: Pickering and Chatto, 2007), I.9.

214 *"while my Hair was dressing"*: Robertson, *Diaries of Elizabeth Inchbald*, I.8.

215 *"became a love match"*: Jenkins, *I'll Tell You What*, 11.

215 *apparently of a heart attack*: Jenkins, *I'll Tell You What*, 49.

216 *"I cannot depend on any other person's attention"*: Quoted in Boaden, *Memoirs*, I.57.

216 *Every play had to be reviewed*: Roger Manvell, *Elizabeth Inchbald: England's Principal Woman Dramatist and Independent Woman of Letters in 18th Century London, a Biographical Study* (Lanham, MD: University Press of America, 1987), 9.

216 *With an "excessively interesting" countenance*: Boaden, *Memoirs*, I.175–76. The detail about her eyelashes being the color of sand comes from what Littlewood

calls an "autoportrait," a description of herself Inchbald wrote down in her thirties. S. R. Littlewood, *Elizabeth Inchbald and Her Circle* (London: Daniel O'Connor, 1921), 62.

217 *"those parts that no person cared"*: Mary Wells, *Memoirs of Mrs. Sumbel Late Wells* (London: C. Chapple, 1811), II.199.

217 *"all her evenings in the theatre"*: Boaden, *Memoirs*, I.115.

217 *"went through all my Farce"*: Robertson, *Diaries of Elizabeth Inchbald*, I.108; I.161; I.196.

217 *gave Inchbald a significant advantage*: See Donkin, *Getting into the Act*, 126, who makes this point in an extended section about Inchbald.

217 *The theater managers were inundated with submissions*: Jenkins, *I'll Tell You What*, 149–50.

218 *"when she did not happen to be invited there"*: Littlewood, *Elizabeth Inchbald and Her Circle*, 60.

218 *"with a little care, I think it can't fail"*: Quoted in Boaden, *Memoirs*, I.185.

218 *the famous courtesan Ann Elliot*: Olive Baldwin and Thelma Wilson, "Elliot, Ann," *Oxford Dictionary of National Biography*, https://doi.org/10.1093/ref:odnb/64332.

219 *"great agitation"*: Wells, *Memoirs*, II:201; also quoted in Jenkins, *I'll Tell You What*, 157.

219 *Inchbald laughed aloud at her fumble*: Boaden, *Memoirs*, I.189–90.

219 *"No, Sir, it is none of the circumstances"*: Wells, *Memoirs*, II:201–2.

220 *"But hold—I say too much—I quite forgot—"*: Colman himself gave the title its name, referring to a very funny (in this reader's opinion) scene describing the moment the wife's infidelity is discovered.

220 *buying the "Navy Fives" stock*: Fergus, "The Professional Woman Writer," 28.

221 *"plainly shews that if a comet is ordained"*: Wells, *Memoirs*, II.200.

221 *requested a special performance*: Jenkins, *I'll Tell You What*, 184.

221 *reached that magic number of £200 a year*: Littlewood, *Elizabeth Inchbald and Her Circle*, 71.

222 *"She had the happiness now of having her door eternally besieged"*: Boaden, *Memoirs*, I.231.

222 *"was productive of more labour"*: Boaden, *Memoirs*, I.264.

222 *Radcliffe's breakout gothic*: Robert D. Hume, citing the £200 number alongside Radcliffe's earnings, observes of their exceptional success that "Radcliffe and Inchbald were probably about as representative as Stephen King and

J. K. Rowling," that is, paid exponentially higher than most other authors. Hume, "The Value of Money in Eighteenth-Century England," 397.

223 *plays an important role in the critical interpretation*: See Margaret Doody, *Jane Austen's Names: Riddles, Persons, Places* (Chicago: University of Chicago Press, 2015), 326–27. Such readings of *Mansfield Park* gained steam in the early nineties: see Moira Ferguson, "Mansfield Park: Slavery, Colonialism, and Gender," *Oxford Literary Review* 13, no. 1/2, Neocolonialism (1991): 118–39; and Edward Said, *Culture and Imperialism* (London: Chatto & Windus, 1993). For the significance of the book's title, see Danielle Christmas, "Lord Mansfield and the Slave Ship *Zong*," *Persuasions* 41, no. 2 (Summer 2021).

223 *"[H]e vowed in the deep torments of his revenge"*: Elizabeth Inchbald, *A Simple Story*, ed. J. M. S. Tompkins, intro. by Jane Spencer (Oxford, UK: Oxford University Press, 1988), 197.

223 *"A vein of elegant simplicity"*: Quoted in Raven and Forster, *The English Novel*, I.536.

224 *including King George III and his daughters*: Jenkins, *I'll Tell You What*, 301.

224 *friends with both Charlotte Smith and Ann Radcliffe*: Radcliffe and Inchbald met at a dinner hosted by Robinson; see Boaden, *Memoirs*, I.342. For a summary of the evidence of the friendship between Inchbald and Smith, see Amy Garnai, *Revolutionary Imaginings in the 1790s: Charlotte Smith, Mary Robinson, Elizabeth Inchbald* (New York: Palgrave Macmillan, 2009), 10.

224 *"secret charm, that gives a grace to the whole"*: The *Monthly Review*, quoted in Raven and Forster, *The English Novel*, I.536; see also Jane Spencer's introduction to the 1988 edition of *A Simple Story*, vii, xvi–xvii.

224 *"I am glad I have never met with a Dorriforth"*: Letter from Maria Edgeworth to Elizabeth Inchbald, January 14, 1810, quoted in Boaden, *Memoirs*, II.151–52. See also Hare, *Maria Edgeworth*, I.178.

224 *"one of the finest novels of any period"*: Terry Castle, *Masquerade and Civilization: The Carnivalesque in Eighteenth-Century English Culture* (Stanford: Stanford University Press, 1986), 290–91.

225 *copied out pieces by both these composers*: Honan, *Jane Austen*, 99.

226 *"'Deceit,' cried Miss Milner"*: Inchbald, *A Simple Story* (1988 edition), 43.

226 *"Miss Milner with apparent satisfaction"*; *"with the most perfect unconcern"*: Inchbald, *A Simple Story* (1988 edition), 45; 54.

227 *"Inchbald's concise, ironic style anticipates Austen"*: Jane Spencer, introduction to Inchbald, *A Simple Story* (1988 edition), vii. It's worth noting that Spencer's

important *The Rise of the Woman Novelist*, was published two years before this introduction.

227 *Garrick famously played a* King Lear *with a happy ending*: Garrick used Nahum Tate's version as a base, but with his own adaptations as well. Harry William Pedicord and Frederick Louis Bergmann, *The Plays of David Garrick, Vol. 3: Garrick's Adaptations of Shakespeare, 1744–1756* (Carbondale: Southern Illinois University Press, 1980), 444; Kalman A. Burnim, *David Garrick, Director* (Pittsburgh: University of Pittsburgh Press, 1961), 144, 210n11.

227 *set the terms for what was considered part of the canon*: See Johnson, "'Let Me Make the Novels of a Country,'" 166.

228 *"you have often made people* laugh till they cry*"*: Quoted in Boaden, *Memoirs*, I.302.

229 "Count: *'I have travelled'"*: Elizabeth Inchbald, *Lovers' Vows*, in *The British Theatre* (London: Printed for Longman, Hurst, Rees, and Orme, 1808), 9.

229 *"a forward young lady"*: Austen, *Mansfield Park*, I.301.

229 *"I shall think her a very obstinate, ungrateful girl"*; *"her spirits sinking"*: Austen, *Mansfield Park*, I.307; I.313.

229 *"the custom of acting plays in private theatres"*: Gisborne, *Enquiry*, 173–74.

230 *"I am glad you recommended 'Gisborne'"*: Letter from Jane Austen to Cassandra Austen, August 30, 1805, in Le Faye, *Letters*, 117.

230 *Austen's neighbor Anne Lefroy once turned down*: Kaplan, *Jane Austen Among Women*, 1.

230 *"be untrue to his science"*: Inchbald, *Lovers' Vows*, 9.

230 *"friend of ours, whom [Austen] never saw or heard of"*: Quoted in Southam, *The Critical Heritage Volume I*, 64–65.

231 *"to set forth the miserable consequences"*: Inchbald, *Lovers' Vows*, 7.

231 *"I was intoxicated by the fervent caresses"*: Inchbald, *Lovers' Vows*, 18.

231 *"shocked to find herself at that moment"*: Austen, *Mansfield Park*, I.305.

232 *"Edward admired Fanny—George disliked her"*: Quoted in Southam, *The Critical Heritage, Volume I*, 48–51.

233 *"poison which is imperceptibly [. . .] taken in"*: Quoted in Boaden, *Memoirs*, I.221.

233 *"the highest art of any time"*: W. D. Howells, *Heroines of Fiction* (New York: Harper & Brothers, 1901), I.76. The essay quoted was first published in *Harper's Bazar* in 1900; see Wells, *New Jane Austen*, 91.

233 *Taking Goodreads as a massive (if imperfect) data set*: "Books by Jane Austen," *Goodreads*, accessed April 29, 2024.

234 *"Didacticism usually puts readers off"*: Barbara D. Stoodt, Linda B. Amspaugh,

and Jane Hunt, *Children's Literature: Discovery for a Lifetime* (Melbourne: Macmillan, 1996), 218. This book focuses on books for children, but the section on didacticism applies across generations.

234 *"angry people are not always wise"*: Austen, *Pride and Prejudice*, III.61.

234 *surveying library holdings in WorldCat*: WorldCat's data, which aggregates information from many different libraries, can be subject to errors, so it is important where possible to supplement it with other methods of research, as here: an antiquarian book dealer's description of a book they had in hand is a wonderful balance to big data that may have ghost records or accidental duplication.

234 *When the novel gave the snotty Miss Milner a happy ending*: See also Anna Lott's introduction to the Broadview Press edition of *A Simple Story* (Ontario, 2007) for a description of how Inchbald continued to revise the novel in subsequent editions to "clarify [its] moral lesson."

234 *Inchbald had to revise it to meet the requirements of her publishers*: Bonnie Nelson argued in 1994 that the early rejected novel may not have been an earlier draft of *A Simple Story*, but I follow Inchbald's most recent authoritative biographer, Jenkins (*I'll Tell You What*, 273–74), in believing it was. See Bonnie Nelson, "Emily Herbert: Forerunner of Jane Austen's *Lady Susan*," *Women's Writing* 1, no. 3 (1994): 317–23.

235 *"evidently had a very useful moral in view"*: May 1791 review of *A Simple Story* signed "M" (for Mary Wollstonecraft), quoted in Appendix B of Inchbald, *A Simple Story*, (2007 edition), 381.

235 *"How are the hero and heroine punished?"*: Quoted in Dorset, "Charlotte Smith," 30.

235 *"made the vehicle of depravity and licentiousness"*: Frances Brooke, *The Excursion: A Novel*, 2nd ed. (London: Printed for T. Cadell, 1785), vi–vii.

235 *"can be read as a kind of atonement"*: Spencer, introduction to Inchbald, *A Simple Story* (1988 edition), xx.

236 *"I always obey my pastor"*: Inchbald, *Lovers' Vows*, 66. This quip isn't in the original German version of the play.

236 *Plato, Ovid, Milton; She also read Radcliffe's* Romance of the Forest: Boaden, *Memoirs*, I.179; I.308.

236 *reviewed one of Edgeworth's works*: In 1814, the year *Mansfield Park* was released, Edgeworth specially sent Inchbald an advance copy of *Patronage* for comment; see Marilyn Butler, *Maria Edgeworth: A Literary Biography* (Oxford, UK: Clarendon Press, 1972), 297–98.

237 *The eleven pocketbooks still known to survive*: Robertson, *Diaries of Elizabeth Inch-bald*, I.xv–xvi.

238 *"In some cases it overlaps"*: Robertson, *Diaries of Elizabeth Inchbald*, I.xviii.

238 *"Lookd at my Old P: Books"*: Robertson, *Diaries of Elizabeth Inchbald*, I.xviii.

239 *rare book catalog tracing the history of romance*: Rebecca Romney, *The Romance Novel in English: A Survey in Rare Books, 1769–1999* (Silver Spring, MD: Type Punch Matrix, 2021), item 2.

CHAPTER EIGHT:
HESTER LYNCH THRALE PIOZZI (1741-1821)

240 *"But all this, as my dear Mrs. Piozzi says"*: Letter from Jane Austen to Cassandra Austen, December 9, 1808, in Le Faye, *Letters*, 162.

240 *listed every one of her "enemies outlived"*: Devoney Looser, *Women Writers and Old Age in Great Britain* (Baltimore: Johns Hopkins University Press, 2008), 99.

240 *debt-inducing birthday celebration in Bath*: Edward Mangin, *Piozziana; or, Recollections of the Late Mrs. Piozzi, with Remarks. By a Friend* (London: Edward Moxon, 1833), 160.

241 *"Miss Owen & Miss Burney asked me if I had never been in Love"*: Piozzi, *Thraliana*, I.492.

242 *"the first world history ever written by an English woman"*: William McCarthy, *Hester Thrale Piozzi: Portrait of a Literary Woman* (Chapel Hill: University of North Carolina Press, 1985), 211.

243 *From childhood she was trained to perform*: From her own account of being taught by the actor Mr. Quin at the house of the Duke and Duchess of Leeds, quoted in McCarthy, *Hester Thrale Piozzi*, 5; and James L. Clifford, *Hester Lynch Piozzi (Mrs. Thrale)*, 2nd ed., with new introduction by Margaret Anne Doody (New York: Columbia University Press, 1987), 12.

243 *"although Education was a Word then unknown"*: One of the most frequently quoted lines about her early life, from Piozzi's manuscript *Biographical Anecdotes*, appearing in Clifford, McCarthy, and elsewhere, but first printed in A. Hayward, *Autobiography, Letters and Literary Remains of Mrs. Piozzi (Thrale) Edited with Notes and an Introductory Account of Her Life and Writings* (London: Longman, Green, Longman, and Roberts, 1861), I.242. My account of Hester Salusbury's early years is indebted particularly to James L. Clifford's

rigorous and comprehensive biography *Hester Lynch Piozzi (Mrs. Thrale)*, cross-checked where applicable with other sources such as Piozzi's own account in *Thraliana* and Piozzi's "Autobiographical Remains" printed in Hayward.

243   *"openly declared he would generously provide for his little niece"*: Clifford, *Hester Lynch Piozzi (Mrs. Thrale)*, 12–13.

243   *he still came back destitute*: Clifford, *Hester Lynch Piozzi (Mrs. Thrale)*, 13–19.

244   *For fun, she would translate her favorite passages from* Don Quixote: Clifford, *Hester Lynch Piozzi (Mrs. Thrale)*, 20. See also Piozzi, *Thraliana*, I.295.

244   *"my Uncle is on the point of being married"*: Quoted in Clifford, *Hester Lynch Piozzi (Mrs. Thrale)*, 31, 44.

244   *"an incomparable young Man"*: Quoted in Clifford, *Hester Lynch Piozzi (Mrs. Thrale)*, 33, and Hayward, *Autobiography*, II.20; see also Piozzi, *Thraliana*, I.300.

245   *her father judged him unfit for Hester*: Clifford, *Hester Lynch Piozzi (Mrs. Thrale)*, 4; see also Piozzi, *Thraliana*, 1.275.

245   *"exchanged for a Barrel of Porter"*: Clifford, *Hester Lynch Piozzi (Mrs. Thrale)*, 36, from Piozzi's manuscript *Biographical Anecdotes*; see also Piozzi, *Thraliana*, 1.302.

245   *"mutual Preference for each other"*: Quoted in Clifford, *Hester Lynch Piozzi (Mrs. Thrale)*, 45.

245   *"Impertinent, or rejected [them] as superfluous"*: Quoted in Clifford, *Hester Lynch Piozzi (Mrs. Thrale)*, 50, from Piozzi's manuscript *Biographical Anecdotes*.

245   *he thought it too "masculine"*: Piozzi, "Autobiographical Remains," II.24.

245   *she hadn't objected to living in such an unfashionable part of town*: Piozzi, "Autobiographical Remains," II.24.

246   *"The illness of this boy frights me for all the rest"*: Letter from Hester Thrale to Samuel Johnson, July 1775, in Hester Lynch Piozzi, *Letters to and from the Late Samuel Johnson, LL.D. To Which Are Added Some Poems Never Before Printed* (London: Printed for A. Strahan and T. Cadell, 1788), I.272.

246   *"often told how little it signified"*: Quoted in Michael John Franklin, *Hester Lynch Thrale Piozzi* (Cardiff: University of Wales Press, 2020), 60.

246   *"the sight of it would not revive the memory of cheerful times"*: Letter from Hester Thrale to Samuel Johnson, August 9, 1775, in Piozzi, *Letters*, I.302.

247   *died suddenly of what was perhaps meningitis*: Mary Hyde (later Eccles), *The Thrales of Streatham Park* (Cambridge, MA: Harvard University Press, 1977), 153.

248   *the Bluestocking leader Elizabeth Montagu*: See Franklin, *Hester Lynch Thrale Piozzi*,

80, for an account of the early relationship of Hester Thrale and Elizabeth Montagu.

248 *"a singular amusement in hearing, instigating, and provoking"*: Burney ("Madame D'Arblay"), *Memoirs of Doctor Burney*, II.105. Also quoted in Clifford, *Hester Lynch Piozzi (Mrs. Thrale)*, 57.

248 *"learn to be as gaily miserable [. . .] as I can"*: Letter from Hester Thrale to Samuel Johnson, November 20, 1773, in Piozzi, *Letters*, I.205.

248 *"I am so much in love with her"*: Burney, *Diary and Letters*, I.61, I.72.

248 *"is a very learned lady"*: Quoted in Hayward, *Autobiography*, I.99–100.

248 *"Grace [was] more acquired than natural"*: Piozzi, *Thraliana*, I.321; also quoted in Franklin, *Hester Lynch Thrale Piozzi*, 9.

249 *lived only ten hours*: Piozzi, "Autobiographical Remains," II.27. A more detailed account is in Clifford, *Hester Lynch Piozzi (Mrs. Thrale)*, 93–94. Piozzi gives an hour as the length that Penelope lived in "Autobiographical Remains," written many years later; but an entry in her *Children's Book* from the time (September 1772, quoted in Hyde, *Thrales of Streatham Park*, 55) states ten hours.

249 *"more famed for his amours than celebrated for his beer"*: *Westminster*, March 1773, quoted in Clifford, *Hester Lynch Piozzi (Mrs. Thrale)*, 98.

249 *"every Night & Morning for an Hour together on my Knees"*: From Thrale's *Children's Book*, April or May 1776 entry, quoted in Hyde, *Thrales of Streatham Park*, 165–66.

249 *won the hearts of a number of men*: Apparently among them was Frances Burney's father, Charles; according to the January 1, 1782, entry in Piozzi, *Thraliana* (I.523): Streatfeild "has begun the new Year nicely with a new Conquest— Poor dear Doctor Burney! He is *now* the reigning Favourite, and She spares neither Pains nor Caresses to turn that good Man's head, much to the Vexation of his Family; particularly my Fanny." Also quoted in Hayward, *Autobiography*, I.115.

249 *"I will not fret about this Rival"*: From Thrale's *Children's Book*, December 31, 1778, entry, quoted in Hyde, *Thrales of Streatham Park*, 218. Also quoted in Clifford, *Hester Lynch Piozzi (Mrs. Thrale)*, 173.

250 *"Mr. Thrale is fallen in Love"*: January 1779 entry in Piozzi, *Thraliana*, I.356.

250 *"I can hardly sometimes help laughing in her Face"*: January 20, 1780, entry and general January 1779 entry in Piozzi, *Thraliana*, I.423 and I.356.

250 *"could have quoted the Lines in the Greek"*: Piozzi, *Thraliana*, October 1780 entry, I.461.

250 *"I cannot help remarking with what blandness and composure"*: Mangin, *Piozziana*, 22–23; also quoted in Hayward, *Autobiography*, I.123.

251 *"Mr Thrale wished me to go, nay insisted on it"*: August 1779 entry in Piozzi, *Thraliana*, I.401.

252 *"they think they are doing me* honour*"*: January 14, 1782, entry in Piozzi, *Thraliana*, I.527.

252 *"see what the world could show me"*: January 1, 1782, entry in Piozzi, *Thraliana*, I.525. In this entry, she talks of it as a plan for years down the road; by the August 22, 1782, entry (*Thraliana*, I.540), she is planning it as an immediate project specifically to save money.

252 *she did have to take out a large loan*: Hyde, *Thrales of Streatham Park*, 233. See also Piozzi, *Thraliana*, I.550–52. The loan was initially planned to be borrowed against her daughters' much larger estate, but one of the other executors took it on instead. See Clifford, *Hester Lynch Piozzi (Mrs. Thrale)*, 214–15, whose account is worth quoting at length: "Crutchley [one of the executors] brutally told Mrs. Thrale to thank her girls for keeping her '*out of Gaol.*' Ironically, after this burst of spleen by one of the trustees, none of the Thrale money had to be used, for Cator [another of the executors] found the interest and security so favourable that he supplied the necessary sum out of his own pocket. He failed to tell Mrs. Thrale what he had done, however [. . .] Her worry meant nothing to Cator and Crutchley, who felt they could maintain better control over her actions by keeping her ignorant of her own financial condition."

252 *"The persecution I endure from men"*: August 22, 1782, entry in Piozzi, *Thraliana*, I.541.

252 *"violently opposed the move"*: Clifford, *Hester Lynch Piozzi (Mrs. Thrale)*, 211. The other guardians were in favor of it; Thrale speculated the single guardian's objection was because he was in love with her eldest daughter Queeney and did not want her to leave the country.

253 *"fills the Mind with Emotions"*: August 8, 1780, entry in Piozzi, *Thraliana*, I.452. This story shows a different side of Thrale's early interactions with Piozzi than the scene that Virginia Woolf made famous in her essay "Dr. Burney's Evening Party."

253 *"that dear little discerning Creature Fanny Burney"*: September 1782 entry in Piozzi, *Thraliana*, I.544. One earlier entry from November 25, 1781 (*Thraliana*, I.519) suggests something of a flirtation between the two; by January 2, 1782 (*Thraliana*, I.525), she is hoping "Piozzi should not pick him up a Wife."

253 *"while She possessed her Reason"*: November 19, 1782, entry in Piozzi, *Thraliana*, I.550.

254 *"To what then am I Guardian?"*: September 1782 entry in Piozzi, *Thraliana*, I.544–45.

255 *"Mr. Darcy's letter, she was in a fair way of soon knowing by heart"*: Austen, *Pride and Prejudice*, II.175–76.

256 *"had more Sense, and would have a better Fortune"*: May 1777 entry in Piozzi, *Thraliana*, I.44.

256 *"duped by ungovernable passions"*: Henry William Edmund Petty-FitzMaurice, Marquis of Lansdowne, *The Queeney Letters: Being Letters Addressed to Hester Maria Thrale by Doctor Johnson, Fanny Burney and Mrs. Thrale-Piozzi* (London: Cassell & Company, 1934), 70.

256 *"fling away [Thrale's] talents"*: Quoted in Lansdowne, *Queeney Letters*, 99.

256 *"discontented when a woman does marry again"*: Austen, *Persuasion*, III.6–7.

256 *"if I would abandon my Children, I must"*: January 1783 entry in Piozzi, *Thraliana*, 559.

256 *"Take your Mama—and make it of her a Countess"*: Quoted in Clifford, *Hester Lynch Piozzi (Mrs. Thrale)*, 217–18, from the *Mainwaring Piozziana*, II.11.

257 *"broken what little resistance there was left"*: Clifford, *Hester Lynch Piozzi (Mrs. Thrale)*, 223.

257 *"I am sorry and feel the worst kind of sorrow"*: Quoted in Clifford, *Hester Lynch Piozzi (Mrs. Thrale)*, 229.

257 *"prayed with true Presbyterian Tenderness"*: Summer 1784 letter from Hester Thrale to Queeney in Lansdowne, *Queeney Letters*, 141.

257 *"would not answer Mrs Thrale's Purpose"*: Letter from Hester Piozzi to Queeney, letter XXI, July 25, 1784, in Lansdowne, *Queeney Letters*, 171.

258 *"Signor Piozzi Ravishing Mrs. Thrale"*: Print by Samuel Collings. See the New York Public Library's Online Collections, last accessed May 10, 2024: https://digitalcollections.nypl.org/items/6073d646-f740-3625-e040 -e00a18067aae. Also in Hyde, *Thrales of Streatham Park*, 243.

258 *"the pursuit of a second husband"*: Lansdowne, *Queeney Letters*, 56.

259 *"was suffering from what we should now call a 'sex complex'"*: Lansdowne, *Queeney Letters*, 57.

259 *"shall never be treated as Friends or even Companions by me"*: Letter from Hester Lynch Piozzi to Queeney, August 17, 1784, in Lansdowne, *Queeney Letters*, 179.

259 *under a hired chaperone*: This chaperone was almost immediately dismissed by

the other executors for being sympathetic to the new marriage; see Hyde, *Thrales of Streatham Park*, 240–44.

260 *"I do sincerely believe there is not so happy a Woman"*: Letter from Hester Thrale to Queeney, July 15, 1784, in Lansdowne, *Queeney Letters*, 167.

260 *They climbed Mount Vesuvius; differences in Italian dialects; Catholic friends kept teasing her; priests tried to convert her*: Clifford, *Hester Lynch Piozzi (Mrs. Thrale)*, 258; Piozzi, *Thraliana*, II.671; II.657; II.676–77.

260 *"Reports of my Husband's having sold my Joynture"*: September 3, 1786, entry in Piozzi, *Thraliana*, II.673.

260 *"informal, indeed intimate and conversational"*: Franklin, *Hester Lynch Thrale Piozzi*, 96.

260 *"the king sent for a copy"*: Hayward, *Autobiography*, I.291; see also Clifford, *Hester Lynch Piozzi (Mrs. Thrale)*, 263–65, and Franklin, *Hester Lynch Thrale Piozzi*, 100.

260 *"Mrs. Piozzi's book is much in fashion"*: Roberts, *Memoirs*, II.15. Also quoted in Hayward, *Autobiography*, I.291.

260 *printed in twice the size*: The first printing of *Anecdotes* was one thousand copies; the first printing of *Letters* was two thousand. See Clifford, *Hester Lynch Piozzi (Mrs. Thrale)*, 265, 314.

261 *"I sat up till four o'clock reading away"*: Quoted in McCarthy, *Hester Thrale Piozzi*, 134. Malone was the main driver behind many of the worst attacks on Piozzi that made it into Boswell's *Life of Johnson*. See Irma S. Lustig, "Boswell at Work: The 'Animadversions' on Mrs Piozzi," *Modern Language Review* 67, no. 1 (January 1972): 11–30.

261 *"How like herself, how characteristic is every line!"*: Burney, *Diary and Letters*, V.38. See also Franklin, *Hester Lynch Thrale Piozzi*, 118.

261 *Ann Radcliffe turned to Piozzi's* Observations: See Marianne D'Ezio, "'As Like as Peppermint Water Is to Good French Brandy': Ann Radcliffe and Hester Lynch Salusbury (Thrale) Piozzi," in *Locating Ann Radcliffe*, ed. Andrew Smith and Mark Bennett (London: Routledge, 2020), 62–73.

261 *A copy of each could be found in the library of Godmersham Park*: A digital re-creation and catalog is available at https://www.readingwithausten.com/index.html.

261 *"that an Italian Name makes an awkward Jumble"*: Letter from Lucas Pepys to Hester Lynch Piozzi, November 30, 1787, quoted in Clifford, *Hester Lynch Piozzi (Mrs. Thrale)*, 289.

261 *Hester Piozzi threw a welcome-home party*: Clifford, *Hester Lynch Piozzi (Mrs. Thrale)*, 293, 303; and Piozzi, *Thraliana*, II.681.

262 *Gabriel Piozzi had locked her mother up*: Piozzi, *Thraliana*, II.681.

262 *fearing that Cecilia would be "corrupted" by their mother*: The word Queeney used when speaking of the topic to Frances Burney in March of 1788, quoted in Piozzi, *Thraliana*, II.686n1.

262 *Queeney sent the Piozzis a lovely tea chest*: Lansdowne, *Queeney Letters*, 180; Lansdowne expresses astonishment that Queeney would do so.

263 *godparents were HRH the Prince of Wales*: Hyde, *Thrales of Streatham Park*, 287.

263 *her "easy irresponsible charm"*: Charles Hughes, *Mrs. Piozzi's Thraliana, with Numerous Extracts Hitherto Unpublished* (London: Simpkin, 1913), 58; originally in Walter Raleigh, *Six Essays on Johnson* (Oxford, UK: Clarendon Press, 1910), 49.

263 *Cecilia compared her to another heroine*: Clifford, *Hester Lynch Piozzi (Mrs. Thrale)*, 379.

263 *"full of spirit & fire, & all herself"*: Letter from Frances Burney to Queeney, January 24, 1785, quoted in Lansdowne, *Queeney Letters*, 108.

263 *"my unprovoked Enemies"; "I will not be taken & left"*: January 1789 entry in Piozzi, *Thraliana*, II.729; May 1789 entry in Piozzi, *Thraliana*, II.744.

264 *"slowly changing into a typical English squire"*: Clifford, *Hester Lynch Piozzi (Mrs. Thrale)*, 406.

264 *"faithful & tender" to his wife, and "doating" on Cecilia*: July 1803 entry in Piozzi, *Thraliana*, II.1039; August 1787 entry in Piozzi, *Thraliana*, II.686.

264 *Many canonical writers were terrible fathers*: See Robert Gottlieb, *Great Expectations: The Sons and Daughters of Charles Dickens* (New York: Farrar, Straus and Giroux, 2012); and Anne E. Bromley, "Faulkner as Father: Student's Prize-Winning Research Reveals Conflicted Portrait," *UVA Today*, November 9, 2016, accessed April 30, 2024, https://news.virginia.edu/content/faulkner-father-students-prize-winning-research-reveals-conflicted-portrait.

264 *"to abandon, forsake, relinquish"*: Hester Lynch Piozzi, *British Synonymy; or, an Attempt at Regulating the Choice of Words in Familiar Conversation. Inscribed with Sentiments of Gratitude and Respect, to Such of Her Foreign Friends as Have Made English Literature Their Peculiar Study* (London: G. G. and J. Robinson, 1794), 1.

264 *"Her position as a woman writer drove her to be resourceful"*: McCarthy, *Hester Thrale Piozzi*, 209; see also 185–56 for discussion of precedents in English.

264 *"the first world history ever written by an English woman"*: McCarthy, *Hester Thrale Piozzi*, 211.

264 *"History cooked up in a novel form reduced to light reading"*: 1801 review in the *Anti-Jacobin*, quoted in Clifford, *Hester Lynch Piozzi (Mrs. Thrale)*, 403n2.

265 *"a work of great daring in every way"*: McCarthy, *Hester Thrale Piozzi*, 210.

265 *an unusual "hybrid quality"*: Marianne D'Ezio, *Hester Lynch Piozzi: A Taste for Eccentricity* (Newcastle upon Tyne, UK: Cambridge Scholars, 2010), 165.

265 *"style is often rendered abrupt and quaint"*: *The Critical Review; or, Annals of Literature*, vol. xxxii (London: Printed by and for S. Hamilton, 1801), 28; also quoted in Clifford, *Hester Lynch Piozzi (Mrs. Thrale)*, 403.

265 *"a literary world still dominated by men"*: D'Ezio, *Hester Lynch Piozzi*, 7.

265 *"Glorious creature! How she writes!"*: Letter from Hester Lynch Piozzi to Penelope Pennington, May 29, 1799, in Oswald G. Knapp, ed., *The Intimate Letters of Hester Piozzi & Penelope Pennington, 1788–1821* (London: John Lane, 1914), 174.

266 *she and More had much in common*: For instance, Piozzi shared More's worries during the French Revolution of Thomas Paine's works influencing lower classes and oversaw the translation into Welsh of More's anti-Paineite story *Village Politics*; see Franklin, *Hester Lynch Thrale Piozzi*, 137.

266 *"gaiety, animation, and cheerfulness"*: Letter from Hannah More to Thomas Sedgwick Whalley, February 19, 1801, in Hill Wickham, ed., *Journals and Correspondence of Thomas Sedgewick Whalley, D.D. of Mendip Lodge, Somerset* (London: Richard Bentley, 1863), II.188. On More and Piozzi as neighbors, see Clifford, *Hester Lynch Piozzi (Mrs. Thrale)*, 406, 413.

266 *"all this, as my dear Mrs. Piozzi says"*: Letter from Jane Austen to Cassandra Austen, December 9, 1808, in Le Faye, *Letters*, 162.

266 *"Well! now all this is nonsense, and fancy, and flight"*: Piozzi, *Letters*, I.270.

266 *"Every thing most dreaded has ensued"*: Piozzi, *Thraliana*, II.1099.

267 *"I am now grown one of the Curiosities of Bath"*: Quoted in McCarthy, *Hester Thrale Piozzi*, 262.

267 *"danced with astonishing elasticity"*: Mangin, *Piozziana*, 160.

267 *"letters are so garbled and distorted"*: Mrs. E. F. Ellet, "Mrs. Piozzi's Love-Letters," *Athenaeum* 1811 (July 12, 1862); also quoted in Looser, *Women Writers and Old Age in Great Britain*, 106.

267 *"painstaking historian and a scholarly collector of books"*: April 1932 Report of the Council of the American Antiquarian Society, 4, https://www.americanantiquarian.org/proceedings/44806896.pdf.

267 *Piozzi as "mentor" and Conway as "would-be protégé"*: Looser, *Women Writers and Old Age in Great Britain*, 113.

268 *"the revolution of years has now produced a generation of Amazons of the pen"*: *The Ad-*

venturer No. 115, quoted in Samuel Johnson, *The Works of Samuel Johnson, LL.D.* (London: J. Buckland et al., 1787), 116; also quoted in William McCarthy, "The Repression of Hester Lynch Piozzi; or, How We Forgot a Revolution in Authorship," *Modern Language Studies* 18, no. 1, Making and Rethinking the Canon: The Eighteenth Century (Winter 1988): 101.

269   *simply as "Dictionary Johnson"*: Boswell, *Life of Samuel Johnson* (1992 edition), 242.

269   *"I doubt not but it was the Lady's Fault"*: Piozzi, *Thraliana*, I.179.

269   *"If you have abandoned your children"*: Letter from Samuel Johnson to Hester Thrale, July 2, 1784, quoted in Lansdowne, *Queeney Letters*, 150.

269   *"I have this morning received from you so rough a letter"*: Letter from Hester Thrale to Samuel Johnson, July 4, 1784, quoted in Lansdowne, *Queeney Letters*, 151.

270   *Johnson had "allegedly left her"*: McCarthy, *Hester Thrale Piozzi*, 187. See also Clifford, *Hester Lynch Piozzi (Mrs. Thrale)*, 372–73.

270   *"I would not accept help from Doctor Johnson"*: Letter from Hester Piozzi to Queeney, August 22, 1793, quoted in Clifford, *Hester Lynch Piozzi (Mrs. Thrale)*, 368; also noted by McCarthy, *Hester Thrale Piozzi*, 186.

270   *newspapers were anonymously suggesting that the eldest Thrale son*: Clifford, *Hester Lynch Piozzi (Mrs. Thrale)*, 99.

270   *showed a "strange lack of taste"*: That Thrale guessed this would happen is recorded by Frances Burney when the jokes began circulating, quoted in Clifford, *Hester Lynch Piozzi (Mrs. Thrale)*, 199.

271   *"Report frequently whispered that a connubial knot"*: Quoted in Clifford, *Hester Lynch Piozzi (Mrs. Thrale)*, 262.

271   *"A Colleague (to me): Who are you writing about?"*: McCarthy, "The Repression of Hester Lynch Piozzi," 99.

271   *"Mrs. Piozzi of Bath and Brynbella"*: Lansdowne, *Queeney Letters*, 127.

272   *"you will never again have the heart of any one so completely"*: The friend was the archaeologist Samuel Lysons, for whom Piozzi once collected fossils. Quoted in Clifford, *Hester Lynch Piozzi (Mrs. Thrale)*, 296.

272   *called her second marriage a "disgrace"*: Quoted in Piozzi, *Thraliana*, I.629n2.

272   *"turn[ing] up the nose of scorn"*: [John Wolcot] "Peter Pindar," *Bozzy and Piozzi: Or the British Biographers. A Town Eclogue*, 9th ed. (London: Printed for G. Kearsley, 1788), 54.

272   *"The kind and generous Thrale was no more"*: "Samuel Johnson," entry by Thomas Babington Macaulay in *The Encyclopaedia Britannica, or Dictionary of Arts, Sci-*

ences, and General Literature, 8th ed. (Edinburgh: Adam & Charles Black, 1856), XXII.802.

273   *"Success!* The Children's Book *was ours!!"*: Mary Hyde Eccles, "Unending Pursuit," *Grolier Club Gazette*, no. 42 (New York: Grolier Club, 1990), 99. *Grolier Gazettes* through number 63 are digitized and available through the New York Heritage Digital Collections website: https://cdm16694.contentdm .oclc.org/digital/collection/Grolier01.

273   *"a rare insight into the life of an eighteenth-century family"*: Hyde, *Thrales of Streatham Park*, vii, viii.

274   *"Welsh-born diarist, author and patron of the arts"*; *"She mentions Samuel Johnson some fifty times"*: Descriptions found on AbeBooks and viaLibri, June 4, 2022, screenshots of each recorded.

274   *"she does so only to disagree with it"*: McCarthy, *Hester Thrale Piozzi*, 186.

275   *"distorted as to change their character"*: Ellet, "Mrs. Piozzi's Love-Letters."

275   *indicates a first issue of the first edition*: Baron Nathaniel Mayer Victor Rothschild, *The Rothschild Library: A Catalogue of the Collection of Eighteenth-Century Printed Books and Manuscripts Formed by Lord Rothschild* (Cambridge, UK: Cambridge University Press, 1954), item 463.

275   *from their very first meeting in 1763*: See Boswell, *Life of Johnson*, 248.

275   *"you and I [are] rivals for that great man"*: Letter from James Boswell to Hester Thrale, September 5, 1769, quoted in James Boswell, *Letters of James Boswell*, ed. Chauncey Brewster Tinker (Oxford, UK: Clarendon Press, 1924), I.173.

276   *sought every opportunity to discredit her books*: Lustig, "Boswell at Work: The 'Animadversions' on Mrs Piozzi," demonstrates that Boswell, in fact, toned down many of the worst attacks on Piozzi before the publication of the first edition of his *Life of Johnson*. My reading is that he included so much in the first place because he had an ulterior motive beyond strict truth to facts (as he claimed): that motive was to discredit Piozzi. Lustig suggests that he took out much of it because "In rereading his draft, Boswell surely noticed how dangerously unprofessional he had become" (24). I agree with this argument, but maintain that his need to surpass Piozzi as the literary representative of Johnson kept him from removing all that he included specifically with the goal of discrediting her.

276   *only quoted from Boswell's prepublication notes*: Clifford, *Hester Lynch Piozzi (Mrs. Thrale)*, 357.

276   *"Boswell's treatment of her"*: McCarthy, *Hester Thrale Piozzi*, 109.

CHAPTER NINE:
MARIA EDGEWORTH (1768-1849)

280   *"I have made up my mind to like no Novels really"*: Letter from Jane Austen to Anna
Austen, September 28, 1814, quoted in Le Faye, *Letters*, 289.

280   *copy of* Emma *that had been owned by Maria Edgeworth*: Lot 96 in the December
16, 2010, sale, "History and Children's Books & Illustrations," at Sotheby's,
https://www.sothebys.com/en/auctions/ecatalogue/2010/english-litera
ture-history-and-children39s-books-illustrations-l10408/lot.96.html.

281   *"easily the most celebrated and successful of practising English novelists"*: Butler, *Maria
Edgeworth*, 1.

281   *"It has been the fashionable novel here"*: Quoted in Hare, *Life and Letters of Maria
Edgeworth*, I.27.

281   *he himself sought to "emulate"*: Walter Scott, *Waverley: Or, 'tis Sixty Years Since* (Edinburgh: Archibald Constable and Co., 1814), III.367. See also John Gibson
Lockhart, *Memoirs of the Life of Sir Walter Scott, Bart* (Edinburgh and London: Robert Cadell and John Murray and Wittaker, 1837-38), III.303-5, for
the letter that Scott's publisher, Ballantyne, wrote to Edgeworth describing
Scott's debt to her. Scott told him, "If I could but hit Miss Edgeworth's wonderful power of vivifying all her persons, and making them live *as beings* in
your mind, I should not be afraid."

281   *"a little, dark, bearded, sharp, withered"*: Published in Mary Wilson Gordon,
"Christopher North": A Memoir of John Wilson (Edinburgh: Edmonston and
Douglas, 1862), 58; and quoted in Butler, *Maria Edgeworth*, 3. The son-in-law
is John Gibson Lockhart, author of *Memoirs of the Life of Sir Walter Scott*.

281   *"the great lioness of Edinburgh"*: Letter from Walter Scott to D. Terry, June 18,
1823, quoted in James Newcomer, *Maria Edgeworth* (Lewisburg, PA: Bucknell
University Press, 1973), 27; originally printed in Lockhart, *Life of Sir Walter
Scott*, V.276.

282   *Maria Edgeworth was the most renowned novelist in England*: Butler opens her 1972
biography, *Maria Edgeworth*, with this point as the first sentence on page one;
Edgeworth's contemporaries also knew it, as Lockhart notes about "the state
of novel literature" before *Waverley* was published: "the only exceptions to its
mediocrity," he says, were "the Irish Tales of Miss Edgeworth." Lockhart,
Memoirs of the Life of Sir Walter Scott, III.124.

283   *"Emma Woodhouse, handsome, clever, and rich"*: Austen, *Emma*, I.1.

284   *There were other books inscribed by Edgeworth*: See lots 114, 1, and 92. Some of the magnificent volumes inscribed by or owned by Edgeworth in this auction included a third edition of *Waverley* presented by Scott to Edgeworth (lot 107); and a set of Burney's first three novels (lot 97): *Evelina* (1794 edition), *Cecilia* (partial set of the 1782 first edition), and *Camilla* (the 1794 first edition).

284   *"you will say that we have been amply repaid"*: Maria Edgeworth, *Letters for Literary Ladies. To Which Is Added, an Essay on the Noble Science of Self-Justification* (London: Printed for J. Johnson, 1795), 8.

285   *"In which of the useful arts"*: Edgeworth, *Letters for Literary Ladies*, 8.

285   *"impression however, which the eloquence of Mr. Day's letter made"*: Maria Edgeworth, *Memoirs of Richard Lovell Edgeworth, Esq. Begun by Himself and Concluded by His Daughter* (London: R. Hunter and Baldwin, Cardock, and Joy, 1820), II.343. This episode also chronicled well in Butler, *Maria Edgeworth*, 147–49.

286   *Maria became indispensable in assisting with the care of children*: Ann Owens Weekes, *Irish Women Writers: An Uncharted Tradition* (Lexington: Kentucky University Press, 1990), 35–36.

286   *"there were no masters of writing for children"*: Butler, *Maria Edgeworth*, 163.

286   *"For though in composition she was equally rapid and correct"*: Austen, "Biographical Notice," vii.

287   *"About the length of Miss Burney's* Evelina*"*: Quoted in Harman, *Jane's Fame*, 20.

287   *"I am very greedy & want to make the most of it"*: Austen, "Biographical Notice," xii; letter from Jane Austen to Fanny Knight, November 18–20, 1814, quoted in Le Faye, *Letters*, 293.

287   *concluding "tho' I like praise as well as anybody"*: Letter from Jane Austen to Fanny Knight, November 30, 1814, quoted in Le Faye, *Letters*, 299–300.

287   *her need to "shrink from notoriety"*: Austen, "Biographical Notice," xiv.

287   *"I shall rather try to make all the Money"*: Letter from Jane Austen to Francis Austen, September 25, 1813, quoted in Le Faye, *Letters*, 241.

287   *"more important to her than anything else in her life"*: Fergus, "The Professional Woman Writer," 13.

290   *"Not at all too late, my dear"*: Maria Edgeworth, *Belinda* (London: Pandora Press, 1986), 14.

290   *"the most fascinating person she [Belinda] had ever beheld"*: Edgeworth, *Belinda*, 4.

290   *"Follow my example, Belinda"*: Edgeworth, *Belinda*, 21.

291   *"Mr. Knightley, in fact, was one of the few people"*: Austen, *Emma*, I.14.

291 *"a heroine whom no one but myself will much like"*: Quoted in Austen-Leigh, *Memoir*, 148.

291 *"the most perfect example in English fiction"*: Edith Wharton, *The Writing of Fiction* (New York: Scribner, 1925), 129.

291 *Edgeworth wrote that she had enjoyed* Mansfield Park: Letter from Maria Edgeworth to Miss Ruxton, December 26, 1814, quoted in Maria Edgeworth, *A Memoir of Maria Edgeworth* (London: Joseph Masters and Son, 1867), I.310; also in Hare, *Life and Letters of Maria Edgeworth*, I.245.

292 *"after reaching the end of the first volume"*: Letter from Maria Edgeworth to Sneyd and Harriet Edgeworth, 1816; while this letter was quoted in Hare, *Life and Letters*, 199, the derogatory comments about *Emma* were left out; they can be found in Butler, *Maria Edgeworth*, 445.

292 *"I am desired not to give you my opinion of 'Pride and Prejudice'"*: Letter from Maria Edgeworth to C. Sneyd Edgeworth, May 1, 1813, quoted in Hare, *Life and Letters*, 218.

292 *"liked them better than ever"*: February 21, 1838, letter quoted in Valerie Pakenham, ed., *Maria Edgeworth's Letters from Ireland* (Dublin: Lilliput Press, 2018), 369.

293 *He did not appreciate novels in the "Burney tradition"*: Butler, *Maria Edgeworth*, 185.

293 *"which entertains me as much at the third reading as it did at the first"*: Letter from Maria Edgeworth to C. Sneyd Edgeworth, May 4, 1808, quoted in Hare, *Life and Letters*, I.150.

293 *"is offered to the public as a Moral Tale"*: Edgeworth, *Belinda*, viii.

293 *"I will not adopt that ungenerous and impolitic custom"*: Austen, *Northanger Abbey*, I.62–64.

294 *"he has pointed out to me that to be a mere writer of pretty stories"*: Letter from Maria Edgeworth to Sophy Ruxton, February 26, 1805, quoted in Butler, *Maria Edgeworth*, 209.

294 *Edgeworth's "epoch-making" work among its biggest catalysts*: Ria Omasreiter, "Maria Edgeworth's Tales: A Contribution to the Science of Happiness," *Functions of Literature: Essays Presented to Erwin Wolff on His Sixtieth Birthday*, ed. Ulrich Broich, Theo Stemmler, and Gerd Stratmann (Tübingen, Germany: M. Niemeyer, 1984), 207.

294 *"the Angora goat [. . .] with long, curling, silky hair"*: Maria Edgeworth, *The Absentee*, in *Stories of Ireland* (London: George Routledge and Sons, 1886), 160.

295 *"actually as perfect as it was possible to make them"*: Quoted in Butler, *Maria Edgeworth*, 1.

295 *he eventually became her biggest champion*: It became Richard Lovell's practice to write prefaces to her novels extolling their moral usefulness.

295 *"literary partnership, which, for so many years, was the pride and joy of my life"*: Edgeworth, *Memoirs of Richard Lovell Edgeworth*, II.190.

295 *"Other writers have caught nothing but the general feature"*: Quoted in Butler, *Maria Edgeworth*, 345.

295 *With Edgeworth, the art of the novel*: See Butler, *Maria Edgeworth*, 304.

296 *"Maria Edgeworth may be said to have invented the modern novel"*: Millicent Fawcett ["Mrs. Henry Fawcett"], *Some Eminent Women of Our Times* (London: Macmillan, 1889), 154.

296 *they became "national sketches"*: Oliphant, *The Literary History of England, 1790–1825*, III.217.

296 *novels about Ireland were viewed as regional novels of "extreme remoteness"*: Josephine McDonagh, "Place, Region, and Migration," in *The Nineteenth Century Novel 1820–1880*, ed. John Kucich and Jenny Bourne Taylor (Oxford, UK: Oxford University Press, 2012), 364.

297 *made her seem "provincial"*: Southam, *Jane Austen: The Critical Heritage, Volume I*, 2.

297 *"Never was life so pinched and narrow"*: Quoted in Southam, *Jane Austen: The Critical Heritage, Volume I*, 28.

297 *"they lacked her own gift of universality"*: Auerbach, *Searching for Jane Austen*, 86–87.

297 *"Edgeworth must certainly be pronounced to have gone out of fashion"*: Minto, *Literature of the Georgian Era*, 239.

297 *"prepare[d] the way for the one prose writer"*: Gosse, *Short History of Modern English Literature*, 295.

297 *"much the better novelist"*: P. H. Newby, *Maria Edgeworth* (London: Arthur Baker, 1950), 94.

298 *"on the one hand there has been the delight of discovering this treasure chest"*: Dale Spender, *Mothers of the Novel: 100 Good Women Writers before Jane Austen* (London: Pandora Press, 1986), 1, 2.

299 *Many other scholars have built upon*: The same year as Spender's *Mothers of the Novel* (1986), for instance, Jane Spencer published *The Rise of the Woman Novelist*, one of the many foundational works on the subject I'm indebted to in writing this book.

300 *"I can only presume that Ian Watt"*: Spender, *Mothers of the Novel*, 290.

300 *"I would dearly love to have a course on Maria Edgeworth's novels"*: Spender, *Mothers of the Novel*, 290–91.

303   *Henry mentions only Samuel Richardson*: Austen, "Biographical Notice," xv. Richardson's *Sir Charles Grandison* was a favorite of Austen's; scholars have carefully traced its influence on her novels. See, e.g., Harris, *Jane Austen's Art of Memory*.

303   *"in which the greatest powers of the mind are displayed"*: Austen, *Northangey Abbey*, I.63.

303   *"a mere common observer of manners, and also a very woman"*: Hazlitt, *Lectures on English Comic Writers*, 245.

303   *"Hazlitt's essay signals a change in the status of the female novelist"*: Runge, "Momentary Fame: Female Novelists in Eighteenth-Century Book Reviews," 295.

304   *"imitating the grandiloquent style of Johnson"*: Austen-Leigh, *Memoir*, 84.

304   *Readers took her relatives as authorities on Austen's taste*: See Halsey, *Jane Austen and Her Readers*, 24–25.

304   *"To-morrow I shall be just like Camilla"*; *"Like Capt. Mirvan to Mde Duval"*: Letter from Jane Austen to Cassandra Austen, September 1, 1796, in Le Faye, *Letters*, 6; letter from Jane Austen to Cassandra Austen, November 26, 1815, in Le Faye, *Letters*, 314.

305   *"None of these parallels have been, or should be"*: Jackel, "Leonora and Lady Susan: A Note on Maria Edgeworth and Jane Austen," 279.

305   *"so strikingly and consistently different"?*: Murphy, *Jane Austen the Reader*, x.

306   *Darwin wasn't the first scientist to suggest a theory of evolution*: See the excellent survey by Edward J. Larson, *Evolution: The Remarkable History of a Scientific Theory* (New York: Modern Library, 2004).

306   *The word "evolution" doesn't even appear*: Gordon Chancellor, "Darwin's *Origin of Species*, Sixth Edition (1872): An Introduction," Darwin Online, accessed May 12, 2024, https://darwin-online.org.uk/EditorialIntroductions/Chancellor_Origin6th.html.

307   *"actively seeking a female precursor"*: Sandra M. Gilbert and Susan Gubar, *The Madwoman in the Attic: The Woman Writer and the Nineteenth-Century Literary Imagination*, 2nd ed. (New Haven, CT: Yale University Press, 2000), 49.

307   *did not begin with Jane Austen. Isn't that exciting?*: Spender had much the same reaction in *Mothers of the Novel*, 2: "I cannot, however, begin to convey a sense of the joy I have experienced in finding these women writers. When I thought that I had read most of the women novelists who had ever been published, the discovery of yet another 100 'new' old novelists was in itself a source of tremendous excitement. And the last two years of avid novel read-

ing has been, for me, one of the most moving and illuminating events of my life."

308   *"[I]nterdependency between women is the only way to [. . .] freedom"*: Audre Lorde, "The Master's Tools Will Never Dismantle the Master's House," in *This Bridge Called My Back: Writings by Radical Women of Color*, 4th ed., ed. Cherríe Moraga and Gloria Anzaldúa (Albany: SUNY Press, 2015), 95.

308   *"first novelistic-canon" in English*: Johnson, "'Let Me Make the Novels of a Country,'" 166.

309   *"As the hackney coachman said"*: Letter from Maria Edgeworth to Sophy Ruxton, December 1809, quoted in Hare, *Life and Letters*, 178.

309   *"landmarks in the history of the novel"*: Butler, *Maria Edgeworth*, 339.

309   *1973 biography of Edgeworth*: See Newcomer's *Maria Edgeworth*.

310   *"led me to discover my life's purpose"*: See https://www.wellreadblackgirl.com /our-story.

310   *"who paved the way for Austen and the Brontës"*: Devoney Looser, *Sister Novelists* (New York: Bloomsbury, 2022).

310   *"Citation is how we acknowledge our debt"*: Ahmed, *Living a Feminist Life*, 16.

312   *"I've been trying to finish this monster"*: Joanna Russ, *How to Suppress Women's Writing* (Austin: University of Texas Press, 1983, 2018), 132.

CONCLUSION

313   *"Jane Austen turns inferior work"*: Bradbrook, *Jane Austen and Her Predecessors*, 104.

313   *"showed her usual critical shrewdness"*: Bradbrook, *Jane Austen and Her Predecessors*, 94.

314   *"skill of Jane Austen in transforming the material"*: Bradbrook, *Jane Austen and Her Predecessors*, 100.

314   *"The influence of Shakespeare on Ann Radcliffe"*: Bradbrook, *Jane Austen and Her Predecessors*, 107, 108.

314   *"Occasionally, Jane Austen may be indebted to Charlotte Smith"*: Bradbrook, *Jane Austen and Her Predecessors*, 103.

315   *"Charlotte Smith's fiction was only of negative use to Jane Austen"*: Bradbrook, *Jane Austen and Her Predecessors*, 105.

315   *I had actually read her books*: I'm not the first to make the observation that critics overlook obvious influences because they are personally unfamiliar with

those texts. I've already alluded to Spender joking that Watt hadn't read Edgeworth (*Mothers of the Novel*, 290)—but the trend goes back much further. In 1928, James R. Foster made this same argument regarding Charlotte Smith's influence on Ann Radcliffe: "modern critics are wont to dismiss the sentimental adventure novel that flourished in the 1780's and 90's [*sic*] with a disdainful smile and the epithet of 'cheap' sentimentality, but their knowledge of this literature is often inexact as is often seen in their having to argue a German influence or, what is just as faulty, to make *Otranto* the sole parent of this body of narratives" (463). Foster, "Charlotte Smith, Pre-Romantic Novelist," 463–75.

315 *"prose is without wit and epigrammatic grace"*: Bradbrook, *Jane Austen and Her Predecessors*, 118.

315 *"Fanny Burney is not able to show a character developing"*: Bradbrook, *Jane Austen and Her Predecessors*, 98. He probably did read *Evelina* and *Cecilia*, the two novels upon which Burney's reputation as a novelist primarily rest: while I don't entirely agree, I can more easily see how this criticism might apply to those novels.

315 *"to freeze responses to the texts"*: Jan Gorak, *The Making of the Modern Canon* (London: Athlone, 1991), 8.

316 *"the first woman to earn repeated comparisons to Shakespeare"*: Auerbach, *Searching for Jane Austen*, 28.

316 *"set more or less in the present day and more or less in the real world"*: Kelly, *Jane Austen*, 25.

316 *"the action in or near the present day"*: Butler, *Maria Edgeworth*, 496.

316 *"afraid" she would satirize them*: Hemlow, *History of Fanny Burney*, 127.

317 *Smith's novels had "forcefulness and originality"*: Fletcher, *Charlotte Smith*, 317.

318 *"What Ann Radcliffe achieved was to place her novels within the Great Tradition of High Art"*: Norton, *Mistress of Udolpho*, 8.

319 *"she* could *have written a Radcliffian best-seller"*: Auerbach, *Searching for Jane Austen*, 88.

319 *"Beware how you imitate Mrs. Radcliffe or Maria Edgeworth"*: "Letter 'To The Artist,'" reprinted in Appendix A of the 2007 Broadside press edition of Inchbald, *A Simple Story*, 343.

319 *"placed on the same shelf as the works of a D'Arblay [i.e., Burney] and an Edgeworth"*: Austen, "Biographical Notice," vii.

320 *kept only Radcliffe and Smith*: Murphy, *Jane Austen the Reader*, 22.

323   *"My discovery of them [. . .] came about"*: Walker, *In Search of Our Mothers' Gardens*, 9.

324   *A number of earlier collectors did just that*: Other examples include Michael Sadleir, who proved by his collection that the "Horrid" gothic romances Isabella Thorpe recommends in *Northanger Abbey* actually existed; and Annibel Jenkins, the major biographer of Inchbald who also collected theatrical prints.

324   *"though he told us that he was much concerned at our Misfortunes"*: Austen, *Love and Freindship*, 23–24; 28.

325   *"A classic is a book that has never finished saying what it has to say"*; *"we find even fresher, more unexpected, and more marvelous"*; *"Your classic author is the one"*: Italo Calvino, "Why Read the Classics?" in *The Uses of Literature* (New York: Harcourt Brace Jovanovich, 1986), 128; 129; 130.

325   *"we don't read classics out of duty or respect"*: Calvino, "Why Read the Classics?" 129.

INDEX

Jenkins, Beverly, 63

Johnson, Samuel, 6, 8, 43, 53, 60, 133,
    137, 139, 144, 146, 248, 268–69,
    273, 304, 313–14
  Adventurer essay of, 268
  Austen and, 313–14, 316
  Boswell and, 269, 270, 271, 275,
    276, 317
  Burney and, 53, 68–69, 241, 268, 304
  death of, 276
  A Dictionary of the English Language, 6,
    121–23, 136, 137, 145, 241, 269,
    274, 339
  illnesses of, 269
  Lennox and, 121, 126, 127,
    132–37, 139, 142–47, 241, 269,
    270, 277, 311, 323
  More and, 155, 156, 241, 269
  Piozzi and, 53, 241, 248, 251,
    260–61, 268–76, 312, 317, 349
  Rasselas, 146
  women as viewed by, 269
*Journal of a Tour to the Hebrides with
    Samuel Johnson, LL.D., The*
    (Boswell), 276
Joyce, James, *Ulysses*, 6, 9, 10, 159

Kaplan, Deborah, 205
Katheryn of Berain, 245
Keats, John, 102, 116
Keith, George Elphinstone, Viscount,
    263
Kennedy, Margaret, 131
Kind der Liebe, Das (Kotzebue), 227, 229
King, Stephen, 50
King Lear (Shakespeare), 91, 212, 214,
    227
Kitt, Sandra, 64
Knapp, Oswald G., 242
Knight, Edward Austen, 19, 20, 23,
    35, 37, 261

Knight, Fanny, 35
Kotzebue, August von, 227, 229

Labbe, Jacqueline M., 191, 197
Lady of the Lake, The (Scott), 281
Lady Susan (Austen), 17, 21, 34, 35
Lamarck, Jean-Baptiste, 306
Lamb, Charles, 104
Lansdowne, Marquis of, 258–59, 271,
    351
LaValle, Victor, 237
Leaves of Grass (Whitman), 192
Lee, Harriet, 265
Lee, Sophia, 92, 265
Le Faye, Deirdre, 323
Lefroy, Anne, 21, 230
Le Guin, Ursula K., 35
Lennox, Alexander, 120, 121, 139
Lennox, Charlotte, 117–48, 151, 155,
    193, 196, 207, 218, 248, 299,
    320, 325
  "anonymity" of, 136, 137
  "The Art of Coquetry," 120, 122,
    129, 132, 153
  Austen compared with, 318
  Austen's reading of, 5, 117, 124–26,
    141, 147, 304, 305, 324
  authorship questions over works of,
    142–46, 311, 323
  biographies of, 138, 146–47
  birth of, 118
  boldness of, 117, 119–22, 127,
    132–34, 137, 147
  disappearance of novels of, 242
  Euphemia, 118
  family and childhood of, 118
  The Female Quixote, 124–29,
    131–32, 136, 137, 141–43,
    145–48, 188, 192, 199, 242,
    269, 270, 299, 304, 311, 323,
    324, 338, 341

ABOUT THE AUTHOR

Rebecca Romney is a rare book dealer and the cofounder of Type Punch Matrix, a rare book company based in Washington, D.C. She is the rare books specialist on the History Channel's show *Pawn Stars* and the co-founder of the Honey & Wax Book Collecting Prize. In 2019, she was featured in the documentary on the rare book trade *The Booksellers*. Romney is the author of *Printer's Error: Irreverent Stories from Book History* (with J. P. Romney) and *The Romance Novel in English: A Survey in Rare Books, 1769–1999*. Her work as a bookseller or writer has been featured in *The New York Times, The Atlantic, Forbes, Variety, The Paris Review,* and more.